The
All-American
Dessert Book

The
All-American
Dessert
Book

Nancy Baggett

PHOTOGRAPHS BY ALAN RICHARDSON

HOUGHTON MIFFLIN COMPANY
BOSTON NEW YORK 2005

For information about permission to reproduce selections from
this book, write to Permissions, Houghton Mifflin Company,
215 Park Avenue South, New York, New York 10003.

Visit our Web site: www.houghtonmifflinbooks.com.

Library of Congress Cataloging-in-Publication Data

Baggett, Nancy.
   The all-American dessert book / Nancy Baggett ; photographs
 by Alan Richardson.
      p. cm.
Includes bibliographical references and index.
   ISBN 0-618-24000-4
1. Desserts—United States. 2. Cookery, American. I. Title.
   TX773.B235   2005
   641.8'6'0973—dc22   2005040429

Book design by Anne Chalmers
Food styling by Anne Disrude, assisted by Nancy Baggett
Prop styling by Betty Alfenito

Printed in the United States of America

QWT 10 9 8 7 6 5 4 3 2 1

For my amazing grandchildren,

CHARLIE AND LIZZIE,

and the rest of their generation,

so they too may enjoy the riches

of our sweets kitchen and

help keep our culinary

heritage alive

acknowledgments

Many people in many ways contributed to this book. The family members who spent time with me in the kitchen and garden, especially my mother, grandmother, and aunt, fostered my lifelong interest in baking and cooking. My husband, Charlie, has steadfastly supported my work on this (and every) project, even when it absorbed far too many of my hours. He has also been a perceptive taster and recipe critic throughout.

My editor, Rux Martin, gave me the freedom to follow my vision and the time to delve deeply into the subject. She also put her formidable editing skills to work, paring a huge manuscript down to size. This book is much the better for her expertise and passionate pursuit of quality. Thanks, too, go to the rest of the Houghton Mifflin cast, particularly Anne Chalmers, who designed the book, Michaela Sullivan, who designed the cover, and publicist Deborah DeLosa.

Photographer Alan Richardson created the delectable, evocative images on these pages, capturing the spirit of my words and the pleasures of American sweets. I am likewise grateful for the talent and hard work of food stylist Anne Disrude and prop stylist Betty Alfenito, who helped make the photographs so spectacular.

My agent, Angela Miller, supported the project enthusiastically and offered me wise counsel when I needed it.

In my kitchen, Dollene Targan helped test and retest many recipes, thoughtfully suggesting corrections and contributing invaluable editorial and organizational support during the years that I worked on this book. Sandy Giangrande, Linda Kirschner, and Greg Hutsell also helped test the recipes.

A number of people invited me into their kitchens or lives to watch, learn, and sample. The Harold J. Howrigan family of Fairfield, Vermont, explained the old-fashioned method of maple sugaring. Jean Jennings of Mountain View, Arkansas, showed me how to make her terrific peach cobbler. Bud Smith gave me an apple-tasting tour of his Seneca Orchards in Clifton Springs, New York. Jeni Makepeace of Naples, New York, let me observe while she made her prizewinning pies for the Naples Grape Festival.

Linda Behrends shared her very special caramel recipe, and Mary Ely outlined the history of how the fabulous caramels of Roswell, New Mexico, came to be. Tom Darlington passed along his heirloom recipe for steamed cranberry pudding, sketched the history of Whitesbog, New Jersey, and gave an illuminating tour of his family's cranberry bogs. David Marvin showed me around Butternut Mountain Farm, his well-tended sugar bush, sugar shack, and maple-processing plant in Johnson, Vermont. Other individuals who shared their time or expertise include Betty Rae Miller of Mountain View,

Arkansas; Kay Thomas, craft coordinator, Ozark Folk Center, Mountain View, Arkansas; Irene Wassell, food editor of the *Arkansas Democrat-Gazette;* Burr Morse, owner of the Morse Farm Maple Sugarworks in Montpelier, Vermont; and Shirley Corriher, food chemist and author of *CookWise.*

A host of people had a hand in providing historical documentation and anecdotal material that I needed to fill in important blanks. Binnie Syril Braunstein helped ferret out the lore and history of candy canes and also provided editorial support. Ann Gasbarre of the *Daily Record* in Wooster, Ohio, furnished information and local articles on the candy cane. Bryce Thomson, longtime editor of the ice cream industry's *Sundae School Newsletter,* sent me back issues and cheerfully answered questions about soda jerks and the origins of the banana split and other sundaes. Lee Jackson, author of *Victorian London* and host of victorianlondon.org, sent me helpful material on the early history of lollipops. New Orleans food writer, publisher, and talk show host Tom Fitzmorris described the local snowball scene, both past and present. Tim Rutherford, managing editor of *Coastal Senior,* in Savannah, Georgia, provided information on fried pies. Colonial Williamsburg historic foodways expert Dennis Cotner and assistant Jim Gay generously helped bring me up to speed on early American desserts and the use of chocolate in the colonial era. The editor of the *Food History News* newsletter, culinary historian Sandra Oliver, provided key information on pandowdies and leavening agents and reviewed my manuscript for historical accuracy.

Former *Washington Post* food editor Renée Schettler and her colleagues at the food section taste-tested and offered invaluable feedback as I re-created the soft gingerbread cookies from Sherrill's Restaurant. Over the years, former *Post* food section editors Nancy McKeon and Jeanne McManus published a number of my reminiscences, giving me the opportunity to begin exploring topics that are covered in this book in more detail.

Finally, my thanks go to the enthusiastic readers of my previous book, *The All-American Cookie Book,* whose heartfelt response to the stories and recipes encouraged me to look deeper into the subject of American sweets. I hope this book will bring pleasure, too.

contents

introduction

For the past four years, I have been out exploring this country, looking for America's most irresistible desserts. Along the way, I ducked into bakeries, restaurants, confectioneries, and old-time soda shops and visited with farmers, growers, and many home cooks. In Montpelier, Vermont, I munched on rustic giant ginger cookies. In Nashville, I sampled four different versions of fudge pie—all in the name of research, of course. In New Jersey, a cranberry grower gave me a cranberry pudding and accompanying sauce that had been in his family for several generations.

Back home in my kitchen, I tested every find and chose the very best for this book. I also reworked and tweaked each choice for clarity and ease of preparation. By the end of the project, I'd gone through 370 pounds of sugar, 130 pounds of butter, and more than 1,100 eggs!

Some of my selections are closely associated with certain regions of the country—a dark, sinful bourbon-pecan fudge cake from New Orleans, for example, or pumpkin whoopie pies from Pennsylvania Dutch country. Other recipes came from acquaintances. A former neighbor shared her recipe for an outstanding vanilla-lemon cheesecake. For the first time ever, a colleague divulged her formula for the chocolate-dipped caramels that are legendary in Roswell, New Mexico—they are out of this world!

I re-created other desserts from memory in my kitchen: a banana-rum ice cream from Virginia's famed Inn at Little Washington, a glossy hot fudge sauce from a Baltimore soda fountain that I visited as a child, and an exceptional mocha swirl cheesecake with a hazelnut crust from Seattle. I raided my family's recipe files, too, plucking a supremely moist, citrusy orange chiffon cake from my grandmother's wooden receipt box and a lemon-pineapple buttermilk sherbet from my mother's collection. And of course I couldn't resist putting in a few gems of my own: my favorite apple pie and a red and black raspberry pudding cake, which the editors of *Gourmet* chose as one of their all-time favorite desserts for their fiftieth-anniversary issue.

Local Treasures

During my travels, I met some extraordinary American dessert makers and confectioners. Although I have been baking and writing about sweets for over three decades, time and time again I found myself thinking, "What a great idea! I'd never have thought of that."

This was the case on a sultry September afternoon in the Ozarks, when I dropped in on Jean Jennings of Mountain View, Arkansas, and looked over her shoulder as she prepared one of her locally famous peach cobblers (see page 160). A veteran cobbler maker myself, I wasn't anticipating any great revelations—but I was in for a surprise. Jean worked without a written recipe and, like her mother, who taught her, measured only by eye. With a confidence born of decades of experience, she pitted, peeled, and thickly sliced big peaches into a pot, poured some water over them, and tossed in what seemed an overly generous scoop of sugar and a big chunk of butter. "My mother always said peaches will take a lot more sugar than you think," she explained as she put them on to simmer.

She added no spices, lemon juice, cornstarch, or flour. "If I want it to be thicker, I just add crumbled-up bits of leftover dough," she said. Instead of the typical biscuit topping, she mixed together a pie pastry, then rolled it out and draped it over the peaches. Finally, in a testament to the dough's extraordinary tenderness, she formed crescent moon-shaped steam vents, not with a knife but with the curved edge of a serving spoon.

About forty-five minutes later, with the fragrance of fruit full in the air, we settled down at her comfortable kitchen table to take our first bite. Awash in a pool of butter-hued sauce, the peaches tasted sweet, fresh, and intensely peachy, perfectly complementing the crisp, flaky pastry. Although made with nothing remarkable and served plain, Jean's creation was hands down the best peach cobbler I've ever eaten. It offered, as so many fine American desserts do, irrefutable evidence that simple ingredients handled with wisdom and respect can yield remarkable results.

I also learned something new from Jeni Makepeace, of Naples, New York, who showed me a no-muss, no-fuss way to roll out pastry as she prepared her prizewinning Concord grape pies. Instead of working on a floured surface or using baking parchment, she rolls out her dough between sheets of grocery-store produce bags. (The plastic layers are much sturdier than parchment, and the dough peels more easily from their smooth surface.) The Harold J. Howrigan family, of Fairfield, Vermont, taught me how to turn maple syrup into an old-fashioned taffylike treat called maple sugar on snow.

Although many food writers claim that supermarket and restaurant chains have obliterated regional dishes, the desserts I found prove that different parts of the country do indeed boast unique repertoires. In New England, for example, many cooks still make Indian pudding, a quietly satisfying cornmeal and molasses dessert that dates back to colonial times. New Englanders also occasionally prepare an old-fashioned dish called apple pandowdy, which is something like a cobbler; it's hard to find anywhere else.

Cooks all over the South serve up banana pudding, a modern, unfussy variant of English trifle. Another dessert that is much loved in some areas of the South is a pan-fried, fruit-filled pastry turnover called the fried pie. In parts of the heartland as well as in the

★ ★ ★ ★ ★ ★ ★ ★ ★ ★ ★ ★ ★ ★ ★

South, cooks are particularly fond of the taste of brown sugar, drizzling caramel sauces over pies, cheesecakes, and puddings and slathering caramel frostings over cakes.

Since good cooks inevitably excel at using what's at hand, it should come as no surprise that many regional desserts feature local ingredients. Missouri, the nation's top producer of our indigenous black walnuts, serves up black walnut ice cream (it's the favorite after vanilla), candies, cookies, and incredibly fragrant, fine-textured black walnut pound cakes. In south Florida and the Keys, where people take pride in the modest Key lime industry that once flourished, Key lime pies, cookies, and all sorts of frozen concoctions are the rule.

ALL-american creativity

Based on my travels and research, I can report that our sweets culture is vibrant, complex, and uniquely American. Those who say that all our desserts are borrowed from Europe are just plain wrong. To see how far we've come, compare the cakes that existed in the colonial era to the ones we enjoy now. Early on we baked seed cakes, gingerbreads, fruitcakes, sponge cakes, and pound cakes. Soon, however, we modified the sponge cake to produce the angel food cake and the pound cake to make the butter layer cake. This in turn led to that quintessentially American creation, the regal frosted layer cake: devil's food cake (see page 104) and a triple-layer white cake with lemon curd, fluffy white frosting, and coconut (see page 100) are two terrific examples from the late nineteenth century.

American cooks rapidly began incorporating New World ingredients such as cranberries, blueberries, pumpkin, and pecans to update existing pie, tart, and pudding recipes. We added flourishes: streusels, cookie crusts, and, in one notable instance, a cloudlike meringue topping that turned a plain lemon pie into an American classic. Homey cobblers, pandowdies, crisps, slumps, and, later, crisps—all riffs on British pies— were clever American timesaving innovations. Yes, ice creams originated in Europe, but it was Yankee ingenuity, with a little push from our temperance movement, that brought about the soda fountain industry and, ultimately, ice cream sodas, sundaes, and milk shakes, to name just a few. It's probably no coincidence that a nation that prizes productivity came up with ice pops, fudge bars, ice cream sandwiches, snow cones, and other sweets that could be eaten on the go. Confections called lollipops date back to Victorian England, but they were stickless lozenges; Americans added the handles. In colonial times, chocolate was just becoming known, but only as a beverage. We've since expanded our dessert options exponentially by coming up with all-American brownies, chocolate chip cookies, fudge, s'mores, and peanut butter–chocolate pie.

Mention the word "dessert," and most Americans picture a generous wedge of pie, cake, or cheesecake. But according to Colonial Williamsburg historic foodways expert Dennis Cotner, this isn't what early Americans meant by the word. Before the nineteenth century, desserts were light and intended as palate cleansers. "Desserts at that time were marzipan, little meringues, fruit pastes and peels, tiny jam tartlets, and other tidbits," Cotner says. "The concept of dessert changed in the next century."

The array of dishes on display at the governor's palace kitchen when I visited Colonial Williamsburg several years ago underscored Cotner's point. Sweet bread puddings, tarts, and cakes were set out for the main course right along with meats and vegetables. The "desserts" were mostly light and dainty, including peach chips (dried sugared peach slices), candied citrus peel, a frothy wine and cream mixture called syllabub, and sugared walnuts.

New food products and updated equipment were very often the mothers of our forebears' culinary invention. Chemical leavening agents enabled cooks to make light cakes and biscuit doughs, which are the foundation of many cobblers and of our beloved strawberry shortcake (see page 178). Our modern, often elaborate cheesecakes, which bear little resemblance to their plain soft-cheese curd predecessors, sprang from a new American product, cream cheese. Perhaps most important, the cast-iron range made preparing many desserts easier than ever before.

Still, the cooks' words in the many cookbooks, magazines, and diaries I pored over make it clear that their work wasn't easy, and that even the various newfangled conveniences didn't make their lives carefree. They describe in exhausting detail, for example, the laborious work of operating a wood- or coal-fueled kitchen stove. A 1902 letter from a stove manufacturer's representative brusquely explained to a housewife who had begged for an oven with a thermostat that such an invention would be impossible: "We have had much experience in this matter, and we find that in order to be absolutely successful in cooking, a lady must have quite a leaning that way, and her knowledge as to the proper heat must be gotten from experience. We can guarantee that if there had been any way to utilize a thermometer in an oven it would have been done long since."

Fortunately, as we move into the twenty-first century, our social roles in the home are less rigid, our kitchens more convenient, and our sweets repertoire more exciting than ever before. I hope that you'll not only enjoy the recipes I've collected but view them as a part of our heritage to be treasured and as components of an American culture that is changing all the time. I can't wait to see what happens next.

techniques and tips for successful dessert making

The individual recipes are your road maps to success, and it's important to follow them carefully. You'll see that they are very detailed, and at first glance some may seem lengthy. However, in an age when fewer and fewer cooks learn basic techniques from mothers and grandmothers, I've found that it's helpful to give plenty of guidance. I've provided enough details that cooks of all levels of expertise can execute even unfamiliar steps properly and enjoy success making a wide range of desserts.

Each recipe has been tested at least three times, most four or five times. A few required more than a dozen tests to get them just right. (I tested the recipes I gathered from other cooks just as carefully as the ones I created myself.) Each recipe was prepared by several different testers, including home cooks, to make sure the directions are clear and easy to follow.

I strongly advise you to prepare the recipes exactly as written at least once before beginning to tinker with them. I know that many cooks like to add their own touches (I certainly do), but switching ingredients can alter the chemistry of a dessert in dramatic, undesirable ways. Take time to look through A Short Course on Ingredients (page 9) first; it will give you valuable insights into which of your alterations will likely work and which won't.

MEASURING METHODS

Careful measuring is a must. It is often possible to cook by "eyeballing" quantities, but not when preparing baked goods and confections. Most desserts depend on a specific ratio of flour, sugar, fat, liquid, and sometimes egg, and unless you are highly experienced and very familiar with a recipe, measuring is the only way to ensure that amounts are right.

Measuring might seem a trivial matter, but it isn't, particularly in the case of flour. The amount will vary considerably depending on whether flour is sifted or stirred or fluffed with a fork first, and whether it is spooned, scooped, or shaken into measures. Unfortunately, there is no standard method that experts suggest for the home cook, although professional bakers and others who bake in large quantities weigh ingredients to ensure accuracy. Because many home cooks don't have accurate kitchen scales, the recipes in this book measure ingredients in cups, not by weight.

When measuring flour and other dry, powdery ingredients for the recipes in this book, always use the dip-and-sweep method. I call for this method throughout because it is the easiest and the most widely used in American home kitchens. It involves simply *dipping lightly down into a bag or container using the appropriate graduated measuring cup and scooping up enough flour or other dry ingredient to overfill the cup.* Then gently sweep across the top of the cup using the straight edge of a knife or long-bladed spatula to remove the excess flour so the quantity remaining is flush with the top of the measure; don't press down while sweeping. The only exception is that when measuring brown sugar, which is not powdery but moist, you need to push it firmly down into the cup to remove any air pockets.

To further ensure that your measuring technique corresponds with the one used for these recipes:

- Don't sift, stir, or fluff up the flour with a fork before you start.
- Don't shake the flour out of the bag or container into the cup.
- Don't tap on the cup or shake it to compact the ingredient.
- Use a graduated measure—that is, a so-called "dry" measure designed to be filled to the top and hold exactly the quantity you need.

Standard graduated measuring sets always include at least ¼-, ⅓-, ½-, and 1-cup measures, but some "gourmet" sets provide ⅛-, ⅔-, ¾-, and even 2-cup measures as well. If you bake often, the more complete sets are particularly convenient and a good investment.

For measuring liquids, use clear 1-, 2-, or 4-cup marked measuring cups (called liquid measures). (Choose the smaller cups for small quantities and the larger cups for large quantities.) Set the cup on a flat surface. After filling to the desired mark, check at eye level to see if the amount is right.

Measure small amounts of ingredients such as vanilla extract, baking powder, and salt using a graduated set of measuring spoons. It's most convenient to have a deluxe set with ⅛-, ¼-, ½-, and 1-teaspoon measures, as well as ½-, 1-, and 2-tablespoon measures. For dry ingredients, use the dip-and-sweep method here, too. Scoop down into the dry ingredient, overfill the spoon, and level off the ingredient flush with the top of the spoon using a small knife.

WORKING WITH DOUGHS AND BATTERS
When preparing doughs and batters, pay close attention to what temperature ingredients are supposed to be. When ingredients are too cold, mixtures can be difficult to blend or dissolve, and they may be stiffer or thicker than expected. Mixtures that are too warm can thin out too fast in the oven, fail to aerate properly, curdle, bake faster than expected, or be limp and difficult to handle during shaping and rolling.

Recipes in this book often call for using an electric mixer. If possible, use a stand model, as this leaves both hands free to proceed with other preparations. If you bake often, consider investing in a heavy-duty mixer such as a KitchenAid. Its powerful motor mixes ingredients more efficiently and quickly than smaller machines and is less likely to labor or overheat when beating heavy doughs for long periods. If you are using a KitchenAid mixer for recipes that call for whipping, as with egg whites or heavy cream, for example, use the wire whip and not the paddle.

Always resist the temptation to add extra flour to firm up overly soft doughs. Overflouring tends to make doughs tough and dry. Whenever pastry or cookie doughs begin to warm up and soften, give them a short stint in the refrigerator or freezer to make them manageable again. Remember, too, that a just-mixed dough may not need either chilling or extra flour; it will stiffen quite a bit if simply allowed to stand for a few minutes, because flour absorbs moisture gradually.

A handy technique to avoid overflouring when working with both pie and cookie doughs is to roll them out between sheets of baking parchment or wax paper instead of on a floured surface. Large plastic bags that have been cut apart to form plastic sheets are a convenient alternative. The best bags to use are the free clear plastic sacks for produce in supermarkets. They are clean and designed for food use, large enough to yield a fifteen- to sixteen-inch square, and surprisingly durable. Plus, the dough can be viewed during rolling and readily peels off the smooth, flexible surface.

The first step is to sandwich the dough between the paper or plastic sheets, then pat or press it flat. The next step is to briskly roll outward in all directions to the desired thickness using a rolling pin. Since the paper sometimes wrinkles on the underside during this process, turn over the dough occasionally and smooth or roll out the underside. (To keep the paper from sliding around, I either tape it to the counter with masking tape or simply drape one end over the counter edge and lean against it.)

At this point, the paper or plastic can be gently peeled from the dough, and the dough can be used. If it is too warm to handle easily, place it on a baking sheet (paper or plastic still attached), then refrigerate or freeze it for a few minutes until firm. To prepare for cutting out cookie dough, I call for peeling off one sheet of paper or plastic, then patting it back into place before flipping the dough over. This step loosens the dough from the bottom sheet so that the cookies can be readily lifted off to the baking sheet later.

Besides avoiding overflouring, this rolling method makes it easy to transfer dough to the refrigerator or freezer as needed. It also makes kitchen cleanup easier.

OVEN CONSIDERATIONS
Turn on the oven at least 15 minutes before baking and adjust the baking racks before preheating. It takes most ovens at least 15 minutes to come up to temperature. Whenever

you open the oven door, the temperature may drop 25 to 50 degrees F, so it's best to adjust the racks before preheating.

It's wise to use an oven thermometer to verify that the temperature you choose is actually reached. In a random check conducted by *Cook's Illustrated* magazine, only two of the sixteen home ovens tested were accurate. Ten ovens ran cool (up to 50 degrees off), and four ran hot (up to 40 degrees off). If baked goods tend to burn or undercook in your oven, the thermostat is likely off.

The first time you prepare a recipe, set the timer to several minutes less than the minimum time specified in the recipe, then bake for as many more minutes as is necessary.
You'll notice that every baked-good recipe in this book includes a range of baking times to guide you. Although these times have all been arrived at through testing, they are simply guides, because there is enormous variation in how ovens perform. This is even true when ovens register the same temperature. For example, I have baked two cake layers from the same batch of batter in identical pans in different ovens registering exactly the same temperature and found that one was done almost 10 minutes before the other. Moreover, one oven browned the cake tops much more evenly and deeply than the other.
If the ingredients are warmer or cooler than usual, the pan used conducts and holds heat more or less efficiently than normal, or other common factors change, the baking times will change, too. Batters baked in metal pans may be ready 10 to 12 minutes sooner than those baked in glass pans.

BAKING PANS

Be sure your pans fit the specifications in the recipes. American manufacturers produce pans that vary greatly in size and volume, and European manufacturers, which produce metric-based sizes, complicate the matter further. Also, many cooks use baking pans that have been handed down and that are not comparable to any on the market now.
Just as there are no standard sizes for bakeware, there are no labeling guidelines. One pan labeled 9 inches may actually be 8½ inches across with two ¼-inch protruding handles, and another labeled 9 inches may really be 9 inches.

To determine the actual size of your pans, measure the distance from one top inside edge to the other using a ruler. Ignore any handles, and don't include the thickness of the edge.

To determine the height of a pan, measure from the outside bottom just to the lip of the pan. The best way to determine whether your pie plate or cake pan will hold the amount of filling specified in the recipe is to check the volume by adding water to the rim.

Some plates labeled as deep-dish are actually fairly shallow, and some so-called regular pie plates are fairly deep. Throughout the book, I define a "deep-dish" plate as 2 inches deep and a "regular" plate as 1½ inches deep. A deep-dish plate should hold 6 to 6½ cups water, and a regular pie plate should hold 4 to 4½ cups.

Round cake pans come in a variety of diameters, too, although they usually have a similar depth: 1½ inches. In this book, I call for 8½- and 9-inch cake pans. If your cake pans are not exactly 8½ by 1½ inches, check the volume by filling a pan to the rim with water; the pan should hold 5¼ to 5½ cups. If your pans are slightly smaller than 9 by 1½ inches, be sure they hold 5¾ to 6 cups water. For information on substituting pans, see page 14.

A short course on ingredients

BUTTER

Having the butter at the right temperature is very important to baking results. You'll find that many recipes in this book call for slightly softened butter. To check for the right consistency, do a "press test." Press a finger into the butter; it should "give" just slightly, and an indentation should remain. Very cold butter will be too stiff to fluff up or cream properly; butter that is too soft will be too thin and squishy to fluff at all.

To warm cold butter quickly, put it in a microwave-safe bowl and microwave on lowest power for brief intervals. Do a press test or stir every 20 seconds, as butter can rapidly change from hard to overly soft. Also, be aware that butter is likely to warm up unevenly in the microwave, staying hard in one spot and melting in another. (Alternatively, you can warm butter by cutting it into chunks and placing it in a metal bowl set inside a larger, shallow bowl of warm water. Stir frequently.)

Though it might seem a sensible approach, simply melting butter and stirring it into a mixture is often not the best method in baking. Cutting cold butter into flour coats the flour particles with fat, which ultimately helps tenderize a baked good. Beating slightly softened butter with sugar (called creaming) incorporates air and helps fluff up and lighten mixtures from cake batters and frostings to some candies.

If you feel you must economize by using margarine in baked goods, use half the butter called for and replace the other half with regular stick margarine. Never use soft, tub-style whipped or "light" margarine, since this often contains extra water and proportionally less fat than butter and can drastically alter results.

Don't substitute margarine for butter in sauces, frostings, and most confections. The finished dish not only will lack the desired buttery taste but also will likely be too salty.

FLOUR

For the best-textured baked goods, be sure to use the kind of flour specified in the recipes. All wheat flour contains a protein called gluten. In baked goods, gluten provides structure and helps the crumb hold together and be sturdy. Chewy, crusty yeast breads need a lot of structure, so they benefit from a lot of gluten. On the other end of the scale, finely textured cakes and pie pastries are not appealing when overly sturdy (they will be tough), so they need far less gluten.

As a rule, cake flour, pastry flour, and soft wheat flour have the lowest percentages of gluten, bread flour has the highest, and all-purpose flour is somewhere in the middle. The recipes in this book call for all-purpose flour (where a moderate amount of gluten is preferable) and, in a few cases, cake flour (where more tenderness is desirable). Cake flour comes in boxes and is found in supermarkets. It's generally heavily bleached, which makes it not only whiter but also more absorbent and thus better suited for cakes with a high fat or sugar content. Cake flour is not the same as pastry flour.

Handle the dough lightly to ensure tenderness. Although the gluten content is important, the way wheat flour is handled once it is wet also affects the toughness or tenderness of a baked good. Stirring, kneading, and other manipulation of wet flour causes its gluten to form long, tough strands and ultimately produces a very sturdy, strong dough. Minimal stirring, beating, and other handling results in short gluten strands, producing a soft, tender pastry or dough. Overbeat, and your baked good may be tough. Underbeat, and it may not have enough structure and be either crumbly or break apart into chunks.

Certain ingredients, such as sugar and various acidic ingredients (lemon juice, vinegar, buttermilk, and sour cream), can also promote tenderness. Sugar binds up the gluten, and acids break it down. Cold butter or shortening that is cut into flour also reduces gluten development, because it works like a raincoat, coating and protecting the flour particles from becoming wet. (Gluten can develop only when flour is wet.)

Although flour draws up a lot of moisture immediately when liquid is added, it continues to absorb liquid for some time. This is why some recipes direct you to set the dough aside to firm up or caution you about adding extra flour too soon. Don't add more flour than is called for. (See page 7 for more details.)

CHOCOLATE

Chocolate never needs to be cooked; it should be heated just enough to melt it and make it fluid. Manufacturers have already cooked the chocolate; high heat and further cooking can cause it to develop an "off" or burned taste and sometimes a crumbly, lumpy, or grainy texture as well. (This is why many recipes in this book have you stir in the chocolate at the end.)

Melt chocolate over very gentle heat. Its melting point is lower than body temperature— usually between 88 and 92 degrees F—and it contains starch that can easily scorch. (This book gives specific directions for melting chocolate in a microwave oven or on a burner.)

Because chocolate can set, or harden, at temperatures that are only a few degrees lower than its melting point (usually between 85 and 88 degrees F), my recipes often tell you to check the consistency and, if necessary, rewarm the melted chocolate before adding it to batters. It's also important to make sure the other ingredients are not too cold.

Follow the directions in the recipe when adding liquid to chocolate. Chocolate doesn't mix readily with liquids. If a tiny amount of liquid, say a teaspoon of vanilla extract or a tablespoon of liqueur, is added to pure melted chocolate, the chocolate's natural starch may grab on to the liquid and cause the chocolate to "seize" into a hard mass. If a large amount of liquid, particularly a cool liquid, is suddenly added to pure melted chocolate, the chocolate is likely to disperse into small bits rather than integrate smoothly. For this reason, recipes often instruct you to warm the liquid before stirring it in gradually. (The starch also causes sauces and frostings to thicken rather than thin out when melted chocolate is added.)

COCOA POWDER

Remember that cocoa is even more susceptible to burning than chocolate. Cocoa is made by removing much of the cocoa butter (the natural fat) from chocolate using a hydraulic press. Since the resulting powder has a lower percentage of fat and a higher percentage of solids, including starch, it burns easily.

If either American or Dutch-process cocoa is specified, don't use them interchangeably. American cocoa still contains its natural acidity, and Dutch-process cocoa has been treated with an alkali to remove its acid. The alkalizing process turns the cocoa darker but gives it a milder flavor. Equally important, since the amount of baking soda in a recipe depends on the level of acidity, switching from one type of cocoa to another can upset the chemical balance. Unfortunately, not all cocoa manufacturers clearly indicate whether their product is alkalized. Assume that American brands are not alkalized and that European brands are treated with alkali unless the labels say otherwise.

In certain recipes—some sauces, fillings, and frostings, for example—the amount of acid isn't critical, and either Dutch-process or American cocoas may be used.

EGGS

Thoroughly boil a pastry cream or pudding mixture containing egg yolks if the recipe instructs you to do so. This step is critical when egg yolks are used along with cornstarch, flour, or another thickening starch. Egg yolks contain an enzyme called alpha amylase, which gradually breaks down thickeners as a mixture stands. A pie filling that seems plenty thick when put in a pastry crust may be quite "soupy" the next day, because the enzyme has destroyed the thickening action of the starch. Boiling eliminates the troublesome enzyme. Don't worry about the egg yolks curdling from the boiling; the starch shields them from the high heat.

SUGAR

Altering the amount of sugar in a dessert changes more than just the level of sweetness. Sugar also increases tenderness and crispness in baked goods (even when added in small quantities), and when cooked down with liquid, it helps thicken sauces and frostings.

Remember that brown sugar not only has more flavor than granulated sugar but also is moister, heavier, coarser, and slightly more acidic, so it will also affect the chemical balance and texture of recipes. Due to its higher moisture content, brown sugar is more prone to lumping than granulated sugar, and even small undissolved bits can have important negative consequences, especially in frostings, candies, sweet sauces, and other recipes with a high sugar content.

In all very sugary solutions, make sure to wash sugar off stirring spoons and wash down pot sides when a recipe tells you to. The dissolved sugar has a natural propensity to turn back into crystals, causing unwanted graining and grittiness. (This tendency results from the fact that sugar, or sucrose, is composed of glucose and fructose molecules that chemically bond together in pairs and then into orderly geometric crystalline patterns.) Adding undissolved sugar crystals back into a mixture can cause it to become grainy, because these sugar crystals can set off a chain reaction. Unnecessary stirring also can cause graining, particularly when the mixture is hot.

To further discourage the candies, syrups, glazes, and frostings from graining, many recipes call for a small amount of corn syrup. The glucose molecules in the syrup effectively disrupt the normal pairing up of the sugar molecules, preventing crystallization. Don't leave out this ingredient, even when the quantity called for seems insignificant.

Baking soda and baking powder are not interchangeable. Although they are both chemical leavening agents, they are not the same. Baking soda, a baking alkali called bicarbonate of soda, bubbles up and aerates only when combined with an acidic ingredient such as sour cream, buttermilk, yogurt, citrus juice, vinegar, or American-style (nonalkalized) cocoa powder. It won't aerate properly when too little acid is present, and unactivated soda can impart an unpleasant chemical aftertaste.

Baking powder, which is a combination of baking soda and acid, will bubble up without any acid from other ingredients. Because moisture causes the activation, store baking powder tightly closed. Since it gradually loses its aerating power over time, replace it every year, or every six to nine months if you open the can frequently.

Frequently Asked Questions

Q. Sometimes a recipe says sift the flour. If I bought flour labeled "presifted," do I still have to sift?

A. Yes. Even if the label doesn't say so, most national brands of flour come presifted, which is why sifting isn't often called for in recipes in this book. However, to ensure a particularly fine, light texture, some recipes call for sifting to fluff up the flour more than usual. If you don't have a flour sifter, simply shake or stir the flour through a fine sieve or very fine strainer. (The recipes in this book always call for measuring the flour before sifting.)

Q. Do I have to use cake flour when it's called for, or can I just use all-purpose flour?

A. If a recipe calls for cake flour, it will definitely yield the best results. I call for cake flour when I want a cake or other baked good to be very tender or have a fine crumb. All-purpose flour has a higher percentage of gluten (see page 10) than cake flour, so it can't deliver the same degree of tenderness. By the way, don't be tempted to use cake flour when it's not called for; the baked good may be so tender it falls apart.

Q. What if I don't have the pan size specified? Does it matter if I substitute?

A. It's fine to substitute another pan, as long as both pans' surface area and depth are fairly similar. For example, if a recipe calls for a 9-by-13-inch pan (117 square inches) and yours happens to be 8 by 14 inches (112 square inches), the substitute will work fine. Likewise, you can substitute a 7-by-11-inch pan (77 square inches) for a 9-inch square pan (81 square inches).

However, both overly large and overly small pans can cause problems. Even if a pan is only a little too small, the layer will be overly thick, which will throw off the baking time (and may hinder proper rising as well). A pan that is overly large will cause the layer to spread too much and be too thin. This may yield an overdone or dry baked good.

Q. My cookies spread too much. What did I do wrong?

A. Frequently, the spreading occurs because the butter in the dough is a little too warm and soft to start with. (See page 9 for how to check for the proper consistency.) When the cookies go into the oven, the butter completely melts, causing them to spread more than they should. Sometimes, though, the butter is fine to start with but softens too much as the dough stands in a warm kitchen. In either case, refrigerating the dough for a few minutes will cool and firm the butter again and will usually correct the problem.

Placing the dough on warm baking sheets also can cause excessive spreading. The residual heat quickly warms and softens the butter too much. Be sure to set your sheets aside between batches and let them cool completely before using them again.

Finally, excess spreading can occur when the ratio of flour to butter is off. To be sure the amount of flour is correct, use the dip-and-sweep measuring method for all recipes in this book (see page 5). Don't stir, sift, or fluff up the flour first. Never use a reduced-fat or reduced-calorie butter spread or soft margarine in place of butter. Not only do these products have a lower percentage of fat for their volume, but the fat is hydrogenated, which makes it more likely to "run" in the oven.

Q. I have small eggs, but the recipe calls for large ones. Can I use what I have?

A. You can, but you must make an adjustment and use more of the smaller eggs. One large egg, lightly beaten, equals a generous 3 tablespoons. Use enough lightly beaten egg of any other size to yield this same amount. Also, if you are substituting small egg whites or yolks, remember that 1 large egg contains 2 tablespoons of white and a generous 1 tablespoon of yolk.

Q. Superfine sugar is hard to find in my area, and it's expensive. Can I substitute regular sugar?

A. Superfine sugar is usually called for because it dissolves more quickly than regular granulated sugar and thus yields a smoother, less grainy texture. It's not a good idea to replace superfine sugar with regular granulated sugar because it may not dissolve fully and can feel gritty on the tongue. However, you can make your own superfine sugar by grinding regular granulated sugar in a food processor until it is very fine (but not completely powdery).

Q. Can I mix up a batter or dough in the food processor instead of using a mixer?

A. It's frequently possible to use either an electric mixer or a food processor, and a number of the desserts in this book provide instructions for both. However, the methods usually differ somewhat and can be arrived at only through testing. A food processor blade rotates much faster than beaters and also chops, so results may be different. Most food processor bowls won't hold as much as mixing bowls, and that can cause problems, too.

Q. Can I substitute salted butter for unsalted?

A. You can substitute salted butter for unsalted in most baked goods but not in frostings and dessert sauces, as they may taste too salty. Moreover, in any recipe where the buttery taste is prominent, unsalted butter is preferable because it usually has a fresher, cleaner flavor. If you do substitute salted butter, reduce the amount of salt called for in the recipe by half.

Q. My baked good came out dry. What did I do wrong?

A. Dryness is most frequently due to overbaking. This often occurs because the oven thermostat is off, a surprisingly common situation. It's a good idea to invest in an oven thermometer to be sure the temperature you set on the dial is really the temperature in the oven. Some baking sheets and pans with a dark finish also absorb and hold heat so efficiently that items bake much more quickly than normal. If you have such pans, set the timer for a few minutes less than the recipe calls for.

Another reason baked goods sometimes come out dry is that the raisins, dates, or other dried fruit called for are too dry and stale. In this case, they will gradually rehydrate and draw moisture from the dough or batter. Despite its name, "dried" fruit should still be fairly plump and moist. Either discard dried-out fruit or rehydrate it by soaking it in a little hot water. (Drain off the water and pat the fruit dry with paper towels before using.)

Q. Why didn't my egg whites (or meringue) whip up?

A. Egg whites have the capacity to whip up into a very light, foamy mixture, but several factors can keep this from happening. The whites need to be completely free of yolk, since yolk contains fat and fat inhibits whipping. Even a small amount of yolk can keep whites from whipping properly. For this reason, it's also important that your bowl, beaters, and rubber spatulas be free of all traces of grease. Be sure not to drop or splash any oily ingredients (chocolate, oil, butter, or nuts, for example) into the whites.

Additionally, whites may not whip up well if the sugar is added too early or too late in the beating process. Follow the recipe carefully. Sugar that's added too soon or too rapidly can make the whites too heavy to fluff up properly. By contrast, since sugar plays a role in keeping beaten whites smooth and stable, if it is not added soon enough, the whites may begin to break apart and weep.

If you prefer to use pasteurized eggs, be aware that the whites will take three or four times longer to beat than unpasteurized eggs and will probably not whip up as much. Add some cream of tartar to facilitate whipping.

1

Pies, Tarts, and Cheesecakes

Favorite Deep-dish Apple pie

Neither apples nor pie originated in the United States, but the expression "as American as apple pie" has a lot of truth to it. During our more than three centuries of pie baking, American cooks have probably turned out more apple pies than any other kind. As soon as the apple trees brought over and planted by the early colonists began to bear fruit, apple pies became popular. Indeed, five of the nine pies in Amelia Simmons's 1796 *American Cookery* featured apples.

This is my favorite apple pie. Because I want the focus to be on the apples, I add only a small amount of lemon juice and cinnamon to bring up their flavor. I cook the filling down a bit before putting it in the pie to ensure that the apples are tender and that there will be no gap between the crust and the filling when they cook down during baking. The pie is large; considering how rapidly it disappears, I've never seen the sense in baking a smaller one.

For fullest flavor, it's best to use a blend of apples in a pie: three or four different kinds is not too much. Bill van Deusen, of Harmony Hollow Orchards in central Virginia, goes even further and recommends using as many different varieties as there are apples in the pie. The apples should be crisp, firm, and, if possible, freshly picked.

Double crust All-Purpose Pie Pastry Dough (page 90)

All-purpose flour for dusting dough

FILLING

10½ cups peeled, cored, and thinly sliced apples (8–11 medium baking apples; choose at least three kinds, such as Stayman, Jonathan, Golden Delicious, Braeburn, Smokehouse, Sunrise, Granny Smith, Grimes Golden, York, and Gala)

1 tablespoon fresh lemon juice, or more to taste

Scant ⅔ cup granulated sugar

⅓ cup packed light brown sugar

3½–4½ tablespoons cornstarch (use larger amount if apples are very juicy)

½ teaspoon ground cinnamon

Pinch of salt

2 tablespoons unsalted butter, cut into bits

1 tablespoon milk for brushing on dough top

1½ tablespoons granulated sugar for sprinkling on dough top

TO ROLL OUT THE PASTRY: Lightly grease a 9½-inch deep-dish pie plate or coat with nonstick spray. If the dough is cold and stiff, let it warm up until slightly pliable but still cool to the touch. Generously dust it on both sides with flour. Roll out one dough portion between large sheets of baking parchment into a 13½-inch round. Occasionally check the underside of the dough during rolling and smooth out any wrinkles. (If the dough seems sticky or limp, place in the freezer for 5 minutes to firm up.) Gently peel off the top sheet of paper, then pat back into place. Flip the dough; peel off the bottom sheet. Center the round, dough side down, in the pie plate. Gently peel off the remaining paper. Smooth the dough into the plate and patch any tears, if necessary. Using kitchen shears or a paring knife, trim the overhang to ¼ inch. Prick the pastry all over with a fork. Loosely cover the pastry and place in the freezer while you roll out the top pastry and prepare the filling.

Roll out the second portion of dough into a 13½-inch round as described above. Transfer the round (paper still attached) to a baking sheet and place in the refrigerator while you prepare the filling.

TO MAKE THE FILLING: Position a rack in the lower third of the oven and preheat to 400 degrees F. In a very large, heavy nonreactive saucepan, toss the apples with the lemon juice. In a medium bowl, stir together the granulated sugar, brown sugar, cornstarch, cinnamon, and salt until well blended. Add the sugar mixture and butter to the apples, tossing until well blended. Bring the mixture to a simmer over medium-high heat. Simmer, stirring and scraping the pan bottom, for about 3 minutes, or until the apples cook down slightly; be careful not to burn. Remove from the burner. Taste and add more lemon juice, if desired.

TO ASSEMBLE THE PIE: Turn out the apple mixture into the bottom crust, mounding it in the center. Gently peel off the top sheet of paper from the second pastry round. Center the round, dough side down, over the filling. Peel off and discard the remaining paper. Trim the overhang to ¾ inch. Fold the overhang under the bottom pastry to form an edge that rests on the lip of the plate. Press the layers together firmly, then flute with your fingers or press the tines of a fork all the way around. Brush the dough top (not the edges) with the milk, then sprinkle with the granulated sugar. Cut generous slashes in the top for steam vents, using a sharp, lightly greased paring knife.

TO BAKE THE PIE: Set the pie on a rimmed baking sheet. Bake for 25 to 35 minutes, or until the crust is lightly browned. Spray the underside of an extra-wide sheet of aluminum foil with nonstick spray (or use

TIP

Experts say that apples soften ten times faster at room temperature than at 32 degrees F. They won't freeze at 32 degrees F because of their high sugar content.

nonstick foil). Make a foil tent over the pie top so the entire crust is covered. Continue baking for 30 to 40 minutes, or until the top is nicely browned and the filling is bubbly. Transfer the pie to a wire rack. Let cool for at least 1½ hours and preferably 4 hours or longer (for neater slices) before serving.

The pie will keep, covered, at room temperature for up to 2 days or refrigerated for up to 2 days longer. Let come to room temperature before serving.

"The pie is an English institution, which, planted on American soil, forthwith ran rampant and burst forth into an untold variety of genera and species. Not merely the old mince pie, but a thousand strictly American seedlings from that main stock, evinced the power of American housewives to adapt old institutions to new uses. Pumpkin pies, cranberry pies, huckleberry pies, cherry pies, green-currant pies, peach, pear, and plum pies, custard pies, apple pies, Marlborough-pudding pies—pies with top crusts and pies without—pies adorned with all sorts of fanciful flutings and architectural strips laid across and around, and otherwise varied, attest to the boundless fertility of the feminine mind."

—Harriet Beecher Stowe,
Oldtown Folks (1869)

Lattice-Topped Deep-Dish Blueberry Pie

I'd forgotten how truly sublime blueberry pie made with fresh blueberries is until I baked this one. The filling has a glorious fruit flavor and pairs perfectly with the pastry crust. Considering that North America's indigenous blueberry is still little known elsewhere—the United States and Canada produce more than four fifths of the total crop—this pie is one of our greatest gifts to the culinary world.

This technique for the lattice top makes it surprisingly easy to form.

FILLING

- 1¼ cups sugar
- 5 tablespoons cornstarch, plus more if berries are very juicy
- ¼ teaspoon ground cinnamon
- 6⅓ cups blueberries
- ¾ teaspoon finely grated lemon zest (yellow part of skin)
- 2 tablespoons fresh lemon juice
- 1½ tablespoons unsalted butter, cut into bits

Sour Cream Pie Pastry Dough (page 92)
All-purpose flour for dusting dough
About 1 tablespoon milk or half-and-half for brushing on lattice top
- 1 tablespoon sugar for sprinkling on lattice top

Lightly grease a 9½-inch deep-dish pie plate or coat with nonstick spray.

TO MAKE THE FILLING: About 20 minutes before baking time, in a large nonreactive saucepan thoroughly stir together the sugar, cornstarch, and cinnamon. Gently stir in the blueberries, lemon zest, lemon juice, and butter until well blended. Set aside.

TO ROLL OUT THE PASTRY: If the dough is cold and stiff, let it warm up until slightly pliable but still cool to the touch, then knead briefly. Generously dust the portions on both sides with flour. Roll out the smaller dough portion between sheets of baking parchment into a 9-inch round. Occasionally check the underside of the dough during rolling and smooth out any wrinkles. Gently peel off the top sheet of paper and pat it loosely back into place so it will be easy to remove later. Flip over the dough and peel off the other sheet. Using a pastry wheel or large knife, cut the dough into ½-inch-wide strips. Peel every other strip off the paper and lay them in the order removed on another sheet of baking parchment. Place the strips you just removed crosswise about ½ inch apart on the strips remaining on the original paper, interweaving them to form a lattice. Using the pastry wheel or knife, trim off any uneven ends so the lattice is about 8¾ inches in diameter. Cover the lattice with plastic wrap. Slide the lattice (paper still attached) onto a baking sheet. Place in the freezer for at least 15 minutes to firm up.

Position a rack in the lower third of the oven and preheat to 400 degrees F. Roll out the larger dough portion between large sheets of baking parchment into a 13½-inch round. Occasionally check the underside of the dough during rolling and smooth out any wrinkles. Gently peel off the top sheet of paper. Center the round, dough side down, in the pie plate. Gently peel off the remaining paper. Smooth the dough into the plate and patch any tears, if necessary. Using kitchen shears or a paring knife, trim the overhang to ¾ inch. Fold the overhang under to form an edge that rests on the lip of the plate. Finish by fluting with your fingers or pressing into the edge with the tines of a fork. Prick the pastry all over with a fork. Loosely cover the pastry and place in the freezer while you heat the filling.

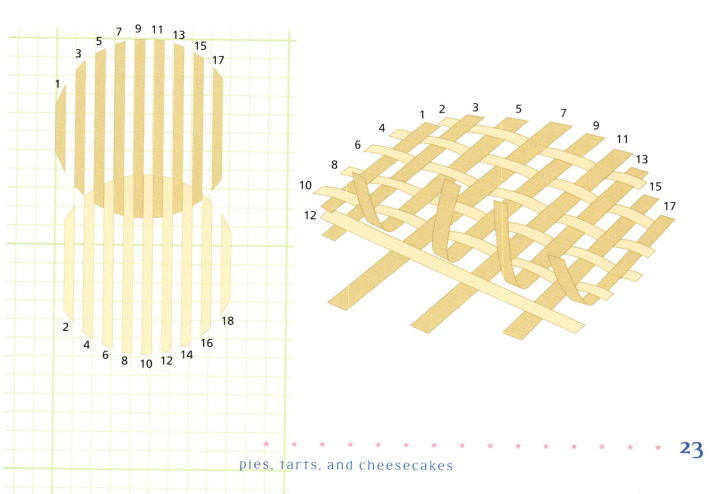

TO ASSEMBLE THE PIE: Transfer the filling to a large saucepan. Stirring gently, bring the filling to a boil over medium-high heat. Cook, stirring, just until piping hot. Turn out the filling into the bottom crust. Remove the plastic wrap from the chilled lattice. Invert the lattice (paper still attached) and center it over the fruit. Gently peel off the paper and discard. Trim off any excess dough, then tuck the lattice ends down into the filling along the edges. Brush the lattice lightly with the milk, then sprinkle with the sugar.

TO BAKE THE PIE: Set the pie on a rimmed baking sheet. Bake for 30 minutes. Remove from the oven and cover the crust edges with foil (or a pie shield) to prevent overbaking. Continue baking for 25 to 35 minutes, or until the top is nicely browned and the filling is bubbly. If the lattice begins to brown too rapidly, loosely cover the entire pie with tented aluminum foil during the last 15 to 20 minutes. Transfer the pie to a wire rack. Let cool for at least 1½ hours and preferably 4 hours or longer (for neater slices) before serving.

The pie will keep, covered, at room temperature for about 36 hours or refrigerated for up to 3 days longer. Let come to room temperature before serving.

VARIATION: Lattice-Topped Deep-Dish Cherry Pie

Prepare as for blueberry pie, substituting 4 cups pitted sour cherries and 2¼ cups pitted, chopped dark sweet cherries for the blueberries and omitting the lemon juice and zest. Drain the juice from the cherries. If there is more than 1 cup cherry juice, boil it down in a nonreactive saucepan until only 1 cup remains. Set the juice aside and stir it into the hot filling just before putting the filling in the pastry.

on Blueberry Hill

I didn't know about New Jersey's lofty place in blueberry history until I visited the eastern New Jersey village of Whitesbog, which held its twentieth annual Blueberry Festival in June 2003. Held in what is now the Pinelands National Reserve, the Whitesbog festival features a mix of lectures, tours, blueberry picking, bake sales, and, of course, a blueberry pie–eating contest.

Whitesbog, originally called White's Bogs, became known for cultivating cranberries in the mid-1800s, but among agriculturalists, it's probably more famous for pioneering the cultivation of the blueberry. Elizabeth C. White, whose father expanded the family's early cranberry operation, is credited with coming up with the idea of raising blueberries commercially. Wild blueberries grew on the higher ground around the cranberry bogs, but attempts to cultivate them had never succeeded. In 1911, White read an article on blueberry culture by Department of Agriculture horticulturist Dr. Frederick Coville and asked him to work with her.

The first key step of their collaboration was to collect the most promising indigenous varieties from the surrounding marshy Pine Barrens area. White sought help from the "Pineys," local woodsmen and country dwellers who knew the swamps and prime blueberry-picking spots intimately. She paid two dollars for every plant they collected that produced tasty berries measuring five eighths of an inch or larger and honored the finders by naming their discoveries after them.

Although only 10 percent of the first plants propagated survived, White and Coville persisted and were able to produce and ship America's first commercial blueberry crop in 1916. Later, Whitesbog helped spawn an entire new industry by providing blueberry plant stock to growers all across North America. Today nearly 90 percent of the annual $178 million U.S. blueberry crop comes from commercially cultivated blueberries.

Lattice-Topped deep-dish raspberry-apricot pie

I love this pie. It's a beautiful golden-red color and has a superb fruit flavor. I think the half-raspberry, half-apricot filling is better than an all-raspberry pie because it's less seedy.

Resist the impulse to cut into the pie until it is completely cool. Better yet, let it stand overnight. The filling and juices will thicken so the slices hold together better, and the pastry and fruit flavors will have time to blend.

Sour Cream Pie Pastry Dough (page 92)
All-purpose flour for dusting dough

FILLING

$1^{1}/_{3}$–$1^{1}/_{2}$ cups sugar (use larger amount if berries or apricots are very tart)

$^{1}/_{4}$ cup plus $^{1}/_{2}$ tablespoon cornstarch

$^{1}/_{8}$ teaspoon ground cardamom (optional)

$3^{1}/_{4}$ cups pitted and coarsely chopped (unpeeled) apricots (7–9 large apricots, or about $1^{1}/_{4}$ pounds)

$3^{1}/_{4}$ cups raspberries

$1^{1}/_{2}$ tablespoons unsalted butter, cut into bits

1 tablespoon whole milk or half-and-half for brushing on lattice top

1 tablespoon sugar for sprinkling on lattice top

TO ROLL OUT THE PASTRY: Lightly grease a $9^{1}/_{2}$-inch deep-dish pie plate or coat with nonstick spray. If the dough is cold and stiff, let it warm up until slightly pliable but still cool to the touch, then knead briefly. Generously dust both portions on both sides with flour. Roll out the smaller dough portion between sheets of baking parchment into a 9-inch round. Occasionally check the underside of the dough during rolling and smooth out any wrinkles. Gently peel off the top sheet of paper and pat it loosely back into place so it will be easy to remove later. Flip over the dough and peel off the other sheet. Using a pastry wheel or large knife, cut the dough into $^{1}/_{2}$-inch-wide strips. Peel every other strip off the paper and lay them in the order removed on another sheet of baking parchment. Place the strips you just removed crosswise about $^{1}/_{2}$ inch apart on the strips remaining on the original paper, interweaving them to form a lattice. (See the illustration on page 23.) Using the pastry wheel or knife, trim off any uneven ends so the lattice is about $8^{3}/_{4}$ inches in diameter. Cover the lattice with plastic wrap. Slide the lattice (paper still attached) onto a baking sheet. Place in the freezer for at least 15 minutes and up to 30 minutes to firm up.

Position a rack in the lower third of the oven and preheat to 400 degrees F. Roll out the larger dough portion between large sheets of baking parchment into a 13½ -inch round. Occasionally check the underside of the dough during rolling and smooth out any wrinkles. Gently peel off the top sheet of paper. Center the round, dough side down, in the pie plate. Gently peel off the remaining paper. Smooth the dough into the plate and patch any tears, if necessary. Using kitchen shears or a pairing knife, trim the overhang to ¾ inch. Fold the overhang under all the way around to form an edge that rests on the lip of the plate. Finish by fluting with your fingers or pressing into the edge with the tines of a fork. Prick the pastry all over with a fork. Loosely cover the pastry and place in the refrigerator while you make the filling.

TO MAKE THE FILLING: In a large nonreactive saucepan, thoroughly stir together the sugar, cornstarch, and cardamom (if using). Stir in the apricots, raspberries, and butter until well blended. (Don't worry if the filling tastes too sweet.) Heat over medium-high heat, gently stirring, just until the mixture comes to a boil. Turn out the filling into the bottom crust, mounding it in the center. Remove the plastic wrap from the chilled lattice. Invert the lattice and center it over the fruit. Gently peel off the paper and discard. Tuck the lattice ends down into the filling along the edges. Brush the lattice strips lightly with the milk, then sprinkle with the sugar.

TO BAKE THE PIE: Set the pie on a rimmed baking sheet. Bake for 30 minutes. Remove from the oven and cover the crust edges with foil (or a pie shield) to prevent overbaking. Continue baking for 25 to 35 minutes, or until the top is nicely browned and the filling is bubbly. If the lattice begins to brown too rapidly, loosely cover the entire pie with tented aluminum foil during the last 15 to 20 minutes. Transfer the pie to a wire rack. Let cool for at least 1½ hours and preferably 4 hours or longer (for neater slices) before serving.

The pie will keep, covered, at room temperature for up to 2 days or refrigerated for up to 2 days longer. Let come to room temperature before serving.

VARIATION: Raspberry-Plum Pie

Prepare as for raspberry-apricot pie, using 3½ cups raspberries and 3 cups pitted and chopped (unpeeled) tart red plums. Substitute ¼ teaspoon ground cinnamon for the cardamom if desired.

Prizewinning concord grape pie

If you like the distinctive fruity taste and bouquet of Concord grape juice, you will love this pie. It's a winner—literally. It received the award for best grape pie at the 2001, 2002, and 2003 Naples Grape Festivals, held in the scenic New York Finger Lakes region. It's an area where both dessert grapes and wine grapes grow in profusion.

The pie's creator, Jeni Makepeace, whose father was a plant manager for the Widmer Wine Cellars in Naples, knows the local grapes well. I spent a morning in her small, cheerful kitchen watching her prepare a few dozen of the eleven hundred homemade pies she turns out during festival week. Although some cooks use a combination of grapes, Jeni bakes only with Concords; she believes they are superior in flavor and texture to other varieties.

Concord grapes are grown in modest quantities in all parts of the country, but especially in New York, Michigan, and Ohio. You can find them in farmers' markets and some supermarkets during the autumn.

FILLING

- 1 cup sugar, plus a little more if grapes are very tart
- 3 tablespoons all-purpose flour
- 5 cups stemmed Concord grapes (about 2 pounds)
- 1 tablespoon unsalted butter, cut into bits

PASTRY

- 3 cups pastry flour, or 2 cups all-purpose flour and 1 cup cake flour, plus extra all-purpose flour for dusting pastry
- Scant 1 teaspoon salt
- 3/4 cup corn oil or other flavorless vegetable oil
- 1/4 cup cold water, plus more if needed

  About 2 teaspoons half-and-half or light cream for brushing on dough top
- 1 tablespoon sugar for sprinkling on dough top

Lightly grease a regular 9-inch pie plate or coat with nonstick spray.

TO MAKE THE FILLING: In a large bowl, thoroughly stir together the sugar and flour. Holding each grape over a heavy, nonreactive 2-quart saucepan (to catch the juice), squeeze until the pulp portion pops out into the pan; reserve the grape skins separately. Gently squeeze the excess juice from the skins and add it to the saucepan. If a fine texture is desired, coarsely chop the grape skins; otherwise, leave as is. Thoroughly stir the grape skins into the flour-sugar mixture and set aside. Bring the grape pulp and seeds and butter to a boil over medium-high heat. Adjust the heat so the pulp simmers gently. Cook, stirring occasionally, for 6 to 9 minutes, or until the pulp is soft and mushy and has boiled down slightly. Remove from the heat and let cool slightly. Carefully turn out the pulp into a food mill or fine sieve set over a bowl. Press through as much liquid and pulp as possible; discard the seeds. Stir the strained pulp into the grape skin mixture until blended; you should have about 3 cups. Set aside. The filling can be refrigerated in an airtight container for up to 3 days. Let come to room temperature before using.

TO MAKE THE PASTRY: Position a rack in the lower third of the oven and preheat to 425 degrees F. In a large bowl, thoroughly stir together the flour and salt. Stir in the oil with a fork just until incorporated. Add the water, gently stirring with the fork until the mixture is moistened and holds together. It may look streaked, but don't overmix. The pastry should not be at all dry; if necessary, add a bit more water until the mixture is evenly moistened but not wet. Lightly knead and shape the dough into a rough ball with your hands. Divide the dough in half, then shape each half into a smooth disk. Wrap one disk in plastic wrap.

TO ROLL OUT THE PASTRY: Generously dust the unwrapped pastry disk on both sides with flour. Roll it out between large sheets of baking parchment into a 13½-inch round. Occasionally check the underside of the dough during rolling and smooth out any wrinkles. Gently peel off the top sheet of paper. Center the round, dough side down, in the pie plate. Gently peel off the remaining paper. Smooth the pastry into the plate and patch any tears, if necessary. Using kitchen shears or a paring knife, trim the overhang to ¼ inch. Turn out the filling into the pastry.

Generously dust the second pastry disk with flour, then roll it out into a 13½-inch round as described above. Gently peel off the top sheet of paper, then pat back into place. Flip the dough; peel off the bottom sheet. Center the round, dough side down, over the filling. Gently peel off the remaining paper and patch any tears, if necessary. Trim the overhang to ¾ inch. Fold the overhang under the bottom pastry to form an edge that rests on the lip of the plate. Press the layers together, then flute with your fingers or press with the tines of a fork all the way around. Brush the dough top (not the edges) with the half-and-half, then sprinkle with the sugar. Cut steam vents in the top, using a sharp, lightly greased paring knife.

TIP

Instead of rolling out dough between sheets of baking parchment, Jeni uses sheets cut from large plastic bags. (The translucent bags grocery stores provide to hold produce work very well.) The plastic is sturdier than parchment, and the dough peels off its surface more readily.

TO BAKE THE PIE: Set the pie on a rimmed baking sheet. Bake for 25 to 35 minutes, or until nicely browned all over. If the edges begin to brown too rapidly, cover with foil (or a pie shield) during the last few minutes of baking. Transfer the pie to a wire rack. Let cool for at least 2 hours and preferably 4 hours (for neater slices) before serving.

The pie will keep, lightly covered, at room temperature for up to 24 hours or refrigerated for 3 days. Let come to room temperature before serving.

The concord connection

America's best-known native grape, the Concord, is named for Concord, Massachusetts. It was developed there by Ephraim Wales Bull, who came up with the uniquely American variety in 1849, after cross-breeding vines of indigenous species for more than ten years. The original parent vine of the Concord grape still grows in a garden near his farmhouse, which is preserved on Lexington Road outside Concord.

Twenty years after Bull's horticultural experiment, physician Thomas Bramwell Welch devised a successful pasteurizing method for unfermented grape juice. His first customers were ministers, who used the juice for Communion services. His son formed Welch's, which has been synonymous with Concord grape juice ever since.

American Grape Festival, Italian Style

The granddaddy of American grape festivals, the Tontitown Grape Festival in northwestern Arkansas, has been held annually since 1988. It began as a ceremony in which a group of Italian immigrants gave thanks for their first harvest. They were originally recruited from Italy's hill country to work on a southern Arkansas cotton and sugar plantation. After the plantation owner died and a malaria epidemic devastated the community, the immigrants resettled in a mountainous area of the state, where they could grow grapes and other fruits as they had in Italy. They soon discovered that Concord grapes thrived in the climate, and eventually they produced enough to support a juice-processing plant for Welch's.

Today the Concord grape industry has dwindled in the region, but the town still honors its past by crowning a "Miss Concordia" and holding a huge spaghetti dinner every year.

meringue-topped Rhubarb-maple pie

This delightful and unusual recipe is adapted from one shared with me by Edith Foulds, a seventh-generation Vermonter who now lives in South Burlington. Her fondness for maple dates back to her childhood in Bennington, where her grandfather made his maple syrup in large kettles behind the house. Like many New Englanders, she is also a great fan of rhubarb.

The mild, light meringue topping adds a slight sweetness, which helps balance the tang of the rhubarb and the richness of the pastry. Because rhubarb has a lot of juice that can make the bottom of the pie soggy, it is briefly boiled with some sugar to release its juices. The juice is then drained off, thickened, and cooked with the rest of the filling.

Single crust All-Purpose Pie Pastry Dough (page 90)

All-purpose flour for dusting dough

FILLING

4½ cups ½- to ¾-inch-long pieces of rhubarb (1½–1¾ pounds trimmed stalks)

¾ cup granulated sugar (divided)

1½ teaspoons fresh lime or lemon juice

¼–⅓ cup orange juice, if needed

3½ tablespoons cornstarch

Pinch of salt

⅔ cup maple syrup, preferably light amber

2 large egg yolks

MERINGUE

4 large egg whites, completely free of yolk and at room temperature

Generous ¼ teaspoon cream of tartar

Pinch of salt

¾ cup plus 2 tablespoons powdered sugar

½ teaspoon vanilla extract

TO ROLL OUT THE PASTRY: Lightly grease a regular 9-inch pie plate or coat with nonstick spray. If the dough is cold and stiff, let it warm up until slightly pliable but still cool to the touch. Generously dust it on both sides with flour. Roll out the dough between large sheets of baking parchment into a 13-inch round. Occasionally check the underside of the dough during rolling and smooth out any wrinkles. Gently peel off the top sheet of paper, then pat it back into place. Flip the dough; peel off the bottom sheet. Center the round, dough side down, in the pie plate. Gently peel off the remaining paper. Smooth the dough into the plate and patch any tears, if necessary. Using kitchen shears or a paring knife, trim the overhang to ¾ inch. Fold the overhang under to form an edge that rests on the lip of the plate. Finish by fluting with your fingers or pressing into the edge with the tines of a fork. Prick the pastry all over with a fork. Loosely cover the pastry and place in the freezer for 15 minutes or in the refrigerator for at least 30 minutes and up to several hours.

TO BAKE THE PASTRY: Position a rack in the lower third of the oven and preheat to 400 degrees F. Insert a large square of aluminum foil coated with nonstick spray (or use nonstick foil) oiled side down into the chilled shell, smoothing the foil over the bottom and sides and folding it out over the rim to cover the pastry. Fill the foil with dried beans, spreading them so they extend up the plate sides. Set the pie shell on a rimmed baking sheet. Bake for 25 minutes. Carefully remove the foil and beans from the shell. Continue baking for 5 to 10 minutes longer, or until the shell is nicely browned all over. If the edges brown too rapidly, cover with strips of foil (or a pie shield). Transfer the pie shell to a wire rack to cool. The pie shell will keep, covered, at room temperature for up to 24 hours.

TO MAKE THE FILLING: In a large nonreactive saucepan, thoroughly stir together the rhubarb, ½ cup of the granulated sugar, and the lime juice. Let stand, stirring once or twice, for about 10 minutes, or until the sugar is mostly dissolved and the mixture looks wet. Bring to a boil over medium-high heat, stirring. Cook, stirring, until the rhubarb pieces exude some juice and just begin to soften but still hold their shape, about 4 minutes. Remove from the heat and let cool for about 10 minutes. Put the rhubarb in a sieve set over a large glass measure. Press down hard on the rhubarb to extract as much juice as possible. You should have ½ to ¾ cup juice; if necessary, add enough orange juice to yield ¾ cup.

Reposition the rack in the middle of the oven and preheat to 350 degrees F. Rinse and dry the saucepan. Put the remaining ¼ cup granulated sugar, the cornstarch, and salt in the pan and whisk until well combined. Add the rhubarb juice, whisking vigorously until the mixture is completely smooth. Bring to a boil over medium-high heat, whisking. Lower the heat slightly and cook, whisking constantly, until very thick, smooth, and translucent, about 1 minute. Remove from the heat. Vigorously whisk in the maple syrup until the mixture is completely smooth.

TIP

To minimize beading on the meringue top, make the pie on a dry day.

In a small deep bowl, whisk the egg yolks until lightly blended. Pouring slowly and whisking constantly, add about ¼ cup of the maple mixture to the yolks. Add the yolk mixture to the saucepan, whisking. Cook over medium-high heat, stirring constantly and frequently scraping the pan bottom with a wooden spoon, until the mixture boils for a full 1½ minutes. Do not undercook, or the filling may thin out later. Stir the reserved rhubarb into the maple mixture. Cook, stirring, just until the rhubarb is piping hot; the filling will be fairly thick. Cover and set aside.

TO MAKE THE MERINGUE: In a completely grease-free large bowl, combine the egg whites, cream of tartar, and salt. Using a mixer on low speed (with a whisk-shaped beater, if available), beat the mixture until frothy. Raise the speed to medium and continue beating until the mixture is smooth, fluffy, and opaque, but still too soft to hold peaks. (Check by stopping and lifting the beater.) Immediately add the powdered sugar 2 tablespoons at a time, beating for about 20 seconds after each addition. Add the vanilla. Raise the speed to medium-high and beat for 2 minutes, scraping down the sides of the bowl as needed. Raise the speed to high and beat for about 1 minute longer, or until the meringue is fluffy and stands in firm but not dry peaks.

TO ASSEMBLE THE PIE: Turn out the hot filling into the prebaked pastry shell. Set the pie on a rimmed baking sheet. Spread half the meringue over the filling, making sure the meringue touches the pastry all the way around. Top with the remaining meringue, mounding it in the center. Attractively swirl the meringue with a table knife or the back of a large spoon.

TO BAKE THE PIE: Bake for 12 to 17 minutes, or until the meringue is evenly tinged with brown all over. For even browning, rotate the pie from front to back after 6 minutes. Transfer the pie to a wire rack. Let cool for at least 2 hours and preferably 3 or 4 hours before chilling or covering to minimize any beading of the meringue.

The pie will keep, covered, at room temperature for up to 12 hours (some beading may occur after the first few hours) or refrigerated for up to 2 days. The crust will soften with longer storage. Let come to room temperature before serving.

AT RIGHT

FRIED PIES

PAGE 36

fried pies

makes 10 to 15
4¼- to 5-inch pies

Enjoyed in parts of the South for at least two hundred years, these hand-size, fruit-filled pastries are likely derived from the fried British turnovers called pasties. They are particularly delicious eaten still warm from the skillet, and I'm surprised they aren't more widely known.

This fine heirloom recipe is from the collection of the late Johnnie Mayo Richardson and was shared with me by her son, food photographer Alan Richardson. Alan, who grew up in Mississippi, recalls that his aunt Coralydia and grandmother Inez always seemed to have a stack of fried pies in the kitchen for snacking. They were also a popular offering at family reunions and on the long dessert tables at church dinners held after the Sunday service. Usually, he says, the pies were apple, but sometimes they were peach or apricot. Depending on the season, the fillings were made with either fresh or dried fruit (see the variation).

These pies were originally made with lard. Since obtaining fresh, clean-tasting lard is difficult today, I call for shortening here.

FRESH FRUIT FILLING

- 3½ cups peeled, cored or pitted, and diced (⅓-inch) apples or peaches
- 7 tablespoons granulated sugar, or more to taste
- ¼ teaspoon ground cinnamon
- ¼ cup cold water (divided)
- 1 tablespoon plus 1 teaspoon cornstarch for apple filling or 2½ tablespoons for peach filling

DOUGH

- 3 cups all-purpose flour
- 1½ teaspoons granulated sugar
- ¾ teaspoon salt
- 1 cup solid white shortening, cut into chunks
- 9–12 tablespoons ice water

Solid white shortening for frying
Powdered sugar for dusting pies (optional)

TO MAKE THE FRESH FRUIT FILLING: In a heavy, nonreactive medium saucepan, stir together the apples, granulated sugar, cinnamon, and 1 tablespoon of the water. Bring to a simmer, stirring, over medium heat. Adjust the heat so the mixture simmers gently. Cook, stirring frequently, until the fruit is tender and boiled down slightly, 4 to 6 minutes. In a small bowl or cup, stir together the remaining 3 tablespoons water and the cornstarch until well blended. Add the mixture to the fruit and cook, stirring, until the filling thickens and clears, about 1 minute. Taste and stir in more sugar, if desired; it's best not to skimp on sweetness. Let cool to room temperature. The filling will keep, refriger-

36

THE ALL-AMERICAN DESSERT BOOK

ated in an airtight container, for up to a week. Let come to room temperature before using.

TO MAKE THE DOUGH: In a large bowl, thoroughly stir together the flour, granulated sugar, and salt. Using a pastry blender, forks, or your fingertips, mix in the shortening until the mixture has the consistency of pea-size crumbs. Add 9 tablespoons ice water, tossing with a fork or mixing with your fingertips until evenly incorporated and the mixture holds together. If it seems dry, mix in more ice water 2 to 3 teaspoons at a time. Knead the dough until smooth, then divide in half and shape into two 4-inch disks. Wrap each in wax paper and refrigerate for at least 30 minutes and up to 1 hour.

TO ROLL OUT THE DOUGH: Working with one disk and keeping the other refrigerated, roll out the dough between sheets of baking parchment until it is a scant ¼ inch thick. Occasionally check the underside of the dough during rolling and smooth out any wrinkles. Lay the dough (paper still attached) on a baking sheet and return to the refrigerator. Repeat with the second dough portion. Refrigerate for at least 15 minutes and up to 30 minutes to firm up.

Working with one dough portion and keeping the other refrigerated, gently peel off the top sheet of paper and pat it loosely back into place so it will be easy to remove later. Flip over the dough and peel off the other sheet. Using a 4- to 5-inch bowl or saucer as a guide, cut the dough into rounds using a paring knife. Stack the rounds between sheets of wax paper on a baking sheet and refrigerate them as you work. Reserve any dough scraps, wrapping them in wax paper. When both dough portions have been cut, combine all the scraps and repeat the rolling, chilling, and cutting until all the dough is used. You can stack the rounds of dough between sheets of wax paper, place in a plastic bag, and refrigerate for 2 or 3 days. Let warm up slightly before using.

TO FORM AND FRY THE PIES: Fill each dough round by placing 1½ to 2 tablespoons of the fruit filling in the center. Fold over the dough to form a half-moon. Using your fingertips or a pastry brush, wet the inside edges of the pastry with a little water. Firmly crimp the edges with your fingertips or a fork to seal them tightly.

Heat a generous ½-inch-deep layer of shortening in a 12-inch skillet over medium-high heat until a small bit of dough sizzles when dropped into the pan. Using a heatproof slotted spoon, or tongs, place 4 or 5 pies, slightly separated, in the skillet, being careful not to splash the fat. Adjust the heat so that they fry gently; if they cook too rapidly on the outside, they will be underdone on the inside. Fry until light golden brown, 3 to 4 minutes. Turn and fry on the other side until golden brown, 2 to 3 minutes longer. Place on a triple thickness of paper towels to drain. If desired, dust the fried pies with powdered sugar before serving.

The pies are best served warm and fresh. They will keep, wrapped airtight at room temperature, for a day or so. For the freshest taste, rewarm them slightly before serving.

VARIATION: Dried Fruit Filling

2	cups finely chopped dried apples, dried peaches, or dried apricots, or a combination
2¹/₂	cups water, plus more if needed
5–8	tablespoons sugar, to taste
¹/₄–¹/₂	teaspoon ground cinnamon, to taste
¹/₈	teaspoon ground allspice

Combine the fruit and water in a heavy, nonreactive medium saucepan. Bring to a boil over medium heat, then lower the heat so the mixture simmers gently. Cook, covered, for 15 minutes; check and add more water if needed. Uncover and continue simmering, stirring occasionally and watching carefully, until the fruit is tender and has the consistency of preserves, 5 to 15 minutes longer depending on the fruit. As necessary, add water to prevent the filling from boiling dry. Stir in the sugar, cinnamon, and allspice and cook until the sugar dissolves. Let cool to room temperature and proceed as for the fresh fruit pies.

church fare

Today the art of making fried pies seems to be disappearing from the South, which is a shame. But Tim Rutherford, a Savannah magazine editor who grew up eating fried pies in Tennessee, reports an encouraging recent sighting of them at a church fair in eastern Tennessee: "A group of church women were cooking them in huge iron skillets over wood-burning stoves—apple, peach and apricot—the Holy Trinity of fried pie flavors."

pumpkin pie with pecan crunch streusel

This recipe bridges the gap between those who want something new on the Thanksgiving dessert menu and those who have to have their pumpkin pie. It's a nice change of pace from classic versions, owing to an abundant, wonderfully crisp streusel topping. The streusel will stay crisp even if the pie is made several days ahead.

Single crust All-Purpose Pie Pastry Dough (page 90)

All-purpose flour for dusting dough

FILLING

4	large eggs
1	cup plus 2 tablespoons packed light brown sugar
1 1/2	teaspoons ground cinnamon
1	teaspoon freshly grated nutmeg or 3/4 teaspoon ground nutmeg
1	teaspoon peeled and finely grated fresh gingerroot or 3/4 teaspoon ground ginger
1/8	teaspoon salt
1	15-ounce can solid-pack pumpkin (not seasoned pie filling)
1/2	cup half-and-half or light cream

PECAN CRUNCH STREUSEL

1 1/4	cups chopped pecans
2/3	cup finely crushed corn flakes
6	tablespoons packed light brown sugar
6	tablespoons all-purpose flour
1/8	teaspoon salt
6	tablespoons (3/4 stick) unsalted butter, melted

TO ROLL OUT THE PASTRY: Lightly grease a 9½-inch deep-dish pie plate or coat with nonstick spray. If the dough is cold and stiff, let it warm up until slightly pliable but still cool to the touch. Generously dust it on both sides with flour. Roll out the dough between large sheets of baking parchment into a 13½-inch round. Occasionally check the underside of the dough during rolling and smooth out any wrinkles. Gently peel off the top sheet of paper, then pat it back into place. Flip the dough; peel off the bottom sheet. Center the round, dough side down, in the pie plate. Gently peel off the remaining paper. Smooth the dough into the plate and patch any tears, if necessary. Using kitchen shears or a paring knife, trim the overhang to ¾ inch. Fold the overhang under to form an edge that rests on the lip of the plate. Finish by fluting with your fingers or pressing into the edge with the tines of a fork. Prick the pastry all over with a fork. Loosely cover the pastry and place in the freezer while you make the filling.

tip

To crush the corn flakes, place them in a heavy plastic bag. Roll a rolling pin back and forth until they are crushed into ⅛-inch or finer bits. Measure out the ⅔ cup after the corn flakes are crushed.

Position a rack in the lower third of the oven and preheat to 375 degrees F.

TO MAKE THE FILLING: In a large bowl, thoroughly whisk together the eggs, brown sugar, cinnamon, nutmeg, ginger, and salt until the sugar dissolves and the mixture is smooth. Add the pumpkin and half-and-half, stirring until well blended. Turn out the filling into the pastry. Set the pie on a rimmed baking sheet. Bake for 35 to 45 minutes, or until the filling looks set except in the center third of the pie, which should jiggle when the plate is shaken.

MEANWHILE, TO MAKE THE STREUSEL: In a medium bowl, using your fingertips or two forks, mix together the pecans, corn flakes, brown sugar, flour, and salt until well blended. Add the butter and continue mixing until evenly incorporated. Evenly sprinkle the streusel over the partially set filling. Reposition the rack in the middle of the oven. Continue baking for 20 to 25 minutes longer, or until the streusel is golden brown and very crisp. Transfer the pie to a wire rack. Let cool, then refrigerate until the pumpkin filling sets, at least 45 minutes, before serving.

Serve at room temperature or lightly chilled.

The pie will keep, covered, in the refrigerator for up to 4 days.

Thanksgiving Treat–but Hold the Fish!

The Pilgrims' first harvest feast in 1621 may have included pumpkin, but probably not in pie form. However, the prominence of pumpkin in the early American diet is underscored in John Josselyn's *Account of Two Voyages to New-England,* a 1674 work in which he detailed his visits to the New World. He referred to stewed pumpkin as an "Ancient New England standing dish," meaning that it was commonplace. Sliced pumpkin, or "pompion," as it was then called, was cooked "upon a gentle fire a whole day" and seasoned with vinegar and some ginger. Josselyn went on to note that it was "tart like an Apple" and recommended serving it with fish or meat.

By the late 1700s, pumpkin pie had arrived on the scene and was becoming linked with regional Thanksgiving celebrations. Two basic recipes—one sweetened with sugar, the other with molasses—appear in Amelia Simmons's 1796 cookbook, *American Cookery.* At first glance, it's easy to miss the pumpkin pie recipes. They're tucked in the pudding section, because colonial cooks rightfully recognized that they are simply puddings baked in a pastry crust.

Later, Sarah Josepha Hale, a noted nineteenth-century editor, novelist, and cookbook author, touted pumpkin pie as *the* Thanksgiving dish in her magazine, *Godey's Lady's Book.* In her 1827 novel *Northwood,* she also described it as "an indispensable part of a good and true Yankee Thanksgiving." Thanks mostly to Hale's efforts, Thanksgiving was declared a national holiday in 1863.

butterscotch custard pie

During the first half of the twentieth century, butterscotch pie was a standard in American dessert collections. Initially, it may have been popular because the essential ingredients—butter, brown sugar, eggs, and milk or cream—were usually on hand in the country cook's larder. It has stayed around because it's so delicious.

If you've never tried a traditional butterscotch custard pie, you'll notice that its flavor is rather different from artificial butterscotch. The brown sugar taste of the real thing is quieter and subtler, but also soothing and memorable. Real butterscotch is made by melting brown sugar and bubbling it together with butter. Oddly, some recipes omit this key step, and I always find their flavor a bit lacking.

This pie is rich and sweet but not cloying, especially when served with a generous dollop of whipped cream. When I yearn for comfort food, this is one of the first desserts I make.

Single crust All-Purpose Pie Pastry Dough (page 90)

All-purpose flour for dusting dough

FILLING

2 cups heavy (whipping) cream (divided)

1 cup packed light brown sugar

3 tablespoons light corn syrup

3 tablespoons unsalted butter, cut into chunks

2 large eggs plus 3 large egg yolks

2½ tablespoons dark rum or bourbon (optional)

⅛ teaspoon salt

2 teaspoons vanilla extract

Unsweetened or very lightly sweetened whipped cream for garnish

TO ROLL OUT THE PASTRY: Lightly grease a regular 9-inch pie plate or coat with nonstick spray. If the dough is cold and stiff, let it warm up until slightly pliable but still cool to the touch. Generously dust it on both sides with flour. Roll out the dough between large sheets of baking parchment into a 13-inch round. Occasionally check the underside of the dough during rolling and smooth out any wrinkles. Gently peel off the top sheet of paper, then pat it back into place. Flip the dough; peel off the bottom sheet. Center the round, dough side down, in the pie plate. Gently peel off the remaining paper. Smooth the dough into the plate and patch any tears, if necessary. Using kitchen shears or a paring knife, trim the overhang to ¾ inch. Fold the overhang under to form an edge that rests on the lip of the plate. Finish by fluting with your fingers or pressing into the edge with the tines of a fork. Prick the pas-

tip

Custard pies sometimes suffer from soggy crusts. To avoid this, fully bake the pie shell ahead and be sure it is hot when you add the filling and return it to the oven.

try all over with a fork. Loosely cover the pastry and place in the freezer until cool and firm, at least 15 minutes and up to 30 minutes.

TO BAKE THE PASTRY: Position a rack in the lower third of the oven and preheat to 400 degrees F. Insert a large square of aluminum foil coated with nonstick spray (or use nonstick foil) oiled side down into the chilled shell, smoothing the foil over the bottom and sides and folding it out over the rim to cover the pastry. Fill the foil with dried beans, spreading them so they extend up the plate sides. Set the pie shell on a rimmed baking sheet. Bake for 25 minutes. Carefully remove the foil and beans from the shell. Continue baking for 5 to 10 minutes longer, or until the shell is nicely browned all over. If the edges brown too rapidly, cover with strips of foil (or a pie shield). Transfer the pie shell to a wire rack. The pie shell will keep, stored airtight, at room temperature for up to 24 hours.

Reposition the rack in the middle of the oven and reset to 325 degrees F.

TO MAKE THE FILLING: Place 1 cup of the cream in a 2-cup glass measure and microwave on high power until hot but not boiling, 1½ to 2 minutes. (Alternatively, heat in a heavy medium saucepan over medium-high heat until hot but not boiling.)

Combine the brown sugar and corn syrup in a heavy 2-quart saucepan over medium heat. Cook, stirring with a wooden spoon, until the sugar completely melts and bubbles, about 2 minutes. Immediately stir in the butter. Adjust the heat so the mixture bubbles and cook, stirring, for 1½ minutes. Standing back to avoid splattering and steam, immediately stir in the hot cream using a long-handled wooden spoon.

Continue simmering, stirring constantly, for about 3 minutes longer, or until the mixture darkens slightly and any sugary lumps dissolve. Remove from the heat. Immediately cool the mixture by stirring in the remaining 1 cup cream. In a large bowl using a wire whisk, beat together the eggs and yolks, rum (if using), salt, and vanilla. Slowly stir the sugar-butter mixture into the egg mixture in a thin stream. Strain the custard through a fine sieve into a 4-cup glass measure.

TO BAKE THE PIE: Set the pie shell on a rimmed baking sheet. Place in the oven, then pour the filling into the pie shell. (Depending on the pie plate, it may be quite full. If there is any leftover filling, bake it in a custard cup.) Bake for 5 minutes. Reduce the oven temperature to 325 degrees F and continue baking for 25 to 35 minutes longer, or until the filling appears set except right in the center, which should jiggle when the plate is shaken. If at any time the filling begins to bubble at the edges, reduce the heat to 300 degrees F. Transfer the pie to a wire rack. Let cool completely. Refrigerate, covered, for at least 1 hour or up to 3 days.

For best flavor, let the chilled pie warm up almost to room temperature before serving. Garnish the whole pie with whipped cream rosettes, or add dollops of whipped cream to individual slices.

pies

"Bread, men say, is the staff of life,
But they will often concede
That were it not for our dainty pies
The staff would be heavy indeed."

—*Recipes Published by the Ladies of the North Congregational Church*
(Nantucket Island, 1902)

American Diner custard Pie

This simple pie has a gentle, comforting custardy flavor and a smooth, slip-across-the-tongue texture. It is a classic offering of American diners, but I was surprised to discover that it was on the scene long before they were. Mrs. Lydia Maria Child, in her 1833 work, *The American Frugal Housewife,* included a recipe strikingly similar to this modern version. It's likely to remain a favorite for at least another hundred years.

Single crust All-Purpose Pie Pastry Dough (page 90)
All-purpose flour for dusting dough

FILLING

2¼ cups half-and-half or whole milk
2 2-by-1-inch strips lemon zest (yellow part of skin)
1 small nutmeg, cut in half (divided)

2¾ cups sugar
4 large eggs
⅛ teaspoon salt
2½ teaspoons vanilla extract

TO ROLL OUT THE PASTRY: Lightly grease a regular 9-inch pie plate or coat with nonstick spray. If the dough is cold and stiff, let it warm up until slightly pliable but still cool to the touch. Generously dust it on both sides with flour. Roll out the dough between large sheets of baking parchment into a 13-inch round. Occasionally check the underside of the dough during rolling and smooth out any wrinkles. Gently peel off the top sheet of paper, then pat it back into place. Flip the dough; peel off the bottom sheet. Center the round, dough side down, in the pie plate. Gently peel off the remaining paper. Smooth the dough into the plate and patch any tears, if necessary. Using kitchen shears or a paring knife, trim the overhang to ¾ inch. Fold the overhang under to form an edge that rests on the lip of the plate. Finish by fluting with your fingers or pressing into the edge with the tines of a fork. Prick the pastry all over with a fork. Loosely cover the pastry and place in the freezer for at least 15 minutes and preferably 30 minutes.

TO BAKE THE PASTRY: Position a rack in the lower third of the oven and preheat to 400 degrees F. Insert a large square of aluminum foil coated with nonstick spray (or use nonstick foil) oiled side down into the chilled shell, smoothing the foil over the bottom and sides and folding it out over the rim to cover the pastry. Fill the foil with dried beans, spreading them so they extend up the plate sides. Set the pie shell on a rimmed baking sheet. Bake for 25 minutes. Carefully remove the foil and beans from the shell. Continue baking for 5 to 10 minutes longer, or until the shell is nicely browned all over. If the edges brown too rapidly, cover with strips of foil (or a pie shield). Transfer the pie shell to a wire rack. The pie shell will keep, stored airtight, at room temperature for up to 24 hours. Place on a rack in the lower third of the oven and reheat at 350 degrees F for 5 minutes, or until piping hot, before adding the filling and baking.

Reposition the rack in the middle of the oven and reduce the heat to 350 degrees F.

TO MAKE THE FILLING: Place the half-and-half and lemon zest in a 4-cup glass measure. Cut one half of the nutmeg in half again and add to the measure. Microwave on high power until very hot but not boiling. (Alternatively, heat in a heavy medium saucepan over medium-high heat, stirring, until very hot but not boiling.)

In a large bowl using a wire whisk, beat the sugar, eggs, salt, and vanilla until well blended. Beating constantly with the whisk, very slowly pour the hot half-and-half mixture into the egg mixture in a thin stream; work gradually to avoid overheating (and possibly curdling) the eggs. Strain the custard through a fine sieve into a 4-cup measure. Set the pie shell on a rimmed baking sheet and place in the oven. Pour the custard into the pie shell. (If there is extra filling, bake it in a custard cup.) Grate the remaining nutmeg half and sprinkle ¼ teaspoon (or more to taste) over the custard.

TO BAKE THE PIE: Bake for 10 minutes. Reduce the oven temperature to 325 degrees F and continue baking for 20 to 25 minutes, or until the filling appears set except in the very center, which should barely jiggle when the plate is shaken. If at any time the filling begins to bubble, reduce the heat to 300 degrees F. Transfer the pie to a wire rack. Let cool completely. Cover and refrigerate for at least 1 hour, or until slightly chilled. Using a large sharp knife dipped in hot water and wiped clean between cuts, cut the pie into wedges and serve.

The pie will keep in the refrigerator for up to 3 days. Let warm up slightly before serving.

brownie Pecan-PraLine mousse Pie

Big, luscious-looking chocolate mousse pies are a standard all over America, though they don't always taste as good as they look. This one does.

The dense brownie pie shell is a deeply chocolatey mixture that puffs up and then falls slightly in the center during baking. The filling is an airy mousse studded with pecan praline, topped with more pecan praline, and drizzled with chocolate. Everyone who tries this pie raves.

CRUST AND GLAZE

- 6 ounces bittersweet (not unsweetened) or semisweet chocolate, broken up or coarsely chopped
- 8 tablespoons (1 stick) unsalted butter, slightly softened
- 2 teaspoons corn oil or other flavorless vegetable oil
- ½ cup plus 2 tablespoons all-purpose flour
- ¼ teaspoon baking powder
- ¼ teaspoon salt
- ½ cup plus 2 tablespoons granulated sugar
- 1 large egg plus 1 large egg yolk
- 2 teaspoons vanilla extract

PECAN PRALINE

- 1⅓ cups chopped pecans
- 3 tablespoons packed light brown sugar
- 1½ tablespoons light corn syrup
- 1 tablespoon unsalted butter, slightly softened

MOUSSE

- 1 tablespoon plus ½ teaspoon unflavored gelatin (about 1½ packets)
- ⅔ cup plus 2 tablespoons water (divided)
- ½ cup plus 2 tablespoons granulated sugar
- ½ cup light corn syrup
- 2 teaspoons vanilla extract
- 1 cup heavy (whipping) cream

TO MAKE THE CRUST AND GLAZE: Position a rack in the middle of the oven and preheat to 325 degrees F. Generously grease a 9-inch regular pie plate or generously coat with nonstick spray. In a microwave-safe medium bowl, melt the chocolate and butter in a microwave on high power for 1 minute. Stop and stir. Continue microwaving on medium power, stopping and stirring at 30-second intervals, until almost melted. Let the residual heat complete the melting. (Alternatively, in a heavy medium saucepan, melt the chocolate and butter over lowest heat, stirring until almost melted, then remove from the heat. Watch carefully so the chocolate does not overheat or burn.) Stir together 2 tablespoons of the melted chocolate mixture and the oil in a small microwave-safe bowl; set aside for the glaze. Set the remaining chocolate mixture aside to cool slightly.

In a medium bowl, thoroughly stir together the flour, baking powder, and salt. Stir the granulated sugar into the chocolate mixture until well blended. Add the egg, yolk, and vanilla to the chocolate mixture and stir vigorously for 1 minute, or until well blended. Stir in the flour mixture just until evenly incorporated. Turn out the batter into the pie plate, spreading it to the edges.

Bake for 26 to 31 minutes, or until a toothpick inserted in the center comes out clean except for the bottom ¼ inch, which should still be wet. Transfer to a wire rack. Let stand for at least 45 minutes, or until thoroughly cooled; the brownie will sink in the center. The crust will keep, tightly covered, at room temperature for up to 24 hours or frozen for several days. Let thaw completely before using.

TO MAKE THE PECAN PRALINE: Preheat the oven to 350 degrees F. Line a rimmed baking sheet with aluminum foil. Spread the pecans on the baking sheet. Toast, stirring occasionally, until fragrant and lightly browned, 7 to 9 minutes. Let cool.

In a medium bowl, stir together the brown sugar, corn syrup, butter, and toasted pecans until the pecans are coated. Return the pecan mixture to the foil-lined baking sheet and bake, stirring once or twice, for 5 to 9 minutes, or until melted, bubbly, and nicely browned. Transfer the sheet to a wire rack. Let cool. Using your fingers, break the praline into small bits.

TO MAKE THE MOUSSE: In a small cup, sprinkle the gelatin over ⅓ cup cold water. Let stand, stirring once or twice, for 5 minutes. In a heavy 2-quart saucepan over medium heat, stir together the granulated sugar, corn syrup, and 2 tablespoons hot water until well blended. Raise the heat to medium-high and bring the mixture to a gentle boil, stirring constantly. Adjust the heat so the mixture boils gently. Cover the pan tightly and boil for 3 minutes to allow steam to dissolve the sugar on the pan sides. Uncover and continue boiling without further stirring; lift the pan and gently swirl the mixture occasionally until it turns a medium amber color (262 to 264 degrees F on a candy thermometer), 4 to 5 minutes. Immediately remove from the heat. Standing back to avoid splatters and steam, and using a long-handled wooden spoon, carefully stir in ⅓ cup hot water. Continue stirring until the bubbling subsides. If the caramel is lumpy or hardened, stir until it dissolves. Stir in the gelatin mixture until it dissolves completely.

pies, tarts, and cheesecakes

Transfer the mixture to a large bowl. Add the vanilla. Using a mixer (with a whisk-shaped beater, if available), beat the mixture for 30 seconds on low, then medium speed. Gradually raise the speed to high and beat until the mixture is stiffened, opaque, and very fluffy, 5 to 6 minutes. Let stand until cooled to barely warm.

TO ASSEMBLE THE PIE: In a separate large bowl, beat the cream (using the cleaned whisk-shaped beater, if available) to soft peaks, about 2 minutes. Fold the whipped cream and a generous half of the praline into the mousse. Spoon the mousse into the pie shell, mounding it in the center. Sprinkle the remaining praline on top. If necessary, rewarm the reserved glaze in the microwave on medium power for a few seconds until fluid. Drizzle decoratively over the pie top. Refrigerate until chilled and set, at least 1 hour and preferably 2 hours. Serve chilled, cut into wedges. The pie slices best with a large sharp knife dipped in hot water and wiped clean after each cut.

The pie will keep, covered, in the refrigerator for up to 5 days.

coconut
chiffon pie

makes 8 servings

This recipe was inspired by a coconut cream pie that writer Greg Schneider described as "life-changing" in a 2002 *Washington Post* article about a visit to the isolated coastal town of Cape Charles, on the southern tip of Virginia's Eastern Shore. He sampled the pie at a restaurant called the Harbor Grille.

I called Julie Delsignore, the owner of the Harbor Grille, to ask for the recipe. It turned out to be the creation of a Virginia Beach caterer friend, Colleen Wallace, who had made Julie promise never to reveal it. Fortunately, Julie was willing to provide tips that were helpful in creating the following recipe. Like its prototype, it is not a traditional coconut custard cream pie, but instead features a light, airy, very flavorful chiffon-style filling. A generous topping of toasted coconut adds both color and contrasting crunch.

Note that the recipe calls for cream of coconut, which is thick and sweet and usually found in the mixed-drinks section of the supermarket. Don't use unsweetened coconut milk, which is thin and won't work. The filling calls for no added sugar; the cream of coconut and the shredded coconut provide all that is needed.

Single crust All-Purpose Pie Pastry Dough (page 90)

All-purpose flour for dusting dough

FILLING AND GARNISH

3 1/3 cups shredded sweetened coconut

1 tablespoon plus 2 teaspoons unflavored gelatin (scant 2 packets)

2 cups whole or low-fat milk

1 15- or 16-ounce can cream of coconut (not coconut milk), stirred well before using

4 large egg yolks

2 1/2 teaspoons vanilla extract

1/2 teaspoon coconut extract (optional)

1 teaspoon finely grated lemon zest (yellow part of skin)

1 1/2 cups chilled heavy (whipping) cream

TO ROLL OUT THE PASTRY: Lightly grease a regular 9-inch pie plate or coat with nonstick spray. If the dough is cold and stiff, let it warm up until slightly pliable but still cool to the touch. Generously dust it on both sides with flour. Roll out the dough between large sheets of baking parchment into a 13-inch round. Occasionally check the underside of the dough during rolling and smooth out any wrinkles. (If the dough seems sticky or limp, place in the freezer for 10 minutes to firm up.) Gently peel off the top sheet of paper, then pat it back into place.

Flip the dough; peel off the bottom sheet. Center the round, dough side down, in the pie plate. Gently peel off the remaining paper. Smooth the dough into the plate and patch any tears, if necessary. Using kitchen shears or a paring knife, trim the overhang to ¾ inch. Fold the overhang under to form an edge that rests on the lip of the plate. Finish by fluting with your fingers or pressing into the edge with the tines of a fork. Prick the pastry all over with a fork. Loosely cover the pastry and place in the freezer for 15 minutes or in the refrigerator for at least 30 minutes and up to several hours.

TO BAKE THE PASTRY: Position a rack in the lower third of the oven and preheat to 400 degrees F. Insert a large square of aluminum foil coated with nonstick spray (or use nonstick foil) oiled side down into the chilled shell, smoothing the foil over the bottom and sides and folding it out over the rim to cover the pastry. Fill the foil with dried beans, spreading them so they extend up the plate sides. Set the pie shell on a rimmed baking sheet. Bake for 25 minutes. Carefully remove the foil and beans from the shell. Continue baking for 5 to 10 minutes longer, or until the shell is nicely browned all over. If the edges brown too rapidly, cover with strips of foil (or a pie shield). Transfer the pie shell to a wire rack. Let cool completely. The shell will keep, stored airtight, at room temperature for 1 to 2 days or frozen for up to a week. Let thaw before using.

TO MAKE THE FILLING AND GARNISH: Reposition the rack in the middle of the oven and preheat to 350 degrees F. Spread the coconut on a large rimmed baking sheet. Toast, watching carefully and stirring every 3 minutes to redistribute the coconut, until crisp and deep golden brown, 10 to 15 minutes; be careful not to burn. Transfer the sheet to a wire rack.

Meanwhile, in a heavy, nonreactive medium saucepan, sprinkle the gelatin over the milk and let stand, stirring once or twice, for 5 minutes. Set aside 1⅓ cups of the toasted coconut for garnish. Stir the remaining toasted coconut and the cream of coconut into the saucepan. Bring the mixture to a simmer over medium-high heat, stirring occasionally. Adjust the heat so the mixture simmers gently and cook, stirring occasionally, for 2 minutes. Remove from the heat.

Put the egg yolks in small deep bowl. Slowly whisk ½ cup of the cream of coconut mixture into the yolks. Add the yolk mixture to the saucepan, stirring vigorously. Return the saucepan to low heat. Cook, stirring constantly, for 3 minutes, or until the mixture is piping hot and slightly thickened; do not boil. If steam rises from the surface and the edges begin to bubble (or the mixture reaches 175 degrees F on a cooking thermometer), immediately lift the pan from the heat and stir vigorously for 30 seconds to cool the mixture before returning it to the heat. Remove from the heat and stir in the vanilla, coconut extract (if using), and lemon zest. Let stand for 10 minutes. Pour the coconut mixture through a fine sieve into a large bowl, pressing down hard on the shredded coconut to extract as much liquid as possible; discard the coconut. Stir the heavy cream into the liquid.

Fill a very large bowl with ice cubes and water. Set the bowl with the filling in the ice water. Every few minutes, scrape down the sides of the bowl and whisk to redistribute the contents. Continue until the coconut mixture is cold and thickly jelled but not completely set, 20 to 30 minutes. Scrape down the bowl sides. Using a mixer (with a whisk-shaped beater, if available), beat the mixture on low, then medium speed until slightly fluffy, about 30 seconds. Gradually raise the speed to high and beat until very light and greatly increased in volume, 1 to 1½ minutes. Return the bowl to the ice water and let stand, whisking once or twice, until the mixture is thick enough to mound into the pie shell, about 5 minutes.

Turn out the filling into the pie shell, mounding it in the center. Sprinkle the reserved toasted coconut over the filling until completely covered. Refrigerate for at least 1½ hours. To serve, cut into wedges with a large sharp knife dipped in hot water and wiped clean between cuts.

The pie will keep, covered, in the refrigerator for up to 4 days.

key Lime mousse Pie

The intense flavor and zip of this pie are similar to that of traditional Key lime pie, but it is light, high, and airy, instead of low and dense. It's more summery and refreshing than the usual version.

CRUST

About 10 whole graham crackers, coarsely broken

5 tablespoons unsalted butter, slightly softened

¼ cup powdered sugar

FILLING

6 tablespoons cold water

1 tablespoon plus 1½ teaspoons unflavored gelatin

1 14-ounce can sweetened condensed milk

1 cup chilled fresh or bottled Key lime juice, or more to taste

1 teaspoon vanilla extract

½ cup granulated sugar, or more to taste

3½ tablespoons finely grated lime zest (green part of skin; from 7–10 Key limes or about 4 regular limes)

6 ounces (two 3-ounce packages) cold cream cheese or Neufchâtel cheese (light cream cheese), cut into 1-inch chunks

1⅓ cups chilled heavy (whipping) cream

Lightly sweetened whipped cream for garnish

Fine slivers of lime zest (green part of skin) for garnish (optional)

TO MAKE THE CRUST: Position a rack in the middle of the oven and preheat to 350 degrees F. Generously grease a regular 9-inch pie plate or generously coat with nonstick spray. In a food processor, grind the graham crackers to fine crumbs; you should have 1½ cups. Add the butter and powdered sugar and pulse for 1 to 1½ minutes, or until the mixture looks oily and just begins to hold together. Press the crumbs evenly and firmly into the bottom and 1 inch up the sides of the pie plate, then even the top edge of the crust by gently pressing down on the crumbs all the way around. Bake until just tinged with brown and very crisp, 7 to 11 minutes. Set aside. Wash and dry the processor bowl and blade.

TO MAKE THE FILLING: In a heavy, nonreactive 1-quart saucepan, stir together the water and gelatin. Let stand, stirring once or twice, for 5 minutes. Heat over low heat, stirring, just until the gelatin completely dissolves and the mixture is smooth, about 1 minute. Remove from the heat. Stir in the condensed milk until smoothly incorporated, then stir in the lime juice and vanilla.

In the food processor, process the granulated sugar and grated lime zest until the zest is very fine and the sugar is colored and wet, about 2 minutes, scraping down the sides of the bowl as needed. With the motor running, add the cream cheese a few chunks at a time and process, scraping down the sides of the bowl as needed, until completely smooth. With the motor still running, slowly add the lime juice mixture until incorporated and the mixture is well blended. Turn out the filling into a large bowl. Stir in the cream.

Fill a very large bowl with ice cubes and water. Set the bowl with the filling in the ice water. Every few minutes, scrape down the sides of the bowl and whisk until the filling is cold and thickly jelled but not completely set, 30 to 40 minutes. (Replenish the ice as it melts.) Using a mixer (with a whisk-shaped beater, if available), beat on low, then medium speed for 30 seconds. Gradually raise the speed to high and beat until very frothy and lightened, 1½ to 2 minutes longer, scraping down the sides of the bowl as needed. Taste and briefly beat in up to 1 tablespoon more lime juice or 1 to 2 tablespoons more granulated sugar, if desired. Return the bowl to the ice water and let stand, whisking every minute or so, until the mixture is stiff enough to mound in the pie plate, about 5 minutes.

Turn out the filling into the pie plate, mounding it in the center. Use the back of a tablespoon to form attractive swirls in the top. Refrigerate until well chilled and firm, at least 4 hours, then loosely cover and return to the refrigerator for at least 12 hours so the flavors can blend. The pie will keep, covered, in the refrigerator for 4 or 5 days.

At serving time, let the pie stand at room temperature for about 5 minutes before cutting. Using a pastry bag fitted with a large open-star tip, pipe large rosettes of whipped cream around the pie top, or add dollops of whipped cream to individual slices. (Use a large sharp knife dipped in hot water and wiped clean between cuts to slice into wedges.) Garnish the rosettes or dollops with the slivered lime zest, if desired.

The Key to Survival

The supremely tart and tangy Key lime, also known as the Mexican or West Indian lime, takes its name from the Florida Keys. These limes are smaller and much seedier than the regular Persian limes sold in American supermarkets. They also have a slightly different flavor. Key limes are green inside and out, but as they ripen, the skin turns yellowish.

Key limes probably originated in Asia and were brought to the New World by the Spaniards. They were readily naturalized in the West Indies and Mexico and eventually in the South Florida mainland and 100-mile-long Keys island chain. Exactly when they came to Florida is not known, but they were said to be "increasing" there in 1839.

By the late nineteenth century, Floridians were raising Key limes commercially. Production increased dramatically when growers began planting limes to replace the pineapple crops destroyed by a 1906 hurricane. The limes ultimately fared no better, however, as a 1926 hurricane decimated the groves. As a result, commercial efforts to raise Key limes waned and local supplies began to dwindle.

In the 1950s, a Key Largo grower and a group of civic leaders launched a campaign highlighting the fruit's local history and encouraging residents to plant it again. Due largely to their efforts, Key limes are now back in Florida gardens in abundance.

Lemon meringue Pie

The combination of bracing yet silky lemon filling, mild, puffy meringue, and crisp crust has made the lemon meringue pie an American classic. Although we didn't invent lemon custard pies, we did come up with the brilliant idea of topping them with meringue. (Some culinary historians credit the nineteenth-century Philadelphia cooking teacher Mrs. Goodfellow with the innovation.)

This voluptuous, generous pie will disappear quickly. The filling is deeply lemony and on the tart side, and the meringue is not overly sweet. Government food safety guidelines recommend that meringue toppings should be thoroughly cooked. The method I've devised to ensure that is close to the old-fashioned approach. The meringue is simply beaten, then baked. So that it will not shrink (a common consequence of thorough baking), I stabilize it through long, slow beating, which produces a finer, more compact meringue. I also use powdered sugar instead of granulated, because it is less grainy and contains a little cornstarch, which helps control the beading. It's best not to bake this pie in humid weather, or the meringue may bead a bit on top after a few hours.

Single crust All-Purpose Pie Pastry Dough (page 90)
All-purpose flour for dusting dough

FILLING

- 1⅓ cups granulated sugar, plus more if needed
- 6 tablespoons cornstarch
- Pinch of salt
- 1⅔ cups cold water
- 2½ tablespoons unsalted butter, cut into bits
- 7 large egg yolks
- ½ cup plus 2 tablespoons fresh lemon juice, plus more if needed

- ½ teaspoon vanilla extract
- 2 tablespoons very finely grated lemon zest (yellow part of skin)

MERINGUE

- 5 large egg whites, completely free of yolk and at room temperature
- Generous ¼ teaspoon cream of tartar
- Pinch of salt
- 1 cup plus 2 tablespoons powdered sugar
- ½ teaspoon vanilla extract

TO ROLL OUT THE PASTRY: Lightly grease a regular 9-inch pie plate or coat with nonstick spray. If the dough is cold and stiff, let it warm up until slightly pliable but still cool to the touch. Generously dust it on both sides with flour. Roll out the dough between large sheets of baking parchment into a 13-inch round. Occasionally check the underside of the dough during rolling and smooth out any wrinkles. (If the dough seems sticky or limp, place in the freezer for 10 minutes to firm up.) Gently peel off the top sheet of paper, then pat it back into place. Flip the dough; peel off the bottom sheet. Center the round, dough side down, in the pie plate. Gently peel off the remaining paper. Smooth the dough evenly into the plate and patch any tears, if necessary. Using kitchen shears or a paring knife, trim the overhang to ¾ inch. Fold the overhang under to form an edge that rests on the lip of the plate. Finish by fluting with your fingers or pressing into the edge with the tines of a fork. Prick the pastry all over with a fork. Loosely cover the pastry and place in the freezer for 15 minutes or in the refrigerator for at least 30 minutes and up to several hours.

TO BAKE THE PASTRY: Position a rack in the lower third of the oven and preheat to 400 degrees F. Insert a large square of aluminum foil coated with nonstick spray (or use nonstick foil) oiled side down into the chilled shell, smoothing the foil over the bottom and sides and folding it out over the rim to cover the pastry. Fill the foil with dried beans, spreading them so they extend up the plate sides. Set the pie shell on a rimmed baking sheet. Bake for 25 minutes. Carefully remove the foil and beans from the shell. Continue baking for 5 to 10 minutes longer, or until the shell is nicely browned all over. If the edges brown too rapidly, cover with strips of foil (or a pie shield). Transfer the pie shell to a wire rack. The pie shell will keep, stored airtight, at room temperature for up to 24 hours.

Reposition the rack in the middle of the oven and reduce the heat to 350 degrees F.

TO MAKE THE FILLING: In a heavy, nonreactive medium saucepan, thoroughly whisk together the granulated sugar, cornstarch, and salt. Whisk in the water until the mixture is completely smooth. Whisking constantly, bring to a boil over medium-high heat. Lower the heat slightly and cook, whisking constantly, until very thick, smooth, and translucent, about 2 minutes. Remove the pan from the heat. Whisk in the butter until melted.

In a deep medium bowl, whisk the egg yolks until blended. Whisk about ½ cup of the cornstarch mixture into the yolks until blended. Whisking vigorously, slowly add the yolk mixture to the cornstarch mixture until well blended. Return the saucepan to medium-high heat and bring to a boil, whisking vigorously and scraping the pan bottom, until the mixture boils for a full 2 minutes. Don't undercook, or the filling may thin out later. Remove from the heat and whisk in the lemon juice and

vanilla. Strain the filling through a fine sieve into a microwave-safe medium bowl or a medium heavy saucepan. Whisk in the lemon zest. Taste the filling and stir in more lemon juice or granulated sugar, if desired. Cover and set aside.

TO MAKE THE MERINGUE: In a completely grease-free large bowl, combine the egg whites, cream of tartar, and salt. Using a mixer on low speed (with a whisk-shaped beater, if available), beat the mixture until frothy. Raise the speed to medium and continue beating until the mixture is smooth, fluffy, and opaque, but still too soft to hold peaks. (Check by stopping and lifting the beater.) Immediately add the powdered sugar 2 tablespoons at a time, beating for about 20 seconds after each addition. Add the vanilla. Raise the speed to medium-high and beat for 2½ minutes, scraping down the sides of the bowl as needed. Raise the speed to high and beat for about 1 minute longer, or until the meringue is fluffy and stands in firm but not dry peaks.

Microwave the filling on medium power, stopping and stirring once, until piping hot, about 1½ minutes. (Alternatively, reheat over medium heat, stirring, just until piping hot.) Turn out the filling into the pie shell, spreading to even the surface. Set the pie on a rimmed baking sheet. Spread about half of the meringue over the filling, making sure the meringue touches the pastry all the way around. Add the remaining meringue, mounding it slightly in the middle. Attractively swirl the meringue with a table knife or the back of a large spoon.

TO BAKE THE PIE: Bake for 12 to 17 minutes, or until the meringue is cooked through and evenly tinged with brown all over. For even browning, rotate the pan from front to back after 6 minutes. Transfer the pie to a wire rack. Let cool for at least 2 hours and then refrigerate until completely cold before covering; this will reduce the beading and weeping of the meringue. Let warm up slightly before serving. Using a large sharp knife dipped in hot water and wiped clean between cuts, cut the pie into wedges and serve.

The pie will keep, covered, in the refrigerator for 3 or 4 days.

fudge pie

Fudge pie is one of those recipes that can be whipped up without much fuss. It appears frequently among the dessert selections at the modest "meat-and-three" establishments that are a fixture in many southern cities and towns. Often open only at lunchtime, these locally owned cafeteria-style eateries offer customers a hot meal featuring an entree (the "meat") and a choice of three sides for a relatively modest price. And they always have a selection of homey desserts.

This fudge pie is in keeping with most I've tried, except it is a little richer, with a fuller chocolate flavor. As the name suggests, it's chewy-moist and fudgy. Home cooks sometimes add pecans, but they are optional.

Single crust All-Purpose Pie Pastry Dough (page 90)

All-purpose flour for dusting dough

FILLING

1 cup light corn syrup

³/₄ cup sugar

¹/₈ teaspoon salt

5 tablespoons unsalted butter, cut into chunks

4 ounces unsweetened chocolate, broken up or coarsely chopped

3 large eggs plus 1 large egg yolk

2 teaspoons vanilla extract

³/₄ cup coarsely chopped pecans (optional)

Very lightly sweetened whipped cream or vanilla ice cream for garnish

TO ROLL OUT THE PASTRY: Lightly grease a regular 9-inch pie plate or coat with nonstick spray. If the dough is cold and stiff, let it warm up until slightly pliable but still cool to the touch. Generously dust it on both sides with flour. Roll out the dough between large sheets of baking parchment into a 13-inch round. Occasionally check the underside of the dough during rolling and smooth out any wrinkles. Gently peel off the top sheet of paper, then pat it back into place. Flip the dough; peel off the bottom sheet. Center the round, dough side down, in the pie plate. Gently peel off the remaining paper. Smooth the dough into the plate and patch any tears, if necessary. Using kitchen shears or a paring knife, trim the overhang to ¾ inch. Fold the overhang under to form an edge that rests on the lip of the plate. Finish by fluting with your fingers or pressing into the edge with the tines of a fork. Prick the pastry all over with a fork. Loosely cover the pastry and place in the freezer for 15 minutes or the refrigerator for at least 30 minutes and up to several hours.

TO MAKE THE FILLING: Position a rack in the lower third of the oven and preheat to 350 degrees F. In a heavy 2-quart saucepan, heat the corn syrup, sugar, and salt over medium-high heat, stirring, just until the mixture boils and the sugar dissolves. Remove from the heat. Stir in the butter and chocolate until completely melted. Let cool to warm. Stirring vigorously with a large wooden spoon, beat in the eggs, yolk, and vanilla until completely smooth. Fold in the pecans, if using.

TO BAKE THE PIE: Turn out the filling into the pastry. Set the pie on a rimmed baking sheet. Bake for 30 to 40 minutes, or until puffed all over and a toothpick inserted in the center comes out clean. Transfer to a wire rack. Let cool to warm, at least 30 minutes. Cover and refrigerate until chilled. Serve garnished with dollops of whipped cream or scoops of ice cream.

The pie will keep in the refrigerator, covered, for up to 4 days. Let warm up slightly before serving.

chocolate to the rescue

"About ten years before the Revolutionary War the first American chocolate mill was erected on the bank of the Neponset River at Dorchester, Massachusetts. Strangely enough, the celebrated Boston Tea Party stimulated the sale of chocolate in those troublous days, for patriotic American colonists, refusing to drink the royally taxed tea, turned to cocoa.

"In 1780 an enterprising doctor, James Baker, bought this factory. At his death it became the property of his grandson, Walter Baker. Since that early day the Walter Baker chocolate mills have steadily grown until, today, a large group of modern buildings stand on the site once occupied by a small wooden mill."

—Walter Baker & Company, *Chocolate Cookery* (1929)

NO-Bake chocoLate-GLazed Peanut Butter Pie

This unpretentious no-bake pie is rich, dense without being heavy, and smooth. It's topped with a tempting chocolate glaze and crunchy peanuts. You can make the chocolate crumb crust with commercial cookies, but it will be better with the homemade dark chocolate cookies on page 280. The flavor becomes fuller if the pie is allowed to mellow overnight.

CRUST

About 2 cups coarsely broken ($1/2$-inch pieces) chocolate wafers, homemade (see page 280) or store-bought

3   tablespoons unsalted butter, melted

$1/4$ cup powdered sugar

2   tablespoons water, if needed

FILLING

Generous $1 1/4$ teaspoons unflavored gelatin

$1/3$ cup whole or low-fat milk

1   cup packed dark brown sugar

1   3-ounce package cream cheese, slightly softened and cut into chunks

1   cup creamy peanut butter

$2 1/2$ teaspoons vanilla extract

1   cup chilled heavy (whipping) cream

GLAZE

3   ounces bittersweet (not unsweetened) or semisweet chocolate, broken up or coarsely chopped

$6 1/2$ tablespoons chilled heavy (whipping) cream

1   tablespoon packed dark brown sugar

$3/4$ cup coarsely chopped salted peanuts

TO MAKE THE CRUST: Generously grease a regular 9-inch pie plate or generously coat with nonstick spray. In a food processor, grind the wafers to very fine crumbs, 20 to 30 seconds; you should have a generous 1¼ cups crumbs. Add the butter and powdered sugar and pulse for 30 to 40 seconds, or until the mixture begins to hold together. (Stop and squeeze it between your fingertips to check the consistency.) If it seems very dry and crumbly, gradually add up to 2 tablespoons water and process a little longer, scraping down the sides of the bowl as needed. Press the crumbs evenly and firmly into the bottom and ⅔ inch up the sides of the pie plate, then even the top edge of the crust by pressing down on the crumbs all the way around. Set aside in the refrigerator. Wash and dry the processor bowl and blade.

TO MAKE THE FILLING: In a 2-cup glass measure, stir together the gelatin and milk. Let stand, stirring once or twice, until the gelatin softens, about 5 minutes. Place the brown sugar and cream cheese in the processor. Heat the gelatin mixture in the microwave oven on high power until hot but not boiling, stopping and stirring at 30-second intervals. (Alternatively, heat the gelatin mixture in a very small saucepan over medium heat, stirring until the mixture is hot but not boiling. Remove from the heat.) Continue stirring until the gelatin completely dissolves. With the motor running, pour the gelatin mixture into the processor and process until the mixture is completely smooth, scraping down the sides of the bowl as needed. Stop and add the peanut butter and vanilla. Process until the filling is thick and smooth, scraping down the sides of the bowl once or twice. With the motor running, gradually add the cream and process just until smoothly incorporated. Turn out the filling into a medium bowl.

Fill a large bowl with ice cubes and water. Set the medium bowl in the ice water. Every few minutes, scrape down the sides of the bowl and whisk until the filling is cold and thickly jelled but not completely set, 15 to 20 minutes. Rinse and dry the processor bowl and blade.

TO MAKE THE GLAZE: Finely chop the chocolate in the food processor. In a 2-cup glass measure, microwave the cream and brown sugar on high power until piping hot but not boiling, 30 to 40 seconds. (Alternatively, heat the cream and brown sugar in a small saucepan over medium-high heat until hot). Stir well. With the motor running, slowly add the cream mixture to the processor and process until the chocolate is melted and smooth, about 1 minute, scraping down the sides of the bowl several times.

TO ASSEMBLE THE PIE: Turn out the peanut butter filling into the pie plate, spreading it evenly to the edges with a table knife. Stir the chocolate glaze well, then carefully pour it over the filling. Sprinkle the peanuts evenly over the chocolate. Cover and refrigerate until the flavors are well blended, at least 8 hours and up to 4 days. Serve chilled, cut into wedges. The pie slices best with a large sharp knife dipped in hot water and wiped clean between cuts.

A nutty idea

Today peanuts and chocolate are one of America's most popular pairings, but a hundred years ago, the combination was virtually unknown. Chocolate started turning up in a number of American baked goods in the second half of the nineteenth century, and peanuts and peanut butter appeared in candies and cookies near the century's end. Commercial peanut butter made its grand debut in 1904 at the Universal Exposition in St. Louis, where a vendor named C. H. Sumner cleared about five hundred dollars in sales.

The idea of putting peanuts and chocolate together may have originated in the candy industry. A Milwaukee firm, the George Ziegler Company, created a locally distributed candy called the Milk Chocolate Peanut Block at some point early in the twentieth century. The Standard Candy Company of Nashville introduced a chocolate-marshmallow-peanut sweet called the Goo Goo Cluster in 1912. Howell Campbell, its creator, may have thought his product was novel; he proclaimed it "America's 1st Combination Candy Bar" and called it "A Nourishing Lunch for a Nickel." The Goo Goo Cluster soon became a hit across the South.

oLd GLory AngeL ice cream pie

The word "angel" is usually a tip-off that a pie is made with a baked meringue shell. My version pairs the meringue with vanilla ice cream, strawberries, and blueberries. The combination of a crisp, light shell; cold, smooth ice cream; and tangy berries is particularly enticing in warm weather, and the red, white, and blue colors are perfect on patriotic holidays such as Memorial Day and the Fourth of July.

Make the meringue on a dry day; humidity can cause it to be sticky rather than crisp.

MERINGUE SHELL

- 3 large egg whites, completely free of yolk and at room temperature
- 1/2 teaspoon cream of tartar
- 1/8 teaspoon salt
- 3/4 cup sugar, preferably superfine
- 1 teaspoon vanilla extract

FILLING

- 3 cups thickly sliced large fresh strawberries or small hulled whole strawberries
- 1/3 cup sugar
- 1 quart vanilla ice cream, slightly softened
- 1 cup fresh blueberries

TO MAKE THE MERINGUE SHELL: Position a rack in the lower third of the oven and preheat to 250 degrees F. Line a 9½-inch deep-dish pie plate with a 12-inch square of aluminum foil coated with nonstick spray, sprayed side up (or use nonstick foil, nonstick side up).

In a completely grease-free large bowl using a mixer (with a whisk-shaped beater, if available), beat the egg whites on low speed for 30 seconds. Add the cream of tartar and salt. Gradually raise the speed to medium and continue beating until the whites are frothy, opaque, and just begin to form soft peaks, about 1½ minutes. Raise the speed to high and add the sugar 2 tablespoons at a time, beating for 20 seconds after each addition and scraping down the sides of the bowl as needed. Add the vanilla. Continue beating until the meringue is glossy and stands in firm but not dry peaks, 1 to 2 minutes longer. Spoon the meringue mixture into the pie plate, smoothing the bottom and sides with a rubber spatula to form an evenly thick pie shell; be sure the bottom is not overly thick. Set the pie plate on a rimmed baking sheet.

Tip

It's easy to vary this dessert by substituting coffee ice cream for vanilla and topping it with chocolate syrup (see page 312) or hot fudge sauce (see page 310). For this version, I also like to enhance the meringue shell by folding in some nuts before baking (see the variation).

Bake for 1 hour. Reduce the heat to 200 degrees F and bake for 1½ hours longer. Turn off the oven and let the pie shell stand in the oven, door slightly ajar, for 30 minutes. Remove from the oven and, using a paring knife, check for doneness by pricking at a point where the bottom and sides join. If the meringue seems very sticky, return the pie shell to the oven and bake at 200 degrees F for 30 minutes longer, then open the oven door and let the shell stand for 30 minutes. Transfer to a wire rack. When the shell is completely cooled, gently peel off and discard the foil; return the shell to the pie plate. Slide it into an airtight container or a large plastic bag. The pie shell will keep, stored airtight, at room temperature for 3 or 4 days.

TO MAKE THE FILLING: Stir together the strawberries and sugar in a medium bowl. Let stand for a few minutes, stirring occasionally, until the sugar dissolves. Spread the ice cream evenly in the pie shell. Spoon the strawberries evenly over the ice cream. Sprinkle the blueberries attractively over the top. Serve immediately, or place the pie in the freezer for up to 1 hour before serving. (Don't store in the freezer longer, or the fruit may freeze.) The pie slices best with a large sharp knife dipped in hot water and wiped clean between cuts.

VARIATION: Coffee-Nut Ice Cream Pie

Make the meringue mixture as for the standard version, except after the meringue is beaten to stiff peaks, sprinkle over ⅓ cup finely chopped skinned hazelnuts or pecans and fold them in just until evenly incorporated. Proceed as directed, but substitute coffee ice cream for the vanilla and omit the fruit. If desired, serve the pie with Crown Candy Kitchen's Chocolate Syrup (page 312) or Real Hot Fudge Sauce (page 310).

FALLEN ANGEL

Meringue cookies, candies, and frostings have been in the American repertoire since colonial days. However, meringue used as a pie shell is probably a twentieth-century invention and may have been inspired by the early twentieth-century Jewish American classic *The Way to a Man's Heart: "The Settlement" Cook Book* by Lizzie Black Kander, a German-born advocate for Milwaukee's immigrant poor. Her "torten" chapter contained many European desserts, including an eye-catching "kiss torte" that featured a meringue baked in a springform pan and garnished with strawberries and whipped cream. Mrs. Kander's work, a community cookbook that went through thirty-four editions over the next seven decades, was used by millions of homemakers, who, lacking springform pans, may well have turned her torte into a pie.

By the 1950s, nearly every American cookbook included at least several angel pies, which were often touted as company or ladies' luncheon fare. Some recipes called for a mousse-type filling; others were filled with ice cream. Meta Given's 1959 edition of the best-selling *Modern Encyclopedia of Cooking* described angel pies as having "plenty of class." By the 1970s, people saw them as precious and passé.

summer Fresh Fruit Tart

Modern dessert makers in the United States often give the classic French fruit tart an American twist by replacing the traditional pastry cream with a simple cream cheese filling. The tart is just as pretty, but the taste is lighter and more refreshing, and the preparation is considerably easier—no fussing over cooking the eggs.

This tart is particularly appealing in warm weather. The shell is flavorful and crisp and holds up nicely even when filled with juicy fruit. The dough is also pressed into the pan, completely eliminating the task of rolling out the dough. (The recipe can also be used to make tartlets; see the variation.)

I've suggested several fruits and berries that complement one another and go well with the cream cheese, but it's fine to substitute whatever is in season or at hand.

ALMOND PASTRY

- 1 cup plus 3 tablespoons all-purpose flour
- ¼ cup sugar
- ¼ teaspoon salt
- 8 tablespoons (1 stick) cold unsalted butter, cut into chunks
- ⅔ cup blanched sliced almonds
- 1–1½ tablespoons ice water, as needed

FILLING

- ½ cup sugar
- 1 teaspoon finely grated lemon zest (yellow part of skin)
- ⅓ cup sour cream (not nonfat)
- 1 teaspoon vanilla extract
- ¼ teaspoon almond extract
- 11 ounces (one 8-ounce package plus one 3-ounce package) cream cheese or Neufchâtel cheese (light cream cheese), slightly softened and cut into chunks

FRUIT

- 1¼ cups small thinly sliced wedges fresh pineapple
- 1 cup fresh raspberries, blueberries, or thinly sliced strawberries, or a combination
- 2 ripe kiwifruit, peeled and cut crosswise into ¼-inch-thick half-moons
- ¼ cup strained apricot preserves (optional)

TO MAKE THE PASTRY: Grease a 10-by-1-inch tart pan with a removable bottom or coat with nonstick spray. In a food processor, combine the flour, sugar, and salt. Pulse several times to mix. Sprinkle the butter and almonds over the flour mixture. Pulse until the butter is evenly incorporated, the almonds are chopped fairly fine, and the mixture has the consistency of fine meal. Sprinkle over ½ tablespoon of the ice water, pulsing until the mixture begins to hold together. (Press between your fingertips to check.) If the mixture seems too dry, sprinkle over ½ to 1 tablespoon more ice water and pulse until just incorporated.

Firmly and evenly press the dough into the bottom and up the sides of the tart pan, smoothing it into the indentations. Cover and freeze until cold and firm, about 20 minutes, or refrigerate for about 40 minutes.

Position the rack in the middle of the oven and preheat to 375 degrees F. Prick the pastry all over with a fork. Cover the pastry with a large sheet of heavy-duty aluminum foil coated with nonstick spray (or use nonstick foil), oiled side down, smoothing the foil into the bottom and up the sides and wrapping the excess foil out over the pan edges to cover the pastry. Fill the foil with dried beans, spreading them so they extend up the pan sides. Set on a rimmed baking sheet.

Bake for 20 minutes. Carefully remove the foil and beans. Prick the pastry bottom again. Reposition the rack in the lower third of the oven. Bake the pastry until tinged with brown on the bottom and golden brown at the edges, 8 to 13 minutes longer. Transfer to a wire rack. Let cool. The tart shell will keep, stored airtight, at room temperature for up to 24 hours.

TO MAKE THE FILLING: In a food processor, combine the sugar and lemon zest and process until the sugar is pale yellow, about 1 minute. Add the sour cream, vanilla, and almond extract and process just until free of lumps, scraping down the sides of the bowl as needed. Add the cream cheese and pulse just until the mixture is completely smooth; don't overprocess. Turn out the filling into the tart shell, smoothing the surface. Refrigerate, covered, until well chilled and slightly firm, at least 1½ hours and up to 24 hours.

TO MAKE THE FRUIT: Pat the fruit dry on paper towels. Arrange the fruit, alternating the colors and shapes, in slightly overlapping concentric circles (or as desired) over the filling, pressing down lightly to embed. Serve immediately, or cover and refrigerate for up to 3 hours. If desired, just before serving, stir the preserves until fluid, or if necessary, heat in the microwave for a few seconds until fluid. Using a pastry brush, lightly brush the fruit with the preserves. The tart slices best with a large sharp knife dipped in hot water and wiped clean between cuts.

The finished tart will keep, covered, in the refrigerator for 2 or 3 days, but the fruit will weep.

VARIATION: Summer Fresh Fruit Tartlets

Generously grease fourteen or fifteen assorted 2½- to 3-inch round, square, or oblong tartlet pans or generously spray with nonstick spray. Press enough dough into each pan to form an even ¼-inch-thick shell; be careful not to make them too thick. Be sure to press the dough into the fluted sides and the bottom. Cover and chill the pastries as directed for the tart pastry. Prick with a fork, cover each with heavy-duty aluminum foil coated with nonstick spray (place it oiled side down) and bake on a rimmed baking sheet as directed for 20 minutes. Remove the foil and bake for 4 to 8 minutes longer, or until nicely browned. Transfer to a wire rack and let cool. Divide the filling among the tartlet shells and arrange fresh fruit on the filling as desired.

BLackBerry-Lemon curd Tart

America is blessed with an abundance of hardy native blackberries. Being an avid forager, I'm delighted that the woods right behind my house contain a patch. Most summers, I gather enough berries to make a cobbler, or pie, and this simple yet amazingly good tart.

If you've never tried blackberries and lemon together, you'll likely be bowled over by this extraordinary pairing. The intense citrus taste of the lemon curd deepens the flavor of the blackberries, and the color combination is a knockout, too.

Nothing beats the lemon-blackberry combo, but when blackberries are unavailable, I've also had great success making this recipe using fresh red raspberries or blueberries. People who have never tasted the blackberry version don't seem to realize they're missing anything.

All-Purpose Tart Pastry Dough (page 94)

LEMON CURD

- ³⁄₄ cup sugar
- 5 large egg yolks
- 2 tablespoons finely grated lemon zest (yellow part of skin)
- ¹⁄₂ cup fresh lemon juice
- 6 tablespoons (³⁄₄ stick) unsalted butter, cut into chunks

BERRIES AND GARNISH

- 2¹⁄₂–3 cups fresh blackberries
  Lightly sweetened whipped cream for garnish (optional)

TO ROLL OUT THE PASTRY: Grease a 9- to 9¹⁄₂-by-1-inch tart pan with a removable bottom or coat with nonstick spray. If the dough is cold and stiff, let it warm up until slightly pliable but still cool to the touch. Roll out the dough between large sheets of baking parchment into a 12¹⁄₂-inch round. Occasionally check the underside of the dough during rolling and smooth out any wrinkles. (If the dough seems sticky or limp, place in the freezer for 5 to 10 minutes to firm up.) Gently peel off the top sheet of paper, then pat it back into place. Flip the dough; peel off the bottom sheet. Center the round, dough side down, in the tart pan. Gently peel off the remaining paper. Smooth the dough into the pan and patch any tears, if necessary. Push the dough firmly into the fluted sides to form an evenly thick edge. Roll a rolling pin across the rim of the pan to trim off the overhanging dough. Prick the pastry all over with a fork.

tip

This recipe calls for 2¹⁄₂ to 3 cups berries. If you have the smaller amount, space them a bit apart on the tart. If you have the larger amount, tuck them close together.

Cover with a sheet of aluminum foil coated with nonstick spray (or use nonstick foil) oiled side down, smoothing the foil into the bottom and up the sides and wrapping the excess foil over the pan edges to cover the pastry. Freeze for at least 20 minutes or refrigerate for 45 minutes and up to 24 hours.

TO BAKE THE PASTRY: Position a rack in the lower third of the oven and preheat to 400 degrees F. Fill the foil-lined shell with dried beans, spreading them so they extend up the pan sides. Set the tart shell on a rimmed baking sheet. Bake for 25 minutes. Carefully remove the foil and beans and continue baking for 5 to 10 minutes, or until tinged with brown on the bottom and golden brown at the edges. If the edges brown too rapidly, cover with strips of foil (or a pie shield). Transfer to a wire rack. Let cool. The tart shell will keep, stored airtight, at room temperature for up to 24 hours or frozen for up to 2 weeks.

TO MAKE THE LEMON CURD: In a heavy, nonreactive medium saucepan, whisk together the sugar, egg yolks, lemon zest, and lemon juice until completely blended. Add the butter. Place over medium heat, whisking and scraping the pan bottom and sides constantly, until the butter melts. Continue whisking and scraping the pan bottom constantly until the mixture reaches a boil. Boil, whisking constantly, for 1 minute. Immediately remove from the heat and whisk for 30 seconds longer. Let stand for 10 minutes. Strain the lemon curd through a fine sieve into a glass bowl or other container. Refrigerate, tightly covered, for at least 1½ hours and up to 4 days.

TO ASSEMBLE AND GARNISH THE TART: Evenly spread the lemon curd in the tart shell. Attractively arrange the berries over the curd, spacing them so the amount you have will fit evenly. To serve, cut into wedges and garnish with small dollops of whipped cream, if desired.

The tart will keep, covered, in the refrigerator for 2 to 3 days. Let warm up slightly before serving.

Harvest cranberry-pear tart

Judging from Amelia Simmons's recipe in her 1796 book *American Cookery,* as well as other early versions I've come across, cranberry tarts were originally rather plain and featured only cranberries, sugar, and, sometimes, spices. (Simmons's version calls for adding spices "until grateful.") In this tart, however, pears and golden raisins team up with cranberries (along with orange zest, allspice, and gingerroot) to lend an enticingly rich fruit flavor. Like the cranberries themselves, the tart is brightly colored and on the tangy side. The zestiness both suits the cranberries and helps clear the palate after a heavy meal.

Considering the popularity of cranberry tarts in colonial America, this seems particularly appropriate for serving at Thanksgiving. It can be made well ahead.

All-Purpose Tart Pastry Dough (page 94)

FILLING

- 1 cup plus 2 tablespoons sugar, or more to taste
- 3½ tablespoons plus 1 teaspoon arrowroot powder or cornstarch
- 3½ cups fresh (or frozen, partially thawed) cranberries, coarsely chopped
- 1 cup golden raisins
- 1 cup peeled, cored, and finely chopped Bartlett or Bosc pear (about 1 medium pear)
- ¼ cup cranberry juice cocktail, orange juice, or water

- 1 teaspoon peeled and finely minced fresh gingerroot
- ½ teaspoon finely grated orange zest (orange part of skin)
- Generous ¼ teaspoon ground allspice
- 3 tablespoons unsalted butter, cut into bits
- ½ teaspoon vanilla extract

Pastry leaves for garnish (see the variation; optional)

Frosted cranberries for garnish (see the variation; optional)

Whipped cream for garnish (optional)

TO ROLL OUT THE PASTRY: Lightly grease a 10-by-1-inch tart pan with a removable bottom or coat with nonstick spray. If the dough is cold and stiff, let it warm up until slightly pliable but still cool to the touch. Roll out the dough between large sheets of baking parchment into a 13-inch round. Occasionally check the underside of the dough during rolling and smooth out any wrinkles. (If the dough seems sticky or limp, place in the freezer for about 5 minutes to firm up slightly.) Gently peel off the top sheet of paper, then pat it back into place. Flip the dough; peel off the bottom sheet. Center the round, dough side down, in the tart pan. Gently peel off the remaining paper. Smooth the dough into the pan and patch any tears, if necessary. Push the dough firmly into the fluted sides to form an evenly thick edge. Roll a rolling pin across the rim of the pan to trim off the overhanging dough. Save the scraps for decorative accents, if desired. Prick the pastry all over with a fork. Cover with a sheet of aluminum foil coated with nonstick spray (or use nonstick foil) oiled side down, smoothing the foil into the bottom and up the sides and wrapping the excess foil over the pan edges to cover the pastry. Freeze for at least 20 minutes and up to 30 minutes or refrigerate, covered, for several hours or overnight.

TO BAKE THE PASTRY: Position a rack in the lower third of the oven and preheat to 400 degrees F. Fill the foil-lined shell with dried beans, spreading them so they extend up the pan sides. Set the tart shell on a rimmed baking sheet. Bake for 25 minutes. Carefully remove the foil and beans and continue baking for 5 to 10 minutes, or until tinged with brown in the bottom and golden brown at the edges. If the edges brown too rapidly, cover with strips of foil (or a pie shield). Transfer to a wire rack. Let cool. The tart shell will keep, stored airtight, at room temperature for up to 24 hours or frozen for up to 2 weeks.

TO MAKE THE FILLING: In a heavy, nonreactive 2-quart saucepan, stir together the sugar and arrowroot powder until thoroughly blended. Stir in the cranberries, raisins, pear, cranberry juice, gingerroot, orange zest, and allspice until incorporated. Bring to a simmer over medium heat, stirring and scraping the pan. Adjust the heat so the mixture boils gently. Cook, stirring constantly, until the filling thickens slightly and turns clear and the cranberries are cooked through, 5 to 7 minutes. Add the butter and vanilla and stir until the butter melts. Taste and stir in a tablespoon or so more sugar, if desired. The filling will keep, covered, in the refrigerator for up to 3 days. Stir well before using.

Turn out the filling into the tart shell, spreading it evenly to the edges. Rap the pan on the counter several times to even the surface. Refrigerate until the filling is cooled and firm, at least 45 minutes.

If desired, arrange some baked pastry leaves attractively in the center of the tart and pile some frosted cranberries in the center of the leaves. Lift the tart and pan bottom from the sides. Carefully slide the tart off the pan bottom onto a serving plate. Serve cut into wedges, with dollops of whipped cream, if desired.

The tart will keep, covered, in the refrigerator, for 2 or 3 days or in the freezer, wrapped airtight, for up to a month. Let come almost to room temperature before serving.

VARIATIONS: OPTIONAL FINISHING TOUCHES

Pastry Leaves

Position a rack in the middle of the oven and preheat to 400 degrees F. Recombine the tart pastry scraps. Roll out ⅛ inch thick between sheets of baking parchment. Place on a small baking sheet and freeze until cold and firm, 20 to 30 minutes. Gently peel off the top sheet of paper. Using a paring knife, cut the pastry into six 1½- to 2½-inch-long leaves. Make shallow cuts in the surface to suggest leaf veining. Slightly crumple sheets of aluminum foil and place on a baking sheet. Drape the leaves over the foil, so that they look slightly curled like real leaves. Sprinkle the leaves lightly with granulated or coarse crystal sugar. Bake for 7 to 12 minutes, or until tinged with brown all over; smaller leaves will bake faster than large ones. Cool completely, then store, covered, for 3 or 4 days.

Frosted Cranberries

After the cranberry filling comes to a boil, add 6 to 8 whole cranberries. As soon as the whole cranberries are coated with the boiling juice, lift them out with a slotted spoon. Immediately toss them in 1 tablespoon sugar until evenly coated. Cover and refrigerate until needed for the garnish.

THE ALL-AMERICAN cranberry

As one of America's indigenous fruits and our most important and colorful cool-weather berry, the cranberry has a special place in our cuisine. Cranberries were part of the diet of Native Americans and quickly gained acceptance by the colonists as well. Although original Plymouth Colony records suggest that cranberry sauce was *not* served at the celebration now called "the first Thanksgiving," cranberry dishes did grace the newcomers' tables once sugar was on hand to make them.

Cranberries were also well known outside New England. In 1680, a settler of Burlington, New Jersey, Mahlon Stacy, wrote to his brother back in Britain that "the cranberries, much like cherries for color and bigness, may be kept until fruit comes in again. An excellent sauce is made of them for venison, turkeys and other great fowl and they are better to make tarts than either gooseberries or cherries."

classic Lemon-vanilla cheesecake

New York City's Jewish delis are usually credited with introducing the modern American style of cheesecake around the turn of the century. The trend away from pastry-lined curd cheese tarts and toward thicker, smoother "cakes" with cookie crusts occurred gradually, with Lindy's on Broadway eventually serving what is now considered the quintessential New York cheesecake by the 1940s.

Inspired by a recipe a neighbor gave me in the 1960s, this version is flavored with lemon and vanilla like the New York–style cheesecakes, but its texture is even smoother, and it features a rich sour cream topping and a graham cracker crust. Whenever I want a good, easy, classically flavored cheesecake, this is the one I bake. It's a winner.

CRUST

About 7 whole graham crackers, coarsely broken

3 tablespoons unsalted butter, melted

1/4 teaspoon vanilla extract

1–3 teaspoons water, if needed

FILLING

1 1/3 cups sugar

2 pounds (four 8-ounce packages) cream cheese, at room temperature

7 large eggs

Very finely grated zest (yellow part of skin) and juice of 1 medium lemon

2 1/2 teaspoons vanilla extract

SOUR CREAM TOPPING

1 1/2 cups sour cream

3 tablespoons sugar

1/2 teaspoon vanilla extract

Quick Strawberry Sauce (page 317) or Fresh Pineapple Sauce (page 318) for serving (optional)

Fresh strawberries or thinly sliced fresh pineapple half rings for garnish (optional)

Position a rack in the middle of the oven and another in the lower third, and preheat to 350 degrees F. Generously grease a 9- to 9½-inch springform pan (at least 2¾ inches deep) or generously coat with nonstick spray.

TO MAKE THE CRUST: In a food processor, grind the graham crackers to very fine crumbs; you should have a generous 1 cup. Add the butter and vanilla and process, scraping down the sides of the bowl once or twice, for 1 minute, or until the mixture begins to hold together. If it seems very dry, gradually add the water, a teaspoon at a time, processing a little longer. Press the crumbs evenly and firmly into the bottom (not the sides) of the pan. Wipe any stray crumbs from the pan sides. Bake for 8 to 13 minutes, or until fragrant and nicely browned. Transfer to a wire rack.

TO MAKE THE FILLING: Reset the oven to 325 degrees F. In a large bowl, combine the sugar and cream cheese. Using a mixer, beat on medium-low speed for 4 to 6 minutes, or until very smooth, scraping down the sides of the bowl as needed. Beat in the eggs one at a time, then the lemon zest and juice and the vanilla. Continue beating on medium-low speed until well blended, 2 to 3 minutes longer, scraping down the sides of the bowl as needed.

Turn out the filling into the crust, spreading it evenly to the edges. Rap the pan on the counter several times to release any air bubbles. Set the cheesecake on a rimmed baking sheet. Place a roasting pan (or broiler pan) on the lower oven rack, directly under the cheesecake, and add ¾ inch hot water. Bake for 15 minutes. Reduce the oven temperature to 300 degrees F and continue baking for 55 to 75 minutes longer, or until the filling barely jiggles in the center when the pan is shaken.

MEANWHILE, TO MAKE THE TOPPING: In a small bowl, stir together the sour cream, sugar, and vanilla until well blended. Remove the cheesecake from the oven and spread the topping evenly over the surface. Bake for about 5 minutes longer, just until the topping looks melted and smooth.

Transfer the cheesecake to a wire rack. Let stand for 10 minutes. Carefully run a paring knife around the cheesecake to loosen it from the pan sides; this helps prevent it from cracking. Let cool completely, at least 1½ hours. Cover and refrigerate for at least 6 hours, or until thoroughly chilled.

At serving time, remove the pan sides. Serve the cheesecake directly from the pan bottom. It slices best with a large sharp knife dipped in hot water and wiped clean between cuts. Serve with strawberry or pineapple sauce, passed separately, if desired. Garnish with strawberries or pineapple, if desired.

The cheesecake will keep, covered airtight, in the refrigerator for 5 or 6 days, although the crust will gradually lose its crispness after a day or so.

who put the philly in philadelphia cream cheese?

The custom of preparing rich, tartlike cheesecakes with eggs, mild fresh cheese, lemon, and often raisins or currants dates back centuries in Europe. Old American recipes generally called for unripened cottage-style cheese curds mashed or sieved to smooth their texture.

Today silky smooth cream cheese forms the basis of most American cheesecakes. It is said to have been developed in about 1870 by New York dairymen who wanted to approximate European Neufchâtel cheese. Kraft Foods, which now makes Philadelphia brand cream cheese, says that New York cheese distributor A. L. Reynolds gave the product its name, introducing it in New York in 1880. According to Kraft, he chose the moniker not because of any Philadelphia connection, but for marketing reasons: in that era, Philadelphia was associated with top-quality food items.

marbled mocha-chocolate cheesecake

This custardy cheesecake was inspired by two favorite ingredients of the Northwest, coffee and hazelnuts. (Seattle is the home of Starbucks, and Oregon's Willamette Valley grows nearly all of the country's hazelnuts.) The crust, made with chocolate wafer crumbs and hazelnuts, is dark, nutty-tasting, and slightly crisp. Chocolate creates dramatic-looking swirls in the ultra-creamy, light mocha filling. The secret to the smooth consistency is to bake the cheesecake in a water bath.

CRUST

- ½ cup (about 1⅔ ounces) whole hazelnuts
- About 2 cups coarsely broken (1-inch pieces) chocolate wafers, homemade (see page 280) or store-bought
- 1 tablespoon unsalted butter, slightly softened
- 1–3 teaspoons water, if needed

FILLING

- 3 ounces bittersweet (not unsweetened) or semisweet chocolate, broken up or coarsely chopped
- 2 pounds (four 8-ounce packages) cream cheese, at room temperature
- 1¼ cups sugar
- 2 teaspoons instant espresso powder or granules, dissolved in 1 tablespoon hot water
- 2 teaspoons vanilla extract
- 6 large eggs, at room temperature
- ½ cup heavy (whipping) cream

TO MAKE THE CRUST: Position a rack in the middle of the oven and preheat to 350 degrees F. Spread the hazelnuts in a baking pan. Toast, stirring occasionally, for 12 to 16 minutes, or until the nuts are slightly colored and their hulls are loosened. Set aside until cool enough to handle. Remove all loose pieces of hull by vigorously rubbing the nuts between your hands or in a clean kitchen towel, discarding the loose bits as you work. (It's not necessary to remove every bit of hull.)

Generously grease a 9- to 9½-by-3-inch springform pan or generously coat with nonstick spray. Center the pan on a double layer of heavy-duty aluminum foil; make sure there are no holes in the foil. Carefully pull the foil up around the pan sides to completely encase it. This prevents water from seeping into the bottom of the pan when you place it in the water bath.

tip

Make sure the cream cheese and eggs are at room temperature when you begin. This will ensure that the chocolate blends in smoothly.

In a food processor, grind the wafers until fine; you should have 1¼ cups. Combine the crumbs, hazelnuts, and butter in the processor. Pulse until the nuts are coarsely chopped. Process, scraping down the sides of the bowl as needed, for 1½ to 2 minutes longer, or until the nuts are finely ground and the mixture just holds together. If it seems very dry, gradually add the water, a teaspoon at a time, processing a little longer. Press the crumbs evenly and firmly into the bottom (not the sides) of the pan. Wipe any stray crumbs from the pan sides. Bake for 10 to 15 minutes, or until fragrant and almost firm. Transfer to a wire rack.

TO MAKE THE FILLING: Reset the oven to 325 degrees F. In a microwave-safe medium bowl, microwave the chocolate on high power for 30 seconds. Stop and stir. Continue microwaving on medium power, stopping and stirring every 30 seconds, until the chocolate is just melted. Set aside in a warm spot or over a bowl of warm water. (Alternatively, melt the chocolate in a metal bowl set over a saucepan of almost simmering water, stirring occasionally, until smooth. Remove the saucepan from the heat; let the bowl sit over the saucepan.)

In a large bowl, combine the cream cheese and sugar. Using a mixer, beat on medium speed for 4 to 5 minutes, or until completely smooth (but not fluffy), scraping down the sides of the bowl as needed. Add 2 tablespoons of the melted chocolate, the espresso mixture, and vanilla and beat until smoothly incorporated, scraping down the sides of the bowl as needed. (Reserve the small amount of chocolate remaining in the bowl used for melting.) Add the eggs one at a time, beating after each addition. Beat in the cream a little at a time until the mixture is well blended and smooth. Scoop up 1 cup of the filling and gradually stir it into the reserved melted chocolate until well blended.

Turn out the filling into the springform pan. Rap the pan on the counter several times to release any air bubbles. Let stand for 5 minutes, then rap again. Spoon the chocolate mixture onto the filling in 7 or 8 pools. Using a table knife held vertically, swirl down through the pools to form decorative marbling throughout.

Place the pan in a roasting pan (or broiler pan). Transfer to the oven and add ¾ inch hot water to the roasting pan. Bake for 15 minutes. Reduce the oven temperature to 300 degrees F and bake for 55 to 65 minutes longer, or until the filling appears barely set in the center when tapped.

Transfer the cheesecake to a wire rack. (For safety's sake, let the roasting pan cool in the oven before removing it.) Let the cheesecake cool for 10 minutes. Carefully run a paring knife around the cheesecake to loosen it from the pan sides; this helps prevent it from cracking. Cover and refrigerate for at least 6 hours, or until thoroughly chilled.

At serving time, remove the pan sides. Serve the cheesecake directly from the pan bottom. The cheesecake slices best with a large sharp knife dipped in hot water and wiped clean between cuts.

The cheesecake will keep, covered airtight, in the refrigerator for up to 4 days. Let warm up slightly before serving.

spiced pumpkin cheesecake with orange-gingersnap crust

A perfect choice for a Thanksgiving menu, this cheesecake is large and handsome, with a dark orange-gingersnap bottom and a brown sugar–sour cream topping setting off a pumpkin-tinged middle layer. The filling is rich and mellowed with spice. It tastes somewhat like pumpkin pie, but since it is baked in a water bath, it is smoother, creamier, and more sumptuous. The crust is gingery and aromatic.

CRUST

About 2¼ cups coarsely broken (1-inch pieces) gingersnaps

2½ tablespoons unsalted butter, melted

½ teaspoon finely grated orange zest (orange part of skin)

1–3 teaspoons water, if needed

FILLING

1 15-ounce can solid-pack pumpkin (not seasoned pie filling)

1 tablespoon plus 1 teaspoon unflavored gelatin (about 1½ packets)

3 tablespoons water

½ cup heavy (whipping) cream

1½ pounds (three 8-ounce packages) cream cheese, at room temperature

1 cup packed light brown sugar

⅓ cup granulated sugar

2 teaspoons ground ginger

2 teaspoons ground cinnamon

1¼ teaspoons ground allspice

½ teaspoon freshly grated or ground nutmeg

6 large eggs

2½ teaspoons vanilla extract

SOUR CREAM TOPPING

1 cup sour cream

¼ cup packed light brown sugar

1 teaspoon vanilla extract

4 or 5 kumquats or a small, thin orange slice for garnish (optional)

TO MAKE THE CRUST: Position a rack in the middle of the oven and preheat to 350 degrees F. Generously grease a 9- to 9½-inch springform pan (at least 2½ inches deep) or generously coat with nonstick spray. Center the pan on a double layer of heavy-duty aluminum foil; make sure there are no holes in the foil. Carefully pull the foil up around the pan sides to completely encase it. This prevents water from seeping into the bottom of the pan when you place it in the water bath.

In a food processor, grind the gingersnaps to very fine crumbs; you should have about 1⅓ cups. Add the butter and orange zest to the processor and process, scraping down the sides of the bowl as needed, for 30 to 40 seconds, or until the mixture begins to hold together. Set aside 2 tablespoons crumbs for garnish. If the remaining crumb mixture seems very dry, gradually add the water, a teaspoon at a time, processing a little

TIP

Use top-quality gingersnaps. To break them into coarse pieces, place them in a heavy-duty plastic bag, close the bag tightly, and whack the gingersnaps with a kitchen mallet, heavy rolling pin, or the back of a large, heavy metal spoon.

longer. Press the crumb mixture evenly and firmly into the bottom and ¼ inch up the sides of the pan. Even the edge by pressing down with a fingertip. Wipe any stray crumbs from the pan sides. Bake for 8 to 12 minutes, or until just barely darker at the edges and almost firm when pressed. Transfer to a wire rack. Rinse and dry the processor bowl and blade.

TO MAKE THE FILLING: Reset the oven to 325 degrees F. Line a large colander with a triple layer of heavy-duty paper towels. Spoon the pumpkin into the colander. Top the pumpkin with a double thickness of paper towels. Press down firmly on the towels to squeeze as much liquid as possible from the pumpkin. Continue pressing down until the pumpkin resembles a paste, replacing the towels as necessary. Turn out the pumpkin onto a triple layer of clean paper towels; pat a double thickness of towels over the top and let stand while you prepare the remaining filling ingredients.

In a small deep microwave-safe bowl or a small saucepan, sprinkle the gelatin over the water. Let stand, stirring once or twice, for 5 minutes. Stir the cream into the gelatin mixture. Microwave on high power for 1 minute. Stir well. If the gelatin is not completely dissolved, microwave for 20 seconds longer. Stir and set aside. (Alternatively, heat over low heat, stirring, until the gelatin dissolves.)

Combine the cream cheese, sugars, ginger, cinnamon, allspice, and nutmeg in a large bowl. Using a mixer, beat on low, then medium speed for 4 to 5 minutes, or until very smooth, scraping down the sides of the bowl and the bottom as needed. Beat in the eggs one at a time until smoothly incorporated. Lift the pumpkin off the paper towels and add to the cream cheese mixture. Beat until smoothly incorporated, 1 to 2 minutes, scraping down the sides of the bowl and the beater as needed. Beat in the cream-gelatin mixture and vanilla just until evenly incorporated.

Pour the filling into the crust, spreading it evenly to the edges. Rap the pan on the counter several times to release any air bubbles. Place in a roasting pan (or broiler pan). Transfer to the oven and add ¾ inch hot water to the roasting pan. Bake for 15 minutes. Reduce the oven temperature to 300 degrees F and continue baking for 50 to 65 minutes longer, or until the filling barely jiggles in the center but springs back when the surface is tapped.

where's the cheese?

Oddly enough, a number of old cheesecake recipes actually contained no cheese at all. One such recipe, titled "To Make Very Good Cheesecakes Without Cheese Curd," comes from *Martha Washington's Booke of Cookery.*

> Take a quart of cream, & when it boyles take 14 eggs; If they be very yallow take out 2 or 3 of the youlks: put them into the cream when it boyles & keep it with continuall stirring till it be thick like curd. Then put into it sugar and currans, of each halfe a pound; the currans must first be plumpt in faire water; then take a pound of butter & put into the curd a quarter of the butter.

MEANWHILE, TO MAKE THE TOPPING: In a small deep bowl, thoroughly stir together the sour cream, brown sugar, and vanilla until the sugar dissolves and the mixture is well blended. Set aside.

Transfer the cheesecake to a wire rack. (For safety's sake, let the roasting pan cool in the oven before removing it.) Let the cheesecake stand for 10 minutes. Carefully run a paring knife around the cheesecake to loosen it from the pan sides; this helps prevent it from cracking. Spread the topping evenly over the surface. Let the cheesecake cool completely, at least 1½ hours. Using a small spoon, sprinkle a narrow border of the reserved crumbs around the cheesecake edge. For additional garnish, place a small, thin orange slice in the center (or at serving time garnish with kumquats). Cover and refrigerate until thoroughly chilled, about 6 hours.

At serving time, remove the pan sides. Serve the cheesecake directly from the pan bottom. It slices best with a large sharp knife dipped in hot water and wiped clean between cuts.

The cheesecake will keep, covered airtight, in the refrigerator for up to 5 days.

very Berry swirl cheesecake

Blackberries and red raspberries add a mellow fruit taste and swirls of pale fuchsia color to the cheesecake filling. Because of the water bath baking method, this cheesecake has an extraordinarily creamy texture. It can be prepared well ahead and makes an impressive dessert for company.

BERRY MIXTURE

- $^2/_3$ cup sugar
- $1^1/_2$ tablespoons unflavored gelatin (about $1^1/_2$ packets)
- 1 tablespoon cornstarch
- 2 cups blackberries
- 2 cups raspberries
- 1 tablespoon blackberry brandy or kirsch (optional)
- 2 teaspoons grated lemon zest (yellow part of skin)

  Orange juice, if needed

  Up to 1 tablespoon fresh lemon juice, to taste (optional)

CRUST

- About 7 whole graham crackers, coarsely broken
- 1 tablespoon sugar
- 3 tablespoons unsalted butter, slightly softened and cut into bits
- 1–2 teaspoons water, if needed

FILLING

- $1^1/_3$ cups sugar
- 2 pounds (four 8-ounce packages) cream cheese, at room temperature
- 6 large eggs
- $^1/_3$ cup all-purpose flour
- 2 tablespoons very finely grated lemon zest (yellow part of skin)
- $1^1/_2$ tablespoons blackberry brandy, kirsch, or orange juice
- $2^1/_2$ teaspoons vanilla extract

  Raspberries and blackberries for garnish (optional)

TO MAKE THE BERRY MIXTURE: In a heavy, nonreactive 2-quart saucepan, stir together the sugar, gelatin, and cornstarch until blended. Stir in the berries, brandy (if using), and lemon zest. Let stand until the gelatin softens, 5 to 10 minutes. Bring to a simmer over medium-high heat and cook, stirring, for 2 minutes, or until the berries soften and the mixture turns clear. Let cool for 5 minutes. Turn out into a fine sieve set over a bowl. Press down hard to force through as much juice and pulp as possible; discard the seeds. (You should have at least 1¼ cups of the berry mixture. If you have less, add orange juice to equal that amount. If you have more, save the extra to toss with the berries for garnish.) Stir in the lemon juice, if desired. Cover and refrigerate for up to 3 days. Reheat until fluid and warm before using if necessary.

TO MAKE THE CRUST: Position a rack in the middle of the oven and preheat to 350 degrees F. Generously grease a 9- to 9½-by-3-inch springform pan or generously coat with nonstick spray. Center the pan on a double layer of heavy-duty aluminum foil; make sure there are no holes in the foil. Carefully pull the foil up around the pan to completely encase it. This prevents water from seeping into the bottom of the pan when you place it in the water bath.

In a food processor, grind the graham crackers to fine crumbs; you should have a generous 1 cup. Add the sugar and butter and process until the mixture begins to hold together, about 1 minute. If the mixture seems too dry to hold together when squeezed between your fingertips, add a teaspoon or two of water and process briefly. Press the crumbs evenly and firmly into the bottom of the pan; wipe any stray crumbs from the pan sides. Bake for 8 to 13 minutes, or until fragrant and nicely browned. Transfer to a wire rack.

TO MAKE THE FILLING: Reset the oven to 325 degrees F. In a large bowl using a mixer on medium speed, beat the sugar and cream cheese for 3 to 4 minutes, or until completely smooth, scraping down the sides of the bowl and the beater several times. Add the eggs one at a time, then the flour, lemon zest, brandy, and vanilla. Continue beating, scraping down the sides of the bowl and the beater several times, until very well blended and smooth.

Measure out a generous 1¾ cups of the filling into a medium bowl and stir in ¾ cup of the berry mixture until incorporated. Stir the remaining ½ cup berry mixture into the remaining filling until smoothly incorporated. Turn out half of the paler filling into the springform pan. Spoon about half of the brighter filling onto the pale filling in about 6 pools. Put the remaining pale filling on top of the bright filling. Spoon the remaining bright filling over the top in about 6 pools. Holding a table knife vertically, swirl down through the pools to form decorative marbling throughout. Rap the pan on the counter several times to release any air bubbles.

Place the pan in a roasting pan (or broiler pan). Transfer to the oven and add ¾ inch hot water to the roasting pan. Bake for 15 minutes. Reduce

Graham the Whole-Grain Cracker Man

The graham cracker gets its name from the nineteenth-century Presbyterian minister and diet reformer Sylvester Graham. An advocate of homemade, high-fiber breads and vegetarianism, and a critic of refined sugar (and nearly every other earthly pleasure), Graham invented his wholesome cracker, made with coarsely ground whole-wheat flour, in 1829. No doubt he would turn over in his grave at the thought of the crackers being incorporated into rich desserts.

85

pies, tarts, and cheesecakes

the oven temperature to 300 degrees F and bake for 1 to 1¼ hours longer, or until the cheesecake is firm at the edges and barely jiggles and springs back in the center when tapped.

Transfer the cheesecake to a wire rack. (For safety's sake, let the roasting pan cool in the oven before removing it.) Let cool for 15 minutes. Carefully run a paring knife around the cheesecake to loosen it from the pan sides; this helps prevent it from cracking. Let the cheesecake cool completely, at least 1½ hours. Cover and refrigerate for at least 6 hours, or until thoroughly chilled.

At serving time, carefully remove the pan sides. Serve the cheesecake directly from the pan bottom. The cheesecake slices best with a large sharp knife dipped in hot water and wiped clean between cuts. If desired, garnish each serving with plain fresh berries, or, if you have extra berry mixture, thin it with hot water until fluid and toss it with the berries first.

The cheesecake will keep, covered airtight, in the refrigerator for up to 4 days.

coconut cream cheesecake with chocolate-coconut glaze

The chocolate-coconut crust, silky coconut-flavored filling, and assertive chocolate glaze place this sumptuous creation about as far out on the spectrum from the original European egg-and-cheese-curd cheesecakes as you can get. Most of the early recipes in sixteenth- and seventeenth-century British cookbooks were really more like dense custard pies or tarts and were baked in pastry, never crumb crusts. The crumb crust—initially prepared with zwieback biscuits or graham crackers—is an American invention, appearing around the 1930s. Chocolate crumb crusts, such as the one used here, are even more recent than that.

Serve this when you want to make a splash.

CRUST

1 cup shredded or flaked sweetened coconut

About 2 cups broken (1-inch pieces) chocolate wafers, homemade (see page 280) or store-bought

1 ounce bittersweet (not unsweetened) or semisweet chocolate, coarsely chopped

1 tablespoon unsalted butter, slightly softened

1–3 tablespoons water, as needed

FILLING

2 pounds (four 8-ounce packages) cream cheese, at room temperature

Generous $3/4$ cup sugar

1 tablespoon light rum or orange juice

$2^1/2$ teaspoons vanilla extract

$1/4$ teaspoon coconut extract or almond extract

2 tablespoons all-purpose flour

5 large eggs, at room temperature

$2/3$ cup canned cream of coconut (not coconut milk), stirred well before using

CHOCOLATE-COCONUT GLAZE

$2/3$ cup canned cream of coconut (not coconut milk), stirred well before using

$6^1/2$ ounces bittersweet (not unsweetened) or semisweet chocolate, broken up or coarsely chopped

1 ounce unsweetened chocolate, broken up or coarsely chopped

2 tablespoons light rum or orange juice

$1/8$ teaspoon coconut extract or almond extract

TO MAKE THE CRUST: Position a rack in the lower third of the oven and preheat to 325 degrees F. Generously grease a 9- to 9½-by-3-inch springform pan or generously coat with nonstick spray.

Spread the coconut on a small rimmed baking sheet. Toast, stirring every 2 to 3 minutes, for 7 to 11 minutes, or until well browned but not burned. In a food processor, grind the wafers into fine crumbs; you should have 1¼ cups. Add the coconut and chocolate to the food processor. Process for 2 to 3 minutes, or until the mixture is very finely ground, scraping down the sides of the bowl as needed. Add the butter and 1 tablespoon water and process until the mixture just holds together, about 30 seconds. If the mixture seems very dry when pressed together with your fingertips, gradually add up to 2 tablespoons more water, processing a little longer. Press the crumbs evenly and firmly into the bottom (not the sides) of the pan. Wipe any stray crumbs from the pan sides. Bake until fragrant and almost firm, 8 to 13 minutes. Transfer to a wire rack.

TO MAKE THE FILLING: In a large bowl, combine the cream cheese, sugar, rum, vanilla, and coconut extract. Using a mixer, beat on medium speed for 4 to 5 minutes, or until completely smooth (but not fluffy), scraping down the sides of the bowl as needed. Beat in the flour until smoothly incorporated. Add the eggs one at a time, beating for about 20 seconds after each addition. A bit at a time, beat in the cream of coconut until the mixture is well blended and smooth.

Gently turn out the filling into the pan. Rap the pan on the counter several times to release any air bubbles. Let stand for 5 minutes, then rap again. Set on a rimmed baking sheet. Bake for 15 minutes. Reset the oven to 300 degrees F and continue baking for 40 to 50 minutes, or until the filling appears barely set in the center when tapped. Turn off the oven. Leave the cheesecake in the oven for 10 to 15 minutes, or until the center just seems firm when the pan is jiggled. Transfer to a wire rack. Let stand for 10 minutes. Carefully run a knife around the cheesecake to loosen it from the pan sides; this helps prevent it from cracking. Let cool completely, at least 1½ hours. Remove the pan sides. Set the cheesecake, pan bottom still attached, on paper towels to catch drips when the glaze is added.

TO MAKE THE GLAZE: In a heavy medium saucepan over medium-high heat, bring the cream of coconut just to a simmer, stirring. Remove from the heat, add the chocolates, and stir until completely smooth and melted. Add the rum and coconut extract, stirring until smoothly incorporated. Pour the glaze evenly over the center of the cheesecake. Using an offset spatula or table knife, spread the glaze smoothly to the cheesecake edges until the chocolate just begins to drip down the sides. Shake the cheesecake to even the glaze. Let cool for 1 hour.

Refrigerate, covered, until well chilled, at least 6 hours. Carefully run a small knife under the cheesecake to loosen it from the pan. To facilitate cutting, let the cheesecake warm up for 5 to 10 minutes. The cheesecake slices best with a large sharp knife dipped in hot water and wiped clean between cuts. Cut into small wedges and serve.

The cheesecake will keep, covered airtight, in the refrigerator for up to 4 days.

ALL-purpose pie pastry Dough

This flavorful, versatile pastry is carefully designed to be easy for cooks of various levels of expertise. It calls for both all-purpose flour and cake flour, a combination that yields a tenderer dough than just all-purpose flour. If you don't have cake flour on hand, replacing it with all-purpose flour will yield acceptable results. A small amount of sugar helps keep the dough from toughening during mixing and rolling, and a little baking powder helps counteract shrinking during baking.

This recipe gives measures for a double crust and a single crust. Since deep-dish (at least 2-inch-deep) pie plates require more pastry, there will be slightly more to trim away from regular (1½-inch-deep or less) pie plates.

If cutting in the fat with a food processor, take care not to overprocess; pulse, watching closely. Once the fat is cut in, turn out the mixture into a bowl and complete the mixing by hand.

PASTRY DOUGH (DOUBLE CRUST)

- 8 tablespoons (1 stick) cold unsalted butter, cut into ⅓-inch cubes
- 7 tablespoons solid white shortening, cut or spooned into 14 pieces
- 2 cups all-purpose flour
- ⅔ cup cake flour
- 1½ tablespoons sugar
- 1 teaspoon salt
- ½ teaspoon baking powder
- 6–9 tablespoons ice water

PASTRY DOUGH (SINGLE CRUST)

- 4 tablespoons (½ stick) cold unsalted butter, cut into ⅓-inch cubes
- 3½ tablespoons solid white shortening, cut or spooned into 7 pieces
- 1 cup all-purpose flour
- ⅓ cup cake flour
- 2½ teaspoons sugar
- ½ teaspoon salt
- ¼ teaspoon baking powder
- 3–5 tablespoons ice water

Freeze the butter cubes and shortening pieces for 20 minutes.

TO MIX BY HAND: In a large bowl, thoroughly stir together the all-purpose flour, cake flour, sugar, salt and baking powder. Sprinkle the chilled butter and shortening over the flour mixture. Using a pastry blender, forks, or your fingertips, cut in the fat until the mixture looks like coarse crumbs with a few bits the size of small peas remaining. Be sure to scrape up the flour mixture on the bottom of the bowl.

TO MIX WITH A FOOD PROCESSOR: Combine the all-purpose flour, cake flour, sugar, salt, and baking powder in the processor. Pulse for 10 seconds to mix. Sprinkle the chilled butter and shortening over the flour mixture. Process with about ten 1-second pulses. Stir, lifting up the contents on the bottom. Pulse about 15 more times, just until the bits of fat are cut in and the mixture looks like coarse crumbs with a few bits the size of small peas remaining; stop halfway through and stir to redistribute the contents on the bottom. Turn out the mixture into a large bowl.

TO MAKE A DOUBLE CRUST: In a small bowl, measure out 6 tablespoons ice water.

TO MAKE A SINGLE CRUST: Measure out 3 tablespoons ice water.

Using a fork, lightly combine the water mixture with the flour mixture, tossing until the water is evenly incorporated and the mixture just begins to form clumps, 15 to 20 strokes. Be sure to reach down to the bottom to be sure the flour underneath is dampened. Check the consistency by pinching a small amount of dough between your fingertips; it should hold together smoothly and be moist but not soggy. If it is crumbly or dry, sprinkle over more ice water, 2 teaspoons at a time, tossing briefly with a fork. When the water is evenly incorporated and the dough is sufficiently moistened to hold together when pinched, gather it up and firmly press it together with your fingertips into a smooth, dense mass.

TO MAKE A SINGLE CRUST: Flatten it into a 5-inch disk.

TO MAKE A DOUBLE CRUST: Divide it into 2 equal portions. Flatten the portions into 5-inch disks.

Wrap in plastic and refrigerate for at least 45 minutes and preferably 1 hour. The dough can be refrigerated for up to 2 days or wrapped airtight and frozen for up to a month; thaw in the refrigerator before using. Roll and bake as directed in the individual recipes.

keys to pastry success

1. Avoid overmanipulating the dough by stirring, mixing, kneading, or rolling any more than is absolutely necessary. Extra pulling, stretching, or handling of pie pastry makes it tough and more likely to shrink.

2. Think of warmth as an enemy and coolness as a friend. Cold butter and shortening are much easier to handle than warm fat and yield a better dough, so chill as directed when you begin. If possible, have your kitchen cool, too. If you can't avoid a warm kitchen, compensate by lightly chilling not only the fat and water but also the dry ingredients, work bowl, rolling pin, and pie plate. Proceed promptly once the chilled ingredients are removed from the refrigerator, and avoid overhandling them, as friction generates heat.

   If the butter and shortening overheat, the dough will become increasingly limp, greasy, and challenging to work with. Don't use flour to correct the situation; working it in will cause toughness and further overheating. Instead, place the dough in the refrigerator; the dough will firm up and become manageable again.

sour cream pie pastry dough for Lattice-topped pies

Makes enough for a 9-inch double-crust Lattice pie

Sour cream and lemon juice help keep this dough for lattice-topped pies and other pies with a decorative upper crust tender in spite of the extra handling the top requires. The sour cream pastry also goes well with fruit fillings.

The lattice method is surprisingly easy, but if it seems too daunting, make a simple cutaway (or cutaways) in the top crust to reveal the filling underneath. To do this, roll the smaller dough portion into a 9½-inch round, then lay a 9-inch plate or saucer on the dough and cut around it using a sharp knife to form a perfect round of dough for the top. Make a single cutaway in the center of the round with a plain or scalloped round cookie cutter or several attractively spaced cutaways using whatever cutters you please.

8 tablespoons (1 stick) cold unsalted butter, cut into ⅓-inch cubes
¼ cup solid white shortening, cut or spooned into 8 pieces
2⅓ cups all-purpose flour
1½ tablespoons sugar

Generous ¾ teaspoon salt
1 tablespoon fresh lemon juice
⅓ cup sour cream
1½–3½ tablespoons ice water

Freeze the butter cubes and shortening pieces for 20 minutes.

Pulse the flour, sugar, and salt in a food processor several times to mix. Sprinkle the butter and shortening over the flour mixture. Process in about twenty 1-second pulses just until the bits of fat are cut in and the mixture looks like coarse crumbs with some bits the size of small peas remaining; stop halfway through and stir to redistribute the contents on the bottom.

Mix the lemon juice into the sour cream. Add the sour cream mixture and 1½ tablespoons ice water to the processor. Process in fifteen to twenty 1-second pulses, or just until the mixture is thoroughly incorporated, stirring to lift the crumbs from the bottom several times. Check frequently and stop processing as soon as the dough holds together when pressed together with your fingertips. If it is too dry, add up to 2 tablespoons more cold water ½ tablespoon at a time and pulse until the mixture begins to hold together.

Turn out the dough onto a sheet of baking parchment. Knead briefly until it holds together smoothly. Shape the pastry into a 6-inch disk. Cut off a generous third. Shape the smaller portion into a 4-inch disk (for the top) and the larger portion into a 5-inch disk (for the bottom). Wrap each portion in plastic wrap and refrigerate for at least 45 minutes and up to 24 hours. Roll and bake as directed in the individual recipes.

ALL-purpose tart pastry dough

This tart pastry dough has a buttery taste and is easy to make and work with. Although it doesn't become soggy from juicy fillings, it's still tender.

9½ tablespoons (1 stick plus 1½ tablespoons) cold unsalted butter, cut into ⅓-inch cubes

1 large egg yolk

2 teaspoons fresh lemon juice

3 tablespoons ice water, plus more if needed

1⅔ cups all-purpose flour

2 tablespoons sugar

½ teaspoon salt

¼ teaspoon baking powder

Freeze the butter cubes for 15 minutes.

In a small bowl using a fork, beat together the egg yolk, lemon juice, and 3 tablespoons ice water until evenly incorporated.

TO MIX WITH A FOOD PROCESSOR: In the processor, combine the flour, sugar, salt, and baking powder. Pulse for a few seconds to blend. Sprinkle the chilled butter over the flour. Process in fifteen to twenty 1-second pulses, or until the butter is cut in and the mixture resembles coarse meal. Stop and scrape up the mixture from the bottom after 10 pulses. Add the egg mixture through the feed tube and process in five to eight 1-second pulses, or until the liquid is evenly incorporated and the particles stick together. If the mixture seems crumbly or at all dry when pressed between your fingertips, sprinkle over more ice water, a teaspoon or two at a time, while processing in 1-second pulses. Frequently stop and press together a small amount of dough to check the consistency. As soon as the mixture holds together and looks slightly moist, stop processing. Don't overprocess, as it can cause toughness.

TO MIX BY HAND: In a medium bowl, thoroughly stir together the flour, sugar, salt, and baking powder. Using a pastry blender, forks, or your fingertips, cut the butter into the flour mixture until the mixture resembles coarse meal. Lift up the mixture on the bottom several times. Add the egg mixture to the flour mixture, blending with a fork just until the mixture holds together. If necessary, mix in more ice water, a teaspoon at a time, until the pastry is moist and holds together but is not wet.

Turn out the pastry onto a sheet of baking parchment. Knead and shape the dough lightly to form a 6-inch disk. Wrap in plastic and refrigerate for at least 45 minutes and up to 24 hours. Roll and bake as directed in the individual recipes.

pastry panache

Experienced pastry makers have long known the importance of keeping ingredients cool. In introducing her pastry, or "paste," recipes in the eponymous 1851 *Miss Leslie's Directions for Cookery,* Eliza Leslie advised, "All paste should be made in a very cool place, as heat renders it heavy. It is far more difficult to get it light in summer than in winter." She also suggested washing the butter in very cold water, one cooling method that was available in the days before refrigeration.

2

Cakes and Frostings

yeLLow sour cream-Butter Layer cake

The layer cake is so much a part of weddings, birthdays, and other celebrations that it's easy to forget it is a fairly recent American innovation, spurred by the appearance of chemical leavenings and modern ovens. The yellow layer cake is a basic in every American cake baker's repertoire, and it's most often the one dressed up and decorated. Nearly any icing desired can be successfully paired with it, although I think a caramel frosting or fudge frosting are best. Light Lemon Cream Cheese-Butter Frosting (page 148) lends a more elegant look and holds up beautifully when piped.

You will notice that the mixing method for this cake is somewhat different than for most cakes. The method of beginning by beating the butter and dry ingredients together was refined and popularized in the 1980s by Rose Levy Beranbaum in *The Cake Bible,* but the idea is not new. In her 1879 work, *Housekeeping in Old Virginia,* Marion Cabell Tyree mentioned that "some of the best housekeepers" preferred to beat together the flour and butter first. The advantage of this is that the flour particles become coated with butter, which helps prevent them from developing tough gluten strands when liquids are added. The result is a velvety tenderness and a fine crumb similar to that of pound cake, but less compact. This cake is moist, aromatic, and very buttery.

$1^2/_3$ cups unsifted cake flour

1 cup all-purpose flour

1 tablespoon baking powder

Scant $3/4$ teaspoon salt

2 cups sugar

12 tablespoons ($1^1/_2$ sticks) unsalted butter, softened but not melted

5 large eggs, at room temperature

$1/2$ cup sour cream, at room temperature

$3/4$ cup milk

1 tablespoon vanilla extract

American Caramel Frosting (page 146) or Rich and Creamy Chocolate Fudge Frosting (page 149)

Position a rack in the middle of the oven and preheat to 350 degrees F. Lightly grease three 8½-inch or two 9-inch round cake pans or coat with nonstick spray. Insert rounds of baking parchment or wax paper into the pans. Lightly grease the paper or lightly coat with nonstick spray. Dust the pans with flour, tip from side to side to coat evenly, and tap out any excess.

Sift the flours, baking powder, and salt into a large bowl. Add the sugar and combine with a mixer on low speed for 30 seconds to blend. Beat in the butter a generous tablespoon at a time until all of it is incorporated and the mixture just has the consistency of coarse crumbs; don't over-beat. In a medium bowl or a 4-cup measure, use a wire whisk to beat together the eggs and sour cream until well blended and smooth. Whisk in the milk and vanilla. Add half the egg mixture to the crumbs and beat on low speed until just blended, about 10 seconds. Raise the speed to medium and beat for 1½ minutes longer. Beating on low speed, slowly pour in the remaining egg mixture until all is incorporated. Raise the speed to medium and beat for 1½ minutes longer, scraping down the sides of the bowl as needed; the mixture may look slightly separated.

Divide the batter evenly among the pans, spreading it to the edges. Rap the pans on the counter to release any air bubbles. Bake for 25 to 35 minutes, or until a toothpick inserted in the center comes out clean, the surface is nicely browned, and the tops spring back slightly when pressed. Transfer the pans to wire racks. Let cool to barely warm, at least 30 minutes. Carefully run a knife around the pans and under the paper all the way around, then rap the pans on the counter to loosen the layers; handle gently. Holding a rack flat against a pan, invert the layers onto the racks. Remove the paper. Let cool completely. The unfrosted layers will keep, stored airtight, at room temperature for up to 24 hours or frozen for up to a month. Let come to room temperature before frosting.

TO FROST THE CAKE: Brush any loose crumbs from the layers. Put several dabs of frosting in the center of a cake plate. Center one cake layer bottom side up on the plate, pressing down lightly to anchor it.

FOR A THREE-LAYER CAKE: Spread a scant quarter of the frosting over the layer. Add the second cake layer. Frost with another scant quarter of the frosting. Top with the third layer. Use the remaining frosting to cover the cake top and sides, swirling it attractively.

FOR A TWO-LAYER CAKE: Spread a scant third of the frosting over the layer. Add the second cake layer. Use the remaining frosting to cover the cake top and sides, smoothing and swirling it attractively.

The cake will keep, stored airtight, in a cool place (not refrigerated) for 3 or 4 days.

nutrispeak

"Because of its high nutritive value, cake is most desirable at a meal that lacks hearty food in the form of meat or fat or their equivalents; but as sugar satisfies hunger almost instantly, cake should be eaten at the end of a meal."

—Swans Down,
Cake Secrets (1919)

Triple-Layer coconut white cake with Lemon curd

The combination of mild, mellow coconut cake and zesty, colorful curd is both delicious and attractive, especially when paired with Fluffy White Frosting (page 144). It's been traditional for decades to garnish the frosting with shredded coconut, but the cake is very good without it, too. The "plain" coconut cake—that is, minus the lemon curd filling—is also excellent frosted with Rich and Creamy Chocolate Fudge Frosting (page 149).

Although some versions call for coconut milk or grated coconut, my cake calls for canned cream of coconut, which not only adds coconut flavor but also helps give the cake a tender, moist crumb. Don't use canned coconut milk; it isn't thick or sweet enough to serve as a substitute for cream of coconut in this recipe.

LEMON CURD

- 1 cup sugar
- 1 tablespoon grated lemon zest (yellow part of skin)
- ½ cup fresh lemon juice
- 5½ tablespoons unsalted butter, slightly softened and cut into chunks
- 7 large egg yolks (reserve whites for cake)
- ½ teaspoon vanilla extract

CAKE

- 2 cups unsifted cake flour
- 1 cup all-purpose flour
- 1 tablespoon baking powder
- ¾ teaspoon salt
- 1⅔ cups sugar
- ⅔ cup (10⅔ tablespoons) unsalted butter, slightly softened
- 2½ teaspoons vanilla extract
- Generous ¼ teaspoon coconut extract or almond extract
- 5 large egg whites, at room temperature
- 1¼ cups milk (divided)
- ½ cup canned cream of coconut (not coconut milk)

- Fluffy White Frosting (page 144)
- 1½ cups shredded sweetened coconut for garnish (optional)

TO MAKE THE CURD: In a heavy, nonreactive medium saucepan, stir together the sugar, lemon zest, and lemon juice until well blended. Heat over medium heat, stirring, until very warm but not hot to the touch. Remove from the heat. Whisk in the butter until melted. Whisk in the egg yolks until smoothly incorporated.

Return the pan to the burner. Whisking constantly, heat over medium-low heat until the mixture becomes more opaque and has the consistency of a pourable, slightly thickened cream sauce, 6 to 8 minutes. If bubbles begin to form at the pan edges, lift the pan from the heat and whisk to cool slightly before continuing cooking. Remove from the heat. Stir in the vanilla. Let stand for 10 minutes; the mixture will thicken further as it cools. Press the mixture through a fine sieve into a storage container. Lay a sheet of plastic wrap directly on the curd. Refrigerate, covered, for at least 1½ hours and up to several days. The curd will thicken to a stiff spreading consistency when chilled. Stir well before using.

TO MAKE THE CAKE: Position a rack in the middle of the oven and preheat to 350 degrees F. Generously grease three 8½-inch (or similar) round cake pans or generously coat with nonstick spray. Dust the pans with flour, tip from side to side to coat evenly, and tap out any excess.

Sift the flours, baking powder, and salt onto a sheet of baking parchment or wax paper. Combine the sugar, butter, vanilla, and coconut extract in a large bowl. With a mixer on medium speed, beat until the mixture is well blended and lightened, 1½ to 2 minutes, scraping down the sides of the bowl as needed. Add the egg whites in 2 batches, beating for about 30 seconds after each addition.

With the mixer on low speed, beat in half the dry ingredients until incorporated, scraping down the sides of the bowl as needed. Then beat on medium speed for 1½ minutes, or until well blended. On low speed, gradually beat in ½ cup of the milk and the cream of coconut until evenly incorporated. Beat in the remaining dry ingredients until smoothly incorporated, then the remaining ¾ cup milk. Beat on low speed for 1 minute, or until well blended and smooth, scraping down the sides of the bowl as needed.

Divide the batter evenly among the pans, spreading it to the edges. Rap the pans on the counter to release any air bubbles. Bake (on two racks, if necessary) for 25 to 35 minutes, or until a toothpick inserted in the center comes out with just a few loose crumbs attached and the tops spring back slightly when pressed; the layers will be drawing away from the pan sides. Transfer the pans to wire racks. Let cool completely.

Carefully run a knife around the pans and under the cake edges, then rap the pans on the counter to loosen the layers. Holding a rack flat against a pan, invert the layers onto the racks. Remove the paper.

cake of many names

Light, multilayered white cakes with coconut and lemon have been a great favorite in the South since at least the mid-nineteenth century. Early on, there were many variations on the basic theme: some versions were leavened with baking soda and cream of tartar; others were lightened with only beaten eggs and were essentially sponge cakes. Some had coconut tucked between the layers; others had a lemon icing or glaze; still others called for an uncooked, beaten egg white icing flavored or garnished with coconut or lemon, or both; and some included a cooked "lemon jelly filling" that we now call lemon curd.

The recipe also went by a number of names—white mountain cake, snow mountain cake, mountain coconut cake, lemon jelly cake, and, very often, Robert E. Lee cake. Some sources say the latter name reflects the fact that General Lee particularly liked the cake; others say it was simply named in his honor.

TO ASSEMBLE THE CAKE: Brush any loose crumbs from the layers. Put several dabs of lemon curd in the center of a cake plate. Center one cake layer bottom side up on the plate, pressing it down lightly to anchor it in the curd. Spread half the lemon curd on the layer to within ⅓ inch of the edge. Repeat the process with the second cake layer, then spread with the remaining curd. Top with the remaining layer. Let the cake stand while you make the frosting.

Generously frost the cake top and sides, smoothing and swirling the frosting attractively. Sprinkle the shredded coconut over the top, if desired. For best flavor, let the cake stand for at least 3 hours to allow the flavors to blend before serving.

Be sure to store the cake airtight, as high humidity can cause the frosting to deflate after a day or so. The cake will keep for up to 3 days.

Triple-Layer Devil's Food Cake

I love this cake not only for its full, rich flavor and almost black color but also for its very soft, tender crumb. With three ample layers, it's tall and impressive-looking.

Chocolate cakes like this began turning up in the late nineteenth century. Caroline B. King, an early-twentieth-century cookbook author who grew up in Chicago, mentioned in a 1941 memoir that devil's food cakes had come on the scene in the Windy City in the mid-1880s, when they became "quite the rage." The first published recipe I've found with the devil's food name is in the 1898 edition of *Mrs. Rorer's New Cook Book* by Sarah Tyson Rorer. No one knows who thought of calling it that, but the fact that a contracting, white-hued cake called angel food was already popular no doubt had something to do with it.

When devil's food cakes first appeared, a variety of recipes—some considerably darker and more chocolatey than others—bore the name. Today "devil's food" usually suggests not just a chocolate cake, but one that is dramatically dark in color and that has a distinctive, pleasantly bitter-edged flavor and aroma. The key to obtaining the striking look and taste is in combining baking soda with nonalkalized, American-style cocoa powder, not Dutch-process cocoa powder. The soda reacts with the natural acid in the untreated cocoa, deepening the color and giving it a reddish tinge and also changing the flavor. Don't substitute Dutch-process cocoa powder, which has already had its acid neutralized and won't react properly with the baking soda.

Top this cake with Rich and Creamy Chocolate Fudge Frosting (page 149) or, for a nice color and textural contrast, Fluffy White Frosting (page 144).

4 ounces unsweetened chocolate, broken up or coarsely chopped	Generous ¼ teaspoon salt
⅔ cup unsweetened, nonalkalized American-style cocoa powder	1¼ cups (2½ sticks) unsalted butter, slightly softened
1¼ teaspoons baking soda	2⅔ cups sugar
¾ cup boiling water	5 large eggs
1⅓ cups unsifted cake flour	1 cup sour cream
1 cup all-purpose flour	2½ teaspoons vanilla extract
¾ teaspoon baking powder	Rich and Creamy Chocolate Fudge Frosting (page 149) or Fluffy White Frosting (page 144)

Position a rack in the middle of the oven and preheat to 350 degrees F. Generously grease three 9-inch (or similar) round cake pans or generously coat with nonstick spray. Insert rounds of baking parchment or wax paper into the pans. Generously grease the paper or coat with nonstick spray. Dust the pans with flour, tip from side to side to coat evenly, and tap out any excess.

In a small microwave-safe bowl, microwave the chocolate on high power for 1 minute. Stop and stir. Continue microwaving on medium power, stopping and stirring at 30-second intervals, until almost melted; allow the residual heat to melt the chocolate completely. (Alternatively, in a small heavy saucepan, melt the chocolate over lowest heat, stirring constantly and watching carefully until almost melted, then remove from the heat and allow the residual heat to finish the job.)

In a medium bowl, stir together the cocoa powder and baking soda until well blended. Pour the boiling water over the mixture, stirring well; it will foam up. Let cool to warm. Sift together the flours, baking powder, and salt onto a sheet of baking parchment or wax paper. In a large bowl with a mixer on medium speed, beat the butter for 1½ minutes, or until very light and fluffy, scraping down the sides of the bowl as needed. Add the sugar and beat for about 1½ minutes longer, or until very light and well blended, scraping down the sides of the bowl as needed. Beat in the eggs one at a time just until blended. Add the cocoa mixture and continue beating until the mixture is free of lumps, scraping down the sides of the bowl several times; the mixture may look slightly curdled. Stir the chocolate; it should still be warm and fluid. (If it has stiffened or cooled, reheat it to warm, but not hot, before adding.) Beat the chocolate into the batter until smoothly incorporated. With the mixer on low speed, beat in half the dry ingredients, then the sour cream and vanilla. Beat for 1 minute, scraping down the sides of the bowl as needed. Beat or stir in the remaining dry ingredients just until smoothly incorporated.

Divide the batter evenly among the pans, spreading it to the edges. Bake for 25 to 35 minutes, or until a toothpick inserted in the center comes out clean but still moist and the layers are just beginning to draw away from the pan sides. Transfer the pans to wire racks. Let cool completely.

Carefully run a knife around the pan sides and under the baking parchment or wax paper all the way around, then rap the pans on the counter to loosen the layers. Holding a rack flat against a pan, invert the layers onto racks. Remove the paper.

TIP

For a moist texture, it's important not to overbake this cake. The best way to tell if it's done is to watch the pan edges. As soon as the layers *just begin* to pull away from the sides, remove the pans from the oven.

TO FROST THE CAKE: Brush any loose crumbs from the layers. Put several dabs of frosting in the center of a cake plate. Center one cake layer bottom side up on the cake plate; press it down lightly to anchor it in the frosting. Spread a generous quarter of the frosting over the layer. Add the second cake layer. Frost with another generous quarter of the frosting. Top with the third layer. Use the remaining frosting to cover the cake top and sides, smoothing and swirling it attractively. Let stand for at least a few minutes until the frosting firms up slightly before serving.

The cake is best fresh but can be stored, covered airtight, in a cool place (not refrigerated) for a day or so.

BLack walnut pound cake

This cake is full of flavor, buttery, and moist, and rather easy to prepare. It bakes up with an appealing brown, slightly crisp crust and fills the kitchen with a heady, unforgettable fragrance. I've adapted the recipe from several versions from Missouri, where black walnuts are popular in pound cakes, cookies, candies, pies, and ice creams.

Black walnuts are abundant all across the state, and organizations such as the Missouri Farmers Association operate black walnut hulling machines at various collection points every autumn. For a modest fee, residents can have their 100-pound bags efficiently husked. Black walnuts—conveniently hulled, cracked, picked, cleaned, and chopped—are also available in grocery stores across America in the fall.

3 cups all-purpose flour
Generous 1/2 teaspoon salt
1/4 teaspoon baking soda
1 1/2 cups (3 sticks) unsalted butter, slightly softened
3 cups minus 2 tablespoons sugar
7 large eggs

1 tablespoon vanilla extract
Finely grated zest (yellow part of skin) and juice of 1 small lemon
1 1/3 cups chopped black walnuts

Position a rack in the middle of the oven and preheat to 350 degrees F. Grease a 10-by-4¼-inch (15-cup or similar large) tube pan with a removable bottom or coat with nonstick spray. Dust the pan with flour, tip from side to side to coat, and tap out any excess.

Sift together the flour, salt, and baking soda onto a sheet of baking parchment or wax paper. In a large bowl with a mixer on medium speed, beat the butter and sugar until lightened and fluffy, about 2 minutes, scraping down the sides of the bowl as needed. Reduce the speed to low and gradually beat in the flour mixture; if the motor labors, stir in the last of the flour by hand. Add the eggs one at a time, beating 10 seconds after each addition. Add the vanilla, lemon zest and juice, and walnuts. Beat on medium speed until well blended and fluffy, 2 to 3 minutes, scraping down the sides of the bowl as needed. (The bowl will be rather full.) Turn out the batter into the pan, smoothing the surface.

Bake for 1¼ hours to 1 hour and 25 minutes, or until the surface is nicely browned and springs back when lightly pressed, and a toothpick in-

tip

The batter may be baked in two 5-by-9-inch (or similar) loaf pans instead of a tube pan, if desired. The baking time will be 55 to 70 minutes. You can also make one black walnut cake and one plain pound cake. In this case, use 2/3 cup nuts and add them to the batter left in the bowl after half has been transferred to a loaf pan.

serted in the thickest part comes out with just a few crumbs clinging to it; do not overbake. Transfer the pan to a wire rack. Let cool completely, about 1 hour. Run a table knife around the pan sides to loosen the cake, then lift out the cake and tube portion. Run a knife under the cake and around the tube until the cake is completely loosened. Carefully lift up the cake and transfer it to a cake plate. Cut into slices and serve.

The cake will keep, stored airtight, at room temperature for up to 4 days or frozen for up to a month. Let thaw at room temperature before serving.

VARIATION: Plain Pound Cake

For a very good plain pound cake, omit the black walnuts from the recipe.

cracking for cake

"Just before Christmas, my mother would set me outside on the sunny side of the house with a hammer and a big bucket of black walnuts gathered from an ancient tree in the pasture. For hours at a time, I'd sit there, my back against the side of the house, an upturned flat iron between my legs, pounding away at the walnuts and then tediously picking the nut meat out with a bobby pin. The payoff was a piece of delicious black walnut cake on Christmas Day."

—A. C. Snow, "Black Walnuts Better Than Stars as Stocking Gifts," *Raleigh News-Observer* (December 29, 2002)

going nutting

In the rolling Maryland farm country where I grew up, towering stands of native black walnut trees shower the ground in many woods and yards with their green-hulled, golf ball–size nuts each August or September. (The black walnut trees in our yard were just beyond the porch off our kitchen, so gathering, or "nutting," as some called it, was easy.)

Harvesting is a tedious process. After the nuts are collected, they must sit in an airy but sheltered (and squirrel-proof) spot for several weeks so the damp green hulls can dry and the meats can cure. Then the slippery, acrid-smelling hulls must be stripped away and the rocklike nuts cracked. Some people put the cured nuts in a sturdy sack and run over them with a car, but I take the plodding route, pulling off the husks by hand and whacking the nuts with a hammer.

The last step is extracting the fine veins of meat embedded in the shells. This is usually done with a nut pick or small, fine paring knife and requires perseverance. Even a lengthy, earnest picking session never yields more than a cup or so of meats.

Although I'm a great fan of these rough-textured North American nuts, they are an acquired taste. Their distinctive, slightly acrid, deeply woodsy flavor dominates any dish they are added to. They are most popular in areas where our hardwood forests still flourish and the autumn custom of going nutting still endures.

These days, I depend on the supermarket for most of my supply, but I can't break the habit of nutting completely. Whenever I see the green-hulled orbs on the ground in the woods behind my Maryland house, my hunter-gatherer urge takes over, and I'm compelled to carry a few nuts back to my kitchen.

applesauce
spice cake

Recipes for applesauce spice cakes turn up all over America, but especially in the heart-land, where applesauce is a popular ingredient in baked goods. This delightful cake, which reminds me of one my mother sometimes made for my birthday, is adapted from a recipe said to be a favorite of a former governor of Iowa, Terry Branstad.

Part of its appeal is the spice and applesauce combination: it yields a cake of exceptional fragrance and flavor. The applesauce also keeps the crumb wonderfully moist. The cake can be baked in two round pans and stacked for a layer cake, or in one 9-by-13-inch pan for a simpler presentation. It is excellent topped with cream cheese frosting, which dresses it up a bit. Or try fluffy white frosting for a more old-fashioned look and taste. I think the raisins are a nice addition, but you can omit them, if you like.

Many traditional layer cake recipes call for separating the yolks and whites, then beating the whites until fluffy before folding them back into the batter. This extra step is unnecessary and sometimes yields a drier cake. It may be a holdover from the time before baking soda and baking powder came on the market, when cooks had to fold in well-beaten egg whites to aerate their cakes.

3/4 cup coarsely chopped dark raisins (optional)

1/4 cup hot water, if using raisins

2 cups all-purpose flour

1 1/2 teaspoons baking powder

1/8 teaspoon baking soda

1 1/2 teaspoons ground cinnamon

1 1/4 teaspoons ground ginger

1 teaspoon ground nutmeg

Generous 3/4 teaspoon ground cloves

1/2 teaspoon salt

16 tablespoons (2 sticks) unsalted butter, slightly softened

1 1/3 cups granulated sugar

1/2 cup packed light brown sugar

1 1/2 teaspoons vanilla extract

4 large eggs

1 1/4 cups sweetened applesauce (divided)

Orange Cream Cheese–Butter Frosting (page 148) or Fluffy White Frosting (page 144)

Position a rack in the middle of the oven and preheat to 350 degrees F. Generously grease a 9-by-13-inch baking pan or two 8 1/2- to 9-inch round cake pans or coat with nonstick spray.

If using the raisins, combine them with the hot water in a small bowl. Sift the flour, baking powder, baking soda, cinnamon, ginger, nutmeg, cloves, and salt onto a sheet of baking parchment or wax paper. In a large bowl, combine the butter, granulated sugar, brown sugar, and vanilla. With a mixer on medium speed, beat until the mixture is very well blended and lightened, about 2 minutes, scraping down the sides of the bowl as needed. Add the eggs one at a time, beating for about 20 seconds after each addition. Add half the flour mixture, beating just until smoothly incorporated. Add half the applesauce and beat for about 30 seconds longer; scrape down the sides of the bowl. Beat in the remaining flour mixture until smoothly incorporated, scraping down the sides of the bowl as needed. Beat in the remaining applesauce just until evenly incorporated. Drain and discard any liquid from the raisins, if using. Blot them dry with paper towels and fold into the batter.

Turn out the batter into the pan(s), spreading it evenly to the edges. For the rectangular pan, bake for 30 to 40 minutes; for round cake pans, bake for 20 to 30 minutes. Bake until the top of the cake is browned and springs back slightly when pressed, and a toothpick inserted in the center comes out clean; the cake should not be drawing away from the pan sides. Transfer the pan(s) to a wire rack. Let cool completely. If making a layer cake, hold a rack flat against a pan and invert the layers onto racks.

TO FROST THE CAKE: For a layer cake, brush any loose crumbs from the layers. Put several dabs of frosting in the center of a cake plate. Center one cake layer bottom side up on the plate, pressing down lightly to anchor it in the frosting. Spread a generous third of the frosting over the layer. Add the second layer. Use the remaining frosting to cover the cake top and sides, smoothing and swirling it attractively. For a single-layer sheet cake, spread the frosting evenly over the cake to the pan edges. Let stand for at least 30 minutes and up to 24 hours before serving.

The cake will keep, stored airtight, in a cool place (not refrigerated) for 2 or 3 days.

LOOK MOM, NO seeds

Before modern agriculture blessed us with seedless raisins, homemakers—or their children or servants—had to remove the seeds from raisins by hand. The machine described in this 1880 advertisement from the X-Ray Raisin Seeder Company promised liberation from the drudgery:

This is a model machine, composed of 38 different parts put together as a true and perfect watch not a single part can possibly get out of order. It will seed raisins as fast as you can drop them into the hopper and turn the crank. When we say seed, we mean every single seed . . . Talk about perfection—this machine is the very acme of it.

cakes and frostings

Nana's orange chiffon cake with orange Glaze

This cake is extremely flavorful, tender, and light, and delightfully homespun. The recipe is from my grandmother's "receipt" box. It is based on an earlier sponge cake from her repertoire, which she altered by adding some vegetable oil.

In modifying her recipe, Nana was undoubtedly picking up on all the fanfare surrounding General Mills' introduction of the chiffon cake a few years earlier. In 1948, *Better Homes and Gardens* touted it as "the first really new cake in one hundred years." The cake was devised by a California insurance salesman, Harry Baker, who created an exceptionally moist cake with a texture similar to that of a fine sponge cake by incorporating vegetable oil. He sold his idea to the giant food company in 1947, and for the next decade chiffon cakes were all the rage.

My grandmother always topped her orange chiffon cake with a zingy, vibrant-tasting orange glaze, and the combination is superb. However, if you really prefer your cakes plain, skip the glaze and dust the cake with a little powdered sugar.

CAKE

- 1½ cups unsifted cake flour
- 1 cup granulated sugar (divided)
- ¾ teaspoon baking powder
- ¼ teaspoon baking soda
- ¼ teaspoon salt
- 6 large eggs, at room temperature
- ½ cup corn oil or other flavorless vegetable oil
- 1 tablespoon finely grated orange zest (orange part of skin)
- 2½ teaspoons finely grated lemon zest (yellow part of skin)
- ½ cup fresh orange juice
- 1½ teaspoons vanilla extract
- ¼ teaspoon lemon extract
- 1 teaspoon fresh lemon juice

ORANGE GLAZE (OPTIONAL)

- 1½ cups powdered sugar
- ⅔ cup fresh orange juice
- ¼ cup fresh lemon juice
- 1 tablespoon unsalted butter, cut into chunks
- ¼ teaspoon vanilla extract

TO MAKE THE CAKE: Position a rack in the middle of the oven and preheat to 350 degrees F. Set out a 10- by 4¼-inch tube pan with a removable bottom.

Sift together the cake flour, ⅔ cup of the granulated sugar, the baking powder, baking soda, and salt onto a sheet of baking parchment or wax paper. Separate the eggs, keeping the whites free of any bits of yolk. Place the whites in a large bowl and 5 yolks in a very large bowl. (Reserve the remaining yolk for another purpose.) Using a whisk, whisk together the egg yolks, oil, orange zest, lemon zest, orange juice, vanilla, and lemon extract until blended. Gradually whisk the flour mixture into the yolk mixture until smoothly incorporated.

Add the lemon juice to the egg whites. Using a mixer (with a whisk-shaped beater, if available), beat on low speed, then medium, for 1½ to 2 minutes, or until the whites just begin to form soft peaks. Add the remaining ⅓ cup granulated sugar a tablespoon at a time, beating for about 15 seconds after each addition. Raise the speed to high and continue beating for 1 to 3 minutes, or until the whites just begin to hold firm peaks but are still moist. Don't overbeat, or the whites will be difficult to incorporate. Gently whisk about a third of the whites into the yolk mixture, then whisk in the remaining whites just until no white streaks remain. For the greatest volume and lightness, don't overmix. Immediately turn out the batter into the ungreased tube pan, spreading it evenly to the edges.

Bake for 30 to 40 minutes, or until the cake is nicely browned on top and a toothpick inserted in the thickest part comes out clean; do not overbake. Invert the cake, resting it on the feet if the pan has them or on top of a wire rack. Let cool completely, at least 1 hour. Run a table knife around the tube and the sides of the pan to loosen the cake. Carefully lift the base from the pan, using the tube. Loosen the cake from the base with the knife and invert it onto a serving plate.

TO MAKE THE GLAZE (IF USING): In a heavy, nonreactive 2-quart saucepan, combine the powdered sugar, orange juice, and lemon juice. Bring to a boil over medium-high heat. Let boil, stirring occasionally, for 4 minutes. Remove from the heat. Stir in the butter and vanilla. Let the glaze stand until cooled and just slightly thickened, about 10 minutes. Slowly pour the glaze over the cake top, then spread it out so it drips down the sides.

The cake will keep, covered airtight, at room temperature for 2 or 3 days.

cake contests

Although my grandmother and the other "girls" in her bridge club (all age fifty-plus) never publicly admitted it, they were fiercely competitive about their cakes. A fine baker, my grandmother was always in a tizzy when she hosted the group, and maintaining her reputation for serving killer cakes was at the heart of her distress. Though normally soft-spoken and impeccably ladylike, she doggedly pursued ingredients and techniques that would give her an edge. I'm sure that this 1935 Swans Down advertisement would have attracted her and many of her contemporaries, whose self-worth and identity came at least in part from their prowess at producing cakes.

Some thirty-five years ago, a bright red and yellow package with the name "Swans Down Cake Flour" printed upon it began to make friends for itself. It found popularity easily, for it held the secret of successful cakes. The good news traveled from kitchen to kitchen—first to thousands, then to millions of women . . . And so Swans Down became the most popular cake flour in the world.

banana cake

Tender and full of banana flavor and aroma, this cake is moist and light. It was adapted from a recipe by Lenore Sborofsky, a Baltimore home cook who has been baking it—and getting raves—at least since the 1940s. It's a particular favorite of her daughter, caterer Linda Kirschner, who also bakes it and shared the recipe with me.

Linda's mother usually tops the cake with a simple mocha icing, which complements the banana taste nicely. Fudge Glaze (page 150) and Rich and Creamy Chocolate Fudge Frosting (page 149) also make people swoon.

CAKE

- 2⅓ cups unsifted cake flour
- ¾ teaspoon baking powder
- ½ teaspoon baking soda
- Scant ½ teaspoon salt
- ⅔ cup (10⅔ tablespoons) unsalted butter, slightly softened
- 1½ cups granulated sugar
- 2 large eggs plus 1 large egg yolk
- ½ cup sour cream
- 1¼ cups well-mashed overripe bananas (about 4 medium bananas)
- 2 teaspoons vanilla extract

EASY MOCHA ICING

- 1¼ teaspoons instant espresso powder or granules, dissolved in 1½ tablespoons hot water
- 1½ tablespoons unsweetened Dutch-process cocoa powder
- ⅓ cup (5⅓ tablespoons) unsalted butter, slightly softened
- ½ teaspoon vanilla extract
- 1½ cups powdered sugar, sifted after measuring if lumpy
- 1–2 teaspoons water, if needed

TO MAKE THE CAKE: Position a rack in the middle of the oven and preheat to 350 degrees F. Generously grease a 9-by-13-inch baking dish or coat with nonstick spray.

Sift together the flour, baking powder, baking soda, and salt into a medium bowl, then stir well. In a large bowl, combine the butter and sugar. Beat with a mixer on medium speed until the mixture is well blended and lightened, about 1½ minutes, scraping down the sides of the bowl as needed. Add the eggs and yolk, beating until well blended, about 30 seconds. Add the sour cream and continue beating for 1 minute longer, or until smoothly incorporated, scraping down the sides of the bowl as needed.

Reduce the mixer speed to low. Add half the flour mixture, beating just until incorporated. Beat in the mashed bananas and vanilla until smoothly incorporated. Beat in the remaining flour mixture until the batter is well blended and smooth, scraping down the sides of the bowl as needed.

Turn out the batter into the pan, spreading it evenly to the edges. Bake for 20 to 30 minutes, or until the top is browned and springs back slightly when pressed, and a toothpick inserted in the center comes out clean; the sides of the cake will begin to draw away from the pan sides. Transfer to a wire rack. Let cool completely, at least 1 hour.

TO MAKE THE ICING: In a large bowl with the mixer on low, then medium speed, beat together the espresso mixture, cocoa powder, butter, and vanilla until very well blended and smooth, scraping down the sides of the bowl as needed. On low, then medium speed, beat in the powdered sugar until the icing is very smooth, scraping down the sides of the bowl several times. The icing should be slightly soft and spreadable; if necessary, beat in a teaspoon or two of water. Immediately spread the icing evenly over the cake top in the pan using an offset spatula or table knife. Let stand for a few minutes until the icing sets before cutting.

The cake will keep, stored airtight, at room temperature for 3 or 4 days.

AT RIGHT

NICELY SPICY
GINGERBREAD

PAGE 118

Nicely spicy gingerbread

No book of American desserts would be complete without a gingerbread or two. Originally, gingerbread was crisp, spicy, and rolled out thinly, much like contemporary gingerbread cookies, but denser. An airier, cakey type, which cooks referred to as "soft gingerbread," appeared later, after chemical leavenings became available.

The following soft gingerbread recipe is modern, being tenderer, lighter on molasses, and a bit richer than typical heirloom versions. It includes the option of adding a light lemon glaze, another modern touch. My spice combination—ginger, cinnamon, allspice, and cloves—is the same one called for in a cake-style gingerbread from an 1828 cookbook, *Seventy-five Receipts, for Pastry, Cakes, and Sweetmeats* by Philadelphia author Eliza Leslie. Use a bit of orange zest and/or crystallized ginger to enhance the flavor, if you like.

GINGERBREAD

- 2²/₃ cups all-purpose flour
- 1¼ teaspoons baking powder
- ½ teaspoon baking soda
- ¼ teaspoon salt
- ²/₃ cup (10²/₃ tablespoons) unsalted butter, slightly softened
- 1 cup packed light brown sugar
- 2½ teaspoons ground ginger
- 1³/₄ teaspoons ground cinnamon
- ³/₄ teaspoon ground allspice
- ½ teaspoon ground cloves
- 1 large egg
- ²/₃ cup light or dark molasses
- ²/₃ cup buttermilk
- 2 tablespoons minced crystallized ginger (optional)
- ½ teaspoon finely grated orange zest (orange part of skin; optional)

LEMON GLAZE (OPTIONAL)

- 1¼ cups powdered sugar, sifted after measuring if lumpy
- 1½ tablespoons unsalted butter, melted and cooled
- 1½ tablespoons hot water, plus more if needed
- ¼ teaspoon finely grated lemon zest (yellow part of skin)
- 1 tablespoon fresh lemon juice

  Whipped cream for garnish (optional)

TO MAKE THE GINGERBREAD: Position a rack in the middle of the oven and preheat to 350 degrees F. Lightly grease a 9-by-13-inch baking dish or coat with nonstick spray.

In a medium bowl, thoroughly stir together the flour, baking powder, baking soda, and salt. In a large bowl with a mixer on low, then medium speed, beat together the butter, brown sugar, ground ginger, cinnamon, allspice, and cloves until well blended and fluffy, about 1½ minutes, scraping down the sides of the bowl as needed. Beat in the egg and molasses until smoothly incorporated; it's all right if the mixture looks slightly curdled. With the mixer on low speed, beat in half the flour mixture just until smoothly incorporated. Beat in the buttermilk, crystallized ginger (if using), and orange zest (if using) just until incorporated. Beat in the remaining flour mixture until evenly incorporated, scraping down the sides of the bowl as needed.

Turn out the batter into the pan, spreading it evenly to the edges. Bake for 35 to 40 minutes, or until the center springs back when lightly pressed and a toothpick inserted in the center comes out clean; the center may crack slightly. Transfer to a wire rack. Let cool to warm, at least 30 minutes.

TO MAKE THE GLAZE (IF USING): In a medium bowl, vigorously stir together the powdered sugar, butter, hot water, lemon zest, and lemon juice until well blended. Let stand for 2 minutes. If the mixture stiffens too much to flow readily, thin it with a little more hot water. Using a pastry brush or a table knife, smoothly spread the glaze over the entire surface.

To serve, cut the gingerbread into thirds lengthwise and quarters crosswise (or as desired). Serve garnished with a dollop of whipped cream, if desired.

The gingerbread, glazed or unglazed, will keep, stored airtight, at room temperature for 3 days.

Lighten up

From the late eighteenth century through the mid-nineteenth century, soft gingerbread was often lightened with a chemical leavening called pearlash. (The first published recipe appears in Amelia Simmons's 1796 *American Cookery.*) Gradually, this leavening agent was replaced with saleratus and then baking soda, which was less likely to leave an aftertaste and fluffed up baked goods more effectively. The next important chemical leavening, baking powder, didn't come on the American home-baking scene until 1859.

Apple-Pecan coffeecake with caramel Glaze

A touch of cinnamon and an abundance of apples flavor this moist, slightly gooey coffeecake. The pecans provide a pleasing contrast to the softness of the cake.

Apple cakes are a favorite with cooks all over the country and have been for almost two centuries. My version is inspired by a recipe from Little Rock caterer Pat Yielding, whose caramel-apple coffeecake won grand prize at the Arkansas State Fair in 1996.

The caramel glaze is to die for, but the cake also is good (and easier to make) with a simple cinnamon-sugar mixture sprinkled on top (see the variation).

PECANS

- 1 cup coarsely chopped pecans
- 2½ tablespoons packed light brown sugar
- 1 tablespoon light or dark corn syrup
- 1 tablespoon unsalted butter, slightly softened

CAKE

- 3½ cups peeled, cored, and diced (⅓ inch) tart, flavorful apples (about 3 large apples)
- ⅓ cup packed light brown sugar
- ½ teaspoon ground cinnamon
- 3 cups all-purpose flour
- 1¼ teaspoons baking powder
  Generous ½ teaspoon salt
- 16 tablespoons (2 sticks) unsalted butter, slightly softened
- 2 cups granulated sugar
- 3 large eggs
- ⅔ cup sour cream
- 2½ teaspoons vanilla extract

CARAMEL GLAZE

- 1 cup heavy (whipping) cream
- 1 cup packed light brown sugar
- 3 tablespoons unsalted butter, cut into chunks
- 2 tablespoons light or dark corn syrup
  Reserved apple juice from preparing cake
- ½ teaspoon vanilla extract

Position a rack in the middle of the oven and preheat to 350 degrees F. Grease a 9-by-13-inch baking dish or coat with nonstick spray. Line a rimmed baking sheet with aluminum foil.

TO MAKE THE PECANS: In a medium bowl, stir together the pecans, brown sugar, corn syrup, and butter until the pecans are coated. Spread the pecan mixture on the foil-lined baking sheet and toast, stirring occasionally, for 9 to 14 minutes, or until nicely browned. Let cool completely. Chop the pecan crunch into ¼-inch bits. The pecans will keep, stored airtight, at room temperature for several days.

TO MAKE THE CAKE: In a large bowl, thoroughly stir together the apples, brown sugar, and cinnamon. Sift together the flour, baking powder, and salt onto a sheet of baking parchment or wax paper. In a large bowl with a mixer on medium speed, beat the butter and granulated sugar until lightened and fluffy, about 2 minutes, scraping down the sides of the bowl as needed. Add the eggs one at a time and beat until well blended, about 2 minutes. On low speed, beat in half the dry ingredients just until thoroughly incorporated, scraping down the sides of the bowl as needed. Add the sour cream and vanilla, beating just until evenly incorporated. Beating on low, then medium speed, add the remaining dry ingredients, mixing until evenly blended; the batter will be stiff.

Spoon half the batter into the pan, spreading it evenly to the edges with a greased table knife; the layer will be thin. Using a slotted spoon and shaking off any excess juice, distribute the apple mixture over the batter. (Reserve the juice for the glaze.) Sprinkle the pecans over the apples. Spoon the remaining batter over the apples and pecans, spreading it to the edges; the batter will seem skimpy.

Bake for 45 to 55 minutes, or until the top is well browned and springs back when lightly pressed, and a toothpick inserted in the center comes out clean. If the top begins to brown too rapidly, cover the pan with aluminum foil during the last few minutes of baking. Transfer the pan to a wire rack. Let cool for at least 20 minutes.

TO MAKE THE GLAZE: In a heavy, nonreactive 3- to 4-quart saucepan, stir together the cream, brown sugar, butter, corn syrup, and reserved apple juice until well blended. Stirring constantly, cook over medium-high heat until the mixture comes to a boil. Boil briskly, stirring, for 5 minutes; lower the heat, if necessary, to keep it from boiling over. Stir in the vanilla. Set aside until the glaze cools and thickens just slightly. Pour the glaze evenly over the cake. Let stand for a few minutes, or until the glaze sets up. To serve, cut the coffeecake into thirds lengthwise and quarters crosswise (or as desired).

The cake will keep, stored airtight, in a cool place for up to 2 days or refrigerated for 2 or 3 days longer. Let come to room temperature before serving.

VARIATION:

Apple-Pecan Coffeecake with Cinnamon-Sugar Topping

Omit the glaze. Combine 3 tablespoons granulated sugar and ½ teaspoon ground cinnamon in a small bowl and sprinkle over the batter just before baking. Bake as directed.

Apple stack cake

Cooks in the Ozarks and Appalachian Mountains have had long experience with hard times and near-empty larders, and their traditional apple stack cake is an excellent example of what can be done with meager supplies. This version of the regionally popular specialty is composed of a half-dozen large, crisp sugar cookie rounds sandwiched together with a simple dried apple filling. Though not a cake in the usual sense, the cookie and fruit layers meld together in a rustic, cakelike stack and are served cut into wedges. The cookie-apple combination is reminiscent of apple or fig Newtons, but fuller-flavored and more succulent.

This recipe is inspired by one shared with me by Betty Rae Miller, whom I met during a trip to the Ozark mountain town of Mountain View, Arkansas. Betty Rae says she used to dry her own apples for stack cakes, but like many other folks in the area, she has given up the practice.

Reflecting the hardscrabble conditions that originally spawned them, most authentic stack cakes call for a minimum of simple pantry staples. The filling often contains only water, apples, and a little sugar, and the dough features economical shortening or lard. I've taken the liberty of using half water and half apple juice and adding some cinnamon and nutmeg to this filling to intensify the apple flavor a bit. If, for the sake of authenticity, you prefer to use all water and omit the spices, the cake will still taste very good. I like to use vanilla extract in the dough, although this, too, is often missing from regional recipes. You may use it or not, as you wish.

FILLING

- 9–10 ounces dried apples
- 1½ cups apple juice
- 1½ cups hot water
- ½ teaspoon ground cinnamon (optional)
- ¼ teaspoon freshly grated or ground nutmeg (optional)
- 1–2 tablespoons water, if needed
- 2–4 tablespoons packed light or dark brown sugar, to taste

DOUGH

- 3⅓ cups all-purpose flour, plus more if needed
- 2¼ teaspoons baking powder
- ¾ teaspoon salt
- 1¼ cups solid white shortening
- ⅔ cup granulated sugar
- ⅓ cup packed light or dark brown sugar
- 1 large egg
- 3 tablespoons milk, plus more if needed
- 2½ teaspoons vanilla extract (optional)

TO MAKE THE FILLING: By hand or using a food processor, finely chop the apples; you should have 3 loosely packed cups. In a medium nonreactive saucepan, stir together the apples, apple juice, water, cinnamon, and nutmeg (if using). Bring the mixture just to a boil over medium-high heat; adjust the heat so the mixture simmers gently. Cover and cook, stirring frequently, for 15 to 20 minutes, or until the apples are softened and almost all the liquid is absorbed. Check frequently and stir to make sure the mixture doesn't burn. If it becomes dry, stir in a tablespoon or two of water to prevent sticking. Stir in 2 tablespoons brown sugar. Taste and add 1 to 2 tablespoons more brown sugar if the filling seems too tart. Let cool to room temperature before using. The filling will keep, covered, in the refrigerator for several days. Let come to room temperature and stir before using.

TO MAKE THE DOUGH: In a medium bowl, thoroughly stir together the flour, baking powder, and salt. In a large bowl using a mixer, beat the shortening and sugars on medium speed until light and well blended, about 1½ minutes. Beat in the egg, milk, and vanilla (if using) until smoothly incorporated and fluffy, scraping down the sides of the bowl as needed. Beat in half the flour mixture just until smoothly incorporated. Stir in the remaining flour until evenly incorporated. If the dough seems too dry to hold together, stir in up to 2 tablespoons more milk. If it seems too soft and wet, stir in up to 3 tablespoons more flour 1 tablespoon at a time. Let the dough stand for 5 minutes to firm up slightly.

Shape the dough into an 8-inch disk, then cut the disk into sixths. Form the 6 portions into balls. Place each portion between sheets of baking parchment. Roll out each portion into a 7-inch round. Occasionally check the underside of the dough during rolling and smooth out any wrinkles. Stack the rolled portions (paper still attached) on a rimmed baking sheet. Refrigerate until cold and firm, at least 1 hour and up to 24 hours, or freeze for 30 to 40 minutes to speed the chilling.

Position a rack in the upper third of the oven and preheat to 375 degrees F. Working with one dough portion at a time and leaving the other portions in the refrigerator, gently peel off the top sheet of paper. Center a 6½-inch (or similar) saucer or bowl upside down on the dough. Using a sharp knife, cut around the saucer to form a round; avoid cutting through the paper. Transfer the round (paper still attached) to a large rimmed baking sheet. Repeat with the remaining dough portions, spac-

ing them slightly apart and using several baking sheets in all. You can save the dough scraps, shape into a ball, and make one more round, if desired.

Bake one sheet at a time for 9 to 13 minutes, or until the rounds are lightly colored on top and slightly darker at the edges. Reverse the pan from front to back about halfway through baking, if necessary, to ensure even browning. Transfer the sheet to a wire rack. Let cool for 10 minutes; the rounds are too tender to move when warm. Transfer the rounds (paper still attached) to wire racks. Let cool completely. Lift the rounds from the paper. The rounds will keep, stored airtight, at room temperature for up to a week.

TO ASSEMBLE THE CAKE: At least 6 hours before serving, put a dab of apple filling on a cake plate. Center one round on the plate, pressing it down lightly to anchor it in the filling. Divide the filling into fifths (or sixths if you made the extra dough round) and place one portion on the round, spreading it out almost to the edges. Then add another round, spreading it with more filling, and continue stacking the rounds and spreading them with filling, ending with a round on top. Press down on the layers just slightly to compact the cake. Cover and let stand at room temperature. Let the cake mellow for at least 6 hours and preferably 12 hours before serving.

The cake will keep, covered, at room temperature for several days or refrigerated for up to 4 days. Let come to room temperature before serving.

string 'em up

It's no coincidence that stack cakes usually feature dried rather than fresh apples. From the time itinerant nurseryman John Chapman, a.k.a. Johnny Appleseed, traveled west establishing nurseries of apple seedlings in the late eighteenth century, American homesteaders routinely planted apple trees and depended on their fruit. Dried apples were particularly important because they could be brought out in winter when supplies had dwindled and fresh fruit was totally absent from the diet. Cooks in rural areas often "put by" huge quantities of cored, sliced apples each autumn. Some people dried them on lines strung across the rafters and took them down as needed.

Not everyone was a fan of dried apples, however. An anonymous poet complained that dried apple pies comprised the farmers' "gnarliest fruit," griping in verse, "Tread on my corns, or tell me lies, / But don't pass me dried apple pies."

Fortunately, the commercial vacuum-packed dried apples stocked in supermarkets and health food stores today are usually of fine quality, moist and flavorful.

peach upside-down cake

Fresh peaches are as much a part of American summers as beach towels draped over back porch railings. They are grown commercially in thirty-four states, and in private gardens in a number of others, and are our most popular stone fruit. First known in China, peaches were introduced here by Christopher Columbus on his second voyage to the New World, then again later as European colonists settled the land.

Peach cakes are popular in Maryland in the summertime, and I like to make this buttery, brown sugary version at least several times each season. The peach-caramel combination is simple yet sublime. Note that because the peaches continue giving off juice as they stand, the cake is best served within a few hours of baking.

3¹⁄₃ cups peeled, pitted, and sliced (¹⁄₃ inch thick) peaches (9–10 medium peaches)

3 tablespoons plus ²⁄₃ cup packed light brown sugar (divided)

2 teaspoons fresh lemon juice

4 tablespoons (¹⁄₂ stick) unsalted butter, cut into chunks

BATTER

1²⁄₃ cups all-purpose flour

1 teaspoon baking powder

¹⁄₄ teaspoon baking soda

Scant ¹⁄₂ teaspoon salt

8 tablespoons (1 stick) unsalted butter, slightly softened

³⁄₄ cup plus 2 tablespoons granulated sugar

1 large egg

1 teaspoon finely grated lemon zest (yellow part of skin)

2 teaspoons vanilla extract

³⁄₄ cup milk (divided)

Caramel or vanilla ice cream for serving (optional)

Position a rack in the middle of the oven and preheat to 375 degrees F. In a large bowl, gently stir together the peaches, 3 tablespoons of the brown sugar, and the lemon juice. Set aside until the sugar dissolves and the peaches begin to release their juice, about 15 minutes. Put the peaches in a strainer or colander set over a bowl and let stand until thoroughly drained, 15 to 20 minutes.

In a 9½- to 10-inch (2-inch-deep) flameproof round casserole or nonreactive ovenproof skillet, stir together the remaining ²⁄₃ cup brown sugar and the butter. Cook over medium-high heat, stirring with a long-handled wooden spoon and watching carefully to prevent burning, until the butter completely melts and the mixture bubbles. Adjust the heat so the mixture bubbles gently and cook, stirring, for 1 minute. Standing back

tip

Be sure to use a nonreactive casserole or skillet, such as one made of stainless steel or enamel-coated cast iron, or one with a nonstick finish.

to avoid steam and splatters, stir all the juice drained from the peaches into the sugar mixture until evenly blended. Cook, stirring, until bubbly. Adjust the heat so the mixture bubbles briskly but doesn't burn. Cook, stirring, for about 2 minutes longer, or until the caramel is boiled down to the consistency of thin gravy. Remove from the heat. Attractively arrange the peaches over the caramel mixture.

TO MAKE THE BATTER: In a medium bowl, thoroughly stir together the flour, baking powder, baking soda, and salt. In a large bowl with a mixer on medium speed, beat together the butter and granulated sugar until well blended and lightened, about 1 minute. Add the egg, lemon zest, and vanilla and beat on medium-high speed for about 2 minutes longer, or until very light and fluffy.

Reduce the mixer speed to low and beat in half the flour mixture just until incorporated. Then beat in half the milk just until incorporated. Lightly beat in the remaining flour mixture, then the remaining milk, scraping down the sides of the bowl as needed. Raise the speed to medium and beat just until the batter is well blended and smooth, 1 to 1½ minutes longer. Pour the batter over the fruit, spreading it evenly with a table knife.

Bake for 30 to 40 minutes, or until a toothpick inserted in the center comes out clean and the cake surface is nicely browned. If it begins to brown too rapidly, reduce the heat to 350 degrees F for the last 10 to 15 minutes. Transfer to a wire rack. Let cool for 15 minutes. Run a knife around the cake to loosen the edges. Center a large serving plate over the casserole or skillet. Holding the two tightly together, invert the cake onto the serving plate. If any caramel or peach pieces remain in the skillet, return them to the cake surface. Let the cake cool for at least 20 minutes and preferably 30 minutes before serving. Add a scoop of ice cream to each serving, if desired.

The cake is best fresh but will keep, covered, for a few hours. Serve warm or at room temperature.

Delaware, the "peach state"?

Georgia is now known as the Peach State, but it hasn't always been. From the mid-1800s to the early twentieth century, Delaware was the peach state, acclaimed for both the quantity and quality of its fruit. The peak production year in Delaware was 1875, when workers called "peach plucks" harvested nearly 6 million baskets of the fruit for market.

According to information in the Delaware Agricultural Museum, the state's peach industry collapsed as a result of a deadly blight called "peach yellows." In the years between 1890 and 1920, many farmers were forced to burn their orchards, and the number of trees plummeted from 5 million to 500,000. Delaware never gained peach prominence again.

Despite its title, Georgia isn't America's top peach producer. Both South Carolina and California have larger annual crops.

BLueberry
Buckle

Because of their quaint-sounding name, buckles are often mistakenly grouped together with nineteenth-century fruit desserts such as betties, slumps, pandowdies, and cobblers. In fact, buckles are simple cakes, made from a single layer of a berry-studded cake batter (nearly always featuring blueberries) sprinkled with streusel.

This one is tender, buttery, and mild. The recipe was inspired by a buckle served at Gwendolyn's Bed & Breakfast, a stately 1872 gambrel mansard mansion in Perkinsville, Vermont. Innkeeper Laurie Hathaway remembers her grandmother baking the cake in the New Jersey Pine Barrens, the state's premier blueberry-growing region.

BATTER

- 1²/₃ cups all-purpose flour
- 1 teaspoon baking powder
- ½ teaspoon salt
- Generous ¾ cup sugar
- 8 tablespoons (1 stick) plus 2 tablespoons unsalted butter, very soft but not melted
- 2 large eggs
- ¼ cup milk
- 1½ teaspoons vanilla extract
- 3 cups blueberries

TOPPING

- ²/₃ cup sugar
- Scant ½ cup all-purpose flour
- ½ teaspoon ground cinnamon
- 6 tablespoons (¾ stick) cold unsalted butter, cut into bits

Whipped cream for serving (optional)

Position a rack in the middle of the oven and preheat to 350 degrees F. Generously grease a 9-by-13-inch baking pan or generously coat with nonstick spray.

TO MAKE THE BATTER: In a large bowl, thoroughly stir together the flour, baking powder, and salt. Add the sugar and butter. Using a mixer on low speed, beat until the mixture is blended and crumbly, about 2 minutes.

In a medium bowl using a fork, thoroughly beat together the eggs, milk, and vanilla. With the mixer on low speed, gradually beat the egg mixture into the flour mixture until well blended. Raise the speed to medium and beat for 1½ minutes, scraping down the sides of the bowl as needed. Gently fold in the blueberries. Turn out the batter into the pan, spreading it evenly to the edges.

TO MAKE THE TOPPING: In a small bowl, thoroughly mix together the sugar, flour, and cinnamon. Sprinkle the butter over the top. Using a pastry blender or fork, cut in the butter until the mixture is crumbly and has the consistency of coarse meal. Sprinkle the topping evenly over the batter.

Bake for 35 to 45 minutes, or until a toothpick inserted in the center comes out clean and the top is crisp and tinged with brown. Transfer the pan to a wire rack. Let cool to warm, at least 20 minutes. Cut into squares. Serve with dollops of whipped cream, if desired.

The buckle will keep, covered, in a cool place for up to 3 days or in the freezer for up to a week. Let come to room temperature before serving.

BUCKLE BUSINESS

I'm not certain how a blueberry coffeecake came to be called a "buckle." One explanation sometimes suggested is that the cake surface tends to buckle from the streusel layer on top, but it's more likely that some creative baker just liked the alliteration.

Today the buckle most frequently turns up in American country cookbooks and in collections from areas that grow blueberries. Perhaps because it's undemanding to prepare, it's a favorite offering of inns and bed-and-breakfasts. It makes a nice addition to breakfast, brunch, lunch, or afternoon tea.

Red and Black Raspberry pudding cake

This is a slightly updated version of a recipe I originally created for *Gourmet* magazine. The editors chose it as one of their all-time favorite desserts for the fiftieth-anniversary issue. The ethereal flavor, aroma, and color of red and black raspberries cooked together and set off by a soft, buttery cake make it memorable.

At first glance, black raspberries look like blackberries, but they are not the same. Black raspberries have the characteristic raspberry indentation in the bottom. They also have an unmistakable raspberry taste but are tangier, more intense, and bolder than the familiar red kind.

Whenever you come upon black raspberries (usually at roadside stands, pick-your-own farms, and specialty produce stores), snap them up. They are a great treat—especially in this cake. If you can't find them, substitute blackberries. It will be enticing, though not quite as spectacular as the original.

SAUCE

- ³/₄ cup sugar
- 2 teaspoons arrowroot powder or cornstarch
- 3 tablespoons cold water
- 2 cups black raspberries
- 1¹/₂ cups red raspberries
- ¹/₄ teaspoon finely grated lemon zest (yellow part of skin)
- 2 tablespoons fresh lemon juice, or more to taste

BATTER

- 1 cup all-purpose flour
- ³/₄ teaspoon baking powder
- ¹/₈ teaspoon baking soda
- ¹/₄ teaspoon salt
- 8 tablespoons (1 stick) unsalted butter, slightly softened
- ¹/₂ cup sugar
- 1 large egg
- 1¹/₂ teaspoons vanilla extract
- ¹/₂ cup milk

Vanilla ice cream, lightly sweetened whipped cream, or heavy (whipping) cream for serving (optional)

Position a rack in the middle of the oven and preheat to 350 degrees F. Generously grease a 9-inch square or 7-by-11-inch baking pan or generously coat with nonstick spray.

TO MAKE THE SAUCE: In a heavy, nonreactive medium saucepan, stir together the sugar and arrowroot powder until well blended. Gently stir in the water, raspberries, and lemon zest until smoothly incorporated. Bring to a gentle boil over medium heat, stirring until the sugar dissolves. Simmer, stirring occasionally, just until the raspberries release their juice and the mixture turns translucent, about 30 seconds longer. Remove from the heat. Stir in the lemon juice. Taste and add more lemon juice, if desired.

TO MAKE THE BATTER: In a medium bowl, thoroughly stir together the flour, baking powder, baking soda, and salt. In a large bowl with a mixer on medium-high speed, beat the butter until lightened, about 1½ minutes. Add the sugar and beat until the mixture is light in color and fluffy, about 2 minutes, scraping down the sides of the bowl as needed. Add the egg and vanilla and beat until smooth, about 1 minute longer. With the mixer on low speed, beat in half the flour mixture until evenly incorporated. Gradually beat in the milk until evenly incorporated. Add the remaining flour and beat on low speed until incorporated. Raise the speed to medium and beat for 1 minute longer, scraping down the sides of the bowl as needed. Turn out the batter into the pan, spreading it evenly to the edges. Pour the sauce over the batter; *do not stir.*

Bake for 30 to 40 minutes, or until the top is puffed and lightly browned. Transfer to a wire rack. Let cool to warm, at least 20 minutes. Spoon the pudding cake into bowls or onto plates. Serve with ice cream, whipped cream, or heavy cream, if desired.

The cake will keep, covered, in the refrigerator for up to 3 days. Let come to room temperature before serving.

tip
The sauce is delicious spooned over ice cream or butter cake, or both.

mississippi mud cake

Laden with chocolate or cocoa, mud cakes and mud pies are said to be named for the rich, dark mud along the Big Muddy's banks. In fact, culinary researchers often question whether these popular sweets originated in Mississippi at all. The late *New York Times* food writer Craig Claiborne, who grew up in the state, was quoted as saying that he had never heard of a Mississippi mud pie or cake until he moved to the North. On the other hand, John Chapman, longtime owner of Chappy's Seafood Restaurant in the Mississippi Gulf Coast town of Long Beach, claims the mud pie tradition started somewhere along the river between Vicksburg and Natchez. He says the original recipe included alternating layers of cake and pudding in a prebaked cookie crust, and was topped with chocolate icing—and sometimes chocolate sauce or ice cream as well. Yikes! The version his restaurant sells today features peanut butter.

Designed to be prepared completely ahead and frozen, my Mississippi mud cake features a chocolate cookie crumb crust, a mousse filling, pecan praline on the sides, and a chocolate glaze garnish on top. It takes a bit of work but is stunning. (You can pass around warm hot fudge sauce to spoon over the cake, but it certainly doesn't need this embellishment.) At serving time, simply pull the cake from the freezer, slice, and serve—and receive your compliments.

BASE

- 2 cups coarsely broken chocolate wafers, homemade (see page 280) or store-bought
- 3 tablespoons unsalted butter, melted
- 1/4 cup powdered sugar
- 2 tablespoons water, if needed

FILLING

- 5 large eggs
- 1 1/2 teaspoons unflavored gelatin
- 6 1/2 tablespoons unsweetened, nonalkalized American-style cocoa powder or unsweetened Dutch-process cocoa powder
- 1 1/2 teaspoons instant coffee powder or granules
- 1/8 teaspoon salt
- 2 1/4 cups granulated sugar
- 1/4 cup light corn syrup
- 5 tablespoons water
- 2 teaspoons vanilla extract
- 1 cup finely chopped pecans
- 2 1/2 cups heavy (whipping) cream

CHOCOLATE DRIZZLE

- 1/4 cup heavy (whipping) cream
- 1 ounce bittersweet (not unsweetened) or semisweet chocolate, broken up or coarsely chopped

Real Hot Fudge Sauce for serving (page 310; optional)

TO MAKE THE BASE: Generously grease an 8-inch (or slightly larger) springform pan (at least 3 inches deep) or generously coat with nonstick spray. In a food processor, grind the wafers to very fine crumbs, 20 to 30 seconds; you should have 1¼ cups. Add the butter and powdered sugar and process for 30 to 40 seconds, or until the mixture begins to hold together. (Stop and squeeze it between your fingertips to check the consistency.) If it seems very dry and crumbly, gradually add up to 2 tablespoons water, processing a little longer. Pat the crust evenly and firmly into the pan bottom (not the sides). Refrigerate while you prepare the filling.

TO MAKE THE FILLING: In a large bowl, thoroughly stir together the eggs, gelatin, cocoa, coffee powder, and salt. Scrape down the sides of the bowl. Set in a larger bowl of very hot water, stirring once or twice, and let stand until the mixture reaches 100 degrees F (or very warm to the touch). If the water cools before the mixture is warm, replace with more very hot water and continue warming.

In a heavy medium saucepan, combine the granulated sugar, corn syrup, and 5 tablespoons water, stirring until well blended. Bring to a boil over medium-high heat. Cover and gently boil for 2½ minutes to allow steam to wash any sugar crystals from the pan sides, then uncover. If necessary, wash down the pan sides using a pastry brush dipped in warm water or a damp paper towel. Continue boiling, lifting the pan and gently swirling the syrup occasionally but never stirring, for about 5 minutes longer, or until the syrup turns a medium amber color. Immediately remove the pan from the heat.

Wearing oven mitts and working carefully (the mixture is extremely hot), pour 1¼ cups of the syrup into a glass measure. Using a mixer (with a whisk-shaped beater, if available), on medium speed beat the egg mixture just until blended. Raise the speed to high and immediately pour in the 1¼ cups syrup in a very slow, thin stream down the bowl sides. Avoid the beaters or whisk, as the syrup will stick to them. Make sure to add the syrup slowly, or the eggs will curdle. Beat in the vanilla, scraping down the sides of the bowl as needed. Continue beating on high speed until the mixture cools to barely warm, about 5 minutes. Refrigerate until cool to the touch, about 30 minutes, stirring once or twice. (To speed chilling, set the bowl in a larger bowl of ice water and let stand, stirring occasionally, until cool to the touch.)

Meanwhile, return the syrup left in the pan to the burner and heat over medium heat, stirring with a wooden spoon, until fluid. Quickly add the pecans, stirring until evenly coated. Immediately spread the pecan mixture on a sheet of aluminum foil coated with nonstick spray (or use nonstick foil). Press out into a ¼-inch-thick layer using the back of a greased spoon. Let cool slightly. Wrap the foil around the pecans and freeze until completely cooled, 15 to 20 minutes. Peel the mixture from the foil and break it into small pieces. In a food processor, pulse the pieces into ⅛-inch or finer bits. Discard any larger bits or process them further. Transfer the pecan bits to an airtight container and refrigerate until needed to garnish the cake.

In a large bowl, beat the cream just to firm but not dry peaks. Using a wire whisk, mix the cream into the cooled chocolate mixture until completely blended and smooth. Turn out the filling into the pan, shaking the pan to even the surface. Freeze for at least 4 hours and preferably 6 hours, or until frozen solid. Carefully run a knife around the cake. Remove the pan sides. Evenly press the pecan mixture onto the cake sides. Return the cake to the freezer while you prepare the chocolate drizzle.

TO MAKE THE CHOCOLATE DRIZZLE: In a small saucepan, bring the cream just to a boil over medium-high heat. Remove from the heat. Stir in the chocolate until completely smooth and well blended. Let cool to room temperature. Using a pastry bag fitted with a fine writing tip or a paper decorating cone, attractively drizzle the chocolate back and forth in fine (1⁄16-inch) lines over the still-frozen cake. (If a pastry bag and writing tip are unavailable, spoon the mixture into a small, sturdy plastic bag and close it tight. Snip off the tip of one corner and squeeze the chocolate into thin lines.) To serve, cut into wedges using a large sharp knife dipped in hot water and wiped clean between cuts. Pass the hot fudge sauce separately, if desired.

The cake will keep, stored airtight, in the freezer for up to 10 days.

GOING DUTCH-OR NOT

From their earliest days, American and European chocolate manufacturers took different tacks in producing cocoa powder. European firms began neutralizing cocoa's natural acid following a method invented in 1828 by the Dutch chemist Coenraad van Houten. Van Houten's technique, which yielded a darker but milder product (eventually known as Dutch-process, or Dutched, cocoa), didn't catch on in America. Manufacturers here usually preferred to leave in the natural acid. A 1908 book, *Choice Recipes,* published by Walter Baker & Company, noted: "The analyst of the Massachusetts State Board of Health states . . . that the treatment of cocoa with alkali for the purpose of producing a more perfect emulsion is objectionable, even if not considered as a form of adulteration. Cocoa thus treated is generally darker in color than the pure article."

Up until the late twentieth century, when imported European cocoas began making inroads into the U.S. market, our recipes were nearly always designed for the standard, untreated, higher-acid American cocoas. (In baked goods, this generally meant including some baking soda to neutralize the cocoa's acidity.) Today all that has changed. Not only are European Dutch-process cocoas in our markets, but some American cocoa manufacturers also produce alkalized cocoas. (Hershey's European Style Dutch Processed Cocoa is one that's widely available.) Unfortunately, manufacturers' labels don't always clearly say which type they're selling. When uncertain, assume that American brands retain their natural acid unless the label says "Dutched," "Dutch-process," or "European-style," and that European brands are Dutched (low in acid) unless the label says otherwise. In some cases—the filling in this mud cake, for example—the level of acidity doesn't matter, so you can use either kind of cocoa. (See page 11 for more discussion and tips.)

Bourbon-pecan Fudge cake

Served along with Fudge Glaze (page 150), this is an immensely rewarding cake—moist, tender, and very chocolatey on the inside, with a glossy, gooey fudge layer on the outside. It's fairly tender, so handle the cake gently when lifting it off the baking pan and plating it. Also, to maintain the beautiful sheen of the fudge glaze, smooth it on with a minimum of strokes.

9 ounces bittersweet (not unsweetened) or semisweet chocolate (divided)

8 tablespoons (1 stick) unsalted butter, cut into chunks

Generous 1/4 teaspoon salt

2 1/2 teaspoons vanilla extract

3 tablespoons bourbon, combined with 2 tablespoons hot water

1 1/2 tablespoons unsweetened, nonalkalized American-style cocoa powder, sifted after measuring if lumpy

2/3 cup sugar

1/2 cup chopped pecans

1/4 cup all-purpose flour

7 large eggs, at room temperature

Fudge Glaze (page 150)

Position a rack in the middle of the oven and preheat to 350 degrees F. Lightly grease the bottom of a 10-inch springform pan (at least 2 1/2 inches deep) or coat with nonstick spray. Line the bottom of the pan with baking parchment or wax paper. Generously grease the paper and pan sides or generously spray with nonstick spray. Dust the pan with flour, tip from side to side to coat, and tap out any excess.

Coarsely chop 6 ounces of the chocolate. In a medium heavy saucepan, combine the chopped chocolate, butter, salt, and vanilla. Warm over lowest heat, stirring frequently and watching carefully to prevent overheating, until the chocolate and butter are completely melted. Remove from the heat. In a thin stream, vigorously stir in the bourbon-water mixture, then the cocoa powder, until the mixture is well blended; it may look slightly curdled. Set aside.

In a food processor, combine the sugar and pecans. Process until the nuts are ground to a powder but not oily, 1 to 1 1/2 minutes. Transfer the pecan mixture to a large bowl. Wipe out the food processor with a paper towel. Coarsely chop the remaining 3 ounces chocolate. Process the chocolate in the food processor until chopped fairly fine. Add the flour and process until the chocolate and flour are well blended and the chocolate is very fine, about 45 seconds.

Tip

For an easier presentation, bake the cake in a greased 7 1/2-by-11-inch rectangular baking pan and let cool in the pan. Pour the finished fudge glaze over the cake top, spreading it quickly to the edges. Cut and serve the cake directly from the pan.

In a large bowl using a mixer (with a whisk-shaped beater, if available), beat the eggs and pecan mixture on medium speed until well blended. Raise the speed to high and beat for 3 to 4 minutes, or until the mixture is lightened and nearly doubled in volume. Reduce the speed to medium and beat for 2 minutes longer; the mixture will deflate slightly but will be more stable. Remove 1 cup of the egg mixture from the bowl and stir it into the melted chocolate mixture until well blended. Add the melted chocolate-egg mixture and the flour mixture to the large bowl. Using a whisk, combine the ingredients just until well blended, but don't over-mix. Immediately turn out the batter into the pan. Rap the pan on the counter to release any air bubbles. Set on a rimmed baking sheet.

Bake for 15 minutes. Lower the temperature to 325 degrees F and continue baking for 20 to 25 minutes longer, or until the center springs back when lightly tapped and a toothpick inserted in the center comes out clean except for some moist crumbs at the bottom.

Transfer the pan to a wire rack. Let cool completely, at least 1½ hours and up to several hours (covered). Run a knife around the cake. Remove the pan sides. The cake will keep, stored airtight, at room temperature for 24 hours or in the freezer for 2 weeks. Let thaw completely before proceeding with the recipe.

TO GLAZE THE CAKE: Center a serving plate over the cake. Holding the cake and plate firmly together, carefully invert the cake onto the plate. Gently peel off the pan bottom, then the paper. Brush off any loose crumbs. Using wide spatulas, slide the inverted cake onto an 8-inch cardboard cake round or back onto the pan bottom.

Pour a generous two thirds of the fudge glaze over the cake top and lightly spread it out to the edges, using a long-bladed metal spatula or large knife; use a minimum of strokes for best appearance. Spread the remaining fudge over the cake sides, smoothing (but avoiding overworking) until the surface is covered. If the fudge stiffens too rapidly to smooth easily, dip the spatula in hot water, shaking off the excess, and continue spreading. Wipe off the plate rim with a damp paper towel, if necessary.

The cake will keep, stored airtight, in the refrigerator for up to 4 days. Let come to room temperature before serving.

Fudge is the Best Revenge

You've probably heard the one about the woman who thought she'd bought a $2.50 Neiman Marcus (or, in some versions, Mrs. Fields) chocolate chip cookie recipe, only to discover that her credit card charge had been $250 instead. In revenge, she gave away the recipe to everybody she could. Well, that tale has been circulating for more than fifty years, except that early on, the recipe in question was for fudge cake (or sometimes red velvet cake), not chocolate chip cookies. A number of fudge cake versions turned up in the 1940s, some accompanied by a story similar to the one that appeared in the 1948 cookbook *Massachusetts Cooking Rules, Old and New.* The specific details of the "$25 Fudge Cake" recipe introduction clearly suggest an earlier social milieu—trains had fine dining cars with chefs, nobody had credit cards, and a dollar was still a lot of money—but the basics have a familiar ring:

> This friend had to pay $25 upon the receipt of the recipe from the chef of one of the railroads. She had asked for the recipe while eating on the train. The chef gladly sent it to her, together with a bill for $25, which her attorney said she had to pay. She then gave the recipe to all her friends, hoping they would get some pleasure from it.

MoLten Lava chocoLate soufflé cakes

The sumptuous texture and death-by-chocolate intensity of molten lava chocolate cakes have made them wildly popular in upscale restaurants. A good molten lava cake is as dense as the richest fudge cake, but with the bonus of a pocket of equally rich chocolate pudding sauce that flows out from the middle.

That sauce is actually cake batter that isn't cooked completely, so baking to just the right degree of doneness is the most critical part of preparing these cakes. (Mixing the ingredients is quite easy.) Check the tops of the cakes frequently: as soon as their surfaces start to puff and appear dry at the edges but still retain a dark, moist, and slightly sunken 1-inch-diameter area in the center, snatch them from the oven.

The flavor and sweetness of the cakes will depend greatly on the brand of chocolate you use. If you choose a very bittersweet chocolate, consider adding an extra tablespoon or two of sugar to the batter.

12 ounces bittersweet (not unsweetened) or semisweet chocolate, broken up or coarsely chopped

16 tablespoons (2 sticks) unsalted butter, cut into chunks

5 large eggs plus 1 large egg yolk

3/4 cup granulated sugar

2 teaspoons vanilla extract

Pinch of salt

2/3 cup all-purpose flour

1/2 cup powdered sugar

2 tablespoons unsweetened Dutch-process cocoa powder

Lightly sweetened whipped cream for serving

Apricot-Orange Sauce for garnish (page 227; optional)

Generously butter six ¾-cup soufflé dishes, ramekins, or shallow custard cups. (It's very difficult to remove the cakes intact from deep custard cups.)

In a microwave-safe medium bowl, combine the chocolate and butter. Microwave on high power for 1 minute, then stop and stir. Continue microwaving on medium power, stopping and stirring at 30-second intervals, until the chocolate and butter are mostly melted, stirring occasionally; let the residual heat finish the job. (Alternatively, in a heavy medium saucepan, warm the chocolate and butter over lowest heat, stirring frequently, until partially melted; be very careful not to burn. Immediately remove from the heat.) Set aside, stirring, until completely melted and cooled slightly.

In a large bowl, whisk the eggs and yolk until blended. Add the granulated sugar, vanilla, and salt and whisk until evenly incorporated. Whisk in the chocolate mixture. Sift the flour, powdered sugar, and cocoa powder over the batter and whisk until smoothly incorporated. Spoon out the batter into the prepared dishes, dividing it equally among them; they should be full. The unbaked cakes will keep, covered, in the refrigerator for up to 48 hours.

Position a rack in the middle of the oven and preheat to 400 degrees F. Place the dishes on a rimmed baking sheet. Bake for 15 to 20 minutes (a little longer if the batter has been refrigerated), or until the tops are browned at the edges and rise above the dish rims. The center tops should be soft to the touch and look underdone, and the consistency should be pudding-like when a toothpick is inserted in the center. Run a paring knife around the dishes and under the bottoms of the cakes until completely loosened. Let cool on a wire rack for 6 to 7 minutes to cool slightly and firm up.

To serve, center a dessert plate directly over a cake top. Using oven mitts and holding the two tightly against each other, invert the cake onto the plate. Repeat with the remaining cakes. Serve immediately, garnished with lightly sweetened whipped cream. For a dressier presentation, also garnish with a few artfully placed drizzles of apricot-orange sauce, if you wish. (Alternatively, the warm cakes can be unmolded and placed on an ovenproof platter, covered, and set aside for a few hours. Reheat in a 325 degree F oven just until warmed through but not hot before serving.)

VARIATION: Mini Molten Lava Cakes
Makes about 40 mini-cakes

Prepare exactly as for the regular cakes, except use 12-cup mini-muffin tins for baking. Butter the tins generously. Most brands of tins will take about 2 tablespoons batter per cup and should be filled almost to the top. Bake for 6 to 10 minutes, or until the tops are browned at the edges and rise above the cup rims; the centers should still look underdone and pudding-like. Carefully run a knife around the cups and under the bottoms of the cakes until completely loosened. Let stand for about 5 minutes to firm up. Press a flat dish or cutting board tightly against the muffin tin. Invert the mini-cakes onto the dish. Repeat until all the cakes are baked. Serve the mini-cakes individually plated with several other mini-desserts (such as tartlets, candies, or pieces of fruit).

chocoLate pudding cake

One of my mother's desserts that entranced me as a child was a soft chocolate cake served warm from the oven with its own puddle of thick chocolate sauce. This homely but wonderfully gratifying pudding cake could be put together fairly quickly, so it was a favorite in many households in the 1950s and 1960s. I don't know why it's not well known today, but it should be. Hopefully, my updated recipe will help spawn a revival.

CAKE

- ¼ cup unsweetened Dutch-process cocoa powder
- ½ cup boiling water
- 8 tablespoons (1 stick) cold unsalted butter, cut into chunks
- ¾ cup sugar
- 1 large egg
- 1½ teaspoons vanilla extract
- 1 cup all-purpose flour
- 1 teaspoon baking powder
- Generous ⅛ teaspoon salt
- ½ cup sour cream

SAUCE

- 4 ounces semisweet chocolate, broken up or coarsely chopped
- 2 tablespoons unsweetened Dutch-process cocoa powder
- ½ cup sugar
- ¾ cup boiling water
- 8 tablespoons (1 stick) unsalted butter, slightly softened and cut into chunks
- 1 teaspoon vanilla extract

Vanilla ice cream or whipped cream for serving (optional)

TO MAKE THE CAKE: Position a rack in the middle of the oven and preheat to 350 degrees F. Generously grease a 9-inch square or 7-by-11-inch baking pan or generously coat with nonstick spray.

In a food processor, combine the cocoa and boiling water, processing until well blended and smooth. Let cool until warm to the touch. Add the butter and sugar and process in pulses, then continuously, until well blended and smooth. Add the egg and vanilla and continue processing until smoothly incorporated.

In a medium bowl, thoroughly stir together the flour, baking powder, and salt. Sprinkle the flour mixture over the cocoa mixture. Pulse a few times; do not overprocess. Add the sour cream and process for about 30 seconds, or just until smoothly incorporated, scraping down the sides of the bowl as needed. Turn out the batter (it will be fairly stiff) into the pan, spreading it to the edges with a greased table knife.

Rinse and dry the processor bowl and blade. Add the chocolate, cocoa, and sugar and process until the chocolate is finely chopped. With the motor running, slowly add the boiling water through the feed tube, processing until the mixture is very smooth and well blended. With the motor running, add the butter and vanilla. Process until the mixture is smooth (it will be thin). Pour the sauce over the batter; do not stir.

Bake for 40 to 45 minutes, or until the cake is puffy all over and a toothpick inserted in the center comes out with only a few crumbs clinging to its bottom. Transfer to a wire rack. Let cool for 10 minutes. Spoon into bowls and serve with scoops of vanilla ice cream or dollops of whipped cream, if desired.

The cake will keep, covered, in the refrigerator for up to 3 days. Let warm up slightly before serving.

Fluffy white frosting

Makes enough to generously cover a 9-by-13-inch cake, a 9-inch 2-layer cake, or an 8½-inch 3-layer cake

Sometimes called white mountain frosting or boiled white frosting, this marshmallowy, luxurious-looking frosting has been a favorite of mine since childhood. It was the topping I most often asked for on cakes for my birthday. Particularly in the South, many folks like to sprinkle shredded coconut over this frosting, but I prefer to let the silky smooth texture and mild vanilla flavor stand alone. The frosting tastes surprisingly rich, particularly considering that it's completely fat-free.

Frosting recipes featuring beaten egg whites originated in Britain and date back at least three centuries in America. Early recipes often called for beating egg whites and sugar until stiff. One version in a 1747 Hannah Glasse cookbook, *The Art of Cookery Made Plain and Easy,* called for four hours of beating by hand! By the late nineteenth century, boiled white frosting recipes similar to this one had become popular in America. ("Boiled" meant that the whites were cooked by beating a boiling sugar syrup mixture into them.) In this version, I've included updated instructions to make sure the whites heat sufficiently to satisfy current government safety guidelines for cooking eggs. Warm the egg white mixture in a stainless steel or other metal bowl, since this conducts heat readily and quickly raises the frosting temperature into the safe zone.

½ cup egg whites (about 4 large), completely free of yolk and at room temperature

1¼ cups sugar

3 tablespoons light corn syrup

¼ cup water, plus up to 3 tablespoons more warm water, if needed (divided)

Scant ½ teaspoon cream of tartar

Pinch of salt

¾ teaspoon vanilla extract

Place the whites in a completely grease-free large bowl. Set the bowl in a larger bowl of very hot water and let stand, gently stirring occasionally, until the whites warm to 100 degrees F (or very warm to the touch), about 10 minutes. (It's usually necessary to replace the water with more hot water once or twice to warm the whites sufficiently.)

Combine the sugar, corn syrup, and ¼ cup water in a heavy 2-quart saucepan, stirring until well blended. Bring to a boil over medium-high heat. With a pastry brush dipped in warm water or a damp paper towel, wipe any sugar from the pan sides. Continue boiling, without stirring further, for 2 to 3 minutes longer, or until the mixture reaches 240 degrees F on a candy thermometer. Remove from the heat. (To test for doneness without a candy thermometer, remove the pan from the heat after 1 minute. Drop a teaspoon of the syrup into ice water. If cooked enough, after 10 seconds the syrup will form a firm ball that softens just slightly when squeezed between your fingertips. If the ball is not firm, cook for 30 seconds longer, remove the pan from the heat, test again, and continue cooking, if necessary, until it is the right consistency.)

Using a mixer (with a whisk-shaped beater, if available) on low speed, beat the whites, cream of tartar, and salt for 30 seconds. Increase the speed to medium and beat until the whites are very frothy and opaque and just begin to peak. Immediately reheat the syrup just to simmering.

Beating the whites on medium speed, immediately begin slowly pouring the syrup in a thin stream down the bowl sides (avoid the beaters, or the syrup will stick to them). Pour so that all the syrup is incorporated in about 30 seconds. Continue beating on medium speed for 2 minutes, scraping down the sides of the bowl as needed. Raise the speed to high and beat until the mixture stands in stiff but not dry peaks and has cooled to warm, 3 to 4 minutes. Beat in the vanilla until evenly incorporated. The frosting is easiest to spread when fluffy and fairly soft (the consistency of stiffly whipped cream). If it seems too stiff or at all gummy, gradually beat in up to 3 tablespoons warm water to soften. (Note that the frosting will continue to stiffen as it cools and stands.)

Frost the cooled cake immediately, following the directions provided in the specific cake recipe.

American caramel Frosting

Makes enough to cover a 9-inch 3-Layer or smaller cake

A favorite all over America, this frosting has been around for more than a hundred years. The first version I've found was called Opera Caramel Frosting and appeared in *The 1896 Boston Cooking-School Cook Book.* Today it's perhaps best known in the South, where it often adorns—with great success—a yellow layer cake.

The traditional American caramel frosting gets its flavor from brown sugar, not caramelized granulated sugar, as classic French caramel does. Misleading or not, the name simply refers to the appealing caramel color and taste. On occasion, the recipe also appears under the name penuche or panocha frosting. (Penuche was a robust tasting brown sugar introduced from Mexico in the 1800s; see page 327.) Like most American caramel frostings, this one is on the sweet side. But unlike some versions, which dry out a bit and become sugary, it is light and creamy and stays that way even after several days of storage.

10 tablespoons (1 stick plus 2 tablespoons) unsalted butter, cut into chunks	1/2 cup heavy (whipping) cream, at room temperature
2 1/2 cups packed light brown sugar	3 cups powdered sugar, plus 1/3 cup if needed
1/4 cup light corn syrup	2 teaspoons vanilla extract
Pinch of salt	1–4 teaspoons water, if needed

In a heavy 2-quart saucepan using a long-handled wooden spoon, combine the butter, brown sugar, corn syrup, and salt. Cook over medium heat, stirring constantly, until the mixture just comes to a boil. Immediately stir in the cream, standing back to avoid any splattering. Bring the mixture back to a boil and cook, stirring, for 1 minute. Strain the mixture through a fine sieve into a large bowl. Let cool for 5 minutes.

Add the 3 cups powdered sugar and vanilla. With a mixer on low, then medium speed, beat until completely smooth and free of lumps, 2 to 3 minutes, scraping down the sides of the bowl as needed. Let stand until cool to the touch and stiff enough for frosting, at least 30 minutes. (To speed cooling, set the bowl in a larger bowl of ice water and let stand, stirring occasionally, until cool to the touch and stiff enough for frosting, 10 to 15 minutes.) If the mixture seems too stiff for frosting when completely cooled, thoroughly stir in a teaspoon or two of water. If the mixture seems too soft when completely cooled, sift ⅓ cup more powdered sugar into the bowl and beat just until incorporated, about 1 minute.

Beat the frosting on medium speed just until lightened in color, slightly fluffy, and creamy but not too soft to spread, about 1 minute. Don't overbeat, or it will overheat and soften too much.

Frost the cooled cake immediately, following the directions provided in the specific cake recipe. If the frosting stiffens as the cake is being frosted, thin it by beating in a teaspoon or two more of water. Due to the butter and cream, the frosting may soften somewhat if the cake is allowed to stand in an overheated room and stiffen if the cake is refrigerated.

orange cream cheese-Butter frosting

Makes enough to generously cover a 9-by-13-inch cake, a 9-inch 2-layer cake, or an 8½-inch 3-layer cake

This modern frosting is easy to make, looks attractive, handles well, and goes beautifully with all kinds of spiced cakes, including carrot cakes and Applesauce Spice Cake (page 110). The lemon variation is also a fine accompaniment to a lemon, yellow, or white cake and pipes nicely when you want a dressy look.

11	ounces (one 8-ounce package plus one 3-ounce package) cream cheese, slightly softened and cut into chunks
8	tablespoons (1 stick) unsalted butter, slightly softened
3–3¾	cups powdered sugar, sifted after measuring if lumpy
2½	teaspoons finely grated orange zest (orange part of skin)
1¼	teaspoons finely grated lemon zest (yellow part of skin)
1	tablespoon fresh lemon juice
1	teaspoon vanilla extract
1–2	teaspoons water, if needed

In a large bowl with a mixer on low, then medium speed, beat together the cream cheese, butter, 3 cups powdered sugar, orange zest, lemon zest, lemon juice, and vanilla until well blended and completely free of lumps, scraping down the sides of the bowl as needed. If the frosting seems too thin to spread, beat in up to ¾ cup more powdered sugar. If the frosting is very stiff, add a teaspoon or two of water to thin it to a spreadable but still firm consistency.

Frost the cooled cake immediately, following the directions provided in the specific cake recipe. Let the cake stand, preferably refrigerated, until the frosting sets, at least 1 hour. In warm weather, it's best to store the frosted cake in the refrigerator and then allow it to come almost to room temperature before serving.

VARIATION: Lemon Cream Cheese–Butter Frosting

Omit the orange zest and use 1 tablespoon plus 1 teaspoon finely grated lemon zest in all.

Rich and creamy chocolate fudge Frosting

makes enough to generously cover a 9-by-13-inch cake, a 9-inch 2-layer cake, or an 8½-inch 3-layer cake

With a particularly satisfying chocolate fudge flavor and a smooth consistency, this frosting enhances many cakes, including white, yellow, banana, and devil's food. It's fairly easy to make and spreads beautifully.

- 2/3 cup heavy (whipping) cream
- 2/3 cup granulated sugar
- 1 tablespoon unsalted butter, cut into chunks
- 1½ tablespoons light or dark corn syrup
- 1 teaspoon vanilla extract, combined with 1½ tablespoons water
- 8 ounces bittersweet (not unsweetened) or semisweet chocolate, broken up or coarsely chopped

- 2½ ounces unsweetened chocolate, broken up or coarsely chopped
- 11 ounces (one 8-ounce package plus one 3-ounce package) cream cheese, slightly softened and cut into chunks
- 2–2½ cups powdered sugar, sifted after measuring if lumpy
- 1–2 teaspoons water, if needed

In a heavy 2-quart saucepan, bring the cream, granulated sugar, butter, and corn syrup just to a full boil over medium-high heat, stirring. Wash any sugar from the pan sides using a pastry brush dipped in warm water or a damp paper towel. Also wash any sugar from the stirring spoon. Boil briskly, stirring frequently, for 3 minutes. Remove from the heat. Stir in the vanilla mixture and the chocolates until they completely melt. (It's all right if the mixture looks slightly separated.)

Transfer the mixture to a large bowl. With a mixer on low speed, beat in the cream cheese a few chunks at a time. Continue beating until well blended, scraping down the sides of the bowl as needed. Beat in 2 cups powdered sugar, scraping down the sides of the bowl as needed. Raise the speed to medium-low and beat until the mixture is completely smooth, 1 to 2 minutes; it should be cool to the touch. If the frosting seems too thin to spread, beat in up to ½ cup more powdered sugar until smoothly incorporated. Let stand to firm up, 5 to 10 minutes. If the frosting is very stiff, add a teaspoon or two of water to thin it to a spreadable but still firm consistency.

Frost the cooled cake immediately, following the directions provided in the specific cake recipe. Let the cake stand until the frosting sets, at least 1 hour.

fudge Glaze

Makes enough for a 9-by-13-inch cake or pan of brownies or a 9-inch Bourbon-Pecan fudge cake (page 137)

A superb topping for Bourbon-Pecan Fudge Cake (page 137), Fudge Brownies (page 272), Banana Cake (page 115), or any 9-by-13-inch cake that pairs well with chocolate, this glaze is dark and glossy and has a fine fudge flavor. It's made exactly like classic American chocolate fudge, except that it's cooked to a softer candy stage and used "unset," so no beating is required.

As when making fudge, the main challenge is determining when the glaze is done. This is easiest with a candy thermometer. If you don't have one, there's more chance of undercooking or overcooking it, but not to worry: cool undercooked, slightly runny glaze for a little longer, and it will thicken; thin overcooked glaze by stirring in a little hot water.

1 cup heavy (whipping) cream
1 cup sugar
3 tablespoons light corn syrup
2 tablespoons unsalted butter, cut into chunks
1/8 teaspoon salt

4 1/2 ounces unsweetened chocolate, broken up or coarsely chopped
1/2 teaspoons vanilla extract
Hot water, if needed

In a heavy 2½- to 3-quart saucepan, combine the cream, sugar, corn syrup, butter, and salt. Bring just to a full boil over medium-high heat, stirring with a long-handled wooden spoon. Immediately cover the pot with a tight-fitting lid and boil for 2 minutes to allow steam to wash the sugar crystals (which might cause graininess) from the pan sides. Meanwhile, completely wash any sugar from the spoon.

Remove the lid and reduce the heat to medium. If any sugar remains, wash down the pan sides using a pastry brush dipped in warm water or a damp paper towel. If using a candy thermometer to gauge doneness, immediately clip it to the pan, with the tip fully submerged but not touching the pan bottom. Gently boil, stirring and occasionally scraping the pan bottom, until the mixture reaches 227 to 228 degrees F; this usually takes only 1 to 1½ minutes. Remove from the heat. (If no candy thermometer is available, cook, stirring gently, for 1 minute. Immediately test for doneness by removing the pan from the heat and dropping a bit of the mixture into ice water. Let the mixture stand for about 15 seconds, then press a bit between your fingertips. If the mixture clings together in a soft mass and is sticky, it is done. If it is runny and disperses in the water, cook for 30 seconds longer and test in the water again. Continue cooking and testing until the right consistency is obtained.)

Gently stir the chocolate, then the vanilla, into the mixture just until the chocolate melts and the glaze is completely smooth. If it looks separated and oily (suggesting overcooking), vigorously and thoroughly stir in hot water a teaspoon or two at a time until the glaze smoothes out and looks glossy. Set aside for 2 to 5 minutes, stirring occasionally, until the glaze thickens and cools slightly. If the glaze seems too thick to flow and spread easily, thin it with a little more hot water a teaspoon at a time until a pourable and spreadable consistency is obtained. If it is too thin and runny to spread, let cool for a few minutes longer so it can stiffen further.

If glazing a 9-by-13-inch cake or a large pan of brownies, pour the glaze over the cooled top and use an offset spatula or table knife to spread evenly with a minimum of strokes. If glazing a cake, follow the directions in the specific cake recipe. Let the brownies or cake stand, covered, at room temperature for at least 30 minutes and preferably 1 hour before serving.

3

Cobblers, Crisps, and Other Fruit Desserts

High-summer cobbler with buttermilk biscuit crust

Cobblers have been part of our American dessert repertoire for well over 150 years. Lettice Bryan noted in her 1839 cookbook, *The Kentucky Housewife*, that they were "very excellent for family use," though not "fashionable" for company.

It's the mingling of three popular summer fruits—peaches, raspberries, and blueberries—that gives this cobbler its outstanding flavor and color. Like many modern cobblers, it features a tender, puffy biscuit dough enlivened with buttermilk. Even Mrs. Bryan would probably agree that it's company-worthy.

FILLING

Generous 1 cup sugar, or more to taste

3 tablespoons cornstarch

4 cups peeled, pitted, and sliced peaches

1¼ cups raspberries

1 cup blueberries

2–4 teaspoons fresh lemon juice, to taste (optional)

DOUGH

1⅓ cups all-purpose flour, plus more if needed

Generous ½ teaspoon salt

¼ teaspoon baking soda

6 tablespoons (¾ stick) cold unsalted butter, cut into bits

⅓ cup buttermilk

Cold water, if needed

About 1 tablespoon sugar for sprinkling on dough top (optional)

Vanilla ice cream for serving (optional)

Position a rack in the middle of the oven and preheat to 375 degrees F.

TO MAKE THE FILLING: In a 2½-quart or similar nonreactive flameproof round casserole or nonreactive skillet with an ovenproof handle, thoroughly stir together 1 cup sugar and cornstarch. Stir the peaches into the sugar mixture until well blended and smooth. Bring to a simmer over medium-high heat. Continue simmering, stirring constantly, until slightly thickened and translucent, 2 to 3 minutes. Gently stir in the raspberries and blueberries. If the mixture tastes too tart, add a little more sugar; if too sweet, add a little lemon juice. Set aside.

TO MAKE THE DOUGH: In a large bowl, thoroughly stir together the flour, salt, and baking soda. Add the butter. Using a pastry blender, forks, or your fingertips, cut in the butter until the mixture resembles very coarse meal. Add the buttermilk, mixing with a fork until evenly incorporated. Knead lightly with greased hands until the dough just holds

Tip

If you don't have a stovetop-proof, ovenproof casserole or skillet, make the fruit filling in a saucepan, then transfer it to an ovenproof round glass casserole and top with the dough.

together. If it seems too wet, sprinkle over and then work in a little flour; if too dry, sprinkle over and then work in a few teaspoons of cold water.

Very lightly dust a 12-inch square of baking parchment or wax paper with flour. Turn out the dough onto the paper. Very lightly dust the dough with flour. Top with a second sheet of paper. Press down on the dough, then roll out into a round just slightly smaller than the diameter of the casserole. Peel off the top sheet of paper. Center the dough, paper side up, on the fruit. Peel off the remaining paper. If desired, sprinkle the dough with about 1 tablespoon sugar. Using a greased paring knife, cut large decorative slashes for steam vents in the top.

Bake for 30 to 40 minutes, or until the top is nicely browned and a toothpick inserted in the center of the dough comes out clean. If the dough begins to brown too rapidly, turn the heat down to 350 degrees F during the last 5 to 10 minutes of baking. Transfer to a wire rack. Let cool for at least 30 minutes. Serve with scoops of vanilla ice cream, if desired.

The cobbler will keep, covered, at room temperature for 24 hours and refrigerated for up to 3 days longer. Let come to room temperature or reheat in a low oven to warm before serving.

rising to the occasion

Lettice Bryan's 1839 "cobler" called for pie pastry. Biscuit doughs—which require a chemical leavening—were still fairly new in her day, and the first widely popular chemical leavening, baking soda, had just come on the scene. It took the rest of the century for a large repertoire of American desserts using biscuit doughs to emerge.

not as old as you think

Considering how widely enjoyed cobblers, shortcakes, betties, fruit dumplings, and crisps are today, it's surprising how infrequently they were published in heirloom collections. A search through several dozen nineteenth-century American cookbooks netted fewer than twenty such desserts. I could find no recipes for crisps published before the twentieth century and no cobblers or betties before the nineteenth century.

One often-cited explanation for the absence of these desserts is that they were so easy to make, no one felt it necessary to write the recipes down. I doubt that this is the reason, however, since heirloom cookbooks routinely contain extremely simple recipes. Rather I think it's due in part to the fact that these dishes were regional inventions and it took time for them to circulate and take hold. Their popularity has increased greatly over the past century, partly because fewer cooks are practiced at making and rolling out pastry and prefer to prepare cobblers and other less demanding fruit desserts in place of pies.

raspberry-plum crumb cobbler

If the idea of attempting a dough is keeping you from making a cobbler, this is the recipe to try. Instead of being rolled out and shaped like most cobbler doughs, the biscuit topping is prepared like a streusel and simply crumbled over the fruit. Besides being easy, it comes out exceptionally crisp.

FILLING

- $^2/_3$–$^3/_4$ cup granulated sugar (use larger amount if filling is very tart)
- 2 tablespoons cornstarch
- 3 cups raspberries
- $2^1/_2$ cups pitted and chopped (unpeeled) firm, slightly underripe tart red or black plums
- 2 cups blueberries or blackberries
- 1 tablespoon fresh lemon or lime juice (optional)

DOUGH

- $1^2/_3$ cups all-purpose flour
- $^1/_3$ cup packed light brown sugar
- $^1/_3$ cup granulated sugar
- $^3/_4$ teaspoon baking powder
- $^1/_4$ teaspoon salt
- 6 tablespoons ($^3/_4$ stick) unsalted butter, melted
- 1 large egg, lightly beaten

Vanilla ice cream or whipped cream for serving (optional)

Position a rack in the middle of the oven and preheat to 375 degrees F. Lightly grease a 9-by-13-inch baking dish or coat with nonstick spray.

TO MAKE THE FILLING: In a large nonreactive bowl, thoroughly stir together the granulated sugar and cornstarch. Gently stir in the raspberries, plums, blueberries, and lemon juice (if using) until well blended. Spread the mixture evenly in the baking dish.

TO MAKE THE DOUGH: In a medium bowl, thoroughly stir together the flour, sugars, baking powder, and salt. Add the melted butter, stirring until incorporated. Add the egg, stirring with a fork until the mixture is blended and forms clumps. Sprinkle the dough clumps evenly over the filling.

Bake for 30 to 40 minutes, or until the top is well browned and the filling is bubbly. Transfer to a wire rack. Let cool for at least 30 minutes. Spoon into bowls and serve with ice cream or whipped cream, if desired. The cobbler will keep, covered, at room temperature for 24 hours or refrigerated for 2 or 3 days longer. Let come to room temperature or reheat in a low oven to barely warm before serving.

TIPS

The cobbler topping is sweeter than most, so make sure the fruit filling is tart. Choose plums that are slightly underripe and have a robust, zingy flavor. If necessary, bring up the fruit flavor with the optional lemon or lime juice.

If you happen to have $7^1/_2$ cups of raspberries on hand, feel free to make an all-raspberry version.

Blackberry
cobbler

I've made this simple cobbler every season for years, and it never ceases to satisfy. The biscuit crust is tender, and the berry flavor, aroma, and color are intense. If the berry pickings are slim, I stretch them with a cup or two of chopped tart apples. When I was growing up, we used apples from our Yellow Transparent trees, an old-fashioned, greenish yellow summer variety with a tangy taste. These apples are hard to find nowadays (except occasionally at Amish stands in Pennsylvania Dutch country), so I usually substitute Granny Smith.

This recipe makes a good red or black raspberry cobbler, too. Use 2 tablespoons lemon juice for that version.

FILLING

Scant 1 cup sugar

2 tablespoons arrowroot powder or cornstarch

6½ cups blackberries (or substitute up to 2 cups peeled, cored, and diced [⅓ inch] tart, flavorful apples for some of the blackberries)

½ teaspoon finely grated lemon zest (yellow part of skin)

1–2 tablespoons fresh lemon juice (use larger amount if berries are very sweet)

DOUGH

1¼ cups all-purpose flour, plus more if needed

2 teaspoons sugar

¾ teaspoon baking powder

⅛ teaspoon baking soda

½ teaspoon salt

6 tablespoons (¾ stick) cold unsalted butter, cut into bits

7–9 tablespoons buttermilk, as needed, plus more for brushing on dough top

1 tablespoon sugar for sprinkling on dough top (optional)

Vanilla ice cream for serving (optional)

Position a rack in the middle of the oven and preheat to 425 degrees F.

TO MAKE THE FILLING: In a 2½-quart or similar nonreactive round casserole or Dutch oven, thoroughly stir together the sugar and arrowroot powder. Gently stir in the berries (and apples, if using), lemon zest, and lemon juice until thoroughly incorporated.

TO MAKE THE DOUGH: In a large bowl, thoroughly stir together the flour, sugar, baking powder, baking soda, and salt. Add the butter. Using a pastry blender, forks, or your fingertips, cut in the butter until the mixture resembles moderately fine meal. Add 7 tablespoons butter-milk to the flour mixture, mixing with a fork until evenly incorporated. If the dough looks dry and crumbly, mix in a little more buttermilk. Knead lightly with greased hands until the dough just holds together. If it seems too wet, sprinkle over and work in a little flour; if too dry, sprinkle over and work in more buttermilk.

Very lightly dust a 12-inch square of baking parchment or wax paper with flour. Turn out the dough onto the paper. Very lightly dust the top of the dough and your fingertips with flour. Shape the dough into a 6-inch disk. Sprinkle over a little more flour. Top the dough with a second sheet of paper. Press down on the dough, then roll out into a round just slightly smaller than the diameter of the casserole. Peel off the top sheet of paper. Center the dough, paper side up, on the filling. Peel off the remaining paper. Using a pastry brush or paper towel dipped in buttermilk, brush the top. If desired, sprinkle the top with the sugar. Using a greased paring knife, cut large decorative slashes for steam vents in the top.

Bake for 10 minutes. Reduce the heat to 400 degrees F and continue baking for 30 to 40 minutes, or until the top is nicely browned and a toothpick inserted in the center of the dough comes out clean. Transfer to a wire rack. Let cool for at least 30 minutes. Serve with scoops of ice cream, if desired.

The cobbler will keep, covered, at room temperature for 24 hours or refrigerated for 2 to 3 days longer. Let come to room temperature or reheat in a low oven to warm before serving.

ozark-style peach cobbler

Makes 10 to 12 servings

When I asked around Mountain View, Arkansas, for the best home bakers in the area, Jean Jennings's name kept popping up. A single bite of her peach cobbler convinced me that her local fame was more than deserved. The pastry dough is unbelievably rich and tender, and the filling tastes sublime. The cobbler is soupier than most I've eaten, but it seems right that way.

FILLING

- 9½ cups peeled, pitted, and coarsely sliced large ripe peaches (about 4½ pounds)
- ¼ cup water
- 1⅓ cups sugar
- 8 tablespoons (1 stick) unsalted butter, cut into chunks

DOUGH

- 2 cups all-purpose flour
- 1 teaspoon salt
- 13 tablespoons (1½ sticks plus 1 tablespoon) butter-flavored or solid white shortening, cut into chunks
- ½ cup cold water, combined with 2 ice cubes
- 1 tablespoon sugar for sprinkling on dough top

Position a rack in the middle of the oven and preheat to 425 degrees F. Grease a 9-by-13-inch (or similar) baking dish or spray with nonstick spray.

TO MAKE THE FILLING: In a large nonreactive saucepan or Dutch oven, gently stir together the peaches, water, and sugar. Add the butter. Bring to a boil over medium-high heat, gently stirring occasionally until the sugar dissolves. Reduce the heat so the mixture simmers gently. Simmer until the peaches begin to release their juices and soften, about 4 minutes; the filling will be soupy. Turn out the filling into the baking dish; set aside.

TO MAKE THE DOUGH: In a large bowl, thoroughly stir together the flour and salt. Add the shortening. Using a pastry blender, forks, or your fingertips, cut in the shortening until the mixture resembles coarse meal. Measure out 7 tablespoons ice water and sprinkle over the flour mixture, tossing with a fork until evenly incorporated. Gently knead until the dough holds together smoothly when pressed between your fingertips. If necessary, add a tablespoon or two more ice water to

TIP

To peel peaches quickly and easily, dip them in boiling water for 30 to 40 seconds. Then immediately dip them in cold water to cool them down. The skins will usually slip right off.

moisten; the dough should not be at all dry. (Alternatively, combine the flour and salt in a food processor. Process briefly to mix. Add the shortening. Pulse until lumpy. Measure out 7 tablespoons ice water and sprinkle over the mixture. Process briefly until the mixture has the consistency of very coarse crumbs. If it seems crumbly or dry, add a tablespoon or two more ice water until it is moist and begins to hold together when pressed between your fingertips. Carefully remove the processor blade.) Turn out the pastry onto a large sheet of baking parchment or wax paper. Gently knead until the dough holds together and is very smooth.

Shape the dough into a 3-by-6-inch log. Lay it between sheets of baking parchment or wax paper. Roll out into a rough rectangle 10½ by 14½ inches (or a generous 1 inch longer and wider than the baking dish). Peel off the top sheet of paper, then loosely pat it back into place so it will be easy to remove later. Flip over the dough and peel off the second sheet. Using a paring knife, trim the dough to a 9½-by-13¾-inch rectangle (about ½ inch wider and ¾ inch longer than the dish used). If a slightly less juicy cobbler is desired, finely crumble several tablespoons of the cut-away dough scraps and stir them into the peaches.

Gently peel off the remaining paper. Lightly fold the dough in half (to make lifting it easier). Center the dough in the dish, then unfold it and tuck it neatly into place. (It will seem a bit large but will shrink to fit during baking.) Using a greased paring knife, cut decorative steam vents in the dough top. Sprinkle the top with the sugar.

Bake for 20 minutes. Reduce the heat to 375 degrees F. Continue baking for 15 to 20 minutes longer, or until the top is nicely browned and the filling is bubbly. Transfer to a wire rack. Let cool for at least 20 minutes before serving.

The cobbler will keep, covered, at room temperature for 24 hours or refrigerated for 2 or 3 days longer. Let come to room temperature before serving.

MOTHER KNOWS BEST

I met Jean Jennings on a sultry September afternoon in her thoroughly modern, homey kitchen. As she deftly sliced peaches, cut shortening into flour, and rolled out a silky soft dough, she recalled growing up in Van Buren County, Arkansas, where "Sunday dinner for the preacher almost always included fried chicken and a cobbler."

"I don't have anything written down. I just mix till things look right," she said. Many of the tips Jean shared with me were ones she'd learned from her mother. "She always said to add more sugar to the peaches than seemed right at first, 'cause once they cook down, they'll take more than you think."

Jean starts by precooking the peaches on the stovetop with water, sugar, and a generous amount of butter. No flour or cornstarch is needed, because she thickens the filling by tossing in small bits of dough, just as her mother did. Instead of a biscuit dough—which is more typical for cobblers—Jean makes a pastry crust. "I use Crisco," she said, "though my mother used lard. Nobody around here bakes with that anymore."

Gingered Pear-Apple cobbler

Pears and apples accent each other nicely in this fragrant cobbler. I particularly like to bake it in autumn, when these two fruits are at their peak. Fresh gingerroot, lemon, and vanilla enhance the taste of the filling, and sour cream lends tenderness and flavor to the easy biscuit topping.

FILLING

Generous ¾ cup sugar

2½ tablespoons cornstarch

2 tablespoons unsalted butter, cut into chunks

2½ teaspoons peeled and finely grated fresh gingerroot

1½ teaspoons finely grated lemon zest (yellow part of skin)

6 tablespoons apple juice or water

1½ tablespoons fresh lemon juice

3½ cups peeled, cored, and sliced tart, flavorful apples, such as Stayman or Granny Smith (about 1¾ pounds)

6 cups peeled, cored, and coarsely sliced slightly underripe Bosc or Bartlett pears (about 3 pounds)

1 teaspoon vanilla extract

DOUGH

1⅓ cups all-purpose flour

1 tablespoon sugar

Generous ½ teaspoon salt

¼ teaspoon baking soda

6 tablespoons (¾ stick) cold unsalted butter, cut into bits

½ cup sour cream, plus about 1½ tablespoons for brushing on dough top

Cold water, if needed

1 tablespoon sugar for sprinkling on dough top (optional)

Vanilla ice cream for serving (optional)

Position a rack in the middle of the oven and preheat to 400 degrees F.

TO MAKE THE FILLING: In a 3- to 4-quart nonreactive, flame-proof round casserole or Dutch oven, thoroughly stir together the sugar and cornstarch. Stir in the butter, ginger, lemon zest, apple juice, and lemon juice until well blended. Heat over medium-high heat, stirring and scraping the bottom of the casserole, just until thickened slightly and translucent. Add the apples. Let the mixture return to a boil. Cook, stirring frequently, for 3 minutes. Add the pears and vanilla (the casserole may be rather full). Cook, stirring gently, for 2 minutes longer. Remove from the heat.

TO MAKE THE DOUGH: In a food processor, combine the flour, sugar, salt, and baking soda. Process to blend. Add the butter. Process in quick pulses, scraping down the sides of the bowl as needed, just until the mixture has the consistency of fine crumbs. Add ½ cup sour cream and process in quick pulses just until it is incorporated and the mixture holds together when pressed between your fingertips; don't overprocess. If the mixture seems dry at all, gradually add cold water a teaspoon at a time and pulse several times, just until the mixture is moistened and holds together but isn't soggy. Remove the processor blade. Turn out the dough onto a sheet of baking parchment or wax paper. Knead briefly until the dough is smooth.

(Alternatively, in a medium bowl, thoroughly stir together the flour, sugar, salt, and baking soda. Using a pastry blender, forks, or your fingertips, cut in the butter until the mixture has the consistency of coarse meal. Lightly stir the sour cream into the flour mixture, tossing until evenly incorporated. Briefly knead the dough in the bowl until it holds together. If necessary, work in cold water a teaspoon at a time until the dough is moistened but not soggy.)

Let the dough stand for 5 minutes to reduce stickiness.

Lightly dust a 12-inch square of baking parchment or wax paper with flour. Turn out the dough onto the paper. Lightly dust the dough on both sides with flour. Top with a second sheet of paper. Roll or press out the dough into a round slightly smaller than the diameter of the casserole. Peel off the top sheet of paper. Center the dough, paper side up, over the fruit. Peel off the remaining paper. Using a greased paring knife, cut large decorative slashes for steam vents in the dough top. Using a pastry brush, lightly brush the dough all over with sour cream. Sprinkle with the sugar, if desired.

Set the casserole on a rimmed baking sheet. Bake for 40 to 50 minutes, or until the top is well browned and a toothpick inserted in the center of the dough comes out clean. Transfer to a wire rack. Let cool for at least 30 minutes. Spoon into bowls and serve with ice cream, if desired.

The cobbler will keep, covered, at room temperature for 24 hours, and refrigerated for 2 days longer. Let come to room temperature before serving.

strawberry-
rhubarb betty

Classified as a vegetable but eaten mostly as a fruit, rhubarb is among the first plants to come up in the spring. Before fresh produce was available year-round, it was an eagerly awaited respite from winter's starchy fare. Rhubarb was so often used in pies that some nineteenth-century cooks referred to it as "pie plant."

I've taken the traditional strawberry-rhubarb pie combination and put it to work in an easier old-fashioned dessert, the betty. The difference between betties and similar fruit dishes is that betties nearly always include day-old bread cubes or cracker crumbs. Considering that Victorian-era cookbook authors and home management authorities routinely exhorted homemakers to avoid wasting food, especially bread, it's likely that betties, like bread puddings, were devised to use up leftover scraps of the "staff of life."

This betty is a nice blend of textures and flavors—the astringency and slight firmness of the rhubarb pieces, the sweet taste of the strawberries, the hints of cinnamon and orange, and the toasted bread cubes all join to make an appealing, colorful dessert. In contrast to early betties, which were like pudding, this one is baked in a shallow dish and comes from the oven crisp on top.

4¾ cups cubed (⅓ inch) day-old sourdough, French, or Italian bread, crust removed

7 tablespoons (1 stick minus 1 tablespoon) unsalted butter, melted

1 cup plus 2 tablespoons packed light brown sugar

¾ teaspoon ground cinnamon

¼ teaspoon finely grated orange zest (orange part of skin)

¼ cup fresh orange juice

1 teaspoon vanilla extract

3 cups ½-inch-long pieces of rhubarb (about 1¼ pounds untrimmed stalks)

3 cups very coarsely sliced strawberries

Vanilla ice cream or sweetened whipped cream for serving (optional)

Position a rack in the upper third of the oven and preheat to 375 degrees F. Lightly grease a 7-by-11-inch (or similar) baking dish or coat with nonstick spray. In a large nonreactive bowl, stir together the bread cubes, butter, brown sugar, cinnamon, orange zest, orange juice, and vanilla until blended. In the baking dish, stir together the rhubarb and a generous half of the bread mixture until well blended.

Bake for 15 minutes. Remove the dish from the oven. Stir the strawberries into the rhubarb mixture; the dish will be fairly full. Top with the remaining bread mixture. Bake for 30 to 40 minutes longer, or until the betty is bubbly, browned, and crisp on top. Transfer to a wire rack. Let cool for at least 20 minutes. Serve warm, garnished with a scoop of ice cream or a dollop of sweetened whipped cream, if desired.

Since the rhubarb exudes a lot of juice, the betty is best eaten promptly but will keep, covered, in the refrigerator for a day or so. Reheat in a medium oven to warm before serving.

pie-plant pie

"Mix half tea-cup white sugar and one heaping tea-spoon flour together, sprinkle over the bottom crust, then add the pie-plant cut up fine; sprinkle over this another half tea-cup sugar and heaping tea-spoon flour; bake fully three-quarters of an hour in a slow oven."

–Mrs. D. Buxton,
in *Buckeye Cookery*
and Practical Housekeeping (1880)

PLum-Berry Betty

Most of the well-buttered crumbs in this betty disappear into the zesty plum-berry blend, while the rest lend a nice crunch to the top. The filling is wonderfully bright-colored and flavorful and artfully stretches 2 cups of pricier raspberries and blackberries with more abundant, less expensive plums.

Either tart red or black plums work well in this recipe. Just be sure to choose ones that are on the slightly underripe side.

BUTTERED CRUMBS

- 5 cups cubed (¹/₃ inch) day-old French, Italian, or other crusty white bread, including crusts
- 8 tablespoons (1 stick) unsalted butter, cut into chunks
- ¹/₈ teaspoon salt

FILLING

- 1¹/₃ cups plus ¹/₄ cup sugar (divided)
- 1¹/₂ tablespoons all-purpose flour
- 1 teaspoon ground cinnamon
- 1¹/₂ teaspoons vanilla extract
- 8¹/₂ cups pitted and coarsely chopped (unpeeled) firm, slightly underripe tart red or black plums
- 1 cup raspberries
- 1 cup blackberries

Vanilla ice cream or frozen yogurt for serving (optional)

Position a rack in the middle of the oven and preheat to 375 degrees F. Lightly grease a 9-by-13-inch (or similar) baking dish or coat with non-stick spray.

TO MAKE THE CRUMBS: On a large rimmed baking sheet, toast the bread cubes, stirring once or twice, until dry and crisp, 9 to 12 minutes. Let cool to barely warm. In two batches, transfer to a food processor and process in pulses into coarse crumbs. (Or place the cubes in a large, heavy plastic bag and crush with a rolling pin into coarse crumbs.) In a large skillet, melt the butter over medium-high heat until it bubbles. Stir in the salt and crumbs and cook, stirring, until they are saturated with the butter and slightly crisp, 3 to 4 minutes.

Tip

You can make the crumb topping and the fruit mixture a day or so ahead, then refrigerate the two separately.

TO MAKE THE FILLING: In a large bowl, stir together the 1⅓ cups sugar, the flour, cinnamon, and vanilla until blended. Add the plums and all but ⅓ cup of the bread crumbs, stirring well. Gently stir in the berries until evenly incorporated. Spread the filling evenly in the baking dish. In a small dish, stir together the remaining ⅓ cup bread crumbs and the remaining ¼ cup sugar; set aside.

Bake for 35 minutes. Sprinkle the reserved crumb mixture evenly over the filling. Bake for 15 to 20 minutes longer, or until the betty is bubbly all over and crisp on top. Transfer to a wire rack. Let cool for at least 20 minutes and preferably 45 minutes. Serve with a scoop of vanilla ice cream or frozen yogurt, if desired.

The betty will keep, covered, in the refrigerator for up to 3 days. Let come to room temperature or reheat in a low oven to warm before serving.

words of kitchen wisdom

"As far as it is possible, have bits of bread eaten up before they become hard. Spread those that are not eaten and let them dry, to be pounded for puddings . . . Above all, do not let crusts accumulate in such quantities that they cannot be used. With proper care, there is no need of losing a particle of bread."

—Mrs. Lydia Maria Child,
The American Frugal Housewife (1833)

FaLL Fruit and cranberry Betty

This is a large betty, so there's plenty for a holiday crowd. The apples and pears contribute a mellow flavor and succulence; the cranberries add color and zip. Neither overly rich nor sweet, this betty is nice after a heavy meal.

FILLING

Generous ¾ cup packed light brown sugar

½ teaspoon ground cinnamon

Generous ¼ teaspoon ground allspice

2¼ cups fresh (or frozen, partially thawed) cranberries, chopped fairly fine

2½ cups peeled, cored, and thinly sliced tart, flavorful apples, such as Stayman, Nittany, or Braeburn

2½ cups peeled, cored, and thinly sliced ripe pears, preferably Bosc

5 cups cubed (½ inch) day-old, crusty, slightly crisp sourdough or French bread, including crust

⅔ cup cranberry juice cocktail or orange juice

1 tablespoon cold unsalted butter, cut into bits

TOPPING

¾ cup all-purpose flour

¾ cup packed light brown sugar

½ teaspoon ground cinnamon

Generous 5 tablespoons cold unsalted butter, cut into chunks

Vanilla ice cream for serving (optional)

Position a rack in the upper third of the oven and preheat to 375 degrees F. Lightly grease a 9-by-13-inch (or similar) baking dish or coat with non-stick spray.

TO MAKE THE FILLING: In a large bowl, stir together the brown sugar, cinnamon, allspice, and cranberries until blended. Add the apples, pears, bread, and cranberry juice to the cranberry mixture, tossing until well mixed. Spread the filling evenly in the baking dish. Sprinkle with the bits of butter. Bake for 10 minutes.

MEANWHILE, TO MAKE THE TOPPING: In a food processor, combine the flour, brown sugar, and cinnamon, pulsing several times to mix. Add the butter. Process until the mixture is well blended, about 1 minute. (Alternatively, in a small bowl, stir together the flour, brown sugar, and cinnamon. With a pastry blender, forks, or your fingertips, work the butter into the dry ingredients until well blended.)

Sprinkle the topping evenly over the filling. Bake for 20 to 30 minutes longer, or until nicely browned and bubbly at the edges. Transfer to a wire rack. Let cool for at least 20 minutes. Serve warm or at room temperature, with a scoop of ice cream, if desired.

The betty will keep, covered, at room temperature for 24 hours or refrigerated for up to 3 days. Let come to room temperature or reheat in a low oven to warm before serving.

wherefore art thou, betty?

Betty recipes started turning up in nineteenth-century America, first featuring apples, then peaches, then various other fruits. The earliest versions usually called for multiple layers of fruit and bread cubes or crumbs baked in a deep dish; they were really fruit puddings. Cookbook author Eliza Leslie discusses an apple bread pudding recipe in her *Directions for Cookery:* "This pudding is in some places called by the homely names of Brown Betty or Pan Dowdy." However, Leslie sheds no light on how the name "betty" came to be.

Since that time, betties have become less like puddings and more like fruit crisps. (Unlike crisps, however, they contain bread crumbs or cracker crumbs.) The current habit of spreading the fruit and bread in a single layer and baking them in a large flat dish allows for the top to brown better and the fruit juices to become more concentrated. The result: a very fine, homey dessert indeed.

farmstead Apple crisp

Apple crisp was a standby in my mother's repertoire, especially in late summer and fall, when most of our old apple trees were bearing fruit. This rich, full-bodied crisp is my own recipe, but it's similar to my mother's: a bit of lemon juice to bring up the apple taste, brown sugar for mellowness, and a hint of cinnamon to enhance the fruit. Most of the year, I make it with a mix of Golden Delicious and Granny Smith apples, but in the fall, when I can get them, fresh, succulent Stayman apples, used alone, are hard to beat. I recently made this recipe with a five-apple combination of Golden Delicious, Nittany, Granny Smith, Stayman, and Braeburn; the flavor was excellent.

The idea of the crisp, which is also occasionally called a crunch, is likely borrowed from Pennsylvania Dutch and Amish cooks, who have been sprinkling desserts with streusel since at least the nineteenth century. The word "streusel" derives from the German verb *streuen*, to strew.

FILLING

- ⅓ cup packed light brown sugar
- 2½ tablespoons all-purpose flour
- ½ teaspoon ground cinnamon
- 7½ cups peeled, cored, and coarsely sliced tart, flavorful apples, such as Stayman, Rome, Granny Smith, or Pippin
- 1½ tablespoons fresh lemon juice
- 2 tablespoons unsalted butter, melted

TOPPING

- ¾ cup all-purpose flour
- ¾ cup old-fashioned rolled oats
- ⅔ cup packed light brown sugar
- ½ cup chopped walnuts or pecans (optional)
- 8 tablespoons (1 stick) unsalted butter, melted

Vanilla ice cream or whipped cream for serving (optional)

Position a rack in the middle of the oven and preheat to 350 degrees F. Grease a 7-by-11-inch (or similar) baking dish or coat with nonstick spray.

TO MAKE THE FILLING: In a large bowl, stir together the brown sugar, flour, and cinnamon until blended. Stir in the apples, lemon juice, and melted butter, tossing until the apples are coated with the brown sugar mixture. Spread the filling evenly in the baking dish. Bake for 25 minutes.

TIP

If the apples you use are very tart and tangy, reduce the lemon juice to 1 tablespoon.

MEANWHILE, TO MAKE THE TOPPING: In a medium bowl, stir together the flour, oats, brown sugar, and nuts (if using). Add the melted butter, stirring until incorporated. Sprinkle the topping evenly over the apples. Press down lightly. Increase the oven temperature to 375 degrees F and bake for 25 to 30 minutes longer, or until the top is nicely browned and the filling is bubbly. Transfer to a wire rack. Let cool to warm for at least 30 minutes. Spoon into bowls and serve with ice cream or whipped cream, if desired.

The crisp will keep, covered, at room temperature for 24 hours or refrigerated for up to 3 days longer. Let come to room temperature before serving.

APPLES OF MY EYE

The apples on our farm were not as big and beautiful as the ones in today's markets (we never sprayed them), but they were more flavorful than many of the currently popular varieties. All originated in the nineteenth century, and they were planted long before I was born. Since they bore fruit at different times, whoever chose them obviously wanted to keep the family supplied with apples for as much of the year as possible.

The earliest trees to bear were called Yellow Transparent. Introduced into America from Russia sometime in the nineteenth century, these tart, medium-size, pale green apples ripened in June and made terrific applesauce and a good crisp. The first of our fall apples was the Smokehouse, a crisp, tangy, flavorful apple that ripened in August and was good for eating and for pies. It's said that this apple was discovered growing near a smokehouse in Lancaster County, Pennsylvania, in the early 1800s.

Two other varieties we depended on, the Jonathan and Stayman, are still popular today. Our only yellow autumn apple, the Grimes Golden, ripened in late October. It's the sweetest and fruitiest apple I've ever tasted.

sour cherry-cranberry crisp

Sour cherries and cranberries are delicious together. You can make this crisp with canned cherries when cranberries are in season, and with frozen cranberries when cherries are in season. (Frozen cranberries keep in airtight plastic bags for nearly a year. It's easiest to chop them using a food processor while they are partially frozen.) Be sure to buy unsweetened sour cherries, not canned cherry pie filling.

FILLING

- 1 cup granulated sugar, or more to taste
- 1½ tablespoons all-purpose flour
- 6 cups pitted fresh sour cherries, or three 15-ounce cans pitted unsweetened sour cherries, well drained
- 2 cups fresh (or frozen, partially thawed) cranberries, coarsely chopped

STREUSEL

- 1 cup all-purpose flour
- 1 cup old-fashioned rolled oats
- ¾ cup packed light brown sugar
- ¾ cup chopped walnuts
- ½ teaspoon ground cinnamon
  Scant ½ teaspoon salt
- 10 tablespoons (1 stick plus 2 tablespoons) unsalted butter, melted

  Vanilla ice cream or whipped cream for serving

Position a rack in the middle of the oven and preheat to 375 degrees F. Grease a 9-by-13-inch (or similar) baking dish or coat with nonstick spray.

TO MAKE THE FILLING: In a large bowl, thoroughly stir together the granulated sugar and flour. Gently stir in the cherries and cranberries until evenly incorporated. Spread the filling evenly in the baking dish.

TO MAKE THE STREUSEL: In a large bowl, thoroughly stir together the flour, oats, brown sugar, walnuts, cinnamon, and salt. Stir in the butter until evenly incorporated and the mixture forms small clumps. Sprinkle the streusel evenly over the filling.

Bake for 40 to 50 minutes, or until the top is well browned and the filling is bubbly. Transfer to a wire rack. Let cool to barely warm or room temperature. Serve the crisp spooned into bowls or onto dessert plates. Top with scoops of vanilla ice cream or dollops of whipped cream.

The crisp will keep, covered, at room temperature for 24 hours or refrigerated for up to 3 days. Let come to room temperature or reheat in a low oven to barely warm before serving.

VARIATION: Plum-Nectarine Crisp

Prepare the recipe as directed, but substitute 6 cups coarsely sliced (unpeeled) pitted plums for the cherries and 2 cups coarsely sliced (unpeeled) nectarines for the cranberries. Increase the flour in the filling to 3 tablespoons.

IT'S THE PITS

"[Fisher's Cherry Stoner will with] five strokes stone one hundred cherries. The rapidity and certainty with which it performs its work will make this machine a necessity in every household. Under or overripe fruit equally well stoned, and can be done five times as rapidly as by the old way by hand, and much neater, as it leaves the fruit round and in perfect shape."

–Advertisement, B. K. Bliss & Sons Seed Catalog (1876)

FIRST FIND A FEATHER BED . . .

A "receipt" in *Martha Washington's Booke of Cookery* called "To Keepe Cherries That You May Have Them For Tarts At Christmass Without Preserveing," suggests the following storage method:

> Take the fayrest cherries you can get, fresh from the trees; without bruising, wipe them one by one with a linnen cloth, then put them into a barrell of hay & lay them in ranks, first laying hay on the bottom, and then cherries & then hay & then cheryes, & then hay agayne. stop them up that noe Ayre get to them. Then set them under a fether bead where one lyeth continually, for the warmer they are kept, the better it is.

apricot crisp

I turn to this recipe whenever fresh apricots are in season. Apricot preserves and a little almond extract intensify their fresh taste. The crumb mixture is somewhat unusual in that it includes egg. This helps the topping stay crisp and stand up to the juiciness of the apricots.

6 cups pitted and quartered (unpeeled) apricots	$^1/_4$ teaspoon salt
$^1/_4$ cup apricot preserves	6 tablespoons ($^3/_4$ stick) cold unsalted butter, cut into chunks
$^3/_4$ cup granulated sugar, or more to taste	1 large egg, beaten with $^1/_4$ teaspoon almond extract
$^1/_4$ teaspoon finely grated orange zest (orange part of skin)	$^1/_3$ cup slivered almonds
1$^1/_3$ cups all-purpose flour	Vanilla ice cream or whipped cream for serving (optional)
$^2/_3$ cup packed light brown sugar	
$^1/_4$ teaspoon ground cinnamon	

Position a rack in the middle of the oven and preheat to 375 degrees F. Grease a 7-by-11-inch (or similar) baking dish or coat with nonstick spray.

In a large bowl, stir together the apricots, preserves, granulated sugar, and orange zest until blended. In a food processor, pulse the flour, brown sugar, cinnamon, and salt to mix. Sprinkle the butter over the flour mixture. Process in pulses until evenly incorporated and the mixture has the consistency of coarse crumbs. Sprinkle the egg mixture over the flour mixture. Process in pulses just until the mixture is crumbly; be careful not to overprocess, or it may clump. (Alternatively, in a medium bowl, stir together the flour, brown sugar, cinnamon, and salt. Using a pastry blender, forks, or your fingertips, work the butter into the dry ingredients until the mixture is well blended and has the consistency of coarse crumbs. Sprinkle the egg mixture over the flour mixture. Stir with a fork until the mixture is crumbly.)

tip

Apricots are sometimes surprisingly tart, so taste after combining them with the preserves and sugar, and sweeten them more, if needed.

Measure out ⅔ cup of the crumb mixture and toss with the apricot mixture. Spread the apricot mixture in the baking dish. Sprinkle the almonds, then the remaining crumb mixture, evenly over the apricots.

Bake for 35 to 40 minutes, or until the top is well browned and the filling is bubbly. Transfer to a wire rack. Let cool to barely warm, at least 30 to 40 minutes. Serve with ice cream or whipped cream, if desired.

The crisp is best fresh; if possible, serve within 8 hours of baking. It will keep, covered, in the refrigerator for several days. Let come to room temperature or reheat in a low oven to barely warm before serving.

Taste of Hawaii Pineapple crisp

Pineapple and brown sugar have a great affinity for each other, and vanilla, coconut, and Hawaiian macadamia nuts make this crisp irresistible, especially when garnished with a scoop of good vanilla ice cream.

If you aren't lucky enough to have fresh pineapple, you can substitute juice-packed canned pineapple.

1³/₄ cups all-purpose flour	¹/₂ teaspoon peeled and finely grated fresh gingerroot (optional)
1 cup packed light brown sugar	1¹/₂ teaspoons vanilla extract
Generous ¹/₄ teaspoon salt	¹/₂ cup shredded or flaked sweetened coconut
12 tablespoons (1¹/₂ sticks) unsalted butter, melted (divided)	¹/₂ cup chopped macadamia nuts, preferably unsalted (optional)
5¹/₂ cups diced (¹/₂ inch) fresh pineapple, or three 15-ounce cans juice-packed pineapple tidbits, well drained	Vanilla ice cream for serving
¹/₂ teaspoon grated lemon zest (yellow part of skin)	

Position a rack in the middle of the oven and preheat to 400 degrees F. Grease a 9-inch square or 7-by-11-inch (or similar) baking dish or coat with nonstick spray. In a medium bowl, thoroughly stir together the flour, brown sugar, and salt. Sprinkle all but 2 tablespoons of the melted butter over the flour mixture. Stir until the streusel is well blended and forms clumps.

In a large bowl, thoroughly stir together the pineapple, ⅔ cup of the streusel mixture, the lemon zest, gingerroot (if using), vanilla, and remaining 2 tablespoons melted butter until blended. Spread the filling evenly in the baking dish. Bake for 20 minutes.

Stir the coconut and macadamia nuts (if using) into the remaining streusel. Spread the streusel evenly over the pineapple, breaking up any large clumps with your fingertips. Bake for 20 to 30 minutes longer, or until the top is well browned. Transfer to a wire rack. Let cool to barely warm, at least 30 to 40 minutes. Serve with scoops of vanilla ice cream.

The crisp is best fresh but will keep, covered, in the refrigerator for 2 or 3 days. Let come to room temperature or reheat in a low oven to barely warm before serving.

strawberry shortcake

I was surprised to find that the shortcake dough that I've been making for many years (roughly based on my mother's recipe) is much like typical nineteenth-century versions. Mine calls for buttermilk and is baked in a round cake pan, then split horizontally into two layers that are stacked to form a cake. It's tender yet firm enough to hold up when the fresh berries are spooned over. Quintessentially American in its simplicity and straightforwardness, the finished dessert tastes wonderful and is pretty. (If you prefer individual shortcakes see the variation.)

SHORTCAKE

- 2 cups all-purpose flour, plus a little more for shaping dough
- 1½ tablespoons sugar
- 1½ teaspoons baking powder
- ½ teaspoon baking soda
- Generous ½ teaspoon salt
- 5½ tablespoons cold unsalted butter, cut into bits
- Generous 1 cup buttermilk, plus more if needed

BERRIES

- 5½ cups thinly sliced fresh strawberries
- ½–¾ cup sugar, to taste

Lightly sweetened whipped cream for garnish

Small, hulled whole fresh strawberries for garnish

TO MAKE THE SHORTCAKE: Position a rack in the middle of the oven and preheat to 450 degrees F. Generously grease an 8- to 8½-inch round cake pan, pie plate, or similar round baking pan or generously coat with nonstick spray.

In a large bowl, thoroughly stir together the flour, sugar, baking powder, baking soda, and salt. Sprinkle the butter over the flour mixture. Using a pastry blender, forks, or your fingertips, cut in until the butter is incorporated in very fine bits; scrape up the flour underneath to be sure it is evenly incorporated. (Alternatively, combine the flour, sugar, baking powder, baking soda, and salt in a food processor. Pulse 4 or 5 times to blend the ingredients. Sprinkle the butter over the flour mixture. Process in pulses until the butter is in very fine bits; scrape up the flour underneath to be sure it is evenly incorporated. Turn out the mixture into a large bowl.)

tip

The fashion today is to undersweeten desserts, but ample sugaring really is in order here. Of course, the exact amount depends on how sweet the berries are to start with; taste and go from there.

Being very careful not to overmix, gently stir the buttermilk into the flour-butter mixture until the dough just comes together. Add more buttermilk, if necessary, to produce a soft, moist dough. Sprinkle evenly with 1½ tablespoons flour. Knead in the bowl 5 or 6 times to form a smooth mass, adding a little more flour to prevent stickiness, if necessary. Let stand for 1 minute. With flour-dusted hands, shape and smooth the dough into a 6-inch disk. Brush any excess flour from the top. Place the disk in the pan. Press and pat out into an evenly thick round. If necessary, dust your hands with flour or lightly dust the dough with flour to prevent sticking.

Bake for 17 to 22 minutes, or until the top is puffy and browned. Carefully lift up the dough and check the underside for doneness; it should be tinged with brown. If necessary, continue baking for several minutes longer. Let cool to warm, then tip out of the pan and let cool completely on a wire rack. The shortcake is best served fresh but will keep, stored airtight, at room temperature for up to 24 hours or frozen for up to a week. Let come to room temperature before using.

TO MAKE THE BERRIES: At least 1 hour and up to 3 hours before serving, combine the strawberries with ½ cup sugar. Taste and add more sugar, if desired. The berries will release their juice and become soupy.

TO ASSEMBLE THE SHORTCAKE: Using a large serrated knife, split the biscuit round in half horizontally. Center the bottom half cut side up on a serving plate and top with half the berries and juice. Top with the second round, cut side down. Top with the remaining berries and juice. Garnish generously with whipped cream and a few small strawberries. Cut into wedges and serve.

VARIATION: Individual Shortcakes
Makes 6 or 7 servings

Position a rack in the middle of the oven and preheat to 425 degrees F. Generously grease a rimmed baking sheet or generously coat with non-stick spray. After the dough is shaped into a 6-inch disk, generously dust a large sheet of baking parchment or wax paper with flour and center the dough on it. Evenly dust the dough with more flour. Top with another sheet of paper. Press or pat out the dough into an 8-inch round. Peel off the top sheet of paper, then loosely pat it back into place so it will be

words of kitchen wisdom

"Perhaps you have never stopped to consider the possibilities of the ordinary biscuit dough . . . It is easily mixed and baked and has the advantage of being one of the most inexpensive mixtures to make."

—Belle De Graf,
Mrs. De Graf's Cook Book (1922)

cobblers, crisps, and other fruit desserts

easy to remove later. Flip over the dough and peel off the second sheet. Using a 3- to 3½-inch round, preferably sharp metal cutter (or a washed and dried empty tuna can), cut out shortcake rounds. Dip the cutter in flour as needed and, for the tenderest biscuits, cut out by punching down firmly rather than twisting, which pulls the dough and toughens it. Recombine the dough scraps and continue forming rounds until all the dough is used. Space the rounds about 2 inches apart on the baking sheet.

Bake for 9 to 14 minutes, or until the tops and bottoms are browned; lift up a round to check. Transfer to a wire rack. Let cool. At serving time, split the rounds horizontally in half with a large serrated knife. Center the bottom halves cut sides up on individual dessert plates. Divide the berries and juice among the servings and proceed as for the large short-cake.

The Long and the short of it

Early shortcakes were basically biscuits, served with tea or a meal. The habit of topping them with well-sugared strawberries or other fruit probably took hold in the 1840s, perhaps as a convenient way for cooks to use up leftovers. The first recipe I know of that pairs biscuits and fresh strawberries appears in Eliza Leslie's 1850 *Miss Leslie's Lady's New Receipt Book.* Miss Leslie commented that because the strawberries were not cooked, they retained "all their natural flavor."

However the original strawberry shortcake came about, it's inspired. Although modern recipes often call for a sweet cake base, this is neither traditional nor as good as the original. Short-cakes made the old-fashioned way are not sweet, so the berries and fruits can be generously sugared, which causes them to give off lots of fragrant juice that soaks into the biscuits and provides a contrast to the plain dough. And unlike most cakes, the biscuits are sturdy enough not to become soggy from the fruit. Originally, shortcakes were garnished with a dollop of either rich custard sauce or whipped cream. Today whipped cream rules.

Dark sweet cherry, Apricot, and Peach shortcakes

The combination of dark sweet cherries, apricots, and peaches produces a shortcake that's dramatically different from the classic strawberry version, but just as lovely. I know of no better way to show off summer's sweet bounty.

The cherries and apricots are cooked briefly to intensify their flavors, set their colors, and release their juices. The peaches are folded in just before serving so they retain their firm texture and fresh-from-the-tree taste.

FRUIT

Scant 1 cup sugar

3 tablespoons cornstarch

2 cups pitted dark sweet cherries (about ³/₄ pound)

2 cups pitted and sliced (unpeeled) apricots (about 1 pound)

3 tablespoons kirsch, peach brandy, or orange juice

1 tablespoon fresh lemon juice (optional)

2¹/₂ cups peeled, pitted, and sliced peaches (5–6 medium peaches)

SHORTCAKES

2 cups all-purpose flour, plus more if needed

1¹/₂ tablespoons sugar

1 teaspoon baking powder

¹/₂ teaspoon baking soda

Generous ¹/₂ teaspoon salt

8 tablespoons (1 stick) cold unsalted butter, cut into bits

²/₃ cup buttermilk

Cold water, if needed

Lightly sweetened whipped cream for serving

TO MAKE THE FRUIT: In a nonreactive 3-quart saucepan, thoroughly stir together the sugar and cornstarch. Stir in the cherries, apricots, and kirsch until well blended and smooth. Bring to a simmer over medium-high heat. Simmer, stirring constantly, until slightly thickened and translucent, about 2 minutes. Remove from the heat. Taste and stir in the lemon juice if desired. Cover and refrigerate until cool, at least 1 hour and up to 24 hours. Stir in the peaches just before serving.

TO MAKE THE SHORTCAKES: Position a rack in the middle of the oven and preheat to 375 degrees F. Grease a rimmed baking sheet or coat with nonstick spray. In a large bowl, thoroughly stir together the flour, sugar, baking powder, baking soda, and salt. Add the butter. Using a pastry blender, forks, or your fingertips, cut in the butter until the mixture resembles very coarse meal. (Alternatively, combine the flour, sugar, baking powder, baking soda, and salt in a food processor. Pulse 4 or 5 times to blend. Sprinkle the butter over the flour mixture. Process until the butter is in very fine bits. Turn out the mixture into a large bowl.)

Add the buttermilk to the flour-butter mixture, mixing with a fork until evenly incorporated. Knead lightly with greased hands until the dough just holds together, rubbing the mixture between your fingertips to check. If it seems too wet, sprinkle over and then work in a little flour; if it's too dry, sprinkle over and then work in a few teaspoons of cold water.

Lightly dust a 12-inch square of baking parchment or wax paper with flour. Turn out the dough onto the paper. Lightly dust the dough with flour. Top with a second sheet of paper. Press, then roll out the dough into a generous 6-by-9-inch rectangle. Peel off the top sheet of paper, then pat it back loosely into place so it will be easy to remove later. Flip over the dough and peel off the second sheet. Using a large sharp knife dusted with flour, trim the rectangle so the sides are even. Cut the dough into six 3-inch square biscuits. Place on the baking sheet about 2 inches apart.

Bake for 12 to 18 minutes, or until the tops are nicely browned and a toothpick inserted in the center of a biscuit comes out clean. Let cool for at least 10 minutes. The biscuits are best used fresh but will keep, stored airtight, at room temperature for up to 24 hours or frozen for up to a week. Let come to room temperature before using.

TO ASSEMBLE THE SHORTCAKES: Using a large serrated knife, split the biscuits in half horizontally. Center the bottom halves cut sides up on individual dessert plates. Top with half the fruit mixture. Cover with the biscuit tops, cut sides down. Top with the remaining fruit mixture. Generously garnish with whipped cream and serve immediately.

AT RIGHT

BLUEBERRY-FRUIT
SLUMP

PAGE 184

Blueberry-Fruit Slump

Slumps are the plain-Jane cousins of cobblers. Slumps differ from their better-known relatives because they are covered and usually cooked on the stovetop, so the dough steams and becomes fluffy and dumpling-like, instead of browning and crisping as a cobbler crust does. (It's been speculated that the dough's softening and slumping down into the fruit may account for the name, but I'm not convinced.)

For the novice cook, the advantage of the dish is that the dough is easily mixed together and dropped from spoons to form the dumplings. Another advantage—at least in summer—is that the recipe doesn't require firing up the oven.

My recipe pairs blueberries with other seasonal fruits. Those with a noticeable acidity best complement the mild dough. Sour cherries, tart plums, rhubarb, raspberries, or blackberries all work well, and their red to purple color contrasts with the light puffs of dough.

FRUIT

Generous ½ cup sugar, or more for very tart fruit

2 tablespoons cornstarch

¼ teaspoon ground cinnamon

½ cup cranberry juice cocktail or orange juice

1 tablespoon fresh lemon juice

2 teaspoons finely grated lemon zest (yellow part of skin)

2½ cups blueberries

2 cups pitted sour red cherries, or 1 cup chopped rhubarb and 1 cup blackberries, sour cherries, sliced tart plums, or raspberries

DOUGH

1 cup all-purpose flour

1 teaspoon baking powder

Generous ¼ teaspoon salt

3 tablespoons cold unsalted butter, cut into bits

About ⅔ cup milk

½ tablespoon sugar, mixed with ¼ teaspoon ground cinnamon for sprinkling on dough

Heavy (whipping) cream, whipped cream, or ice cream for serving (optional)

TO MAKE THE FRUIT: In a 9- to 10-inch nonreactive, deep-sided skillet or 2½- to 3-quart saucepan, stir together the sugar, cornstarch, and cinnamon. Stir in the cranberry juice, lemon juice, and lemon zest. Stir in the blueberries and cherries until incorporated. Bring to a simmer, stirring, over medium heat. Simmer, stirring occasionally, until the fruits just begin to soften and release their juices, about 2 minutes. Set aside.

TO MAKE THE DOUGH: In a medium bowl, thoroughly stir together the flour, baking powder, and salt. Add the butter. Using a pastry blender, forks, or your fingertips, cut in the butter until the mixture resembles coarse meal. Add a scant ⅔ cup milk to the flour mixture, mixing with a fork until evenly incorporated. The dough should be very soft and slightly wet; if necessary, stir in a little more milk. Let the dough stand for a minute or two to firm up slightly. With several wet soup spoons, scoop up the dough and drop it in 1-inch mounds on the fruit, spacing the portions evenly over the top.

Return the fruit to the burner and adjust the heat so it simmers very gently. Cover the pan tightly and continue simmering for 16 to 20 minutes, or until the dumplings are puffy and cooked through. Sprinkle the cinnamon-sugar mixture over the dough. Transfer the pan to a wire rack. Let cool, uncovered, for at least 20 minutes. Serve warm, spooned into bowls, with cream, whipped cream, or ice cream, if desired.

The slump will keep, covered, in the refrigerator for up to 4 days. Let come to room temperature or reheat to slightly warm before serving.

cobblers, crisps, and other fruit desserts

Apple Pandowdy, Eliza Leslie's Way

"Shoo-fly pie and apple pandowdy—makes your eyes light up and your tummy say howdy." Despite the endorsement from the popular 1946 Dinah Shore song, few Americans outside New England have ever eaten pandowdy.

My version is based on a recipe from the 1851 edition of *Miss Leslie's Directions for Cookery* by the popular Philadelphia author Eliza Leslie. It's unique in calling for covering the apples with a layer of thick sour milk. I've substituted sour cream—with delicious results. The finished dish looks like a very simple cobbler, tastes like a sour cream apple pie, and, if my family and friends are any indication, does indeed make the eyes light up and the tummy say howdy!

Single crust All-Purpose Pie Pastry Dough (page 90)

All-purpose flour for dusting dough

FILLING

3/4 cup plus 2 tablespoons packed light brown sugar (divided)

5 tablespoons all-purpose flour (divided)

1 teaspoon ground cinnamon

1/8 teaspoon ground cloves

9 cups peeled, cored, and thinly sliced tart, flavorful apples, such as Stayman, Granny Smith, Empire, Cortland, or McIntosh (about 3 pounds)

1 tablespoon fresh lemon juice

1 1/2 cups sour cream

1/8 teaspoon baking soda

Vanilla ice cream for serving (optional)

Position a rack in the middle of the oven and preheat to 400 degrees F. Lightly grease a 9-by-13-inch (or similar) baking dish or coat with nonstick spray.

TO ROLL OUT THE DOUGH: If the dough is cold and stiff, let it warm up until slightly pliable but still cool to the touch. Shape it into a 7-inch-long log. Generously dust it all over with flour. Roll out the dough between sheets of baking parchment or wax paper into a 9½-by-13½-inch rectangle (or just slightly larger than the baking dish). Occasionally check the underside of the dough during rolling and smooth out any wrinkles. Gently peel off the top sheet of paper, then pat back into place. Flip the dough; peel off the bottom sheet. Using a sharp knife, trim off the uneven edges to form an even rectangle just barely larger than the baking dish. Slide the dough (paper still attached) onto a baking sheet. Refrigerate, lightly covered, while you prepare the filling.

TO MAKE THE FILLING: In a small bowl, thoroughly stir together the ¾ cup brown sugar, 2 tablespoons of the flour, the cinnamon, and cloves. In a large bowl, stir together the apples and lemon juice. Add the sugar mixture to the apples and stir until they are coated. Spread the apple mixture evenly in the baking dish. In the bowl used for the apples, thoroughly stir together the sour cream, the remaining 2 tablespoons brown sugar, the remaining 3 tablespoons flour, and the baking soda. Spread the mixture evenly over the apples.

TO ASSEMBLE THE PANDOWDY: Center the dough, paper side up, over the apples. Peel off the remaining paper. Using a greased paring knife, cut several steam vents in the top. Set the dish on a rimmed baking sheet.

Bake for 40 to 50 minutes, or until the pastry is browned all over and the filling is bubbly. (It's normal for the filling to look slightly separated.) Transfer to a wire rack. Let cool for at least 25 minutes and preferably 1 hour. Spoon into bowls and serve with scoops of ice cream, if desired.

The pandowdy will keep, covered, at room temperature for a day or so or refrigerated for 3 or 4 days. Let come to room temperature before serving.

DOWDY-LOOKING?

Despite the rather plain look of the dowdy, many culinary historians, including *Food History News* editor Sandra Oliver, believe that the odd name does not refer to the appearance of the dish but to the fact that it is covered with a "dow," a variation on the word "dough."

PANDOWDY—SERVED WITH ATTITUDE

Pandowdy was known in different parts of the country in the early nineteenth century, but New England is where it lives on today. Perhaps the place most closely associated with the dessert is Boston's Durgin-Park, a landmark Faneuil Hall Market Place eatery with the deadpan tag line "Established Before You Were Born." In fact, the crowded, boisterous establishment has been serving its unabashedly New England fare since before anyone living today was born (for 130 years), although the original clientele of local workers and seamen has now been mostly replaced by tourists and college students.

Apple pandowdy isn't always available at the restaurant, but chef Tommy Ryan says he's been making it there for more than forty years. "The recipe's older than that, though," he says. "Helen, the person here before me, made it for thirty years before that." The Durgin-Park pandowdy contains molasses (long a staple in New England cooking) and is topped with a traditional pastry crust. Ryan uses Cortland or McIntosh apples.

"I tell people pandowdy is like apple pie," the chef says, "except the filling is a little darker and has some molasses flavor. It's baked in a different pan and served cut in squares."

COLORFUL OLD-TIMERS

It's hard to imagine our country without apple trees, but with the exception of crab apples, they are not native to America. The colonists promptly planted them upon arrival here, however, probably from seeds hand-carried or saved from apples that were eaten on the voyage. By the eighteenth century, according to a Boston area homemaker quoted in Richard J. Hooker's *Food and Drink in America,* hay and apples were "the chief produce of the Land."

One of the first apple varieties to be propagated here was the Roxbury Russet, developed in the seventeenth century in Roxbury, Massachusetts. Hundreds of regionally popular varieties — many with catchy names and colorful histories — followed. Some are still being grown in limited quantities.

BLACK SHEEPNOSE — As the name implies, this eighteenth-century baking and dessert apple boasted a deep red, almost black skin. The shape was distinctively elongated, suggesting a black sheep's nose.

EARLY STRAWBERRY — This tart, flavorful apple was small, intensely red, and among the first varieties to ripen, which likely accounts for its name. In the early 1800s, it was very popular in New York markets.

ESOPUS SPITZENBURG — Originally found in the Hudson Valley, in the town of Esopus, New York, this apple was Thomas Jefferson's favorite. Still grown in small quantities in Virginia, it has a fine aroma and zesty fruit flavor, and it makes excellent pies.

GRIMES GOLDEN — Found on the Grimes farm in West Virginia in the early nineteenth century, this very sweet, fruity, yellow apple is an ancestor of one of our favorite eating and cooking apples today, the Golden Delicious.

HUNT RUSSET — Known in the mid-nineteenth century, this long-keeping variety is said to have originated on the property of the Hunt family in Concord, Massachusetts. The name "russet" refers to the brownish patches on the skin.

JONATHAN — This zesty-sweet, shiny red apple was discovered on a Woodstock, New York, farm in the early 1800s and named for the man who found it, Jonathan Hasbrouck. A great favorite for both cooking and eating, it has superior flavor and is pleasingly crisp.

NORTHERN SPY — Discovered in New York in the early 1800s and very hardy, this large, tart, greenish yellow apple is still popular in some northern areas, especially for making pies.

PORTER — A Reverend Samuel Porter gets credit for discovering this red-tinged yellow apple in Massachusetts in 1840.

RHODE ISLAND GREENING — Originating in the early 1600s, the Greening was one of America's favorite cooking apples for more than two hundred years. Although the tart, juicy Greening (which is indeed green) was popularized in Rhode Island, some sources say that it was first planted on Beacon Hill in Boston by a clergyman named William Blaxton. Blaxton is said to have then moved to Rhode Island and introduced the variety there. Other sources say that the Greening was the result of a chance seedling found in the town of Green's End, Rhode Island, around 1650.

YELLOW NEWTOWN PIPPIN — A green apple with a slight red blush, this may have originated along Newtown Creek, across the East River from Manhattan, in the early 1700s. It gradually gained favor in Williamsburg, Virginia, in the mid-eighteenth century, and later it was grown as a cash crop by Thomas Jefferson and others in Albemarle County, Virginia. Sometimes called the Albemarle Pippin, it is a good keeper and was successfully exported to Britain throughout the nineteenth and early twentieth centuries. Queen Victoria was said to have favored this apple.

YORK IMPERIAL — This green-streaked red apple is named for York, Pennsylvania, where it was discovered in the nineteenth century. It is known for its crispness, tangy-sweet flavor, and good keeping qualities, and it is grown in the Cumberland-Shenandoah area.

colorado peach dumplings

The word "dumpling" often refers to steamed or baked doughs, but not in this case. These dumplings are little packages of rich pastry enveloping a juicy peach, baked and served with a brown sugar–butter sauce. They're so good that I make them whenever peaches are in season. The recipe was inspired by one in the *Colorado Cook Book;* it was contributed by Cascade resident Barbara Sabol.

PASTRY

- 4 cups all-purpose flour
- ³/₄ teaspoon salt
- 1¹/₂ cups chilled solid white shortening, cut into chunks
- ¹/₂ teaspoon almond extract
- ³/₄ cup ice water, plus more if needed

PEACHES

- 8 small peaches (4¹/₂–5 ounces each), peeled, halved, and pitted
- 1 cup packed light brown sugar (divided)
- 4 tablespoons (¹/₂ stick) unsalted butter, cut into 8 pieces
- About 2 tablespoons whole milk or half-and-half

SAUCE

- 1 cup packed light brown sugar
- ³/₄ cup hot water
- 3 tablespoons unsalted butter, cut into chunks
- 2 tablespoons fresh lemon juice
- 2 tablespoons peach schnapps or peach brandy, or 2 tablespoons water plus ¹/₈ teaspoon almond extract
- ¹/₈ teaspoon ground cinnamon
- ¹/₂ teaspoon vanilla extract

Position a rack in the middle of the oven and preheat to 400 degrees F. Grease a 9-by-13-inch baking dish or coat with nonstick spray.

TO MAKE THE PASTRY: In a large bowl, thoroughly stir together the flour and salt. Add the shortening. Using a pastry blender, forks, or your fingertips, cut in until it is incorporated and the mixture has the consistency of coarse crumbs. Stir the almond extract into the ³/₄ cup ice water. Drizzle the water mixture over the flour mixture, tossing with a fork or mixing with your fingertips until evenly incorporated and the mixture holds together. If necessary, sprinkle more ice water a tablespoon at a time over the mixture until it holds together when pressed with your fingertips and is not at all dry. Knead until fairly smooth. Divide the dough in half. Shape each dough portion into a 3-by-8-inch log.

TIP

I prefer to peel peaches that are going to be cooked, but if you wish, you can leave the skins intact for this recipe. In this case, do as Mrs. D. A. Lincoln advised in her *Boston Cook Book* (1887) and wipe off the "wool" from the peaches first. A damp kitchen towel or paper towel works well.

Roll out one of the dough logs between sheets of baking parchment or wax paper until 12 inches wide and about 12½ inches long; if necessary, patch the dough to make the edges of the rectangle as even as possible. Occasionally check the underside of the dough during rolling and smooth out any wrinkles. Gently peel off the top sheet of paper, then pat back into place. Flip the dough; peel off the bottom sheet. Trim off any uneven edges. Using a sharp knife or pastry wheel, cut the dough in half lengthwise and crosswise to form four 6-inch squares. Repeat the process with the second dough portion. If the dough is warm and hard to handle, refrigerate briefly.

TO PREPARE THE PEACHES AND ASSEMBLE THE DUMPLINGS: One at a time, peel the pastry squares from the paper and lay on a clean sheet of baking parchment or wax paper. Center a peach half cut side up in the center of a pastry square. Sprinkle 2 tablespoons of the brown sugar on the peach half and top with 1 piece of the butter. Put a second peach half on top of the first and pull the four corners of the pastry up around the peach. (If the pastry square seems too small to wrap around the peach, press the dough out with your fingertips to make the square a little larger.) Pinch the four seams together very firmly so the peach is encased in the pastry; trim away any excess dough from the sides. Repeat with the remaining pastry squares and peaches. Arrange in the baking dish.

If desired, reserve any dough scraps and cut into small squares or other shapes and use to decorate the tops of the dumplings. Using a pastry brush, evenly brush the dumplings with milk.

Bake for 40 to 50 minutes, or until the dumplings are browned and the peaches are tender when pierced with a fork. If the dough begins to brown too rapidly, cover the dish with aluminum foil for the last 10 to 15 minutes of baking.

TO MAKE THE SAUCE: In a heavy 2-quart saucepan , stir together the brown sugar, hot water, butter, lemon juice, peach schnapps, and cinnamon. Bring to a gentle boil, stirring, over medium heat. Boil gently, stirring occasionally, for 3 minutes. Remove from the heat and add the vanilla; the sauce will be thin. When you remove the dumplings from the oven, drizzle about half the sauce over them. Reserve the remaining

REWRITING HISTORY

"It seems strange to many that there can be anything better than butter for cooking, or of greater utility than lard, and the advent of Crisco has been a shock to the older generation, born in an age less progressive than our own . . .

"But these good folk, when convinced are the greatest enthusiasts. Grandmother was glad to give up the fatiguing spinning wheel. So the modern woman is glad to stop cooking with expensive butter, animal lard and their inadequate substitutes.

"And so, the nation's cook book has been hauled out and is being revised. Upon thousands of pages, the words, 'lard' and 'butter' have been crossed out and the word 'Crisco' written in their place."

—Marion Harris Neil,
A Calendar of Dinners (1914)

sauce for serving. Let the dumplings stand for at least 30 minutes and preferably 1 hour. Spoon more sauce over each dumpling as they are served, or pass the sauce in a sauceboat.

The dumplings, sauced, will keep, covered, at room temperature for up to 24 hours or refrigerated for a day or so longer. Reheat to slightly warm before serving. Reheat the sauce to hot.

VARIATION: Apple Dumplings

Use 8 small, tart, flavorful apples (2½ inches in diameter); Jonathan, Empire, and Braeburn are good choices. To speed cooking, cut the apples into quarters rather than halves. Use apple brandy or apple juice in place of the peach brandy or peach schnapps. Proceed as for the peach dumplings.

A Peachy Reputation

When I visited Colorado several years ago and asked about the local food traditions, people immediately mentioned peaches, often boasting that those grown on the western slope of the Rocky Mountains are the sweetest, juiciest, best-tasting peaches in the nation.

Originally, much of the current western slope farmland was arid, rugged, and untamed. Then, in the late nineteenth and early twentieth centuries, irrigation canals and systems were dug to provide water from the Colorado, Gunnison, and Yampa rivers, and the northwestern part of the western slope became the region's fruit basket. Peaches, as well as apples, have long been premier crops there. The region's largest town, Grand Junction, held its first Peach Day in 1891 and celebrated it annually for a number of years. In 1909, President William Howard Taft visited the town's peach festival on his way to dedicate the Gunnison Tunnel and spoke glowingly of the fruit produced in the area. Colorado natives claim that certain minerals in the western slope soil are responsible for the exceptional flavor of their fruit.

cobblers, crisps, and other fruit desserts

4

Puddings, Custards, and Trifles

indian pudding

Many New Englanders have a fierce fondness for the comforting baked dessert known as Indian pudding. In my search for a good one, I went to those who know—Sheryl Julian and Julie Riven, writers for the *Boston Globe* and authors of *The Way We Cook*. This recipe is adapted from one that appeared in their *Boston Globe Magazine* column in 2001. It features an enticing spice combination—cinnamon, ginger, nutmeg, and cloves—and smells a little like gingerbread as it bakes. As is true of all authentic Indian puddings, this one is plain and honest, with a creamy texture and mild taste. It's guaranteed to take you back to a simpler time and place.

½ cup yellow cornmeal	½ cup maple syrup
1 teaspoon ground cinnamon	3 tablespoons packed dark brown sugar
1 teaspoon ground ginger	⅔ cup dried sweetened cranberries or dark raisins, or a combination
¼ teaspoon ground cloves	
¼ teaspoon freshly grated or ground nutmeg	2 large eggs
½ teaspoon salt	⅓ cup light or heavy (whipping) cream
3 cups whole milk	
1 tablespoon unsalted butter	Whipped cream or vanilla ice cream for serving (optional)

Position a rack in the middle of the oven and preheat to 300 degrees F. Grease an 8-inch square or 7-by-11-inch baking dish or coat with nonstick spray.

In a large heavy saucepan, whisk together the cornmeal, spices, and salt until blended. Gradually whisk in the milk until smooth. Cook over medium-high heat, whisking constantly, until the mixture comes to a full boil. Reduce the heat to medium and cook, whisking, until smooth and thickened, 2 to 3 minutes; be careful that the mixture doesn't scorch on the bottom. Immediately remove from the heat. Thoroughly whisk in the butter, maple syrup, brown sugar, and dried cranberries.

In a large bowl, lightly beat the eggs with a fork. A bit at a time, add the cornmeal mixture to the eggs, stirring constantly. Do this very gradually to avoid scrambling the eggs. Pour the mixture into the prepared dish.

Bake for 1 hour. Drizzle the pudding with the cream, tipping the dish back and forth until it covers the top. Continue baking for 15 to 20 minutes longer, or until the consistency is a little loose when the dish is jiggled. Transfer to a wire rack. Let cool for about 15 minutes. Spoon into bowls and serve with dollops of whipped cream or scoops of vanilla ice cream, if desired.

The pudding will keep, covered, in the refrigerator for 3 or 4 days. Reheat in a low oven to warm, if desired, before serving.

corn of plenty

Indian pudding has had a prominent position in the New England sweets repertoire for more than two centuries. Amelia Simmons's slender 1796 volume, *American Cookery*, included three recipes under the heading "A Nice Indian Pudding." The affection for the dish is doubtless partly due to the fact that a key ingredient, cornmeal, was a dietary staple and part of the region's history from the time the Pilgrims first struggled to survive at Plymouth. The dish was not made by the Native Americans there, but corn was so closely associated with them that the pudding was often called simply "Indian."

In a collection of letters (now known as *Mourt's Relation*) first published in 1622, an unidentified Pilgrim recounts:

> We set the last spring some twenty acres of Indian corn, and sowed some six acres of barley and pease, and according to the manner of the Indians, we manured our ground with herrings . . . Our corn did prove well, and God be praised, we had a good increase in Indian corn, and our barley indifferent good, and our pease not worth the gathering.

Roasted Pear Bread Pudding

I can't think of a more satisfying autumn fruit dessert than this one. The pear slices meld with the flavors of fresh ginger and lemon zest in a custardy base. The secret to this dish is in roasting the pears first, so don't be tempted to skip this step. The roasting concentrates the pear juices, heightening their gentle flavor and making the pears meltingly tender.

5 large Bosc or Bartlett pears (about 2 pounds), peeled, cored, and cut into 1/4-inch-thick slices

1 cup packed light brown sugar (divided)

1 tablespoon fresh lemon juice

3–4 tablespoons unsalted butter, softened

10–12 slices (1/3 inch thick) Italian or French bread, crust removed (scant half of a 1-pound loaf)

5 large eggs plus 2 large egg yolks

1 cup heavy (whipping) cream

2 1/3 cups milk

1 1/2 tablespoons peeled and finely minced fresh gingerroot

1 tablespoon very finely grated lemon zest (yellow part of skin)

2 teaspoons vanilla extract

1/4 teaspoon almond extract (optional)

1 tablespoon granulated sugar, combined with 1/4 teaspoon ground cinnamon, for garnish

Butterscotch Sauce (page 314) or Bourbon Sauce (page 230), warmed, for serving (optional)

Position a rack in the middle of the oven and preheat to 425 degrees F. Grease a 9-by-13-inch baking dish and a 10-by-15-inch or larger rimmed baking sheet or coat with nonstick spray. Spread the pears on the baking sheet. Sprinkle with 1/4 cup of the brown sugar and the lemon juice, gently turning to coat. Roast the pears, gently stirring and spooning their juice over them once or twice, until tender when tested with a fork, 8 to 12 minutes. Set aside. Turn off the oven.

Generously butter one side of each bread slice. Lay the slices buttered sides up in the baking dish, arranging them so that the bottom is completely covered. If necessary, cut or tear the slices so they fit snugly. Drizzle the juice from the pears evenly over the bread. Arrange the pear slices attractively on top.

In a large bowl using a fork, beat together the eggs, yolks, and remaining ¾ cup brown sugar until well blended. Add the cream and stir until the sugar completely dissolves. Stir in the milk, gingerroot, lemon zest, vanilla, and almond extract (if using). Pour the custard over the bread and pears. Lay a large sheet of baking parchment or wax paper over the top and press down to keep the bread submerged. Let stand for at least 20 minutes or refrigerate for several hours. Peel off the paper.

Preheat the oven to 325 degrees F. Carefully set the dish in a slightly larger roasting pan (or broiler pan). Place on the oven rack. Add ¾ inch hot water to the pan. Bake for 50 to 60 minutes, or until the pudding appears set except in the center, which should still be slightly jiggly when tapped. (A refrigerated pudding may take a little longer.) Transfer to a wire rack. Let cool for at least 30 minutes and preferably 1 hour. Sprinkle with the cinnamon-sugar mixture. Serve with warm sauce, if desired.

The pudding will keep, covered, in the refrigerator for up to 3 days. Let come to room temperature before serving.

steamed cranberry pudding with creamy butter-orange sauce

This is my updated version of a fine heirloom recipe shared with me by retired New Jersey cranberry grower Tom Darlington. His family has been prominent in the cranberry business in the Whitesbog area of the New Jersey Pine Barrens since the late 1860s. His grandfather J. J. White was the first to dig bogs and raise cranberries where they didn't originally grow. At the time, this approach was considered so preposterous that it was dubbed "White's Folly." By the early twentieth century, however, the J.J. White Company had become the largest cranberry operation in the state.

Tom says that his family has been enjoying this dessert at Thanksgiving and on other holidays for as long as he can remember. It was handed down from his aunt Elizabeth White. The pudding and sauce are a perfect pair: the cranberry pudding is moist, light, and bright with bits of berries, and the mild, buttery sauce provides balancing richness and sweetness. (Don't consider serving one without the other!)

PUDDING

- 2¼ cups fresh (or frozen, partially thawed) cranberries, coarsely chopped
- ½ cup sugar (divided)
- 1½ cups all-purpose flour
- 1 teaspoon baking soda
- ½ teaspoon ground cinnamon
- ¼ teaspoon ground cloves
- ¼ teaspoon ground nutmeg
- ¼ teaspoon salt
- ¾ teaspoon finely grated orange zest (orange part of skin)
- ⅓ cup orange juice
- ¼ cup light molasses
- 3 tablespoons unsalted butter, melted

SAUCE

- ⅔ cup sugar
- ⅔ cup heavy (whipping) cream
- 8 tablespoons (1 stick) unsalted butter, cut into chunks
- 2 tablespoons light corn syrup
- Generous ¼ teaspoon finely grated orange zest (orange part of skin)
- 1 teaspoon vanilla extract

TO MAKE THE PUDDING: Generously grease a 1½-quart pudding mold, small one-piece heatproof tube pan, or similar ring mold or generously coat with nonstick spray. Set out a deep pot or saucepan that is large enough to hold the mold. Place a wire rack (or collapsible vegetable steaming basket) in the pot bottom.

In a medium bowl, stir together the cranberries and 3 tablespoons of the sugar; set aside. In a large bowl, thoroughly stir together the flour, baking soda, cinnamon, cloves, nutmeg, and salt.

In a small bowl, stir together the orange zest, orange juice, molasses, and remaining 5 tablespoons sugar until the sugar dissolves. Add the molasses mixture and the butter to the dry ingredients, stirring just until evenly incorporated. Stir in the cranberries until evenly distributed. Turn out the batter into the mold or pan, spreading it to the edges. Cover the mold tightly with a lid or aluminum foil.

Add ¾ inch hot water to the pot. Set the mold on the rack in the pot, cover the pot, and bring the water to a simmer over medium-high heat. Lower the heat so the water simmers very gently. Gently simmer, checking the pot occasionally and replenishing the water, if needed, for 1½ to 2 hours, or until a wooden skewer inserted in the thickest part of the pudding comes out clean; the time will vary considerably depending on the mold. Transfer the pudding to a wire rack. Let cool until firmed up somewhat, about 30 minutes, but not completely cooled, or it may be difficult to unmold. Carefully run the tip of a table knife around the sides and center tube to loosen the pudding; invert and slide onto a serving plate. The pudding will keep, covered, in the refrigerator for up to 4 days. Reheat in a low oven (or in a microwave oven on medium power) until slightly warm before serving.

TO MAKE THE SAUCE: In a heavy 2-quart saucepan, thoroughly stir together the sugar, cream, butter, corn syrup, and orange zest. Cook over medium heat, stirring, until the sugar completely dissolves and the butter melts. Bring to a boil. Boil gently, stirring occasionally, for 2 minutes. Remove from the heat. Stir in the vanilla. The sauce will keep, covered, in the refrigerator for up to 4 days. Reheat in a saucepan over low heat, stirring (or in a microwave oven on medium power, stopping and stirring once), until the sugar dissolves and the mixture is warm and fluid. If necessary, thin it with a little hot water before serving.

Drizzle a little sauce over the pudding, cut into slices, and serve. Pass the remaining sauce in a pitcher or sauceboat.

Pecan-Coconut Bread Pudding

Toasted pecans and coconut give this easy but delicious bread pudding a decidedly southern feel, particularly if it's served with Bourbon Sauce (page 230).

- 4 cups cubed (¹/₃ inch) crusty French or Italian bread, including crust
- 1 cup shredded or flaked sweetened coconut
- ²/₃ cup coarsely chopped pecans
- 4 large eggs
- Scant ²/₃ cup packed light brown sugar
- 1¹/₄ cups whole milk
- 1 cup heavy (whipping) cream
- 1¹/₄ teaspoons vanilla extract
- ¹/₂ cup (3 ounces) semisweet chocolate morsels or mini-morsels (optional)
- Bourbon Sauce (page 230) or sweetened whipped cream for serving (optional)

Position a rack in the middle of the oven and preheat to 325 degrees F. Lightly grease a 7-by-11-inch (or similar) baking dish or coat with non-stick spray. Spread the bread cubes in the dish. Toast in the oven, stirring once or twice, until crisp, 11 to 15 minutes; set aside. Spread the coconut and pecans in a 10-by-15-inch rimmed baking sheet and toast in the oven, stirring every 3 minutes, until the pecans are fragrant and the coconut is nicely browned, 8 to 10 minutes; set aside.

In a medium bowl using a fork, beat the eggs until frothy and smooth. Add the brown sugar, stirring until it dissolves. Stir in the milk, cream, and vanilla until well blended. Sprinkle a generous half of the pecans and coconut, along with all the chocolate morsels (if using), over the bread. Pour the egg mixture on top. Lay a sheet of baking parchment or wax paper over the top and press down to keep the bread submerged. Let stand for 10 minutes. Peel off the paper. Evenly sprinkle the remaining pecans and coconut over the surface.

Set the dish in a slightly larger roasting pan (or broiler pan). Place on the oven rack. Add ¾ inch hot water to the pan. Bake just until the pudding feels set in the center when lightly tapped and is nicely browned on top, 35 to 45 minutes. Transfer to a wire rack. Let cool for at least 15 minutes. Serve spooned into bowls with the bourbon sauce or whipped cream, if desired.

The pudding will keep, covered, in the refrigerator for up to 4 days. Reheat to very warm but not hot just before serving.

chocolate
bread pudding

Early British colonists brought the custom of eating bread pudding with them to America, but no bread puddings of that era included chocolate. Chocolate bread pudding didn't start turning up until the end of the nineteenth century, when the American taste for all sorts of chocolate baked goods began to take hold.

This pudding features not only chocolate but also a little bourbon, some raisins, and a hint of spice—an indulgent combination. I like to serve it with bourbon sauce, but it is optional.

- 6 ounces bittersweet (not unsweetened) or semisweet chocolate, broken up or coarsely chopped
- 4 tablespoons (1/2 stick) unsalted butter, slightly softened
- 10 slices (1/3 inch thick) French or Italian bread, crust removed (scant half of a 1-pound loaf)
- 1/3 cup dark raisins
- 2 cups whole milk
- 1 cup heavy (whipping) cream
- 3 tablespoons good bourbon (optional)
- Scant 2/3 cup granulated sugar
- 4 large eggs, at room temperature
- 1/8 teaspoon freshly grated or ground nutmeg
- Generous pinch of ground cinnamon
- 1 1/2 teaspoons vanilla extract
- About 1 tablespoon powdered sugar for garnish
- Bourbon Sauce (page 230) or whipped cream for serving (optional)

Lightly grease a 7-by-11-inch (or similar) baking dish or coat with non-stick spray. In a microwave-safe medium bowl, microwave the chocolate on high power for 1 minute, stopping and stirring after 30 seconds. Continue microwaving on medium power, stopping and stirring at 30-second intervals, until the chocolate is mostly melted; let the residual heat finish the job. (Alternatively, in a heavy medium saucepan, warm the chocolate over lowest heat, stirring frequently, until just melted; be very careful not to let it burn. Immediately remove from the heat.)

Generously butter one side of each bread slice. Lay the slices buttered sides up in two overlapping rows in the dish. Sprinkle the raisins over and around the bread. In a 2-quart saucepan, heat the milk, cream, bourbon (if using), and granulated sugar over medium-high heat, stirring occasionally, until hot but not boiling. Remove from the heat. Gradually whisk 3/4 cup of the hot cream mixture into the melted chocolate until well blended. Whisk the chocolate mixture into the cream mixture.

In a medium bowl using a fork, beat together the eggs, nutmeg, cinnamon, and vanilla until well blended. In a thin stream, beat 1 cup of the chocolate mixture into the egg mixture. Add the egg mixture to the chocolate mixture, stirring until well blended. Slowly pour the chocolate mixture through a fine sieve over the bread. Lay a large sheet of baking parchment or wax paper over the top and press down to keep the bread submerged. Let the pudding stand for 15 minutes. Meanwhile, position a rack in the middle of the oven and preheat to 350 degrees F. Peel the paper from the pudding.

Carefully set the dish in a slightly larger roasting pan (or broiler pan). Place on the oven rack. Add ¾ inch hot water to the pan. Bake for 30 minutes. Lower the oven temperature to 325 degrees F. Bake just until the pudding puffs slightly and the center feels set when lightly tapped, 7 to 12 minutes longer. Transfer to a wire rack. Let cool for at least 15 minutes. Just before serving, lightly sift powdered sugar over the pudding. Serve with bourbon sauce or whipped cream, if desired.

The pudding will keep, covered, in the refrigerator for up to 3 days. Reheat to very warm but not hot just before serving.

pumpkin and cranberry bread pudding

When I came upon a pumpkin bread pudding a few years ago, it seemed like a tempting twentieth-century twist on an old English classic. Then a few weeks later, I read a 1749 entry in *Travels into North America,* in which the Swedish visitor Peter Kalm noted that settlers used pumpkin to make puddings and tarts.

Considering how long pumpkin puddings have been around, it's surprising that they aren't more widely prepared. This one has a soothing pumpkin-and-spice flavor and aroma, and it makes a fine, never-fail substitute for pumpkin pie at Thanksgiving. It's also ideal for fall and winter brunches.

4	large eggs
1	cup packed light or dark brown sugar, plus 3 tablespoons for sprinkling on pudding
1	cup whole milk
1	cup light or heavy (whipping) cream
1	15-ounce can solid-pack pumpkin (not seasoned pie filling)
2³⁄₄	teaspoons ground cinnamon
1	teaspoon ground ginger
³⁄₄	teaspoon ground allspice

5½ cups cubed (⅓ inch) crusty French or Italian bread, crust removed

¾ cup dried sweetened cranberries

Bourbon Sauce (page 230) or Brown Sugar–Orange Sauce (page 231) for serving (optional)

Ice cream or lightly sweetened whipped cream for serving (optional)

Position a rack in the middle of the oven and preheat to 325 degrees F. Lightly grease a 7-by-11-inch or 9-inch square baking dish or coat with nonstick spray.

In a large bowl using a wire whisk, beat the eggs until frothy and smooth. Add the brown sugar, whisking until the sugar dissolves. Whisk in the milk, cream, pumpkin, and spices until completely blended and smooth. Stir in the bread cubes and cranberries. Turn out the mixture into the dish, spreading to the edges. Lay a sheet of baking parchment or wax paper on the surface and press down to keep the bread submerged. Let stand for 10 minutes. Peel off and discard the paper.

Bake for 25 minutes. Sprinkle the remaining 3 tablespoons brown sugar over the pudding and continue baking just until the center of the pudding is firm when lightly tapped, 12 to 17 minutes longer. Transfer to a

tip

If preparing this recipe for a crowd, you may want to double it. Bake it in a 9-by-13-inch baking dish (which will be very full) for 35 minutes, then sprinkle on the brown sugar and continue baking until the center is firm when lightly tapped, 20 to 30 minutes longer.

wire rack. Let cool for at least 15 minutes. Serve spooned into bowls. Drizzle with sauce and/or garnish with scoops of ice cream or dollops of whipped cream, if desired.

The pudding will keep, covered, in the refrigerator for up to 4 days. Reheat to very warm but not hot just before serving.

souffLéd whiskey bread pudding with meringue

Meringue-topped bread puddings are popular in parishes around New Orleans. The recipe for this one was inspired by a signature dessert long served at the famed New Orleans restaurant Commander's Palace. An important part of its appeal is the contrasting texture of the fruit-studded pudding and the puffy, not-too-sweet meringue. Thanks to the bourbon, both the pudding and the accompanying sauce pack a punch. A good all-American bourbon is de rigueur.

Note that the recipe is unusual in that the bread-and-custard part of the dish is twice-baked.

BREAD PUDDING

- ¾ cup dried sweetened cherries or golden raisins
- ⅓ cup good bourbon
- 4½ cups cubed (½ inch) airy French or Italian bread, crust removed
- 3 large eggs plus 4 large egg yolks
  Generous ½ cup sugar
- 1 cup whole milk
- ½ cup heavy (whipping) cream
- 2½ teaspoons vanilla extract
- ¾ teaspoon ground nutmeg
- ½ teaspoon ground cinnamon
- ⅛ teaspoon salt
  Scant ½ teaspoon finely grated orange zest (orange part of skin)

MERINGUE

- 1¼ cups egg whites (about 10 large), completely free of yolk and at room temperature
- ½ teaspoon cream of tartar
- ⅛ teaspoon salt
- 1 cup sugar
- 1 teaspoon vanilla extract

  Bourbon Sauce (page 230) for serving

TO MAKE THE PUDDING: Position a rack in the middle of the oven and preheat to 350 degrees F. Lightly grease a 7-by-11-inch (or similar) baking dish or coat with nonstick spray. In a small bowl, combine the cherries and bourbon. Set aside.

Spread the bread cubes on a rimmed baking sheet. Toast in the oven, stirring once or twice, until just slightly crisp, about 10 minutes. Turn out the bread into the dish. Sprinkle the bourbon and cherries evenly over the bread.

In a medium bowl using a fork, beat the eggs and yolks until frothy and smooth. Add the sugar, stirring until dissolved. Stir in the milk, cream, vanilla, nutmeg, cinnamon, salt, and orange zest until well blended. Pour the egg mixture over the bread. Lay a large sheet of baking parchment or wax paper over the top and press down to keep the bread submerged. Let stand for 10 minutes. Peel off and discard the paper.

Carefully set the dish in a slightly larger roasting pan or broiler pan. Place on the oven rack. Add ¾ inch hot water to the pan. Bake just until the pudding feels set in the center when lightly tapped and is lightly browned on top, 30 to 35 minutes. Transfer to a wire rack. Let cool while you prepare the meringue. Or let cool completely, then cover and refrigerate for up to 48 hours. Rewarm slightly in a 325 degree F oven before continuing.

TO MAKE THE MERINGUE: In a completely grease-free large bowl using a mixer (with a whisk-shaped beater, if available), beat the egg whites, cream of tartar, and salt on low speed for 30 seconds. Gradually raise the speed to medium and continue beating until the whites are frothy and opaque. As soon as the whites just begin to form soft peaks (lift the beater[s] to check), add 2 tablespoons of the sugar. Raise the speed to medium-high and beat for 30 seconds. Add the remaining sugar 2 tablespoons at a time, beating for about 20 seconds after each addition and scraping down the sides of the bowl as needed. Add the vanilla. Beat on high speed just until the meringue stands in glossy but not dry peaks, 1 to 2 minutes longer.

TO BAKE THE SOUFFLÉD PUDDING AND MERINGUE: Reduce the oven temperature to 325 degrees F. Generously grease a 9-by-13-inch baking dish or generously coat with nonstick spray. Scoop up all of the bread pudding by spoonfuls and place in a large bowl. Lightly fold half the meringue mixture into the pudding until mostly incorporated; some streaks may remain. Spread the pudding mixture evenly in the baking dish. Using an offset spatula or a table knife, spread the remaining meringue evenly over the pudding top until it touches the edges all around, swirling it attractively.

Bake for 15 to 20 minutes, or until the meringue is tinged with brown all over. If necessary to promote even browning, reverse the pan from front to back halfway through baking. Serve immediately, spooning the pudding onto dessert plates or into bowls. Pass the bourbon sauce separately.

"Promptitude is necessary in all our actions, but never more so than when engaged in making cakes and puddings."

—Mary Randolph,
The Virginia Housewife (1860)

Lemon Fluff pudding

Makes 6 to 8 servings

This easy lemony pudding has been on the American scene in its present form since about 1930, though it probably evolved from several somewhat similar late-nineteenth-century pudding-like desserts. It is sometimes called magical pudding, or mystery or amazing pudding, because the thin batter separates into a light cakelike layer on top and lemon custard sauce on the bottom. It's reminiscent of a very fluffy pudding cake.

The recipe was inspired partly by the enormously popular lemon chiffon pudding featured at Zola restaurant in Washington, D.C. Former Zola chef Phillip Carroll says he based the dessert on one that his mom used to serve him. Another inspiration was a lemon pudding from *The Fannie Farmer Cookbook* that my mother occasionally made when I was a child. Both Carroll's recipe and *Fannie Farmer*'s call for serving it chilled. In cool weather, however, the pudding is also good served slightly warm.

Zola presents its pudding in individual baking dishes, with a few raspberries baked into the bottom and with fresh raspberries and whipped cream garnishing the top. The baked-in raspberries are a particularly nice touch. To make individual puddings, see the variation.

Generous 1 cup raspberries (divided; optional)
1 cup sugar (divided)
6 tablespoons all-purpose flour
1/8 teaspoon salt
Pinch of baking soda
Generous 1 1/2 tablespoons very finely grated lemon zest (yellow part of skin)
Generous 1/2 cup fresh lemon juice

5 tablespoons unsalted butter, melted
1 1/2 teaspoons vanilla extract
6 large egg yolks
1 1/2 cups whole milk
5 large egg whites, completely free of yolk and at room temperature
Whipped cream for serving (optional)

Position a rack in the middle of the oven and preheat to 325 degrees F. Generously grease a 2-quart round casserole or soufflé dish or generously coat with nonstick spray. Sprinkle half the berries, if using, in the bottom of the casserole.

In a large bowl, thoroughly stir together 3/4 cup of the sugar, the flour, salt, and baking soda. Using a wire whisk, gradually mix in the lemon zest, lemon juice, butter, and vanilla until well blended and free of lumps. Thoroughly whisk in the egg yolks, then the milk, until smooth.

In a completely grease-free large bowl using a mixer (with a whisk-shaped beater, if available), beat the egg whites on medium speed until frothy and opaque. Continue beating for several minutes, or until soft peaks just begin to form. Gradually add 1 tablespoon of the remaining sugar and beat for 30 seconds. Raise the speed to medium-high. Very slowly add the remaining 3 tablespoons sugar, beating until the mixture just stands in soft peaks; be careful not to overbeat. Fold the egg white mixture into the yolk mixture just until no white streaks remain. Turn out the mixture into the casserole.

Carefully set the dish in a slightly larger roasting pan (or broiler pan). Place on the oven rack. Add ¾ inch hot water to the pan. Bake for 45 to 55 minutes, or until the pudding is barely firm when tapped in the center and the top is tinged with brown. Transfer to a wire rack. Let cool for at least 15 minutes. Spoon the pudding into bowls and serve warm, or refrigerate for at least 1 hour before serving. Garnish with the remaining raspberries, if using, and whipped cream, if desired.

The pudding will keep, covered, in the refrigerator for 3 or 4 days. If desired, rewarm it, covered, in a 250 degree F oven before serving.

VARIATION: Individual Puddings

Spread a few raspberries in the bottom of each of six 6-ounce custard cups or ramekins. Divide the pudding evenly among the cups. Place them in a roasting pan. Proceed exactly as for the original recipe, except bake for 30 to 40 minutes, or until the puddings are barely firm when tapped in the centers and the tops are tinged with brown. Makes 6 servings.

banana pudding

makes about 8 servings

If you grew up in the South, chances are you like banana pudding. According to southern cooking expert Bill Neal, this comfy, home-kitchen dessert evolved from English
and colonial American trifle recipes, which incorporate fruit and pastry cream or
vanilla custard. Today banana puddings are standard fare in restaurants in the region,
although most versions substitute commercial vanilla wafers for a traditional trifle's
ladyfingers or chunks of cake. They also omit brandy, sherry, or other spirits, which trifles often contain.

This fine banana pudding is adapted from an old family recipe shared with me by
Marie Kahn of Wilmington, North Carolina. Her grandmother "Ma-maw" prepared the
pudding for her when she had her tonsils out at age three. She says that when she
makes it for her own children and grandchildren, "they think they've died and gone to
heaven." Her recipe predates the vanilla wafer era of the 1920s and calls for ladyfingers
or sponge cake. I prefer the pudding made with ladyfingers (I use store-bought ones),
but good vanilla wafers are fine, too. Don't substitute boxed vanilla pudding for homemade: it's the combination of real vanilla custard and ripe bananas that makes this
recipe.

3 cups whole milk

4 large eggs plus 4 large egg yolks

Scant ⅔ cup sugar

Generous ¼ teaspoon salt

2½ tablespoons unsalted butter, cut into chunks

1¼ teaspoons vanilla extract

⅛ teaspoon almond extract

About 36 ladyfingers, 4 cups cubed sponge
cake, or 2½ cups vanilla wafers (divided)

4–5 large ripe bananas

2 tablespoons orange juice

Lightly sweetened whipped cream
for garnish

About ¼ cup unblanched sliced almonds
for garnish (optional)

In a 4-cup measure using a fork, beat together the milk, eggs, and yolks
until well blended. Microwave on high power for 5 to 7 minutes, stopping
and stirring after each minute, until the mixture is just hot to the touch;
do not let boil. (Alternatively, heat the milk, eggs, and yolks in a heavy
medium saucepan over low heat, stirring, until hot. Remove from the
heat.)

212   THE ALL-AMERICAN DESSERT BOOK

In a double-boiler top, stir together the sugar and salt. Set over 1 inch of gently boiling water. Stirring briskly, slowly add the hot milk mixture until smoothly incorporated. Cook, stirring constantly, until the custard thickens to the consistency of very thick heavy cream and coats the spoon, 8 to 12 minutes. Stir in the butter, vanilla, and almond extract until the butter melts. Strain the custard through a medium-fine sieve into a large bowl. Lay a sheet of plastic wrap directly on the custard surface. Refrigerate until thoroughly cooled, at least 1½ hours and up to 2 days.

Arrange half the ladyfingers in the bottom of a 2-quart glass serving bowl or trifle bowl. Peel the bananas; cut into ¼-inch-thick slices. Sprinkle with the orange juice. Arrange half the bananas over the ladyfingers. Pour half the cooled custard evenly over the bananas. Rap the bowl on the counter several times to even the surface. Repeat with the remaining ladyfingers, remaining bananas, and remaining custard. Just before serving, generously top with rosettes of whipped cream. Sprinkle with sliced almonds, if desired.

The pudding will keep, tightly covered, in the refrigerator for up to 4 days.

TOP BANANA TOWN

Joseph Dabney, author of the award-winning *Smokehouse Ham, Spoon Bread, & Scuppernong Wine*, says that the South's taste for bananas dates back to the late 1800s, when the fruit first started arriving at port cities such as Charleston and New Orleans. The bananas then went by rail to the nation's interior, where they were enthusiastically received.

Until recently the town of Fulton, Kentucky, which was once a distribution and repacking center for more than half of all the bananas imported into the country, called itself the Banana Capital of the United States. For many years the town celebrated its former top-banana status by making a one-ton banana pudding at an annual banana festival.

chocoLate pudding

Fewer and fewer children these days have experienced the simple, soothing pleasure of homemade chocolate pudding. And that's a shame. From-scratch chocolate pudding is smooth and not too thick and has an enormously satisfying, though not overwhelming, chocolate taste. The flavor comes from including both cocoa powder and chocolate and from not adding the chocolate until the end. (Chocolate tastes best when it is simply melted, not cooked.) The ample addition of good vanilla helps round out the taste, too.

Note that the basic pudding recipe can be altered to make an excellent chocolate pie filling (see the variation).

²/₃ cup sugar

3¹/₂ tablespoons cornstarch

3 tablespoons unsweetened, nonalkalized American-style cocoa powder or unsweetened Dutch-process cocoa powder, sifted after measuring if lumpy

¹/₈ teaspoon salt

3¹/₂ cups whole or reduced-fat (not skim) milk (divided)

2 tablespoons unsalted butter (optional)

4 ounces bittersweet (not unsweetened) or semisweet chocolate, broken up or coarsely chopped

2¹/₂ teaspoons vanilla extract

Lightly sweetened whipped cream for serving (optional)

In a large heavy saucepan, stir together the sugar, cornstarch, cocoa powder, and salt until well blended. Add about ¾ cup of the milk, stirring until smoothly incorporated. Gradually stir in the remaining milk and the butter (if using). Bring to a boil over medium heat, stirring. Constantly stirring and scraping the pan bottom to prevent scorching, continue cooking until the mixture bubbles and thickens slightly, 2 to 2½ minutes. Immediately remove from the heat. Add the chocolate, stirring until it completely melts and the mixture is smooth. Stir in the vanilla.

Strain the pudding through a medium-fine sieve into individual pudding dishes or a serving bowl. If you wish to prevent a skin from forming on the surface, lay plastic wrap directly on the pudding. Cover and refrigerate for at least 2½ hours. Serve with dollops of whipped cream, if desired.

The pudding will keep in the refrigerator for up to 2 days.

tip

It's fine to use low-fat milk in this recipe, but if you wish to enrich the pudding a bit, add the optional butter. If you use skim milk, the pudding will lack flavor.

VARIATION: Chocolate Pie Filling

Make the recipe exactly as for the pudding, but use ¼ cup cornstarch. After adding the vanilla, strain the mixture through a fine sieve into a fully baked and cooled 9-inch pie shell. Cover and refrigerate for at least 8 hours and up to 24 hours before serving. Serve generously topped with whipped cream.

maple-glazed maple custards

This baked custard dessert is reminiscent of classic French crème caramel but features a regional American twist. Instead of being lined with caramel, the custard cups are coated with boiled-down maple syrup, which becomes a sauce for the finished custards when they are turned out of their cups. I've also played up the maple flavor by substituting maple syrup for sugar in the custard mixture.

Pure maple syrup has such a subtle fragrance and taste that it is overwhelmed in many desserts. Here, however, its enticing mellow essence comes through.

MAPLE GLAZE

Generous ½ cup maple syrup

1½ tablespoons light corn syrup

CUSTARDS

2⅔ cups whole milk

Pinch of salt

3 large eggs plus 3 large egg yolks

½ cup maple syrup

1 teaspoon vanilla extract

¼ cup Pecan Praline (page 46) for garnish (optional)

Position a rack in the middle of the oven and preheat to 325 degrees F. Set eight 6- to 8-ounce custard cups or ramekins in a roasting pan large enough to hold the cups without touching one another. Warm the cups by adding about ½ inch hot water to the pan. If testing doneness using the ice water method, set out a small cup of cold water and add 3 ice cubes.

TO MAKE THE MAPLE GLAZE: In a heavy, nonreactive 2-quart saucepan, bring the maple syrup and corn syrup to a boil over medium heat. Boil, occasionally lifting the pan and gently swirling, for 2 minutes. If using a candy thermometer, clip to the pan side, with the tip submerged but not touching the pan bottom. Boil until the mixture registers 238 to 240 degrees F, 2 to 5 minutes longer, swirling the pan occasionally; the temperature may rise very rapidly as it nears 240 degrees. (Alternatively, to test without a thermometer, begin occasionally checking the syrup for doneness by dropping a small amount into the ice water. When the syrup forms a firm, almost hard ball when squeezed, it is done.) Immediately remove from the heat.

TIPS

The maple glaze is most easily prepared using a candy thermometer, but you can also check for doneness by using the ice water test (see page 323).

Be sure to include the corn syrup in the maple glaze. Maple syrup often becomes grainy when cooked down, and the corn syrup keeps the glaze smooth.

Working very carefully (the glaze is extremely hot) and dividing the syrup equally, pour it into the cups; immediately tip each cup to coat the entire bottom. Set the coated cups aside to allow the glaze to harden. If the syrup stiffens as you are pouring it, reheat it just until fluid and continue pouring.

TO MAKE THE CUSTARDS: In a 4-cup measure, microwave the milk and salt on high power for 4 to 5 minutes, stopping and stirring every minute, until steaming hot but not boiling. (Alternatively, heat the milk and salt in a medium saucepan over medium-high heat until steaming hot. Remove from the heat.) Set aside to let cool slightly. In a large bowl, beat the eggs, yolks, and maple syrup with a fork until well blended. Gradually beat in about a third of the milk, then slowly beat the remaining milk into the egg mixture. Stir in the vanilla. Strain the mixture through a fine sieve into a large measure and divide the mixture among the cups. Discard the water in the roasting pan and return the custard cups to it. Place the pan on the oven rack. Add hot water until it comes ¾ inch up the sides of the cups.

Bake for 33 to 43 minutes, or until the custards appear set when the cups are jiggled and tapped in the center. (The baking time will vary considerably depending on whether glass or ceramic cups are used; glass will take longer.) Transfer the roasting pan to a wire rack. Let cool for a few minutes. Transfer the cups to the rack and let cool completely. Cover and refrigerate until cold, at least 1½ hours and up to 3 days. (After 1½ days, the maple will thin out somewhat, but the custards will taste just as good.)

To serve, run a knife around each custard to loosen it, then invert it onto a serving plate. Sprinkle with bits of pecan praline, if desired.

sipping sap

"The Maple is also a good wood . . . That tree has sap different from that of all others. There it is made from a beverage very pleasing to drink, of the colour of Spanish wine but not so good. It has a sweetness which renders it of very good taste; it does not inconvenience the stomach . . . This is the drink of the Indians, and even of the French, who are fond of it."

–Nicolas Denys,
Histoire naturelle des Peuples, des Animaux, des Arbres et Plantes de l'Amérique Septentrionale
(Natural History of the People, Animals, Trees and Plants of North America, 1672)

caramel-Butterscotch baked custards

There's no more soothing dessert than a simple baked custard. It's the kind of fare American mothers have successfully supplied to cure cranky or ailing children for several centuries, no doubt because it's mild and smooth enough to slip down easily. My mother offered me traditional, nutmeg-dusted egg custard whenever I had a sore throat, and just like chicken soup, it always made me feel better.

This custard has the same silky texture as the classic version, but it has more body and richness, as well as a seductive caramel and brown sugar flavor. Somehow it is both plain enough to satisfy children's tastes and sophisticated enough to appeal to adults.

6 tablespoons granulated sugar	3 large eggs plus 3 large egg yolks, well beaten
1 tablespoon light or dark corn syrup	2 teaspoons vanilla extract
3 tablespoons water	Lightly sweetened whipped cream for serving (optional)
1 cup heavy (whipping) cream (divided)	
1/2 cup packed dark brown sugar	
1/8 teaspoon salt	
2 1/4 cups whole milk	

Position a rack in the middle of the oven and preheat to 325 degrees F. Lightly grease six 6-ounce or eight 4-ounce custard cups or ramekins or coat with nonstick spray. Lay a tea towel or several thicknesses of paper towels in the bottom of a roasting pan large enough to hold the cups compactly but without touching one another; this will insulate the cups from the heat of the pan bottom. Arrange the cups, slightly separated, in the pan.

In a heavy 2-quart saucepan, stir together the granulated sugar, corn syrup, and water with a wooden spoon. Bring to a boil over medium-high heat, stirring until the sugar dissolves. Wipe any sugar from the pan sides using a pastry brush dipped in warm water or a damp paper towel. Continue cooking without stirring, but swirling the mixture in the pan occasionally, until it colors and turns a rich amber, 4 to 5 minutes. To avoid overcooking, immediately remove the pan from the heat. Standing back to avoid splattering and steam and using a clean long-handled wooden spoon, gradually stir half the cream into the pan. Continue stirring until the bubbling subsides and the mixture is smooth. Stir in the remaining cream, the brown sugar, and salt until the sugar completely

tip

It takes gentle, even heat to yield voluptuously smooth baked custards, which is why the cups are set in a hot water bath. If your oven has hot spots, carefully rotate the pan from front to back halfway through baking.

dissolves. Whisk in the milk, then the eggs and yolks and the vanilla, until well blended. Pour the mixture through a fine sieve into a 4-cup measure. Pour the custard into the cups, which should be fairly full.

Place the roasting pan on the oven rack. Add hot water until it comes at least two thirds up the sides of the cups. Bake until the custards appear set except in the centers when the cups are jiggled and a small knife inserted halfway between the edge and the center of one custard comes out clean, 25 to 35 minutes. (Ceramic cups tend to bake much more quickly than glass ones, and smaller ones faster than larger ones.) Carefully transfer the cups to a wire rack. Let cool. Cover and refrigerate for at least 3 hours. Serve with dollops of whipped cream, if desired.

The custards will keep in the refrigerator for up to 3 days.

words of
kitchen wisdom

"For all baked Puddings butter your Pan or Dish you bake in."

—Anne Gibbons Gardiner,
Mrs. Gardiner's Family Receipts from 1763

Blackberry or Raspberry FOOLS

Kin to custards, puddings, and creams, fools originated in sixteenth-century England and eventually became part of the dessert repertoire of colonial America. Today they rarely turn up, which is too bad, since they make a light and festive ending to a warm-weather meal.

Originally, fools were simple custard and fruit desserts, but by the nineteenth century the custard had sometimes been replaced by cream. Gradually, these desserts became more like parfaits. Early English fools very often called for gooseberries, but blackberry or raspberry versions are tastier and more colorful. My updated fool has an airy yet creamy texture, a rich berry flavor, and a very pretty, summery appearance. I like it best with blackberries, but raspberries are good, too.

6–7 tablespoons sugar (use larger amount if berries are very tart)

1 tablespoon arrowroot powder or cornstarch

3 cups blackberries or raspberries, plus 1 cup whole blackberries or raspberries for garnish

Generous pinch of grated lemon zest (yellow part of skin)

1 tablespoon fresh lemon juice

1 tablespoon blackberry brandy, peach brandy, or kirsch (optional)

1/2 cup heavy (whipping) cream

3/4 cup vanilla yogurt (not nonfat), preferably creamy or custard-style containing gelatin

Mint leaves for garnish (optional)

In a nonreactive medium saucepan, stir together the sugar and arrowroot powder until well blended. Stir in the blackberries, lemon zest, lemon juice, and brandy (if using) until thoroughly incorporated. Bring to a simmer over medium heat, stirring until the sugar dissolves. Continue simmering, stirring occasionally, for about 2 minutes, or until the berries release their juice and the mixture turns translucent. Let stand off the heat for 5 minutes. Press the mixture through a fine sieve into a bowl, forcing through as much juice and pulp as possible; discard the seeds. Refrigerate for at least 45 minutes, or until cold. The mixture will keep, covered, in the refrigerator for 3 or 4 days.

In a medium bowl, whip the cream to firm peaks. Lightly fold the yogurt and all but 1/3 cup of the blackberry mixture into the cream until smooth.

Tip

If you use a vanilla yogurt containing gelatin, you can make the fools up to 2 days in advance. Otherwise, make them no more than a few hours ahead, or the yogurt may weep.

Spoon the mixture into parfait, sherbet, or other attractive glass dishes, drizzling each layer with a little of the reserved blackberry mixture and tucking a few blackberries here and there. Garnish each dish with several blackberries. To serve, garnish with mint leaves, if desired.

The fools will keep, carefully covered with plastic wrap, in the refrigerator for up to 2 days.

AT RIGHT

VANILLA AND
CHOCOLATE TRIFLE
WITH BLACKBERRY AND
APRICOT SAUCES

PAGE 224

vanilla and chocolate trifle with blackberry and apricot sauces

The flavors of this large, striking trifle are complex yet complementary—berry, fruit, chocolate, vanilla, and fruit brandy. The brilliant, rippled colors of the blackberry and apricot sauces set each other off perfectly. Presented in a dramatic glass trifle bowl, this party dish draws raves.

To save time, you can use a store-bought pound cake, but for best flavor, make Plain Pound Cake (page 109). (You'll need only about a third of the homemade cake.)

VANILLA AND CHOCOLATE PASTRY CREAMS

- 1 cup granulated sugar
- ¼ cup cornstarch
- 1 teaspoon grated lemon zest (yellow part of skin)
- 6 tablespoons apricot brandy, peach brandy, or orange juice (divided)
- 8 large egg yolks
- 2½ cups milk
- 2 cups heavy (whipping) cream
- ¼ teaspoon salt
- 1 tablespoon vanilla extract
- 4 ounces bittersweet (not unsweetened) or semisweet chocolate, broken up or coarsely chopped

SAUCES, CAKE, AND BERRIES

- Blackberry Sauce (page 319; divided)
- Apricot-Orange Sauce (page 227; divided)
- 6½ cups cubed (¾ inch) vanilla pound cake, crust removed (12–14 ounces cake; divided)
- 4 tablespoons apricot brandy, peach brandy, or orange juice (divided)
- 2½–3 cups blackberries (divided)

WHIPPED CREAM

- 1¼ cups heavy (whipping) cream
- ¼ cup powdered sugar
- ½ teaspoon vanilla extract

Whole blackberries and/or dried apricot slivers for garnish

TO MAKE THE PASTRY CREAMS: In a large heavy saucepan, whisk together the sugar, cornstarch, and lemon zest until well blended. Whisk in the brandy and egg yolks until smoothly combined. Whisk in the milk, cream, and salt. Bring to a boil over medium heat, whisking. Gently boil, whisking, for 2 minutes. Don't undercook, or the pastry creams may thin out later. Remove from the heat and stir in the vanilla. Strain through a fine sieve into a large bowl. Measure out 2½ cups of the pastry cream and transfer to a storage container. Lay a piece of plastic wrap directly on the pastry cream. Cover and refrigerate for at least 1½ hours and up to 3 days. Stir the chocolate into the remaining mixture

Tip

To prepare the trifle, including the whipped cream, ahead, make it with Stabilized Whipped Cream (page 226). It will hold its shape.

until the chocolate melts and the pastry cream is smooth and slightly thickened. Lay a sheet of plastic wrap directly on the pastry cream. Cover and refrigerate for at least 1½ hours and up to 3 days.

TO ASSEMBLE THE TRIFLE: Pour ⅓ cup of the blackberry sauce and ⅓ cup of the apricot sauce into a 3- to 4-quart footed trifle bowl or similar glass serving bowl. Swirl with a spoon to mingle the sauces slightly. Tip the bowl from side to side to form an even layer of sauce on the bottom. Lay half the cake cubes over the sauce. Sprinkle with 2 tablespoons of the brandy. Sprinkle half of the fresh berries on the cake, arranging a few against the glass so they will be visible from the outside. Pour half of the chocolate pastry cream over the berries, smoothing to form an even layer. (If the chocolate mixture is very stiff, thin it before using by stirring in up to 2 tablespoons warm water.) Stir the vanilla pastry cream. Pour half of it over the chocolate pastry cream. Using half the remaining blackberry sauce and half the remaining apricot sauce, pour 4 or 5 pools of each on the vanilla mixture; let some of the fruit sauces drip attractively down the insides of the bowl. Holding a table knife vertically, swirl the blackberry and apricot sauces together just slightly.

Repeat the process by adding the remaining cake cubes, brandy, berries, chocolate pastry cream, and vanilla pastry cream. Neatly add pools of the remaining blackberry and apricot sauces. Using a knife, swirl the two together to form an attractive rippled surface. Cover the trifle with plastic wrap (it should not touch the sauces) and refrigerate for at least 2 hours and up to 3 days.

TO MAKE THE WHIPPED CREAM: Shortly before serving, in a large bowl using a mixer (with a whisk-shaped beater, if available), beat the cream on high speed just to soft peaks. On low, then medium speed, beat in the powdered sugar and vanilla until stiff but not dry. Using a pastry bag fitted with a large open-star tip, pipe whipped cream rosettes in a ring around the edge of the bowl. If desired, finish with a group of rosettes in the center. (Alternatively, dollop the whipped cream attractively over the top.) Garnish the rosettes (or dollops) with whole berries and/or dried apricot slivers. Serve any leftover whipped cream separately in a small bowl, if desired.

VARIATION: Stabilized Whipped Cream

For convenience, prepare stabilized whipped cream using the following variation and complete the piping of the trifle in advance.

Sprinkle ½ teaspoon unflavored gelatin over 2 teaspoons cold water in a small cup. Stir and set aside until the gelatin softens, about 5 minutes. Combine the gelatin mixture and ¼ cup heavy (whipping) cream in a small saucepan. Heat over medium-high heat, stirring just until the gelatin completely dissolves. Remove from the heat and stir ¼ cup more cream into the gelatin mixture until well blended. Combine the gelatin-cream mixture and the remaining ¾ cup cream in large bowl. Refrigerate until well chilled, at least 30 minutes and preferably 45 minutes.

Using a mixer (with a whisk-shaped beater, if available), whip the cream on high speed to soft peaks. Reduce the speed and beat in the powdered sugar and vanilla. Increase the speed to high and beat for 1 minute more. (It's normal for stabilized whipped cream to be softer and less airy than regular whipped cream.) Cover and refrigerate the whipped cream until it firms up enough to pipe, at least 25 to 30 minutes and up to 2 days. Up to 8 hours ahead, pipe the whipped cream on the trifle. Cover and refrigerate until serving time. Garnish with the dried apricot slivers and/or fresh berries shortly before serving.

apricot-orange
sauce

Makes a scant 2 cups

The vivid apricot-orange color and intense fruit flavor of this trifle sauce comes from combining orange juice and zest with dried and canned apricots. It also looks beautiful drizzled on a dessert plate with a slice of Bourbon-Pecan Fudge Cake (page 137) or Molten Lava Chocolate Soufflé Cakes (page 140).

1¼ cups orange juice, plus more if needed (divided)

¾ cup finely chopped dried apricots, preferably American

5 tablespoons sugar

Generous ¼ teaspoon grated orange zest (orange part of skin)

3 tablespoons apricot brandy, peach brandy, or peach schnapps, or 3 tablespoons water plus ¼ teaspoon almond extract

4 canned whole apricots (or 8 halves) in syrup, pitted and drained

1–2 teaspoons fresh lemon juice, to taste (optional)

In a heavy, nonreactive medium saucepan, combine 1 cup of the orange juice, the dried apricots, sugar, and orange zest. Bring to a simmer over medium heat. Adjust the heat so the mixture simmers gently. Cook, stirring occasionally, for 15 to 20 minutes, or until most of the juice is absorbed and the apricots are very tender. Watch to be sure the pan doesn't boil dry and add a tablespoon of water, if necessary. Transfer to a food processor. Add the brandy and canned apricots. Process for 4 to 5 minutes, or until completely smooth. Add the remaining ¼ cup orange juice and process to incorporate. The sauce should be slightly fluid; if necessary, add a bit more orange juice to thin it further. Taste and add the lemon juice, if desired.

Pour the sauce into an airtight storage container. Refrigerate for at least 1 hour. Stir before serving.

The sauce will keep in the refrigerator for up to 1 week.

Tip
If possible, use American apricots in this sauce; they have a brighter orange color and a more intense, tarter flavor than most imported varieties.

very Berry Trifle

This is an eye-catching confection of liquor-spiked pastry cream, cake, strawberries and raspberries, and whipped cream. Trifles date back to England and were popular in the colonial era. Records show that Martha Washington served them at official presidential functions. Lately they have had a resurgence in America, turning up more splendiferous and delectable than ever before. Since they are best made ahead, they are a good choice for dinner parties and dessert buffets.

PASTRY CREAM

- ¾ cup plus 2 tablespoons granulated sugar
- ¼ cup cornstarch
- 1 teaspoon grated lemon zest (yellow part of skin)
- ¼ cup medium-dry sherry or orange juice
- 7 large egg yolks
- 2½ cups milk
- 1 cup heavy (whipping) cream
- ⅛ teaspoon salt
- 2½ teaspoons vanilla extract
  Generous ¼–½ teaspoon almond extract (use larger amount if using orange juice)

BERRY SAUCE

- 2 cups frozen (thawed) raspberries in sugar or syrup (about a 1-pound package)
- 2 tablespoons cornstarch or arrowroot powder
- 3 tablespoons medium-dry sherry or orange juice
- 2 cups frozen (thawed) sliced strawberries in sugar or syrup (about a 1-pound package)
- 2–4 teaspoons fresh lemon juice, to taste

CAKE AND BERRIES

- 6½ cups cubed (¾ inch) pound cake, crust removed (12–15 ounces cake; divided)
- ¼ cup medium-dry sherry or orange juice (divided)
- 4 cups small, hulled whole strawberries or coarsely sliced large strawberries (divided)
- 2½ cup raspberries (divided)

WHIPPED CREAM

- 1½ cups heavy (whipping) cream
- ¼ cup powdered sugar
- ½ teaspoon vanilla extract

  Hulled whole strawberries and whole red raspberries for garnish

TO MAKE THE PASTRY CREAM: In a heavy medium saucepan, stir together the sugar, cornstarch, and lemon zest until well blended. Whisk in the sherry and egg yolks until smooth. Whisk in the milk, cream, and salt. Bring to a boil over medium heat, whisking. Boil gently, whisking constantly, for 2½ minutes, then remove from the heat. Don't undercook, or the pastry cream may thin out later. Stir in the vanilla and almond extract. Let cool for 5 minutes. Strain through a fine sieve into a storage container. Lay a sheet of plastic wrap directly on the pastry cream. Cover and refrigerate for at least 1½ hours and up to 3 days. Stir before using.

TO MAKE THE SAUCE: Press the raspberry juice and pulp through a fine sieve into a nonreactive medium saucepan; discard the seeds. Add the cornstarch and sherry. Stir until the mixture is well blended and smooth. Bring to a boil, stirring, over medium-high heat. Cook, stirring, until the sauce thickens and turns translucent, 1 to 2 minutes. Remove from the heat. Stir in the strawberries and their syrup. Taste and add lemon juice as desired. Transfer to a storage container, cover, and refrigerate for at least 1½ hours and up to 3 days. Stir well before using.

TO ASSEMBLE THE TRIFLE: Spread half the cake cubes in a 3- to 4-quart footed trifle bowl or similar glass serving bowl. Sprinkle with 2 tablespoons of the sherry. Sprinkle half the strawberries and raspberries over the cake, arranging a few against the glass so they will be visible from the outside. Spoon half the pastry cream over the berries, then half the berry sauce, attractively drizzling some down the bowl sides. Repeat the layering of cake, sherry, berries, pastry cream, and berry sauce. Cover and refrigerate for at least 2 hours and up to 24 hours to allow the flavors to blend. (After about 24 hours, the berry colors may begin to fade.)

TO MAKE THE WHIPPED CREAM: Shortly before serving, in a large bowl using a mixer (with a whisk-shaped beater, if available), beat the cream on high speed just to soft peaks. Reduce the speed and beat in the powdered sugar, then the vanilla. Increase the speed to high and beat until stiff but not dry. Using a pastry bag fitted with a large open-star tip, pipe the whipped cream into puffy rosettes over the entire trifle top. (Or simply top the trifle with the whipped cream and swirl it into peaks using a rubber spatula.) Garnish the rosettes (or peaks) with whole berries. Serve immediately.

bourbon sauce

America's bourbon whiskey derives much of its distinctive flavor from sour mash (a special mix of mashed, fermented corn, malt, and rye) and the charred oak barrels in which it's aged. The unique taste comes through clearly in this not-too-sweet, slightly boozy dessert sauce. Designed for adult palates, it makes a fine accompaniment to Souffléd Whiskey Bread Pudding with Meringue (page 208), Pecan-Coconut Bread Pudding (page 203), or Chocolate Bread Pudding (page 204). For an alcohol-free sauce, see Brown Sugar–Orange Sauce (opposite).

⅔ cup packed light brown sugar

2½ teaspoons cornstarch

1½ cups heavy (whipping) cream

6½ tablespoons good bourbon

1½ tablespoons light or dark corn syrup

⅛ teaspoon salt

½ teaspoon vanilla extract

In a heavy 2-quart saucepan, stir together the brown sugar and cornstarch until well blended. Gradually stir in the cream, bourbon, corn syrup, and salt until well blended. Bring to a full boil, stirring, over medium-high heat. Cook, stirring frequently, for 1 to 2 minutes, or until the sauce thickens slightly. (It will thicken a little more as it cools.) Transfer to a wire rack. Stir in the vanilla. Let cool to warm and serve.

The sauce may be stored, tightly covered, in the refrigerator for up to 4 days. At serving time, gently heat to warm in a microwave oven on medium power, stirring every 30 seconds. (Alternatively, place in a small heavy saucepan and heat to warm over medium heat, stirring.) The sauce should flow readily; if it seems too thick, thin it slightly with a few teaspoons of hot water.

Brown sugar-orange sauce

A nice complement to many bread puddings, this sauce can dress up other puddings and fruit desserts featuring peaches, cranberries, or raisins.

- 1¼ cups heavy (whipping) cream
- ¼ cup light corn syrup
- 1 cup packed light brown sugar
- 1 tablespoon unsalted butter, cut into chunks
- ½ teaspoon finely grated orange zest (orange part of skin)
- Pinch of salt
- 1 teaspoon vanilla extract

In a heavy, nonreactive 2-quart saucepan, thoroughly stir together the cream, corn syrup, brown sugar, butter, orange zest, and salt. Cook over medium heat, stirring, until the sugar completely dissolves and the butter melts. Bring to a gentle boil and cook, stirring frequently, for 4 minutes. (The sauce will thicken just slightly as it cooks and a bit more as it cools.) Remove from the heat and let stand for 5 minutes so the orange zest can flavor the sauce. Stir in the vanilla.

Strain through a fine sieve into a sauceboat or pitcher and serve.

The sauce will keep, covered, for up to 1 week in the refrigerator. Reheat in a saucepan over low heat, stirring (or in a microwave oven on medium power, stopping and stirring at 30-second intervals), until warm and fluid.

Big, soft sugar cookies with strawberry icing

If my grandchildren are any indication, these soft, mild sugar cookies are irresistible. The kids particularly love the intense pink icing, which gets its color not from red food coloring but from real strawberries. For an over-the-top gift or child's party presentation, adorn the cookies with a tiny piped strawberry and leaves. For a more adult variation, ice the cookies with a sprightly lemon or lime glaze (see the variation).

COOKIES

- 3⅓ cups all-purpose flour
- ¾ teaspoon salt
- ¾ teaspoon baking powder
- 1¼ cups granulated sugar
- ⅔ cup (10⅔ tablespoons) unsalted butter, slightly softened
- ⅔ cup solid white shortening, at room temperature
- 2 large eggs
- 1 tablespoon light corn syrup
- 1 tablespoon vanilla extract
- 1 teaspoon finely grated lemon zest (yellow part of skin)
- ¼ teaspoon lemon extract
- ¼ cup sour cream

STRAWBERRY ICING

- 1 cup strawberries, at room temperature
- ½ teaspoon grated lemon zest (yellow part of skin)
- About 4 cups powdered sugar, sifted after measuring if lumpy (divided)
- 2 tablespoons unsalted butter, very soft but not melted
- 1½ tablespoons light corn syrup
- ½ teaspoon vanilla extract
- Water, if needed

TO MAKE THE COOKIES: In a medium bowl, thoroughly stir together the flour, salt, and baking powder; set aside. In a large bowl, combine the sugar, butter, and shortening. With an electric mixer on medium speed, beat until well blended and fluffy, about 1½ minutes, scraping down the sides of the bowl as needed. Beat in the eggs, corn syrup, vanilla, lemon zest, and lemon extract until smoothly incorporated. Beat in half the dry ingredients, stopping and scraping down the sides of the bowl as needed. On low speed, beat in the sour cream. Then beat or stir in the remaining dry ingredients just until the mixture is well blended and smooth. Cover tightly and refrigerate for at least 6 hours and up to 2 days.

tip

If you don't have a food processor, it's best to use thawed frozen strawberries. They are much easier to mash by hand than fresh berries.

Position a rack in the middle of the oven and preheat to 350 degrees F. Generously grease several large baking sheets or generously coat with nonstick spray.

On a sheet of plastic wrap or wax paper, shape the chilled dough into a 6-inch disk. Cut the disk into quarters. Wrap 3 of the quarters in plastic wrap or wax paper and return to the refrigerator. Cut the remaining quarter into 6 equal pieces. With greased hands, shape each piece into a ball. Arrange the balls on baking sheets, spacing them about 3 inches apart; don't crowd, as the cookies will spread. Lightly dust your palm with flour, then press down each ball until it is a scant ½ inch thick and about 2¾ inches in diameter. Continue shaping the cookies, leaving each dough portion refrigerated until needed.

Bake for 10 to 14 minutes, or until the edges are lightly browned and the tops just spring back when lightly pressed in the center. Transfer the sheets to wire racks. Let the cookies stand for 1 to 2 minutes to firm up. Using a wide spatula, transfer to the racks. Let cool completely. Set the racks with the cookies over baking parchment or wax paper.

TO MAKE THE ICING: Coarsely chop the strawberries. In a food processor, combine the berries, lemon zest, and ¼ cup of the powdered sugar. Process until the strawberries are completely pureed, about 1½ minutes. (Alternatively, in a small bowl, combine the strawberries, lemon zest, and ¼ cup of the powdered sugar and mash well with a fork. Let stand to soften for a few minutes, then mash again until very soft and pulpy.)

Using a wooden spoon, press as much of the strawberry pulp and juice as possible through a fine sieve into a large bowl; discard the seeds. Stir the butter, corn syrup, and vanilla into the strawberries. Stir in 3¾ cups more powdered sugar until well blended and smooth. If the icing is too stiff, stir in a little water to thin it to a slightly runny consistency. If it's too runny, stir in more powdered sugar until slightly thickened.

Using a small wide-bladed spatula, spreader, or table knife, immediately ice the cookies. For best appearance, swirl the icing in the center of each cookie, leaving ¼ inch all around un-iced; the icing will then flow out toward the edges. (If the icing stiffens as you work, thin with a few drops of water.) Let the cookies stand until the icing sets, at least 2 hours.

The cookies will keep, stored airtight in a single layer, for up to 10 days at room temperature or frozen for up to 6 weeks.

VARIATION: Lemon or Lime Icing

Combine 1 tablespoon grated lemon or lime zest (colored part of skin) and ½ cup granulated sugar in a food processor. Process until the zest is very fine and the sugar is lemon- or lime-colored, 3 to 4 minutes. Add ¼ cup fresh lemon or lime juice, 2 tablespoons very soft butter, 1½ tablespoons corn syrup, and ½ teaspoon vanilla. If desired, add a drop of yellow or green food color. Process until the sugar dissolves. In 3 or 4 batches, add 3½ cups powdered sugar, processing after each addition. If the icing is too stiff, add a little water. If it's too thin, add more powdered sugar. It should have a slightly runny consistency. Ice the cookies as directed.

OLd-Fashioned Tinting Trick

"You may colour icing of a pale or deep yellow, by rubbing the lumps of loaf-sugar (before they are powdered) upon the outside of a large lemon or orange. This will also flavour it finely."

—Eliza Leslie,
Miss Leslie's Directions for Cookery (1851)

giant ginger cookies

Fresh gingerroot gives these sugar cookies a particularly appealing flavor and aroma. They're large and crispy-chewy, and somehow both gingery and mellow. They remind me of snickerdoodles, but since most of the usual cinnamon is replaced with ginger, the taste is different. They were inspired by some big, crisp ginger sugar cookies I bought from an old-fashioned cookie jar at the Morse Farm Maple Sugarworks shop in Montpelier, Vermont.

2¾	cups all-purpose flour
2½	teaspoons ground ginger
¼	teaspoon ground cinnamon
2	teaspoons baking powder
½	teaspoon salt
16	tablespoons (2 sticks) unsalted butter, slightly softened
1¾	cups granulated sugar
1½	tablespoons light corn syrup

2	large eggs
	Generous 1 tablespoon peeled and finely minced fresh gingerroot
1	teaspoon finely grated lemon zest (yellow part of skin)
2½	teaspoons vanilla extract
	About ¼ cup coarse crystal sugar, turbinado sugar, or granulated sugar for garnish

Position a rack in the upper third of the oven and preheat to 375 degrees F. Grease several baking sheets or coat with nonstick spray.

In a medium bowl, thoroughly stir together the flour, ground ginger, cinnamon, baking powder, and salt. In a large bowl with a mixer on medium speed, beat together the butter, granulated sugar, and corn syrup until well blended and fluffy, about 2 minutes. Add the eggs, gingerroot, lemon zest, and vanilla and continue beating until well blended and smooth.

Beat half the flour mixture into the butter mixture until smoothly incorporated. Stir in the remaining flour mixture until evenly incorporated. Cover and refrigerate for 10 minutes to firm up slightly. Don't chill longer, or the cookies may not spread properly.

tip

Garnishing with coarse crystal or turbinado sugar will give the cookies a little crunch. Turbinado sugar is available in many supermarkets; coarse sugar is found in specialty shops with cookie decorating supplies. If you don't have coarse sugar or prefer "crunchless" cookies, use granulated sugar instead.

Place the crystal sugar in a saucer. With lightly greased hands, pull off portions of the dough, rolling each between your palms to form generous 1½-inch balls; the dough will be soft. Lightly dip the top of each ball in the crystal sugar. Space the balls sugar sides up a generous 3 inches apart on the baking sheets; don't crowd, as the cookies will spread. Pat down the cookie tops just slightly.

Bake one sheet at a time for 11 to 15 minutes, or until the cookies are just golden brown around the edges. If necessary, reverse the sheet from front to back halfway through baking to ensure even browning. Transfer the sheet to a wire rack. Let the cookies stand for about 2 minutes to firm up just slightly. Using a wide spatula, transfer to the rack. Let cool completely. Let the baking sheets cool between batches, or the cookies may spread too much.

The cookies will keep, stored airtight, for up to 10 days at room temperature or frozen for 1 to 2 months.

soft gingerbread boys

Rolled gingerbread cookies are usually on the crisp and crunchy side, but these are plump, lightly glazed, sweet and not too spicy, and, most important, noticeably chewy-soft. They are my re-creation of an enormously popular cookie once sold by a now de-funct Capitol Hill diner called Sherrill's Restaurant. I first became aware of the cookies in 2000, when *Washington Post* reporter Douglas Hanks wrote a story about his unsuc-cessful attempts to obtain the recipe for the diner's special soft gingerbread boys from its creator, retired baker Howard Ward.

I, too, failed at persuading Mr. Ward to part with the recipe, but I decided to try to duplicate it. Renée Schettler and her colleagues at the *Washington Post* food section who had sampled the cookies in the past provided me with a detailed description. After numerous attempts and a lot of helpful feedback, I finally produced a batch that they declared "very, very close to the original." Note that this recipe does not contain any eggs.

16 tablespoons (2 sticks) unsalted butter, cut into chunks

²/₃ cup light molasses

Generous ½ cup clover (or other mild) honey

⅓ cup corn oil or other flavorless vegetable oil

⅓ cup packed light brown sugar

3⅓ cups all-purpose flour

2½ teaspoons ground cinnamon

1½ teaspoons ground ginger

½ teaspoon ground cloves

1½ teaspoons baking powder

Scant ½ teaspoon baking soda

Scant ½ teaspoon salt

Dark raisins or dried currants for eyes and buttons

GLAZE

1⅓ cups powdered sugar, sifted after measuring if lumpy

3½ tablespoons water

1½ tablespoons corn oil or other flavorless vegetable oil

In a large saucepan, stir together the butter, molasses, honey, oil, and brown sugar until blended. Cook, stirring, over medium-high heat until the butter melts and the mixture just comes to a full boil. Immediately start timing and cook, stirring occasionally, for exactly 1 minute. Remove from the heat. Let cool slightly.

tip

To keep this dough from warming up and softening too quickly, thoroughly chill a large baking sheet. Then lay the dough on it as you cut out the cookies. Chill the baking sheet as needed for successive batches.

In a large bowl, thoroughly stir together the flour, cinnamon, ginger, cloves, baking powder, baking soda, and salt. Working carefully to avoid splashes, pour the molasses mixture over the flour mixture. Beat with a mixer on low, then medium speed until very well blended. If the mixer motor labors, stop and complete the mixing by hand. Cover and refrigerate for 30 to 40 minutes, or until barely warm and stiffened.

Divide the dough into thirds. Roll out each portion between sheets of baking parchment or wax paper until a generous ¼ inch thick. Stack the rolled portions (paper still attached) on a baking sheet. Refrigerate for at least 1 hour and up to 12 hours, or freeze for 30 to 40 minutes, or until very cold and firm.

Position a rack in the middle of the oven and preheat to 350 degrees F. Grease several baking sheets or coat with nonstick spray. Working with one dough portion at a time and leaving the others in the refrigerator, gently peel off the top sheet of paper, then pat loosely back into place so it will be easy to remove later. Invert the dough and peel off the second sheet.

Using a 4- to 5-inch gingerbread boy (or girl) cutter, cut out the cookies. Using a spatula, transfer the cookies to the baking sheets, spacing them about 2 inches apart. If at any point the dough softens too much to handle easily, transfer the paper and cookies to a baking sheet and refrigerate or freeze until firm. Re-roll any dough scraps. Continue cutting out the cookies until all the dough is used. Very firmly press raisins into the cookies for eyes and buttons.

Bake for 9 to 14 minutes, or until the tops are lightly colored and the edges are slightly darker; don't underbake. Transfer the baking sheets to wire racks set over sheets of baking parchment or wax paper. Let the cookies stand for 4 minutes to firm up. Using a wide spatula, transfer them to the racks.

TO MAKE THE GLAZE: In a 1-quart saucepan, stir together the powdered sugar, water, and oil until well blended. Bring to a boil, stirring, over medium-high heat. Boil just until the mixture is smooth and translucent, 30 to 45 seconds. Stir to recombine the glaze, then use immediately while it is still hot. (If the glaze is allowed to stand and cool, it may thicken and become sugary. In this case, add a teaspoon of hot water to thin it again, place over medium heat, and continue stirring until the sugar dissolves. Immediately remove from the heat and use.)

Using a pastry brush or paper towel, brush the cookies with glaze until their tops are coated all over with an even layer; the more glaze you use, the softer the cookies will be. Stir the glaze frequently to prevent it from separating. Let the cookies cool completely, at least 1 hour. It's normal for the glaze to become slightly sugary.

The cookies will keep, packed flat with baking parchment or wax paper between the layers and stored airtight, at room temperature for up to a week or frozen for up to 2 months.

muddy pond Jumbo sorghum cookies

This big, lightly spiced cookie is adapted from a recipe of Judy Wilson, whose family owns the Muddy Pond Sorghum Mill in the Cumberland Mountains in Monterey, Tennessee. The twenty-three-year-old mill turns out 6,000 to 8,000 gallons of syrup annually, most of which is sold to visitors day-tripping from the Knoxville and Nashville areas each autumn. The family's shop across from the mill sells the syrup and an array of homemade baked goods, including Judy's popular cookies.

Sorghum syrup looks and tastes like a mild, slightly sweet molasses, and I've successfully substituted light molasses when I can't find it. Sometimes health food stores carry it, and it can also be purchased by phone or e-mail. Contact the Muddy Pond Sorghum Mill at (931) 445-3589 or petendoreen@twlakes.net. Or try Maasdam Sorghum Mills at www.maasdamsorghum.com or (641) 594-4369.

4 cups all-purpose flour	8 tablespoons (1 stick) unsalted butter, slightly softened
2¼ teaspoons baking soda	1¾ cups sugar, plus about 3 tablespoons for garnish
1½ teaspoons ground cinnamon	½ cup sorghum syrup or light molasses
¾ teaspoon ground ginger	2 large eggs, at room temperature
½ teaspoon ground cloves	
½ teaspoon salt	
1 cup solid white shortening, at room temperature	

In a large bowl, thoroughly stir together the flour, baking soda, cinnamon, ginger, cloves, and salt. In a large bowl with a mixer on medium speed, beat together the shortening, butter, sugar, and sorghum syrup until well blended and lightened. Add the eggs and continue beating until very well blended, scraping down the sides of the bowl as needed.

Beat half the flour mixture into the sorghum mixture until smoothly incorporated. Beat or stir in the remaining flour mixture until evenly incorporated. Cover and refrigerate until firm, at least 2½ hours and up to 24 hours.

Position a rack in the middle of the oven and preheat to 350 degrees F. Grease several baking sheets or coat with nonstick spray. Remove about a third of the dough from the refrigerator; keep the rest refrigerated until needed. Using a ¼-cup measure, measure out the dough into portions. With lightly greased hands, roll each portion into a ball. Put the garnishing sugar in a shallow bowl. Dip the top of each ball in the sugar. Space the balls sugar sides up about 3 inches apart on the baking sheets; don't crowd. Using a lightly greased palm, flatten the balls to about 2 inches in diameter.

Bake one sheet at a time for 14 to 18 minutes, or until the cookies are barely firm in the center and faintly tinged with color at the edges. Transfer the baking sheet to a wire rack. Let the cookies stand for 3 to 4 minutes to firm up. Using a wide spatula, transfer to the rack. Let cool completely.

The cookies will keep, stored airtight, at room temperature for up to 10 days or frozen for up to 2 months.

sorghum syrup

Sorghum syrup is produced from the juice of a ten- to twelve-foot-tall African grass called sweet sorghum. Introduced in America in 1853, the plants look somewhat like cornstalks. From the mid-1800s through the early twentieth century, rural families across the South, heartland, and upper Midwest often planted sweet sorghum to provide an alternative to cane sugar, which was then beyond the means of many households. As refined cane sugar became more affordable and inexpensive corn syrups came on the market, the production of sorghum syrup gradually declined. It has been on the upswing again in the past several decades, however, as small farmers look for profitable crops to replace tobacco. Operations such as the Muddy Pond Sorghum Mill in Tennessee have found a receptive local clientele.

santa's sorghum candy

Sorghum syrup played a particularly important role in brightening the hardscrabble lives of nineteenth-century subsistence farm families. In the 1916 book *On the Old Plantation: Reminiscences of His Childhood,* South Carolinian John George Clinkscale recalled his childhood Christmases during the Civil War and Reconstruction:

> But these were war times, and Santa Claus is . . . handicapped in war times . . . But mother said he'd come, and he did. He never failed us. The Yankees bothered him, mother said, and he couldn't get rich, fine candy and beautiful dolls as he wished to do. So he did the next best thing: he brought us candy made of sorghum syrup and rag dolls that were as beautiful as deft, loving fingers could make them.

chocoLate chunk coconut-Pecan chews

Pecans, coconut, brown sugar, and condensed milk give these drop cookies a sweet, nutty flavor that complements the little chunks of chocolate nicely. They also have a pleasing toothsomeness.

2½ cups shredded or flaked sweetened coconut	2 teaspoons vanilla extract
1½ cups chopped pecans	¾ cup plus 2 tablespoons all-purpose flour
1 14-ounce can sweetened condensed milk	Scant ½ teaspoon baking soda
⅓ cup packed dark brown sugar	3 ounces semisweet chocolate, chopped into ¼-inch chunks, or ½ cup (3 ounces) semisweet chocolate morsels
3 tablespoons unsalted butter, melted	
1 large egg	
¼ teaspoon salt	

Position a rack in the middle of the oven and preheat to 350 degrees F. Line several large baking sheets with baking parchment or aluminum foil. Stir together the coconut and pecans in a roasting pan. Toast for 9 to 12 minutes, stirring every 3 or 4 minutes, until well browned. Let cool to warm. Reserve 1 cup of the coconut-pecan mixture for garnish.

In a large bowl, thoroughly stir together the condensed milk, brown sugar, butter, egg, salt, and vanilla until well blended. In a small bowl, thoroughly stir together the flour and baking soda. Stir in the flour mixture, then the remaining coconut-pecan mixture and the chocolate chunks, until smoothly incorporated. Refrigerate for 10 minutes, or until slightly firm.

Drop the dough by heaping measuring tablespoonfuls onto the baking sheets, spacing the cookies about 2½ inches apart. Generously sprinkle the reserved coconut-pecan mixture over the tops. Bake one sheet at a time for 10 to 15 minutes, or until nicely browned and barely firm when pressed in the centers. Transfer the sheet to a wire rack. Let the cookies stand for 5 minutes to firm up. Using a spatula, transfer to the rack. Let cool completely.

The cookies will keep, covered, in a cool place for 3 or 4 days or in the freezer for up to a month.

Lemon shortbread sandwiches with Tangerine-Lemon curd

My inspiration for this recipe came from the tangerine curd served at the charming 120-year-old Dunbar House, a bed-and-breakfast establishment situated southeast of Sacramento, California, in the gold-country town of Murphys. Formerly owned by Barbara and Bob Costa, the Italianate Victorian house was built in 1880. Barbara Costa liked to offer her citrus curd with breakfast biscuits, and I've found that it also makes a superb filling for shortbread sandwich cookies. Its intense flavor and glorious golden-orange color pair beautifully with the buttery, lightly lemony shortbreads.

This recipe requires a food processor.

TANGERINE-LEMON CURD

- ½ cup granulated sugar, plus a little more if needed
- 1 tablespoon grated tangerine zest (orange part of skin)
- 1 tablespoon grated lemon zest (yellow part of skin)
- ⅓ cup fresh tangerine juice
- 3 tablespoons fresh lemon juice, plus a little more if needed
- 6 large egg yolks
- 8 tablespoons (1 stick) unsalted butter, cut into chunks
- 1 teaspoon vanilla extract

LEMON SHORTBREAD COOKIES

- 2⅓ cups all-purpose flour
- Generous ¼ teaspoon salt
- ½ cup plus 1 tablespoon granulated sugar
- 1½ tablespoons grated lemon zest (yellow part of skin)
- 1 teaspoon grated tangerine zest (orange part of skin)
- 16 tablespoons (2 sticks) unsalted butter, slightly softened and cut into chunks
- 1½ tablespoons milk
- 2 teaspoons vanilla extract
- ½ teaspoon lemon extract

- 1–2 tablespoons powdered sugar for garnish (optional)

TO MAKE THE CURD: In a heavy, nonreactive 2-quart saucepan, whisk together the sugar, zests, tangerine juice, lemon juice, and egg yolks until completely blended. Add the butter. Heat over medium heat, whisking and scraping the pan bottom and sides constantly, until the butter melts and the mixture just comes to a boil. Whisking vigorously and scraping the pan bottom, gently boil for 2 minutes. Immediately remove from the heat, whisking; the curd may seem thin but will thicken somewhat when refrigerated. Taste and, if desired, whisk in a little more sugar until dissolved or a little more lemon juice. Whisk in the vanilla. Let stand for 15 minutes. Strain through a fine sieve into an airtight storage container. Refrigerate for at least 2 hours and up to 5 days.

TO MAKE THE COOKIES: In a medium bowl, thoroughly stir together the flour and salt. In a food processor, combine the granulated sugar, lemon zest, and tangerine zest. Process until the sugar is orange-colored and the zest is very fine, 1 to 2 minutes. Add the butter, processing until the mixture is well blended and lightened, about 2 minutes, scraping down the sides of the bowl as needed. Add the milk, vanilla, and lemon extract and process until evenly incorporated. Sprinkle the flour mixture over the top. Process in pulses until the flour is just smoothly incorporated, scraping down the sides of the bowl as needed. Carefully remove the blade. Turn out the dough onto a sheet of baking parchment or wax paper and briefly knead to form a mass.

Divide the dough in half. Roll out each portion between sheets of baking parchment or wax paper until ⅛ inch thick. Occasionally check the underside of the dough during rolling and smooth out any wrinkles. Stack the rolled portions (paper still attached) on a baking sheet. Refrigerate for about 30 minutes or freeze for 15 to 20 minutes, or until cold and firm.

Position a rack in the upper third of the oven and preheat to 350 degrees F. Grease several baking sheets or coat with nonstick spray. Working with one portion at a time and keeping the other refrigerated, gently peel off the top sheet of paper, then pat loosely back into place so it will be easy to remove later. Invert the dough and peel off the second sheet.

Using a 2- to 2¼-inch fluted, scalloped, or plain round, square, or oval cutter, cut out the cookies. If you wish to create cut-away cookie tops, cut away a small round from the centers of half the cookies using a thimble, a mini-cutter, or the large end of a metal piping tip. (The tip may need to be cleaned after each use.) If at any point the dough softens too much to handle easily, transfer the paper and cookies to a baking sheet and refrigerate or freeze until firm.

Using a spatula, carefully transfer the cookies to the baking sheets, spacing them 1 inch apart. (If preparing cut-away cookie tops, place these on the interior of the sheets, where the heat is not as intense.) Reroll any dough scraps. Continue cutting out the cookies until all the dough is used.

Bake one sheet at a time for 9 to 13 minutes, or until the cookies are barely colored on top and slightly darker at the edges. If necessary, reverse the sheet from front to back halfway through baking to ensure

TIP

If fresh refrigerated tangerine juice is available, it makes a very satisfactory substitute for tangerine juice squeezed at home.

even browning. Transfer the sheet to a wire rack. Let the cookies stand for 2 to 3 minutes to firm up. Using a wide spatula, gently transfer to the rack. Let cool completely. The cookies will keep, stored airtight, in a cool place for up to a week or frozen for up to 2 months.

TO ASSEMBLE THE COOKIES: If cut-away cookie tops have been prepared, pair each up with a plain cookie. Stir the curd well. Spread about 1 teaspoon of the curd on the underside of a cookie to within ¼ inch of the edge, mounding it slightly in the center. Cover with another cookie, aligning the scalloped edges as needed. If the cookie tops have cut-away centers, squeeze down the tops just slightly so the curd shows through attractively. Repeat until as many sandwiches as desired are assembled. Lightly sift powdered sugar over the cookie tops, if desired.

The assembled cookies will keep, stored airtight, in the refrigerator for up to 12 hours. They'll soften too much if stored any longer. Remove from the refrigerator about 30 minutes before serving and let come almost to room temperature.

pumpkin
whoopie pies

Whoopie pies are big in New England and Pennsylvania. Nearly every bakery and farmers' market in Pennsylvania's Amish country sells them, as do convenience stores and sweet shops all over New England. The classic whoopie pie consists of two hamburger bun-size cakes stuck together with a billowy marshmallow or cream filling. (Some hard-core fans feel that using anything other than marshmallow is a sin.)

Commercial whoopie pies are often too dry, sweet, or bland, but these are nicely spiced, moist, and pleasantly pumpkiny. The easy homemade marshmallow filling is unusual in that it is enriched with cream cheese, which goes especially well with the pumpkin.

COOKIES

- 4¼ cups all-purpose flour
- 2 tablespoons ground cinnamon
- 2½ teaspoons ground ginger
- 1¾ teaspoons ground cloves
- 1½ teaspoons freshly grated nutmeg or 1¼ teaspoons ground nutmeg
- 1¼ teaspoons baking soda
- ½ teaspoon salt
- 16 tablespoons (2 sticks) unsalted butter, slightly softened
- 1 cup solid white shortening, at room temperature
- 1⅔ cups packed dark brown sugar
- ¼ cup light molasses
- ⅓ cup sour cream
- 1 large egg
- 2½ teaspoons vanilla extract
- 1⅓ cups solid-pack canned pumpkin (not seasoned pie filling)

FILLING

- 1 tablespoon plus 1 teaspoon unflavored gelatin (about 1½ packets)
- ⅓ cup plus ¼ cup water (divided)
- ¾ cup granulated sugar
- ½ cup light corn syrup
- 2 teaspoons vanilla extract
- 1 cup powdered sugar
- 16 ounces (two 8-ounce packages) cream cheese, slightly softened and cut into chunks

TO MAKE THE COOKIES: In a large bowl, thoroughly stir together the flour, cinnamon, ginger, cloves, nutmeg, baking soda, and salt. In a large bowl, combine the butter, shortening, brown sugar, and molasses. With a mixer on medium speed, beat until well blended and lightened, about 2 minutes, scraping down the sides of the bowl as needed. Reduce the mixer speed slightly and add the sour cream, egg, and vanilla, beating until very light and fluffy, about 1 minute longer. Beat in about half the flour mixture, scraping down the sides of the bowl as needed. Beat in the pumpkin just until smoothly incorporated. Beat or stir in the remaining flour mixture until smoothly incorporated, scraping down the sides of the bowl as needed. Refrigerate until slightly firmer, 20 to 30 minutes.

Position a rack in the middle of the oven and preheat to 350 degrees F. Generously grease several large baking sheets or generously coat with nonstick spray. Using a heaping ¼-cup measure or similar-size ice cream scoop, place uniformly shaped dough portions on the baking sheets, spacing them about 3½ inches apart. Lightly dust your palm with flour and pat down the dough tops until the cookies are flattened to 3 inches in diameter. Re-dust your palm as needed to prevent the dough from sticking, but avoid overflouring.

Bake for 12 to 16 minutes, or until tinged with brown all over and just firm when lightly pressed in the centers. Transfer the sheets to wire racks. Let the cookies stand for about 2 minutes to firm up slightly. Using a spatula, transfer to the racks. Let cool completely.

TO MAKE THE FILLING: In a small measuring cup, sprinkle the gelatin over ⅓ cup cold water. Let stand, stirring once or twice until the gelatin softens, about 5 minutes. In a heavy 2-quart saucepan over medium-high heat, stir together the granulated sugar, corn syrup, and ¼ cup hot water until well blended. Continuing to stir, raise the heat to high and bring to a full boil. Continue boiling for 30 seconds. Immediately remove from the heat. Stir in the gelatin mixture until it dissolves completely.

Transfer the mixture to a large bowl. Add the vanilla. With a mixer on medium speed (using a whisk-shaped beater, if available), beat for 20 seconds. Gradually raise the speed to high and beat until the mixture is stiffened, white, very fluffy, and cooled to barely warm, about 5 minutes. Reduce the mixer speed to low and beat in the powdered sugar. On medium speed, gradually add the cream cheese, beating just until the mixture is completely smooth. If the filling seems too runny to spread, cover and refrigerate for a few minutes until firmed up slightly.

TO ASSEMBLE THE COOKIES: Lay half the cookies underside up. Spread a generous ¼ cup of the filling in the center of each. Top with a second cookie, pairing up ones that are of similar size. Press down lightly on each whoopie pie so the filling almost squeezes out the edges.

The whoopie pies will keep, packed in an airtight container or individual plastic bags, in the refrigerator for up to a week or in the freezer for up to a month. Let come to room temperature before serving.

whoopie History

Pennsylvanians often say that the whoopie pie originated with early Amish cooks, but my fairly thorough search through late-nineteenth- and early-twentieth-century Pennsylvania Dutch cookbooks failed to turn up a single one—or anything similar. In fact, I've only found whoopie pie recipes in Pennsylvania community cookbooks published during the past three or four decades.

In Massachusetts, the now defunct Berwick Cake Company, which was located in the Roxbury section of Boston and closed in 1977, boasted of having invented the sweet in 1926 or 1927. Although I haven't verified those dates, the original building still stands in Roxbury's Dudley Square, and the words "Whoopee! Pies" are readable on the side. Longtime whoopie pie fan Frank Broderick, who grew up in West Roxbury and now lives in West Newton, Massachusetts, remembers buying them from the company in the 1940s. "I support the contention that Berwick originated whoopie pies, and I have a high cholesterol level to prove it!" he wrote me.

As to how the whoopie pie got its name, the story I've heard is attributed to Betty Groff, a tenth-generation Pennsylvania Dutch cookbook author. She tells the tale of a cook with some leftover cake batter dropping it onto baking sheets and ending up with generous cookie-size rounds. Her children were supposedly so excited with the results that they yelled, "Whoopie! Pies!"

My own guess is that "whoopie pie" is a takeoff on the name "moon pie," a similar-size sweet featuring a round, chocolate-coated graham cracker sandwich with a marshmallow filling. It was created by the Chattanooga Bakery in Tennessee in 1917, and by the time whoopie pies began to appear, the moon pie was already a success in the American baking industry.

In western Pennsylvania, whoopie pies are more often known as "gobs." Susan Kalcik, an archivist with the Southwestern Pennsylvania Heritage Preservation Commission, near Johnstown, points out that the huge mounds and piles of coal refuse around the region's coal mines are called gob piles. She speculates that the cookies may have been named by miners who carried them to work in their lunch buckets.

lemon snowflake cookies

Joy Hare, a Baltimore home cook who shared this heirloom recipe with me, remembers sampling these whisper-crisp sugar cookies every Christmas from a cut-glass plate on her grandmother's sideboard in Quincy, Illinois. She recalls that her grandmother Elsa Emma Albright had an artistic bent, and the unusual look of the cookies hints at her creativity. Instead of pressing down the dough with a plain drinking glass or the tines of a fork, Mrs. Albright used a cut-glass tumbler with a starburst design etched in the bottom, which produced a simple, elegant snowflake imprint in the cookie tops. "For many years, I used that same tumbler for my cookies," Joy says, "but it broke, so now I use a crystal saltshaker with a similar pattern cut into the bottom." For her efforts, Joy earned first prize in a holiday cookie contest sponsored by the American Visionary Art Museum in Baltimore in 2003.

I duplicated the look using a $2.50 glass tumbler embossed with the same pattern. (A cookie stamp with a snowflake design didn't work nearly as well, because its surface wasn't as deeply etched.)

In keeping with the snowflake theme, I like to dust the cookies very lightly with powdered sugar and snow-colored edible glitter. (Edible glitter is often sold with colored sprinkles and other cake-decorating supplies. If it isn't available, white sanding sugar or crystal sugar will give a similar sparkly look but can detract from the distinctive tender texture of the cookies.)

2 cups all-purpose flour	1 large egg
½ teaspoon baking soda	Finely grated zest (yellow part of skin) of 1 large lemon
½ teaspoon cream of tartar	1½ teaspoons fresh lemon juice
⅛ teaspoon salt	¾ teaspoon lemon extract
8 tablespoons (1 stick) unsalted butter, slightly softened	½ teaspoon vanilla extract
⅓ cup corn oil or other flavorless vegetable oil	White or clear edible glitter (optional)
½ cup granulated sugar, plus about 2 tablespoons for shaping cookies	
½ cup powdered sugar, plus about 3 tablespoons for garnish	

Position a rack in the upper third of the oven and preheat to 350 degrees F. Grease several baking sheets or coat with nonstick spray.

In a large bowl, thoroughly stir together the flour, baking soda, cream of tartar, and salt. In a large bowl with a mixer on low speed, beat together the butter, oil, and sugars until well blended. Raise the speed to medium and beat for 1 to 2 minutes, or until lightened in color. Add the egg, lemon zest, lemon juice, lemon extract, and vanilla and continue beating until well blended, 1 to 1½ minutes longer. Beat in half the dry ingredients until evenly incorporated. Stir in the remaining dry ingredients until evenly incorporated, scraping down the sides of the bowl as needed. The dough will be very soft. For easier handling, let stand for 5 to 10 minutes to firm up slightly.

Put 2 tablespoons granulated sugar in a saucer. Lightly oil the etched bottom of a glass tumbler, saltshaker, or small bowl or vase, being sure to coat the grooves. With lightly greased hands, pull off portions of the dough. Working gently, roll each portion between your palms to form ¾-inch balls. Dip the top of each ball in the sugar until lightly coated. Space the balls sugar sides up about 2½ inches apart on the baking sheets. Using the tumbler, press down on the cookie tops until the design is imprinted and the cookies are flattened to about 2 inches in diameter. If sugar builds up on the tumbler bottom, wipe off and re-oil the etched surface. Garnish the cookie tops with a pinch or two of edible glitter, if desired.

Bake one sheet at a time for 10 to 15 minutes, or until the cookies are barely firm in the centers and faintly tinged with color at the edges. Transfer the baking sheet to a wire rack. Let the cookies stand for 2 to 3 minutes to firm up. Using a wide spatula, transfer to the rack. Put a little powdered sugar in a fine sieve. Lightly shake the sieve over the cookies until they are barely dusted with powdered sugar. Let cool completely.

The cookies will keep, stored airtight, at room temperature for up to 10 days or frozen for up to a month.

oatmeal-raisin cookies

Oatmeal cookies come in several styles, from crunchy-hard to cakey-soft to chewy. These plain, homey rounds are definitely in the latter category, boasting a nubby texture, a straightforward wholesome look, and a quiet oat flavor that is greatly enhanced by the addition of a little honey. The honey also helps keep the cookies moist.

2¼ cups all-purpose flour
1½ teaspoons ground cinnamon
¾ teaspoon ground nutmeg
1 teaspoon baking powder
½ teaspoon baking soda
½ teaspoon salt
16 tablespoons (2 sticks) unsalted butter, slightly softened
1 cup packed dark brown sugar
¾ cup granulated sugar

2 large eggs
3 tablespoons clover or other mild-flavored honey
2½ teaspoons vanilla extract
3 cups old-fashioned rolled oats
1½ cups dark or golden raisins
1 cup chopped walnuts or pecans (optional)

Position a rack in the middle of the oven and preheat to 350 degrees F. Generously grease several large baking sheets or generously coat with nonstick spray.

In a medium bowl, thoroughly stir together the flour, cinnamon, nutmeg, baking powder, baking soda, and salt. In a large bowl, combine the butter and sugars. With a mixer on low, then medium speed, beat until the mixture is well blended and lightened, about 1½ minutes, scraping down the sides of the bowl as needed. Add the eggs, honey, and vanilla and beat on medium speed until light and fluffy, about 2 minutes longer. Beat in the flour mixture on low, then medium speed, scraping down the sides of the bowl as needed. Stir in the oats, raisins, and walnuts (if using) until evenly distributed. Let stand to firm up for 10 minutes.

With lightly greased hands, pull off portions of the dough and shape into golf ball-size balls. (Alternatively, use an ice cream scoop that yields balls about this size.) Space them a generous 3 inches apart on the baking sheets. Press down the dough tops until the cookies are flat and about 2 inches in diameter.

tip

Be sure the raisins are plump and moist. Overly dry raisins will draw moisture out of the cookie dough, producing dry cookies. If necessary, toss dried-out raisins with about ⅓ cup very hot water and let stand for 1 to 2 hours. Drain the raisins and pat completely dry on paper towels before using.

Bake for 9 to 14 minutes, or until just slightly darker at the edges and almost firm when lightly pressed in the centers. If necessary, reverse the sheets from front to back about halfway through baking to ensure even browning. Transfer the sheets to wire racks. Let the cookies stand for about 4 minutes to firm up slightly. Using a spatula, transfer to the racks. Let cool completely.

The cookies will keep, stored airtight, at room temperature for up to 2 weeks or frozen for up to a month.

VARIATION: Oatmeal–Chocolate Chip Cookies

Omit the cinnamon and nutmeg and replace the raisins with 1½ cups (9 ounces) semisweet chocolate morsels. Proceed as directed.

neigh·sayers

Because they seem so old-fashioned, I always assumed that oatmeal cookies dated back to colonial America. In fact, they were little known until the late 1800s, and most versions prepared today were created in the twentieth century. Before the 1850s, many Americans looked down on those who ate oats, because the grain was regarded as animal feed. Scottish and Irish immigrants, who had a taste for oats, were ridiculed for eating them and told they might start neighing!

The aversion to oats began changing in the 1860s and 1870s, when an enterprising German immigrant miller named Ferdinand Schumacher promoted his new steel-cut oats as a nutritious, economical breakfast dish. Later, he devised an even more convenient and well-received product called rolled oats. Unlike steel-cut oats, which were hard and gritty, rolled oats were soft and flaky, suitable not only for cooking for breakfast but also for adding to various doughs. They caught on quickly with bakers. An 1881 commercial bakers' reference titled *The Complete Bread, Cake and Cracker Baker in Two Parts* included recipes for oatmeal muffins and rolls, and a rolled oatmeal-molasses cookie called oatmeal snaps or Scotch perkins. Presumably Scottish in origin, the thin, rolled, waferlike snaps are the earliest oatmeal cookie I've found in American cookbooks.

key Lime sugar cookies

My Key lime sugar cookies combine the bracing bite, tantalizing citrus aroma, and sweet tartness of a good Florida Key lime pie. They also have a very crisp texture and slight crunch from the sprinkling of sugar on top. (You can use lime-colored sugar, if desired.)

- 1 tablespoon plus 1 teaspoon corn oil or other flavorless vegetable oil
- 1 tablespoon plus 1 teaspoon finely grated Key lime or regular lime zest (green part of skin)
- 6 tablespoons fresh or bottled Key lime juice
- 1³/4 cups all-purpose flour
- ¹/2 teaspoon baking soda
- ¹/2 teaspoon baking powder
-   Pinch of salt
- ²/3 cup granulated sugar
- 7 tablespoons (1 stick minus 1 tablespoon) unsalted butter, slightly softened and cut into chunks
- 1 teaspoon vanilla extract

- ¹/2 teaspoon lemon extract or 1 teaspoon lime flavoring oil, such as Boyajian
-   Up to 1 tablespoon water, if needed
-   About 3 tablespoons lime-colored decorating sugar, or crystal sugar or granulated sugar for garnish

ICING (OPTIONAL)

-   About 1¹/2 cups powdered sugar
- 2¹/2–3 tablespoons fresh or bottled Key lime juice (see Tip, page 260)
- 1–2 drops yellow liquid food color (optional)
- 1–2 drops green liquid food color (optional)

TO MAKE THE COOKIES: In a small bowl, combine the oil and lime zest. Let stand, covered, for at least 30 minutes and up to several hours. Microwave the lime juice in a 2-cup microwave-safe measure on high power for 2¹/2 to 5 minutes, stopping and checking after 2 minutes, then every 30 seconds, until the lime juice is reduced to 2¹/2 tablespoons; it's normal for the juice to darken in color slightly. (Alternatively, heat the juice in a small nonreactive saucepan over medium heat until reduced to 2¹/2 tablespoons.) If the juice is inadvertently reduced to less than 2¹/2 tablespoons, add enough water to yield 2¹/2 tablespoons. Let cool to room temperature.

In a medium bowl, stir together the flour, baking soda, baking powder, and salt. In a large bowl with a mixer on medium speed, beat together the oil mixture and granulated sugar until well blended. Add the butter, beating until light and fluffy, about 2 minutes. Beat in the lime juice, vanilla, and lemon extract until well blended and smooth. Gradually beat or stir in the flour mixture to form a smooth dough. If the dough seems soft, let stand for 5 minutes to firm up slightly. If it seems dry, stir in up to 1 tablespoon water.

Divide the dough in half. Roll out each portion between sheets of baking parchment or wax paper until a scant ¼ inch thick. Occasionally check the underside of the dough during rolling and smooth out any wrinkles. Stack the rolled portions (paper still attached) on a baking sheet. Refrigerate for about 30 minutes or freeze for about 15 minutes, or until cold.

Position a rack in the middle of the oven and preheat to 350 degrees F. Grease several baking sheets or coat with nonstick spray. Working with one portion at a time and keeping the other refrigerated, gently peel off the top sheet of paper, then pat loosely back into place so it will be easy to remove later. Invert the dough and peel off the second sheet.

Using a 2¼-inch round cutter, cut out the cookies, then cut each round in half with a sharp knife. If at any point the dough softens too much to handle easily, transfer the paper and cookies to a baking sheet and refrigerate or freeze until firm.

Using a spatula, transfer the cookies to the baking sheets, spacing them about 1 inch apart. Re-roll any dough scraps. Continue cutting out the cookies until all the dough is used. Generously sprinkle the cookie tops with the decorating sugar.

Bake one sheet at a time for 7 to 11 minutes, or until the cookies just begin to brown at the edges. If necessary, reverse the sheet from front to back halfway through baking to ensure even browning. Using a wide spatula, immediately transfer the cookies to a wire rack. Let cool completely.

TO MAKE THE ICING (IF USING): In a small bowl, stir together 1½ cups powdered sugar and 2½ tablespoons lime juice until well blended and smooth. If desired, stir in the yellow and green food color. If necessary, stir in more sugar or juice to yield a piping consistency (stiff enough to hold its shape but soft enough to pipe through a fine tip). Place the icing in a paper decorating cone or pastry bag fitted with a fine writing tip. Space the cookies slightly apart on a rack set over baking parchment or wax paper. To suggest lime slices, pipe a thin line around the perimeter of each cookie, then add "segments" by piping a dot in the center and 7 thin spokes radiating out from the dot to the perimeter. Let stand until the icing sets, at least 30 minutes.

The cookies will keep, stored airtight, at room temperature for up to 2 weeks or frozen for up to 2 months.

TIPS

Fresh Key limes are often hard to find except in south Florida or in Latino ethnic markets, but bottled Key lime juice, which works perfectly in these cookies, is stocked in many supermarkets and gourmet shops. You can also use grated zest from either Key limes or ordinary limes with excellent results.

You can make your own lime-colored decorating sugar by combining drops of green and yellow food color, then adding 3 to 4 tablespoons sugar and stirring to blend. Let stand or place in a barely warm (200 degree F) oven for a few minutes until the sugar dries.

Maple-Caramel Nut Crisps

There was a time—before electricity became commonplace in American homes—when cookies that were shaped into logs, then chilled for slicing and baking later, were called icebox cookies. Even though iceboxes are largely gone from the scene (except as curiosities in antique collections), I still like the old-fashioned name.

In fact, although this recipe is completely updated and requires the use of a food processor, it is roughly based on a recipe called icebox slices from my grandmother's collection. The slices are homey and rustic-looking, and they have an outstanding flavor and a wonderful light, crisp texture that always elicits comments. This, of course, is why I call them crisps.

3 tablespoons maple syrup, preferably medium amber

²/₃ cup plus 3 tablespoons granulated sugar (divided)

2 cups coarsely chopped walnuts or pecans

2 tablespoons water

3 cups all-purpose flour

2 teaspoons baking powder

2 teaspoons baking soda
   Generous ¼ teaspoon salt

16 tablespoons (2 sticks) unsalted butter, slightly softened

1 cup packed light brown sugar

2 large eggs

2 teaspoons vanilla extract

Position a rack in the middle of the oven and preheat to 350 degrees F. Line a large pie plate or similar-size heatproof dish with aluminum foil coated with nonstick spray (or use nonstick foil); set aside. Line a 10-by-15-inch (or similar) rimmed baking sheet with aluminum foil coated with nonstick spray (or use nonstick foil).

In a medium bowl, stir together the maple syrup, 3 tablespoons of the granulated sugar, and the pecans until the nuts are well coated. Spread them out on the baking sheet. Toast for 8 to 13 minutes, stirring every 3 or 4 minutes, until nicely browned. Remove from the oven and set aside until thoroughly cooled.

In a heavy 2-quart saucepan over medium heat, stir together the remaining ²/₃ cup granulated sugar and the water until the sugar dissolves. Wipe any sugar from the pan sides with a pastry brush dipped in warm water or a damp paper towel. Without further stirring, bring the mixture to a boil over medium-high heat. Adjust the heat so the mixture boils briskly. Continue boiling, lifting the pan and gently swirling the syrup

occasionally but never stirring, for 3 to 4 minutes. Watch carefully and remove the pan from the heat as soon as the syrup just turns a medium amber color. Wearing kitchen mitts and working carefully, immediately pour the syrup into the pie plate. Let stand until cooled and hard, about 10 minutes. Break the caramel into small chunks. Transfer to a food processor and pulse until fairly finely ground but with some bits visible.

In a large bowl, thoroughly stir together the flour, baking powder, baking soda, and salt. In a large bowl using a mixer on medium speed, beat together the butter, brown sugar, and ground caramel until very fluffy and well blended. Beat in the eggs and vanilla until smoothly incorporated. Beat in half the flour mixture. Beat or stir in the remaining flour mixture, then the toasted nuts, just until smoothly incorporated.

Spoon half the dough onto a 16-inch-long sheet of baking parchment or wax paper. Smoothing and shaping the dough with lightly greased hands, form it into an evenly thick log about 12 inches long. Twist the ends of the paper to keep the log from unrolling. Repeat with the remaining dough. Place the logs on a rimmed baking sheet and refrigerate until completely firm, at least 3 hours and up to 2 days. (For more cylindrical logs, once they are cold and fairly stiff, reshape them to eliminate the flat side. Return to the refrigerator until very cold and stiff.) The logs will keep, stored airtight, in the freezer for up to 12 months. Partially thaw in the refrigerator before using.

Position a rack in the upper third of the oven and preheat to 375 degrees F. Generously grease several baking sheets or generously coat with nonstick spray. Peel the paper off one log. Cut into generous ⅛-inch-thick slices using a large sharp knife. Because of the nuts, the dough may not cut neatly. Using a spatula, immediately transfer the slices to baking sheets, spacing them about 2 inches apart. If desired, repeat with the second log, or save it to bake at another time.

Bake one sheet at a time for 7 to 11 minutes, or until the cookies are golden all over and just slightly darker around the edges. Transfer the sheet to a wire rack. Let the cookies stand for about 5 minutes to firm up just slightly. Using a spatula, transfer to the rack. Let cool completely.

The cookies will keep, stored airtight, at room temperature for up to a week or frozen for a month.

nut mates

Nuts and maple are perfect partners, but which nut you prefer may depend on where you live. Old-time New Englanders think butternuts are the best match for maple syrup. When I visited David Marvin, the owner of Butternut Mountain Farm, in Johnson, Vermont, he presented me with a little box of the creamy-tasting nuts, both shelled and unshelled, furnished by his neighbor, Ed Perkins. (Ed included a note saying the shelling had taken forty minutes.) The box contained only about half a cup of shelled nuts—underscoring the fact that the meats are notoriously difficult to pick out.

The hard, rough-ridged shells made me think of black walnuts, which is not surprising, since the two trees are close relatives. Butternuts are often described as being creamy or buttery, but like black walnuts, they seem to me to have a slightly acrid flavor.

peanut BUTTER munchies

Loaded with dried cranberries, raisins, peanuts, peanut butter, coconut, and chocolate morsels, these are hearty, filling cookies with a robust flavor. They make an appealing and fortifying snack. The slight sweetness of the fruit and chocolate morsels provides a nice counterpoint to the peanut butter and salted peanuts.

2⅓ cups all-purpose flour	1½ teaspoons vanilla extract
½ teaspoon baking soda	1 cup (6 ounces) semisweet chocolate morsels
⅛ teaspoon salt	1 cup dried sweetened cranberries
12 tablespoons (1½ sticks) unsalted butter, slightly softened	1 cup dark raisins
⅔ cup creamy peanut butter	1 cup shredded or flaked sweetened coconut (optional)
¼ cup corn oil or other flavorless vegetable oil	About 1⅓ cups coarsely chopped salted peanuts (divided)
1½ cups packed light brown sugar	
2 large eggs	

In a medium bowl, thoroughly stir together the flour, baking soda, and salt. In a large bowl with a mixer on low, then medium speed, beat the butter, peanut butter, and oil until blended, about 1 minute. Add the brown sugar and continue beating until well blended, about 2 minutes longer. Add the eggs and vanilla. Continue beating until very light and fluffy, about 1½ minutes longer.

On low, then medium speed, beat half the flour mixture into the butter mixture until smoothly incorporated. Beat or stir in the remaining flour mixture, the chocolate morsels, cranberries, raisins, coconut (if using), and ⅔ cup of the peanuts until evenly incorporated. Cover and refrigerate for about 20 minutes or until firmed up slightly.

Position a rack in the upper third of the oven and preheat to 350 degrees F. Grease several baking sheets or coat with nonstick spray. Put the remaining ⅔ cup peanuts in a shallow bowl.

On baking parchment or wax paper, shape the dough into a 6-inch disk, then cut into quarters. Divide and shape each quarter into 8 balls. Dip the tops of the balls in the chopped peanuts. Space the cookies nut sides up about 3 inches apart on the baking sheets. Pat down each cookie until about ½ inch thick.

Bake one sheet at a time for 10 to 15 minutes, or until the cookies are tinged with brown, just darker at the edges, and almost firm when pressed in the centers. If necessary, reverse the sheet from front to back halfway through baking to ensure even browning. Transfer the sheet to a wire rack. Let the cookies stand for 4 minutes to firm up slightly. Using a wide spatula, transfer to the rack. Let cool completely.

The cookies will keep, stored airtight, at room temperature for up to 2 weeks or frozen for up to 1½ months.

Big, easy chocolate chip cookies

Makes about 35 cookies

These cookies have a buttery, brown sugary flavor, are full of chocolate chips, and are crisp on the edges but slightly soft in the centers. The dough is mixed in a large saucepan; no electric mixer is required.

- 2¼ cups all-purpose flour
- 1¼ teaspoons baking powder
- ¼ teaspoon baking soda
- ¾ teaspoon salt
- 16 tablespoons (2 sticks) unsalted butter, cut into chunks
- 1 cup packed light brown sugar
- Scant ⅔ cup granulated sugar
- 2½ teaspoons vanilla extract
- 2 large eggs
- 2 cups (12 ounces) semisweet chocolate morsels
- ¾ cup chopped walnuts or pecans (optional)

In a medium bowl, thoroughly stir together the flour, baking powder, baking soda, and salt. In a large saucepan, melt the butter over medium heat. Immediately remove from the heat. Vigorously stir in the sugars and vanilla until smoothly incorporated. Stir in the eggs until well blended and the mixture is free of lumps. Stir in the flour mixture just until evenly distributed. Let cool for 10 minutes. Stir in the chocolate morsels and nuts (if using). Cover and refrigerate until well chilled and firm, at least 3 hours and up to 24 hours.

Position a rack in the upper third of the oven and preheat to 350 degrees F. Grease several baking sheets or coat with nonstick spray. If the dough is very stiff, let it warm up for about 10 minutes. Use a medium ice cream scoop to scoop up generous 1½-inch rounded dough portions, or, with lightly greased hands, roll portions of dough between your palms to form 1½-inch balls. Space the cookies about 3 inches apart on the baking sheets; don't crowd. With your palm, pat down the dough tops until the cookies are about 2½ inches in diameter.

Tip

Throughout this book, I call for the "dip-and-sweep" method of measuring flour, and it's especially important in this recipe. To ensure the right amount, scoop down into the flour canister or bag with a graduated measuring cup and overfill the cup. Then use a knife blade to sweep off the excess flour even with the cup top. Don't fluff up the flour by stirring it first, and don't try to compact it by tapping or shaking the cup.

Bake one sheet at a time for 10 to 15 minutes, or until the cookies are golden brown around the edges but still slightly soft and underdone in the center. (The baking time will vary considerably depending on the coldness of the dough.) If necessary, reverse the sheet from front to back halfway through baking to ensure even browning. Transfer the sheet to a wire rack. Let the cookies stand for 1 to 2 minutes to firm up just slightly. Using a wide spatula, transfer to the rack. Let cool completely. Let the baking sheets cool between batches, or the cookies may spread too much.

The cookies will keep, stored airtight, at room temperature for up to a week or frozen for up to a month. Let come to room temperature before serving.

cookie of the commonwealth

Considering that chocolate chip cookies are this nation's favorite cookie, it's amazing to realize that they didn't exist until 1930. The creator was a Whitman, Massachusetts, innkeeper named Ruth Wakefield, who added a chopped-up chocolate bar to a cookie dough when she ran out of nuts. She was surprised to find that the chocolate stayed in appealing chunks instead of melting.

In response to public demand for bits of chocolate to add to the exciting new cookie, the Nestlé company began manufacturing prescored chocolate bars that cooks could conveniently break into small pieces. Then in 1939, the company devised an even better solution — little packages containing ready-to-use chocolate morsels and imprinted with Mrs. Wakefield's authentic Toll House Inn recipe.

In honor of her culinary achievement, Massachusetts declared in its 1997 General Laws, "The chocolate chip cookie shall be the official cookie of the commonwealth."

Hazelnut-chocolate chip cookies

Rather refined and sophisticated, these are chocolate chip cookies for grownups. They are tender, buttery, not too sweet, and rich with hazelnuts and chocolate morsels. They taste great with coffee or tea. Evenly shaped and not too large, they also look nice on a dessert tray.

1⅓ cups whole hazelnuts	Generous 1⅓ cups powdered sugar
2¼ cups all-purpose flour	1 large egg
¼ teaspoon salt	2¼ teaspoons vanilla extract
¼ teaspoon baking soda	1 cup (6 ounces) semisweet chocolate morsels
16 tablespoons (2 sticks) unsalted butter, slightly softened	

Position a rack in the upper third of the oven and preheat to 350 degrees F. Grease several large baking sheets or coat with nonstick spray. Spread the hazelnuts on a rimmed baking sheet and toast, stirring occasionally, for 14 to 18 minutes, or until the hulls loosen and the nuts are nicely browned; be careful not to burn. Set aside until cool enough to handle. Rub the nuts between your hands or in a clean kitchen towel, loosening and discarding as much of the hulls as possible. (It's all right if some bits of hull remain.) Chop the nuts moderately fine.

In a medium bowl, thoroughly stir together half the nuts, the flour, salt, and baking soda. Place the remaining nuts in a medium shallow bowl and reserve for rolling the cookies.

In a large bowl with a mixer on medium speed, beat together the butter, powdered sugar, egg, and vanilla until very fluffy and well blended, about 2 minutes. Reduce the speed to low and beat in half the flour mixture until well blended and smooth. Beat or stir in the remaining flour mixture until smoothly incorporated. Fold in the chocolate morsels until evenly distributed. Let stand for 10 minutes, or until the dough firms up just slightly.

Pull off dough portions and roll between your palms to form generous 1-inch balls. Roll the balls in the reserved nuts until lightly coated. Transfer to baking sheets, spacing them 2½ inches apart. Using your palm, press down on the balls until the cookies are 2 inches in diameter.

Bake one sheet at a time for 10 to 15 minutes, or until the cookies are tinged with brown at the edges. If necessary, reverse the sheet from front to back halfway through baking to ensure even browning. Transfer the sheet to a wire rack. Let the cookies stand for 2 or 3 minutes to firm up. Using a spatula, transfer to the rack. Let cool completely.

The cookies will keep, stored airtight, at room temperature for up to 2 weeks or frozen for up to 2 months. Let come to room temperature before serving.

peppermint fudgies

MAKES 40 TO 45 COOKIES

Easy to mix and bake, these festive drop cookies are a good choice for busy cooks or older children who are helping with the family baking. The condensed milk gives them a fudgy consistency, and the peppermint oil in the candy makes them intensely minty.

Notice that the recipe calls for sweetened condensed milk, not evaporated milk. (Evaporated milk is not thick or sweet enough and won't work.) No sugar is added: the condensed milk, chocolate, and candy provide all the sweetness needed.

2 cups (12 ounces) semisweet chocolate morsels (divided)

4 tablespoons (½ stick) unsalted butter

1 14-ounce can sweetened condensed milk

6 tablespoons finely crushed peppermint candy canes, peppermint sticks, or peppermint pinwheel hard candies (divided)

1 large egg

¼ teaspoon peppermint extract or ½ teaspoon vanilla extract

1 cup all-purpose flour

5 tablespoons unsweetened, nonalkalized American-style cocoa powder or unsweetened Dutch-process cocoa powder

Position a rack in the middle of the oven and preheat to 350 degrees F. Line several baking sheets with baking parchment or aluminum foil.

In a large microwave-safe bowl, microwave 1 cup of the chocolate morsels and the butter on high power for 1 minute. Stir well. Continue microwaving on medium power, stopping and stirring at 30-second intervals. Stop microwaving before the chocolate completely melts and let the residual heat finish the job. (Alternatively, in a large heavy saucepan, warm 1 cup of the chocolate morsels and the butter over lowest heat, stirring frequently, until melted; be careful not to burn. Immediately remove from the heat.)

Stir the condensed milk, 3 tablespoons of the crushed candy, the egg, and peppermint extract into the chocolate mixture until well blended. In a medium bowl, stir together the flour and cocoa. Stir the flour mixture into the chocolate mixture until well blended. Stir in the remaining 1 cup chocolate morsels. If the dough seems too soft to drop, let stand for 5 minutes to firm up slightly.

Drop the dough by heaping measuring tablespoonfuls on the baking sheets, spacing the cookies about 2 inches apart. (Don't make the cookies too big, as they are very rich.) Bake one sheet at a time for 6 to 9 min-

TIP

To crush the candy, break the candy canes or peppermint sticks into roughly 1-inch pieces; leave the hard candies whole. Place in a triple layer of heavy plastic bags, closing the bags tightly. Using a kitchen mallet or the back of a heavy metal spoon, whack the candies into ⅛-inch or finer pieces. Discard any pieces that are larger than ⅛ inch or continue crushing them until fine.

utes, or until the centers are almost firm when pressed; be careful not to overbake.

Remove from the oven and garnish each cookie with a pinch or two of the remaining crushed candy. Bake for 1 to 2 minutes longer, or until the candy bits begin to melt. Transfer the sheet to a wire rack. Let the cookies stand for about 5 minutes to firm up. Using a spatula, transfer to the rack. Let cool completely.

The cookies will keep, covered, in a cool place for 3 or 4 days or in the freezer for up to a month.

A New Twist on an Old Idea

Peppermint candy canes are now as much a part of American Christmas celebrations as holly, mistletoe, Christmas trees, and Santa Claus. But surprisingly, prior to the twentieth century, these red-and-white-striped treats were absent from the scene. Examining a large collection of Victorian-era and turn-of-the-century Christmas cards, posters, and decorative papers, I found numerous images of Saint Nick and the usual Christmas greenery, but no candy canes. Nor could I find any reference to them in nineteenth-century cookbooks, periodicals, or personal reminiscences.

I did see several mentions that peppermint sticks purchased from the general store were a favorite children's treat in the 1880s. The first association of peppermint sticks with Christmas that I found appears in a recollection called "A Desert Christmas Memory" by Theresa Kane McCarthy. She remembers that in Randsburg, California, on Christmas Day, 1897, "a popcorn ball and a long stick of peppermint candy peeked out the top of [my] Christmas stocking."

Red-and-white candy canes must have started appearing shortly thereafter, because they were replacing peppermint sticks as Christmas sweets by the following decade. A writer/researcher friend of mine, Binnie Syril Braunstein, uncovered a December 1909 *Good Housekeeping* photograph of a candy cane–decorated Christmas tree and additional references to them in 1910 and 1914 publications.

Nobody knows who came up with the idea of candy canes, but they are probably a turn-of-the-century American secular invention. My guess is that an enterprising peppermint stick maker bent his sticks of candy into a crook on the spur of the moment, creating a permanent twist in candy history. By the 1920s, candy canes were a standard in commercial confectioners' holiday inventories.

fudge brownies

The gloriously good all-American bar cookies called brownies first turned up in two Boston cookbooks about a hundred years ago. No one knows who created them. The early versions were somewhat similar to mine, though a little less chocolatey.

Designed for traditionalists who still think the plain old-fashioned style of brownies is the best, these have a smooth, satisfying chocolate flavor, a moist texture, and a shiny top. If you are in the mood for opulence, they are wonderful topped with Fudge Glaze (page 150) or Rich and Creamy Chocolate Fudge Frosting (page 149).

1¾ cups all-purpose flour

½ teaspoon salt

16 tablespoons (2 sticks) unsalted butter, cut into chunks

2 cups sugar

¼ cup brewed coffee or water

11 ounces bittersweet (not unsweetened) or semisweet chocolate, broken up or coarsely chopped

2 ounces unsweetened chocolate, broken up or coarsely chopped

1 tablespoon vanilla extract

4 large eggs

2 cups chopped walnuts (optional)

Fudge Glaze (page 150) or Rich and Creamy Chocolate Fudge Frosting (page 149) (optional)

Position a rack in the middle of the oven and preheat to 350 degrees F. If you aren't adding the fudge glaze or frosting, line a 9-by-13-inch baking pan with aluminum foil, allowing the foil to overhang the two ends of the pan by about 2 inches. Coat the foil with nonstick spray (or use nonstick foil). If adding a topping, omit the foil lining and grease the pan or coat with nonstick spray.

In a medium bowl, thoroughly stir together the flour and salt; set aside. In a large saucepan, bring the butter, sugar, and coffee just to a boil over medium-high heat, stirring. Remove from the heat. Stir the chocolates into the sugar mixture until completely melted. Let cool to warm (if the mixture is hot, the eggs may curdle when added). Stir the vanilla into the chocolate mixture, then add the eggs and mix thoroughly. Stir the dry ingredients into the chocolate mixture just until the batter is evenly blended. Stir in the nuts, if using. Turn out the batter into the pan, spreading it evenly to the edges.

tip

The baking time depends greatly on the pan used, so check frequently for signs of doneness. In a dull metal pan that absorbs and holds heat readily, the brownies bake through in only about 20 minutes. In a glass or shiny metal pan, they may take 5 to 10 minutes longer.

Bake for 20 to 30 minutes, or until the center is barely firm when tapped and a toothpick inserted in the center comes out clean except for the bottom ⅛ inch, which should have wet crumbs clinging to it. Transfer the pan to a wire rack. Let cool to warm, about 20 minutes.

TO GLAZE OR FROST THE BROWNIES: Pour the fudge glaze or frosting over the brownie surface and immediately spread out with a long-bladed offset spatula to even the surface. Let cool completely, at least 1 hour. The glazed brownie slab can be frozen for up to a month. Uncover and partially thaw before cutting into bars.

Using a large sharp knife wiped clean between cuts, cut the brownies into 2⅛-by-2¼-inch bars (or as desired). Serve them directly from the pan or transfer to a serving plate using a wide spatula.

TO CUT PLAIN BROWNIES: To prepare the brownies for cutting, cover and refrigerate until well chilled and firm, at least 30 minutes.

Using the overhanging foil as handles, carefully transfer the brownie slab to a cutting board. If desired, trim away the uneven edges using a large sharp knife. Cut the slab in half crosswise, cutting through the foil. Carefully peel off and discard the foil.

The slabs will keep, stored airtight, in the freezer for up to a month. Let thaw partially before cutting into bars. Cut the brownies into 2⅛-by-2¼-inch bars (or as desired), wiping the knife clean between cuts.

The glazed or plain brownies will keep, stored airtight, at room temperature for 2 or 3 days.

Glazed cocoa-cheesecake Brownies

This decadent recipe for triple-layer brownies, which I've modified for easier preparation, was shared with me by St. Louis food lover Patty Padawer. She says that she worked on the components over a number of years. The original brownie batter recipe evolved from one she found in an elementary school cookbook. She devised the cheesecake part by altering a recipe from an old friend. I've topped off her masterpiece with an easy, very chocolatey glaze. The result is dense, moist, and as rich as sin.

BROWNIE LAYER

- ¾ cup unsweetened Dutch-process cocoa powder
- 2 cups superfine sugar
- ½ teaspoon salt
- 4 large eggs
- 18 tablespoons (2¼ sticks) unsalted butter, melted and cooled to warm
- 2½ tablespoons light corn syrup
- 2 teaspoons vanilla extract
- 1½ cups all-purpose flour
- 1 cup semisweet chocolate mini-morsels

CREAM CHEESE LAYER

- 1 pound (two 8-ounce packages) cream cheese, at room temperature
- ⅔ cup granulated sugar
- 2 large eggs
- 1 teaspoon vanilla extract

GLAZE

- ⅔ cup heavy (whipping) cream
- ¼ cup powdered sugar, sifted after measuring if lumpy
- 6 ounces bittersweet (not unsweetened) or semisweet chocolate, broken up or coarsely chopped
- ½ teaspoon vanilla extract

Position a rack in the middle of the oven and preheat to 350 degrees F. Generously grease a 9-by-13-inch baking pan or generously coat with nonstick spray.

TO MAKE THE BROWNIE LAYER: Sift the cocoa into a large bowl. Stir in the superfine sugar and salt. Vigorously stir in the eggs one at a time until well blended and smooth. Stir in the melted butter, corn syrup, and vanilla until thoroughly incorporated. Stir in the flour and mini-morsels, mixing until very well blended. Pour the batter into the

tip

If you don't have superfine sugar, you can make it by processing granulated sugar in a food processor until very fine and almost powdery.

baking pan, spreading it evenly to the edges. Bake for 20 to 24 minutes, or until a toothpick inserted in the center comes out clean except for the bottom ¼ inch, which should still look wet.

MEANWHILE, TO MAKE THE CREAM CHEESE LAYER: In a large bowl with a mixer on medium speed, beat the cream cheese and granulated sugar for 2 to 3 minutes, or until completely smooth and well blended, scraping down the sides of the bowl as needed. Add the eggs one at a time, beating for 20 seconds after each addition. Add the vanilla. Continue beating until the mixture is very smooth.

Top the hot brownie layer with the cream cheese mixture, spreading it evenly to the edges. Bake for 15 to 19 minutes, or until all but the very center looks set when tapped; the center should still be jiggly. Transfer to a wire rack. Let cool to warm.

TO MAKE THE GLAZE: Stir together the cream and sugar in a microwave-safe 4-cup measure. Microwave on high power for 1½ minutes, or until steaming hot. Stop and stir. Add the chocolate, without stirring, and microwave on medium power for 1 minute longer. Remove from the microwave and let stand for 1 minute. Add the vanilla and gently stir for 1 to 2 minutes until the chocolate completely melts and the glaze is very smooth and glossy. (Alternatively, stir together the cream and sugar in a 1-quart saucepan. Heat over medium-high heat, stirring, until it comes almost to a boil. Remove from the heat. Immediately add the chocolate and vanilla without stirring. Let stand for 5 minutes. Stir until the chocolate completely melts and the glaze is very smooth and glossy.)

TO GLAZE AND CUT THE BROWNIES: Using a long-bladed offset spatula, spreader, or table knife, spread the glaze smoothly and evenly over the brownie. For the best appearance, smooth out quickly and don't overwork the glaze. Let stand for at least 1½ hours at room temperature or 1 hour in the refrigerator before cutting. Using a large sharp knife dipped in hot water and wiped dry between cuts, cut into quarters lengthwise and sixths crosswise (or as desired).

The brownies will keep, tightly covered, in the refrigerator for 4 or 5 days or in the freezer for up to a month. (If frozen, let thaw in the refrigerator.) Let warm up slightly before serving.

Almond-coconut Joy Bars

Yes, these bars were inspired by Almond Joy candy, but I take the almond part more seriously than the candy bar maker does. Instead of having just a couple of nuts, my chocolate-topped bar cookies are loaded with them: in the chocolate crumb base, throughout the mellow coconut filling, and studding the chocolate on top. Despite the multiple layers, this recipe is relatively easy to make.

Because the bars are rich, I serve them cut fairly small. Coconut fans love them.

2 cups blanched sliced almonds

7–8 whole graham crackers, coarsely broken (2¼ cups)

1½ cups (9 ounces) semisweet chocolate morsels, preferably mini-morsels (divided)

3 tablespoons packed light brown sugar

2 tablespoons unsweetened, nonalkalized American-style cocoa powder or unsweetened Dutch-process cocoa powder

5 tablespoons unsalted butter, melted (divided)

1 tablespoon hot water, plus more if needed

1 14-ounce can sweetened condensed milk

1 large egg

1¼ teaspoons vanilla extract

½ teaspoon almond extract

2¼ cups shredded or flaked sweetened coconut

Position a rack in the middle of the oven and preheat to 350 degrees F. Lightly grease a 9-by-13-inch baking pan or coat with nonstick spray. Line the pan with aluminum foil, letting the foil overhang the two ends of the pan by about 2 inches. Coat the foil with nonstick spray (or use nonstick foil). Spread the almonds on a rimmed baking sheet. Toast, stirring once or twice, until lightly tinged with brown, 5 to 8 minutes. Let cool.

In a food processor, combine ⅓ cup of the toasted almonds, the graham cracker pieces, ¼ cup of the chocolate morsels, the brown sugar, and cocoa. Process until the nuts and chocolate are finely ground and the mixture is well blended, about 1½ minutes, scraping down the sides of the bowl as needed. Add 3 tablespoons of the melted butter and the hot water and process until the mixture is well blended and holds together. Press between your fingertips to check. If necessary, blend in a little more water and check again. Firmly press the mixture into the bottom (not sides) of the pan, forming an even layer. Refrigerate while you prepare the filling.

In a large bowl, stir together the remaining 2 tablespoons melted butter, the condensed milk, egg, vanilla, and almond extract until well blended. Stir in the coconut and ⅔ cup of the remaining almonds. Pour the filling over the crumb layer and spread it evenly to the edges. Bake until lightly browned at the edges and tinged with brown on top, and a toothpick inserted in the center comes out clean, 18 to 23 minutes. Transfer to a wire rack. Let cool for 10 minutes.

Sprinkle the remaining 1¼ cups chocolate morsels evenly over the filling. When the morsels melt, use an offset spatula or table knife to spread evenly over the entire surface. Sprinkle the remaining 1 cup almonds evenly over the glaze. Shake the pan back and forth to embed the almonds in the surface. Refrigerate, uncovered, until completely cooled, at least 1 hour.

Shortly before serving time, using the overhanging foil as handles, transfer the slab to a cutting board. Cut in half crosswise, cutting through the foil. Carefully peel off the foil. Cut each half crosswise into fifths and lengthwise into thirds (or as desired). Let warm up slightly before serving.

The bars will keep, covered, in the refrigerator for up to a week.

chewy peanut-caramel Bars

These are what one of our most popular candy bars, Snickers, would be like if it came in cookie form and was homemade: rich and wonderfully peanutty, with a really gooey, full-bodied caramel. Take them to a bake sale, PTA meeting, or family get-together, then stand back and wait for the raves.

CRUST

- 1¼ cups all-purpose flour
- 2½ tablespoons granulated sugar
- Generous ¼ teaspoon salt
- 6 tablespoons (¾ stick) cold unsalted butter, cut into chunks
- 5 tablespoons heavy (whipping) cream
- 1 teaspoon vanilla extract

TOPPING

- 1¼ cups packed light brown sugar
- ½ cup light corn syrup
- ½ cup heavy (whipping) cream
- 3 tablespoons unsalted butter, cut into chunks
- ⅛ teaspoon salt
- 3 cups chopped unsalted peanuts (divided)
- 1½ teaspoons vanilla extract
- 1½ cups (9 ounces) semisweet chocolate morsels or mini-morsels

Position a rack in the middle of the oven and preheat to 375 degrees F. Line a 9-by-13-inch baking dish with aluminum foil and coat the foil with nonstick spray (or use nonstick foil).

TO MAKE THE CRUST: In a food processor, process the flour, sugar, and salt to blend. Add the butter. Process in pulses until the butter is cut in and the mixture resembles coarse crumbs. Sprinkle the cream and vanilla over the flour mixture. Process in pulses until the dough holds together, being very careful not to overprocess. Very firmly press the mixture into the baking dish in an even layer. Prick the crust all over with a fork. Bake for 20 to 25 minutes, or until just tinged with brown all over and slightly darker at the edges. Transfer to a wire rack.

TO MAKE THE TOPPING: In a heavy 2-quart saucepan, stir together the brown sugar, corn syrup, cream, butter, and salt. Bring the mixture to a boil over medium-high heat, stirring frequently. Stir in 2½ cups of the peanuts. Adjust the heat so that the mixture boils briskly. Cook, stirring frequently, for 2½ minutes. Immediately remove from the heat. Stir in the vanilla.

Pour the topping over the crust, drizzling to cover the entire surface as evenly as possible. Spread out with a greased table knife, if necessary. Let cool and firm up for 20 minutes. Sprinkle the top with the chocolate morsels. Let stand for a few minutes longer, or until the chocolate is partially melted. Using a table knife, spread the melted chocolate over the topping. Sprinkle the top with the remaining ½ cup peanuts.

Let cool completely. Remove the slab from the pan and transfer to a cutting board. Carefully peel off the foil. If desired, using a large sharp knife, trim away the uneven edges. Carefully cut the slab crosswise into eighths and lengthwise into quarters (or as desired).

The bars will keep, stored airtight, at room temperature for up to 10 days or frozen for up to 2 months. Let come to room temperature before serving.

NOTE TO TRIVIA FANS

"Snickers" was said to be the name of a favorite horse owned by the Mars family, the creators of the candy bar.

The Great Goober

Almost everybody who grew up in America in the twentieth century knows Mr. Peanut, the spiffy, stick-legged peanut man on Planters containers who sports a cane, top hat, white gloves, and monocle. (In images where his feet are visible, he also wears spats.) Dating from 1916, he is one of the best-known food advertising mascots and probably the longest-lived. (Elsie the Cow dates from the 1940s, and the Pillsbury Doughboy, the Jolly Green Giant, Tony the Tiger, and the Keebler elves are all post–World War II.)

A thirteen-year-old boy is credited with creating the original Mr. Peanut for a Planters contest, although a professional illustrator later added the distinctive clothing accessories and monocle. Mr. Peanut's odd charm has won him a big fan club: a group of peanut-memorabilia collectors, called Peanut Pals, boasts nine hundred members from the United States, Canada, and Japan.

But even a peanut, it seems, needs an image manager these days. In her March 2000 article in *Salon,* "The Mr. Peanut Chronicles," Ruth Shalit quotes David Hale of Planters: "We wouldn't . . . make him look foolish or silly. We wouldn't . . . dress him up in inappropriate outfits." Added Nancy Anderson, the Planters account supervisor for Foote, Cone & Belding, "He's someone who doesn't change to adapt to the situation. He's comfortable just being himself." In other words, he's a nut who's comfortable in his own shell.

chocolate cookie ice cream sandwiches

Homemade ice cream sandwiches are easy to make, and the cookies for them are much tastier and stay crisper than the store-bought kind. Plus, you can customize your sandwiches by using any flavor of ice cream you want. (I especially like mint chocolate chip, banana, or dark cherry ice cream.) It's also fun to dress up the sandwiches by rolling or dipping the ice cream edges in finely chopped nuts or chocolate, sprinkles, or toasted coconut. (Keep the bits and pieces small, as large items are too hard to eat when frozen.)

The cookies themselves can be crumbled and folded into ice cream or crushed to make wonderfully tasty chocolate crumb crusts. They also are good served as is.

3 ounces bittersweet (not unsweetened) or semisweet chocolate, broken up or coarsely chopped

2¹/₂ cups all-purpose flour

³/₄ cup unsweetened Dutch-process cocoa powder

¹/₄ teaspoon baking soda

¹/₈ teaspoon salt

²/₃ cup (10²/₃ tablespoons) unsalted butter, slightly softened

¹/₄ cup corn oil or other flavorless vegetable oil

1 cup granulated sugar

¹/₄ cup light corn syrup

1 large egg

1 tablespoon milk

2¹/₂ teaspoons vanilla extract

¹/₃ cup powdered sugar for coating cutter, plus more if needed

SANDWICH FILLING AND OPTIONAL GARNISHES

About 1¹/₂ pints vanilla, coffee, mint chip, mocha, banana, cherry, raspberry, or other ice cream, slightly softened

Assorted sprinkles, finely chopped nuts or chocolate, and/or toasted coconut (optional)

In a small microwave-safe bowl, microwave the chocolate on high power for 1 minute. Stir well. Continue microwaving on medium power, stirring every 20 seconds, until the chocolate is almost melted. Set aside, stirring occasionally, and let the residual heat finish the job. (Alternatively, melt the chocolate over the lowest heat, stirring frequently, until barely melted; be careful not to burn.)

In a large bowl, thoroughly stir together the flour, cocoa, baking soda, and salt. In a large bowl with a mixer on low, then medium speed, beat together the butter, oil, granulated sugar, and corn syrup until lightened and fluffy. Beat in the melted chocolate until smoothly incorporated. Beat in the egg, then the milk, and then the vanilla until well blended and smooth. Gradually beat or stir in the flour mixture until well blended. Let stand for about 10 minutes to firm up slightly.

TIP

Don't omit the oil from the recipe. It keeps the frozen cookies from becoming too hard and breaking apart as they are eaten.

Divide the dough in half. Roll out each portion between sheets of baking parchment or wax paper until a scant ¼ inch thick. Occasionally check the underside of the dough during rolling and smooth out any wrinkles. Slide the dough portions and paper onto a baking sheet. Refrigerate for about 45 minutes or freeze for about 25 minutes, or until cold and firm. The dough may be frozen for up to 24 hours. Let warm up slightly before using.

Position a rack in the middle of the oven and preheat to 350 degrees F. Grease several large baking sheets or coat with nonstick spray. Working with one dough portion and keeping the other refrigerated, peel off the top sheet of paper, then pat loosely back into place so it will be easy to re-move later. Invert the dough and peel off the second sheet. Put the pow-dered sugar in a shallow saucer. Using a 3¼-inch round cutter or a clean empty tuna can that has been dipped in the powdered sugar, cut out the cookies. Dip the cutter in the powdered sugar after cutting each cookie to prevent the dough from sticking to it. If the dough softens and be-comes difficult to handle, briefly return it to the refrigerator or freezer until firm. Using a spatula, transfer the cookies to the baking sheets, spacing them about 1½ inches apart. If desired, using the lightly oiled tines of a fork, deeply prick each cookie in a decorative pattern. Repeat the cutting-out process with the remaining dough portion. Re-roll any scraps and continue cutting out cookies until all the dough is used.

Bake one sheet at a time for 8 to 13 minutes, or until the cookies are just firm when pressed in the centers. Transfer the sheet to a wire rack. Let the cookies stand for 1 to 2 minutes to firm up. Using a spatula, transfer to the rack. Let cool completely. Refrigerate for at least 1 hour or freeze for at least 30 minutes before assembling the ice cream sandwiches. The cookies will keep, stored airtight, in the freezer for up to a month.

TO ASSEMBLE THE SANDWICHES: Spread about ⅓ cup ice cream over a cookie bottom. Place a second cookie, bottom side down, over the ice cream, pressing down slightly until the ice cream squeezes out to the edges. Run a knife around the edges to remove any excess ice cream. As the sandwiches are assembled, place them on a baking sheet in the freezer to harden. Freeze for at least 1 hour. Set out shallow bowls of the garnishes, if using, and roll the ice cream edges in them until coated. Immediately pack the sandwiches in plastic bags and return to the freezer or serve.

The assembled sandwiches will keep, stored airtight, in the freezer for up to 2 weeks.

penny sandwich

New York City can probably claim credit for the first ice cream sandwiches, according to Anne Cooper Funderburg's meticulously researched book *Chocolate, Strawberry, and Vanilla: A History of American Ice Cream*. She cites a 1902 *New York Daily Tribune* story detailing how street vendors made them on the spot by placing a long wafer in a mold, adding ice cream, topping with a second wafer, and then clamping down the mold top to press the layers together. When the sandwiches were first offered (as early as 1899), they sold for two or three cents each. Children complained about the high price, so the purveyors accommodated by making the wafers smaller and dropping the price to a penny.

6

Ice Creams, Sauces, and Soda Fountain Treats

vaniLLa FROZEN custard

Frozen custards were among the earliest ice creams introduced and have been prepared in this country since at least the eighteenth century. The ingredients in frozen custard recipes haven't changed much since Thomas Jefferson brought back one from France. Provided by his personal French chef and written down by Jefferson himself, it called for two bottles of "good" cream, six egg yolks, a half pound of sugar, and a "stick" of vanilla. At the time, vanilla was still little known in America, and according to Anne Cooper Funderburg's *Chocolate, Strawberry, and Vanilla: A History of American Ice Cream,* Jefferson complained about its unavailability and ordered "50 pods" from France in 1791.

One taste will convince you that the initial step of making the custard mixture is more than worth the trouble. The flavor is much richer and fuller, the color creamier, and the texture smoother than that of "regular" vanilla ice cream. Although it is delicious plain, this frozen custard is sheer heaven with some Fresh Pineapple Sauce (page 318) or Maple–Butter Pecan Sauce (page 316) spooned over the top.

2 cups half-and-half or whole milk	Generous ³/₄ cup sugar
1¹/₂ cups heavy (whipping) cream	¹/₈ teaspoon salt
1 3-inch-long piece of vanilla bean, split in half lengthwise	1¹/₂ teaspoons vanilla extract
3–4 nickel-size pieces of lemon zest (yellow part of skin)	
4 large egg yolks	

In a heavy 2-quart saucepan, bring the half-and-half, cream, vanilla bean, and lemon zest almost to a boil over high heat. Remove from the heat and let steep for at least 30 minutes and preferably 45 minutes. Reheat the cream mixture just to hot over medium-high heat.

In a small deep bowl, beat the egg yolks, sugar, and salt with a fork until well blended. In a thin stream, stir 1 cup of the cream mixture into the yolk mixture. Slowly stir the yolk mixture back into the cream mixture. Cook over medium heat, stirring constantly and scraping the bottom of the pan with a large wooden spoon; do not boil. If bubbles appear at the edges, immediately lift the pan from the burner and stir vigorously to cool the mixture slightly. Continue cooking and stirring until the mix-

tip

If you (like Thomas Jefferson) have trouble obtaining vanilla beans, you can make the frozen custard without one. In this case, increase the vanilla extract to 1 tablespoon. The frozen custard will still be delicious.

ture thickens slightly and is very hot to the touch, 4 to 5 minutes. Immediately remove from the heat. Stir in the vanilla extract. Pour the mixture through a fine sieve into a storage container. Cover and refrigerate until very cold, at least 4½ hours and up to 24 hours.

Pour the chilled mixture into an ice cream maker and proceed according to the manufacturer's directions. When the custard finishes processing, turn out into a chilled plastic storage container. Let firm up for at least 1 hour in the freezer before serving.

The custard will keep, tightly covered, in the freezer for up to 2 weeks.

the ice cream presidencies

It seems as though anybody who was anybody in post–Revolutionary War government circles ate ice cream. Washington, D.C., was awash with it. Anne Cooper Funderburg's *Chocolate, Strawberry, and Vanilla* notes that Mrs. Alexander Hamilton served it to President George Washington during a dinner in 1789. Later, in August of the same year, President and Mrs. Washington served ice cream at a party attended by Vice President and Mrs. John Adams and Mr. and Mrs. John Jay. When James Madison was Jefferson's secretary of state, he and his wife, Dolley, also served ice cream at a party at their Washington home. She later served it at her husband's inaugural ball in 1813.

Thomas Jefferson was a great ice cream fan, and both during his presidency and afterward at his home, Monticello, he liked to present it encased in warm pastry. This generated "great astonishment and murmurings" from his dinner guests, according to Barbara G. Carson's *Ambitious Appetites: Dining, Behavior, and Patterns of Consumption in Federal Washington*.

With all the ice cream eating of the nation's early political elite, it is surprising that only Dolley Madison is widely associated with it in popular culture. At least two ice cream manufacturers, the Dolly Madison Ice Cream Company and the Dolly Madison Dairy Company, used her name. This may be why she is sometimes erroneously credited with creating it or being the first in America to serve it.

Maple frozen custard

Maple syrup not only imparts a lovely flavor but also, because it's not granular like sugar, produces a frozen custard with an unusually silky texture.

This recipe was inspired by a maple-flavored soft ice cream in a cone that I enjoyed at Morse Farm Maple Sugarworks in Montpelier, Vermont. Some New Englanders call these popular ice cream treats "creamees," for very good reason.

1⅓ cups maple syrup, preferably medium amber	4 large egg yolks
1¼ cups milk	1½ teaspoons vanilla extract
1 cup heavy (whipping) cream	

In a heavy 3- to 4-quart nonreactive saucepan, bring the maple syrup to a boil over medium heat. Boil for 1 minute, stirring frequently. Slowly stir in the milk and cream. Reheat almost to boiling. Set aside.

In a medium bowl, whisk the egg yolks until well blended. Whisking constantly, add 1 cup of the hot maple syrup mixture in a thin stream until well blended. Whisk the egg mixture into the maple mixture.

Cook over medium heat, stirring constantly and scraping the bottom of the pan with a large wooden spoon; do not boil. If bubbles appear at the pan edges or steam rises from the surface, immediately lift the pan from the burner and stir vigorously. Reduce the heat slightly and continue cooking and stirring until the mixture thickens slightly and is hot to the touch but not boiling, 4 to 5 minutes. Remove from the heat. Stir in the vanilla.

Pour the mixture through a fine sieve into a storage container. Cover and refrigerate until very cold, at least 4½ hours and preferably overnight.

Pour the chilled mixture into an ice cream maker and proceed according to the manufacturer's directions. When the custard finishes processing, turn out into a chilled plastic storage container. Let firm up for at least 1 hour in the freezer before serving.

The frozen custard will keep, tightly covered, in the freezer for up to 2 weeks.

sugarhouse hours

"I remember the long hours spent with my father in the sugarhouse. Our old beagle, Nipper, lay curled up under the big wood-fired arch, soakin' up all that heat. I hauled wood in from the shed and Father drew off batches of maple syrup. For two Vermonters with sugarin' in their blood, that's all romantic stuff. At 12:00 o'clock midnight, however, when you're bone tired and still have a tank full of sap yet to boil, the romance does just kinda wear out."

–Burr Morse, "Sugarhouse Music," *News from Vermont*
(e-newsletter; April 21, 2003)

Banana ice cream, inn at Little washington style

makes about 1 quart ice cream

This sumptuously flavored ice cream is much like one I tasted at Virginia's acclaimed Inn at Little Washington, where the food is splendid, the service distinguished, and the décor elegantly overdone. The ice cream was served along with a warm bittersweet chocolate cake, but it could have stood very comfortably on its own.

Part of the secret to achieving the exceptional flavor of this ice cream is starting with ripe bananas, then roasting them to bring out their distinctive creamy taste even more. The other key is to blend them with a rich custard base that's been spiked with a little rum (orange juice can be substituted if you wish). The resulting ice cream is amazing as is, but folding some top-quality grated chocolate into it (my improvisation) or drizzling some hot fudge sauce over it doesn't do a bit of harm.

4 ripe medium bananas, unpeeled	Pinch of salt
1½ cups heavy (whipping) cream	1½ teaspoons vanilla extract
1½ cups whole milk	¾ cup very finely chopped or grated bittersweet (not unsweetened) chocolate (optional)
1 cup sugar	
2 tablespoons light or dark rum or orange juice	
5 large egg yolks	

Position a rack in the middle of the oven and preheat to 350 degrees F. Line a rimmed baking sheet with aluminum foil. Using a paring knife, poke several holes in the bananas so they don't burst their skins. Place the bananas on the baking sheet. Roast until the skins turn dark, 10 to 15 minutes; they will release some liquid. Let cool.

In a heavy medium saucepan, bring the cream, milk, sugar, and rum almost to a boil over medium-high heat, stirring occasionally. Remove from the heat. In a medium bowl, lightly whisk the egg yolks and salt. Whisking constantly, add about 1 cup of the hot cream mixture in a thin stream until evenly incorporated. Whisk the yolk mixture into the cream mixture.

Cook over medium heat, stirring constantly and scraping the pan bottom with a large wooden spoon; do not boil. If bubbles appear at the pan edges or steam rises from the surface, immediately lift the pan from the burner and stir vigorously. Reduce the heat slightly and continue cooking and stirring until the mixture thickens slightly and is very hot to the touch, 4 to 5 minutes. Remove from the heat. Stir in the vanilla.

Peel the bananas and place their pulp in a food processor. Add about 1 cup of the cooked custard. Process for 2 minutes, or until completely pureed, scraping down the sides of the bowl as needed. Stir the banana mixture into the custard.

Pour the custard through a fine sieve into a storage container. Refrigerate until thoroughly chilled, at least 4½ hours and preferably overnight.

Pour the chilled mixture into an ice cream maker and proceed according to the manufacturer's directions. When the ice cream finishes processing, fold in the chocolate, if using, until evenly distributed. Turn out the ice cream into a chilled plastic storage container. Let firm up for at least 1 hour in the freezer before serving.

The ice cream will keep, tightly covered, in the freezer for up to 2 weeks.

strawberry-banana cheesecake ice cream

Cheesecake ice creams—usually the name for ice creams that contain some cream cheese—have become increasingly popular over the past several decades, and there are some good reasons why. The slight tang of cream cheese pairs exceptionally well with fruit, especially strawberries. Plus, the cream cheese provides a shortcut method of producing a very creamy ice cream: normally this texture is achieved only by preparing an egg-custard base, which takes not only time but careful attention.

This ice cream is a favorite of mine: it's creamy and wonderfully colorful, and it has a lovely berry flavor. The cream cheese lends smoothness without making the ice cream too dense, and its taste enhances but doesn't dominate. The banana rounds out the flavor and helps smooth the texture. As an added bonus, the recipe is easy to make.

2½ cups hulled whole strawberries, coarsely chopped

¾ cup plus 2 tablespoons sugar (divided)

1 teaspoon unflavored gelatin

½ cup milk

1 tablespoon fresh lemon juice

1 cup heavy (whipping) cream

1 small slightly overripe banana, peeled and coarsely chopped

4 ounces (half an 8-ounce package) cold cream cheese, cut into chunks

In a medium bowl, thoroughly stir together the strawberries and ¼ cup of the sugar. Let stand until the juices are released and the sugar dissolves. In a small bowl, sprinkle the gelatin over the milk. Let stand, stirring once or twice, until the gelatin softens, about 5 minutes.

In a heavy, nonreactive medium saucepan, stir together the remaining ½ cup plus 2 tablespoons sugar, the lemon juice, cream, and gelatin mixture. Bring almost to a boil over medium-high heat, stirring, until the gelatin dissolves. Let cool slightly.

Transfer the cream mixture to a food processor. Add the banana. With the motor running, add the cream cheese, several chunks at a time. Process until the mixture is completely smooth, scraping down the sides of the bowl as needed. Add the strawberries, processing in pulses just until the berries are chopped moderately fine.

Turn out the mixture into a large bowl. Refrigerate, covered, until very cold, at least 4½ hours and up to 24 hours.

Pour the chilled mixture into an ice cream maker and proceed according to the manufacturer's directions. When the ice cream finishes processing, turn out into a chilled plastic storage container. Let firm up for at least 1 hour in the freezer before serving.

The ice cream will keep, tightly covered, in the freezer for up to 2 weeks.

A Rare and "curious" Dessert

Vanilla is America's favorite ice cream flavor, but the earliest-known mention of ice cream in this country is of strawberry ice cream, eaten in Annapolis, Maryland, in 1744. In *Chocolate, Strawberry, and Vanilla,* Anne Cooper Funderburg quotes a journal entry of William Black, a Virginia official who dined at the Maryland governor's mansion:

> We were Received by his Excellency and Lady in the Hall, where we were an hour Entertain'd by them, with some Glasses of Punch . . . then the Scene was chang'd to the Dining Room, where you saw a plain proof of the Great Plenty of the Country . . . after which came a dessert no less Curious; Among the Rarities . . . was some fine Ice Cream, which with the Strawberries and Milk, eat most Deliciously.

ice creams, sauces, and soda fountain treats

Brandied Dark cherry Ice cream

It's hard to beat eating juicy dark cherries right from their stems, but I like them even better in this incredibly creamy and seductively flavored ice cream. Generously studded with burgundy-colored cherries, it is a beautiful, deep purple-pink and far more fragrant and flavorful than the usual commercial black cherry ice creams. Besides not stinting on the cherries, the key is steeping them in kirsch (clear cherry brandy), which both intensifies their fruitiness and adds some oomph.

You can leave out the cherry brandy and still produce a good ice cream. In this case, substitute orange juice for the kirsch.

1 teaspoon unflavored gelatin	1 cup heavy (whipping) cream
3 tablespoons kirsch or orange juice	1½ teaspoons vanilla extract
3½ cups pitted and chopped dark sweet cherries	¼ teaspoon almond extract
Scant 1 cup sugar	1–2 teaspoons fresh lemon juice, to taste
1⅓ cups half-and-half or light cream	

In a small bowl, sprinkle the gelatin over the kirsch. Let stand, stirring once or twice, until the gelatin softens, about 5 minutes. In a nonreactive 2-quart saucepan, stir together the cherries, sugar, and kirsch mixture. Bring to a boil over medium-high heat. Adjust the heat so the mixture boils gently. Cook, stirring occasionally, for 4 minutes. Stir in the half-and-half and heavy cream. Return the mixture almost to a boil, then remove from the heat. Stir in the vanilla, almond extract, and lemon juice.

Transfer the mixture to a storage container. Refrigerate until very cold, at least 4½ hours and up to 24 hours.

Pour the chilled mixture into an ice cream maker and proceed according to the manufacturer's directions. When the ice cream finishes processing, turn out into a chilled plastic storage container. Let firm up for at least 1 hour in the freezer before serving.

The ice cream will keep, tightly covered, in the freezer for up to 2 weeks.

The Bing Thing

Many Americans refer to dark sweet cherries as Bing cherries, but this is only one of our "black" cherry varieties; Lambert, Lapins, and Sweetheart are others. All of these are grown in the Pacific Northwest, which produces more than half of America's dark sweet cherry crop.

The most popular explanation of how the Bing cherry got its name is that Bing was a Chinese worker employed by Henderson Lewelling, a pioneer nurseryman who in 1847 arrived in Oregon by ox team from Iowa with his large family and more than seven hundred fruit trees. (Lewelling is sometimes called the father of the Pacific Northwest fruit industry.) A variation of this account is that Bing was the Chinese foreman of a crew employed by Seth Lewelling, Henderson's brother. Still a third story is that Bing was the Chinese cook of William Meeks (Henderson's son-in-law), who first used the cherries to make superb pies—unlikely, since sour cherries, not black cherries, are usually used for pies.

ice creams, sauces, and soda fountain treats

mocha ice cream with Hazelnuts

makes generous
1 quart ice cream

The offerings at today's coffee bars inspired this sophisticated, bold mocha ice cream, which is delicious even without the hazelnuts. Its depth and character depend greatly on the flavor and aroma of the coffee beans used, so be sure to choose a roast you like.

- 2/3 cup whole coffee beans, preferably dark roasted
- 2 cups whole milk or half-and-half
- 1½ cups heavy (whipping) cream
- 2/3 cup chopped toasted hazelnuts (see tip; divided)
- Pinch of salt
- 3 ounces bittersweet (not unsweetened) or semisweet chocolate, chopped moderately fine
- ¾ cup plus 2 tablespoons sugar
- 4 large eggs
- 1½ teaspoons vanilla extract

Put the coffee beans in a heavy plastic bag. Tightly close the bag and lightly crush the beans with a rolling pin; the bits should not be too fine. In a large, heavy nonreactive saucepan, bring the crushed coffee beans, milk, cream, ⅓ cup of the hazelnuts, and the salt almost to a boil over high heat. Lower the heat and simmer for 5 minutes. Remove from the heat. Strain through a very fine sieve into a bowl.

Rinse the saucepan; wipe dry with paper towels. Put the chocolate in the saucepan. Gradually whisk ½ cup of the hot milk mixture into the chocolate until it completely melts. Slowly whisk the remaining milk mixture into the chocolate mixture. Set aside.

In a large bowl, whisk together the sugar and eggs until well blended. Whisking constantly, gradually add about 1 cup of the chocolate mixture to the egg mixture until thoroughly incorporated. Whisk the egg mixture into the chocolate mixture.

Cook over medium heat, stirring constantly and scraping the bottom of the pan with a large wooden spoon; do not boil. If bubbles appear at the pan edges or steam rises from the surface, immediately lift the pan from the burner and stir vigorously. Reduce the heat slightly and continue cooking and stirring until the mixture thickens slightly and is very hot to the touch, 4 to 5 minutes.

tip

To toast the hazelnuts, spread them in a large roasting pan. Toast in a preheated 350 degree F oven, stirring occasionally, for 10 to 15 minutes, or until the hulls loosen and the nuts are nicely browned but not at all burned. Set aside until cool enough to handle. Vigorously rub the nuts between your palms or in a clean kitchen towel, discarding any loose bits of hull as you work. (It's not necessary to remove all bits of hull.) Coarsely chop the hazelnuts. Store airtight, preferably in the refrigerator, until needed. The nuts will keep for 3 or 4 days at room temperature or 2 weeks refrigerated.

Remove from the heat. Stir in the vanilla. Pour the mixture through a fine sieve into a storage container. Cover and refrigerate until very cold, at least 5 hours and preferably overnight. Refrigerate the remaining ⅓ cup hazelnuts until thoroughly chilled, at least 1 hour.

Pour the chilled mixture into an ice cream maker and proceed according to the manufacturer's directions. When the ice cream finishes processing, fold in the chilled hazelnuts until evenly distributed. Turn out the ice cream into a chilled plastic storage container. Freeze for at least 2 hours before serving.

The ice cream will keep, tightly covered, in the freezer for up to a week.

An Ice cream maker in every kitchen

"Directions for Freezing Ice-Creams and Custards—Ice-creams . . . are so delightful and refreshing for summer desserts and tea, it is to me a matter of astonishment that every family is not supplied with a patent ice-cream freezer, of which there are many in the market. By the use of one of these, the process of freezing is rendered so much more expeditious and satisfactory as to more than compensate for the trifling expense involved in its purpose."

—Annabelle P. Hill,
Mrs. Hill's New Family Receipt Book (1870)

ice creams, sauces, and soda fountain treats

chocolate
Double-malted milk
ice cream

* makes a generous
1 quart ice cream

When I was growing up, most mothers, including mine, kept a firm rein on how many sweets their offspring ate. But when it came to malted milk drinks, shakes, and even malted milk candy—all of which were popular in the 1930s, 1940s, and 1950s—my mother and many of her contemporaries relaxed their restrictions, convinced that malt conveyed special health benefits.

I won't claim (as some purveyors did) that my malted milk ice cream will boost your energy or help you sleep. But I will say that it's delicious. The mild, toasty malted milk taste is enhanced with just a little chocolate, and I've studded the ice cream with chocolate-coated malted milk balls, which add nubbins of flavor and texture.

If you grew up in malted milk's golden age, I predict that this ice cream will stir fond memories. If you are new to the charms of malted milk, the ice cream will win you over to a taste that richly deserves to live on in the American repertoire.

1 teaspoon unflavored gelatin

2 tablespoons cold water

Scant 2/3 cup sugar

3 tablespoons unsweetened Dutch-process cocoa powder

Pinch of salt

1 1/2 cups heavy (whipping) cream

1 cup plain malted milk powder (not chocolate-flavored)

1 1/2 cups half-and-half or light cream

2 teaspoons vanilla extract

1/2–3/4 cup chopped malted milk balls, frozen (to taste)

In a small bowl, stir the gelatin into the water. Let stand, stirring once or twice, until the gelatin softens, about 5 minutes. In a heavy 2-quart saucepan, thoroughly stir together the sugar, cocoa, and salt until well blended. Slowly whisk in the heavy cream and the gelatin mixture until well blended. Heat the mixture over medium-high heat, whisking until the gelatin dissolves. Remove from the heat.

In a medium bowl, whisk the malted milk powder into the half-and-half until the mixture is completely smooth. Stir the half-and-half mixture and vanilla into the cocoa mixture until smooth. Return the saucepan to the heat and cook over medium-high heat, stirring constantly, until hot. Remove from the heat and let cool slightly. Cover and refrigerate until very cold, at least 4½ hours and up to 24 hours.

Pour the chilled mixture into an ice cream maker and proceed according to the manufacturer's directions. When the ice cream finishes processing, fold in the chopped malted milk balls until evenly incorporated. Turn out the ice cream into a chilled plastic storage container. Let firm up for at least 1 hour in the freezer before serving.

The ice cream will keep, tightly covered, in the freezer for up to 2 weeks.

Diastoid Milk Balls, Anyone?

English-born James and William Horlick settled in Racine, Wisconsin, and patented malted milk powder in 1883. Originally, they called their product Diastoid; not surprisingly, it failed to catch on. After this unappetizing name was changed in 1886, however, the product became a hit. The brothers successfully promoted it as an easy-to-digest, high-protein, and high-carbohydrate food for infants, young children, and invalids. And it was convenient: it could be mixed with boiled water to provide a milk beverage that was complete, satisfying, and—most important in an era before refrigeration and modern food safety regulations—sterile.

Later, in the early twentieth century, Horlick's advertised its malted milk drinks as energy-boosting tonics, further expanding the company's already considerable visibility and customer base. In the 1930s, this effort spawned the "Puppetoons," a series of primitive soft-sell movie-theater cartoons featuring Horlick's drinkers performing amazing feats. The campaign generated print ads with the same basic message. One from 1937 features Amelia Earhart standing by an airplane and holding a can of Horlick's malted milk; a large, very noticeable Horlick's can sits in the background. Polar explorers from Robert E. Peary to Richard Byrd also took along Horlick's on expeditions; Byrd even named an Antarctic mountain range Horlick's. Additionally, in an extensive "night starvation" campaign, Horlick's promoted its malted milk as a natural bedtime sleep aid for adults whose rest was said to be disrupted by hunger. Horlick's was just one of the malted milk makers in the late nineteenth and early twentieth centuries. Others included Duffy's, Thompson's, Borden's, Carnation, National Dairy, and Coors (of Coors beer fame). Adolph Coors was said to be disgusted at having to produce anything other than beer, but prohibition forced him (and some other beer and liquor manufacturers as well) to market malted milk to stay in business.

Today the only malted milk powder widely available in our supermarkets is Carnation. (Ovaltine, a chocolate drink, also contains malt.) Horlick's Malted Milk Corporation was purchased by the family's British company in the mid-1940s, and although the product lives on elsewhere, it's seldom seen in the United States. Most of the other purveyors are out of the malted milk business or gone entirely.

AT RIGHT

CLASSIC BANANA SPLIT

PAGE 300

cLassic banana spLits

makes 4 banana spLits

Soda fountains first began serving sundaes in the 1880s, and since then hundreds of them have been devised. The 1919 edition of an ice cream trade reference called *Spatula Soda Water Guide* contained formulas for 154 sauces and more than one hundred sundaes, including twenty-five different banana splits!

This banana split is the one that's had staying power: dramatic, banana-flanked scoops of vanilla, chocolate, and strawberry ice cream topped with three sauces. It's garnished with whipped cream swirls and maraschino cherries. Showy and extravagant to the point of excess, it fits right in with today's razzle-dazzle, super-size desserts. Made with top-quality sauces and ice creams, it's also delectable—I can never decide whether I prefer the strawberry-strawberry, or pineapple-vanilla, or chocolate-chocolate combo. Happily, I don't have to.

4 small ripe bananas, peeled and halved lengthwise
1 pint strawberry ice cream or Strawberry-Banana Cheesecake Ice Cream (page 290)
1 pint chocolate ice cream or Chocolate Double-Malted Milk Ice Cream (page 296)
1 pint vanilla ice cream, Vanilla Frozen Custard (page 284), or Banana Ice Cream (page 288)
   Real Hot Fudge Sauce, warmed (page 310), or Crown Candy Kitchen's Chocolate Syrup (page 312)

Fresh Pineapple Sauce (page 318)
Quick Strawberry Sauce (page 317)
1 7-ounce can ready-to-use whipped cream or Stabilized Whipped Cream (page 226)
   About ½ cup chopped pecans or walnuts (optional)
   About ¼ cup shaved chocolate or chocolate sprinkles (optional)
12 maraschino cherries, preferably with stems

On each side of four banana split dishes, arrange the pairs of banana halves cut sides up. Place a scoop of strawberry, then chocolate, then vanilla ice cream down the center of each dish. Top the ice cream scoops with about ¼ cup each of the hot fudge, pineapple, and strawberry sauces; usually the chocolate goes over the chocolate, the pineapple over the vanilla, and the strawberry over the strawberry, but this can be varied, if desired. Generously top each scoop with a dollop of whipped cream. Sprinkle the chopped nuts and/or shaved chocolate over the whipped cream, if using. Top each whipped cream dollop with a cherry and serve immediately.

spLit decision

The banana split is an American invention. However, exactly who invented it—and where and when—has generated a hot debate.

According to a 2002 article in the Clinton County Convention and Visitor's Bureau archives, Wilmington, Ohio, a Clinton County town southwest of Columbus, is the birthplace of the banana split. In 1907, the story goes, restaurateur Ernest Hazard devised a large, lavish three-scoop sundae with chocolate, strawberry, and pineapple toppings, all tucked between a banana cut lengthwise. His idea was to attract more business from the students at nearby Wilmington College. The family lore passed down to Hazard's daughter and grandson holds that he decided to call his concoction a banana split, even though his cousin Clifton felt the name wouldn't catch on. To celebrate Hazard's momentous culinary creation, Wilmington holds an annual banana split festival every June.

But in a 2001 article in the *Cincinnati Enquirer,* reporter Chuck Martin suggests that Wilmington missed the banana boat by several years. He points out that about 275 miles east of Wilmington, the folks in Latrobe, Pennsylvania (near Pittsburgh), claim that the banana split was invented there in 1904. The Latrobe story also comes with some convincing-sounding specifics: Dr. David Strickler, a downtown pharmacist, supposedly created the banana split while he was still a young soda jerk working in the Tassell Pharmacy (it later became Strickler's). In several published interviews, Dr. Strickler always said that the original owner, Miss Tassell, had asked him to come up with a new sundae that would draw in more customers. His concoction became a hit, especially with the students of nearby St. Vincent College. Like their rivals in Wilmington, St. Vincent's students hold an annual banana split bash celebrating their school's role in the banana split's birth.

Faced with this banana split decision, I sought the opinion of octogenarian Bryce Thomson, who has been in the ice cream business nearly all his life and has a huge collection of ice cream memorabilia, newspaper clippings, books, and other historical information. After starting out as a soda jerk, then working his way up through sales and management to become CEO of an ice cream company, Bryce retired twenty years ago and took on the job of writing the *Sundae School News,* the ice cream industry's newsletter. He says his research indicates that the banana split originated in Latrobe, Pennsylvania. Sorry, Wilmington, I'm going to take his word for it!

ambrosia sherbet

Inspired by an outing to Beck Grove, a beautifully tended San Diego County fruit farm that produces specialty citrus, I created a refreshing sherbet using the flavors of the classic American orange-banana-coconut fruit cup called ambrosia. The taste is boldly citrusy, with faintly nutty undertones from the banana and toasted coconut. The sherbet is at its best when prepared with blood oranges and kumquats, but it's well worth making with regular oranges and some of their zest. There is a big color difference, however: the blood orange version will be a beautiful, vivid pink, the ordinary orange version a creamy yellow.

1½ cups shredded or flaked sweetened coconut

Generous 3 tablespoons penny-size pieces of kumquat peel or 2 tablespoons penny-size pieces of orange zest (orange part of skin)

⅓ cup sugar

⅓ cup light corn syrup

3 tablespoons water

1¼ teaspoons grated lemon zest (yellow part of skin)

2¼ cups fresh blood orange juice or regular orange juice (9–12 oranges; divided)

1 slightly overripe medium banana

2–4 teaspoons fresh lemon juice, to taste

⅓ cup heavy (whipping) cream

Position a rack in the middle of the oven and preheat to 350 degrees F. Spread the coconut on a small rimmed baking sheet. Toast, watching carefully and stirring every 3 or 4 minutes, until crisp and light golden all over, 10 to 15 minutes. Let cool completely. The coconut will keep, stored airtight, at room temperature for up to a week.

In a heavy, nonreactive 1-quart saucepan, stir together the kumquat peel and sugar, firmly pressing the peel into the sugar to infuse it with flavor. Stir in the corn syrup and water until well blended. Heat over medium-high heat, stirring until the sugar completely dissolves. Bring to a boil, then adjust the heat so the mixture boils gently. Cook, stirring occasionally, for 5 minutes. Remove from the heat. Stir in the lemon zest and ½ cup of the toasted coconut.

In a 4-cup measure, combine 1¾ cups of the orange juice and the kumquat mixture, stirring well. Cover and refrigerate until well chilled, at least 6 hours and preferably 12 to 24 hours. Meanwhile, peel the banana, remove any fibrous strings, and cut into chunks. Place in a small airtight plastic bag and freeze until firm, at least 4 hours and up to 24 hours.

In a blender or food processor, puree the frozen banana and the remaining ½ cup orange juice until smooth, scraping down the sides of the bowl as needed. Stir the banana puree into the chilled orange juice mixture. Strain the mixture through a medium-fine sieve into a bowl, pressing down on the solids to force through as much liquid as possible. Taste and add lemon juice as desired. Stir in the cream.

Pour the chilled mixture into an ice cream maker and proceed according to the manufacturer's directions. When the sherbet finishes processing, turn out into a chilled plastic storage container. Let firm up for at least 1 hour in the freezer before serving. If the sherbet is very hard, let it soften just slightly before serving. Sprinkle a little of the remaining 1 cup toasted coconut over each serving.

The sherbet will keep, tightly covered, in the freezer for up to 1 week.

American purple, Red, or Green Grape sorbet

The Concord is our best-known native American table grape, but many other varieties can also be used in this recipe and, depending on their color, they will produce a pale green, purple, or rose-hued sorbet. Although our various indigenous grapes have differing levels of tartness and pungency, they are all aromatic and flavorful, and all yield sorbets with a clear, fresh-fruit taste. I like to make two sorbets of contrasting colors and serve them together as a palate refresher or light, eye-catching autumn dessert.

Except for Concord grapes, which are fairly widely available in the fall, the grape varieties called for are usually found only at farmers' markets and pick-your-own farms and vineyards. If you come upon some of these beauties, be sure to give them a try.

If you wish, the more commonplace European seedless table grapes, such as Thompson, Perlette, or Red Flame, may be substituted for a pleasant but much milder-tasting sorbet. Since these varieties are less juicy, you'll need 5 to 6 cups of stemmed seedless grapes; process them until finely chopped.

---

4 cups stemmed seedless or seeded purple, green, or red American table grapes, such as Concord, Fredonia, Niagara, Ontario, Himrod, Interlaken, Canadice, Delaware, Vanessa, or Catawba (1¼–1½ pounds)

¼ teaspoon finely grated lemon zest (yellow part of skin)

⅓ cup undiluted Concord grape juice concentrate for purple or red grape sorbets or undiluted Niagara grape juice concentrate for green grape sorbets, plus more to taste

1–3 teaspoons fresh lemon juice, to taste

Combine the grapes and lemon zest in a food processor. Process in on/off pulses just until the grapes are coarsely chopped. If they have seeds, be careful not to overprocess, or the bruised seeds will give the sorbet a bitter taste. Turn out the grapes into a medium sieve or fine colander set over a bowl. Press down hard using a large spoon or the bottom of a wide-mouthed jar to force through as much juice and pulp as possible. Depending on the grape variety and juiciness, you should have 1⅔ to 2 cups of the strained mixture.

For purple-black or red grapes, stir in ⅓ cup Concord grape juice concentrate; for green or yellow grapes, stir in ⅓ cup Niagara grape juice concentrate. Add more grape juice concentrate and fresh lemon juice to taste. Cover and freeze the mixture until completely frozen, at least 4½ hours and up to 2 days.

Tip

American table grapes are easily distinguished from European species not only by their heady fragrance but also by the fact that their skins readily separate from and slip off the pulpy interiors. As a result, they are sometimes called slip-skin grapes.

When the mixture is completely frozen, transfer to a clean food processor. (If it is very firm, break up into chunks with a spoon.) Process, stopping and stirring occasionally to redistribute the contents, until lightened in color and completely smooth. Transfer the sorbet to a well-chilled plastic storage container. Return to the freezer for at least 2 hours to firm up before serving.

The sorbet can be stored, tightly covered, in the freezer for up to 10 days.

going to grape school

Until I visited the Naples Grape Festival in the New York Finger Lakes region in 2003, my knowledge of American grapes was rudimentary. Growing up, I enjoyed the sweet, intensely flavored, purple-black fox grapes that grew wild in the woods on our Maryland farm. This native grape, *Vitis labrusca,* is the ancestor of the Concord, Catawba, and many other modern American varieties.

My education began as soon as I arrived in Naples and dropped in at a picturesque produce center called Joseph's Wayside Market. Several tables were loaded with the most fragrant and eye-catching display of grapes I'd ever seen. Each of the dozens of baskets and trays held three plump, contrasting, jewel-toned bunches neatly laid side by side— the familiar blue-black Concord, plus some lustrous green grapes called Niagara and some equally handsome red grapes called Canadice. Not only did the Niagara and Canadice grapes look somewhat different from our typical European (*Vitis vinifera*) green Thompson and Red Flame supermarket varieties, but also, because of their fox grape ancestry, their taste and aroma were much more floral and complex.

My education continued when I made an impromptu stop at Barron's Pratt Barn & Vineyard, a table-grape vineyard north of Naples. The owner, Len Barron, let me wander through his tidy, well-tended rows of grapes, pointed out varieties, and gave me tasting samples. He grows fifteen different kinds of green, red, and purple American table grapes on five acres and sells everything he produces to local markets. The names he rattled off were mostly unfamiliar—Van Buren, Steuben, Fredonia, Sheridan, Lakemont, and Price. Every kind I tried was sweet, succulent, oh-so-fragrant, and worthy of being well known.

Grapes thrive in the Finger Lakes climate—the luxuriant growth and large, abundant, picture-perfect clusters of fruit made that clear. The main obstacle to success, Len said, has been the deer, which on several occasions nearly destroyed his plantings. He eventually discovered a solution: Toby, a pleasant half-Lab, half–German shepherd mix, who was rescued from a shelter and trained to keep the hungry foragers at bay. "Toby's good at his work," Len said, "and he loves his life."

Pineapple-Lemon Buttermilk Sherbet

Buttermilk, the tangy liquid left over whenever butter was churned, was once a commonplace ingredient in rural American kitchens. Cooks used it to make pancakes, biscuits, cakes, and other baked goods. My grandmother loved an ice-cold glass of buttermilk, and my mother made a great pineapple sherbet with it. It was light, zingy-tart, and wonderfully refreshing.

This recipe is adapted from my mother's version, which I helped her prepare many times over the years. She used canned pineapple, which was all that was available then. I use fresh, since it has a brighter flavor. The buttermilk gives the sherbet a slight creaminess and body. Cored fresh pineapple is available in many supermarkets.

1 cup light corn syrup	1 cup fresh or frozen (reconstituted) pineapple juice
½ cup sugar	1²/₃ cups buttermilk
¼ cup water	
1 cup finely diced fresh pineapple	
Finely grated zest (yellow part of skin) of 1 large lemon	
6½ tablespoons fresh lemon juice, plus more if needed	

In a nonreactive 2-quart saucepan, stir together the corn syrup, sugar, and water. Bring to a gentle boil over medium-high heat. Cover and gently boil for 2 minutes. Stir in the pineapple using a clean spoon and gently boil, uncovered, for 2 minutes longer. Remove from the heat. Stir in the lemon zest, lemon juice, pineapple juice, and buttermilk.

Transfer the mixture to a storage container. Cover and refrigerate until well chilled, at least 4½ hours. Taste and add more lemon juice if more tartness is desired.

Pour the chilled mixture into an ice cream maker and proceed according to the manufacturer's directions. When the sherbet finishes processing, turn out into a chilled plastic storage container. Freeze for at least 1 hour to firm up before serving.

The sherbet will keep, tightly covered, in the freezer for up to a week.

Tip

I prepare this sherbet in an electric ice cream maker, but if you don't have one, you can make it the old-fashioned way. Pour the mixture into some shallow nonreactive pans or bowls and place in the freezer. Three or four times during the freezing process, break up and stir the mixture with a fork. It won't be quite as smooth as the machine-made kind, but it will taste the same and cool you off just as well.

chocoLate-banana maLteds

Legend has it that in the early 1920s, a Walgreens drugstore soda jerk invented the malted milk shake as a tasty way to boost the nutrition (and sales) of regular chocolate shakes. Malted milk shakes, or "malteds," eventually became so popular around the country that they spawned "malt shops," and by the 1940s and 1950s, hip teens were routinely meeting there to sip malteds and play the jukebox.

This chocolate-banana malted was inspired by one I enjoyed at the Crown Candy Kitchen, a traditional malt shop that's been a St. Louis landmark for more than ninety years. You can duplicate the tantalizing flavor and cool, creamy goodness of the original using the shop's chocolate syrup recipe (page 312), super-premium ice cream, and a tablespoon of plain (not chocolate) malted milk powder. But unless you have a top-of-the-line home soda fountain machine or super-powerful blender with a special blade, your malteds will likely not be quite as thick and creamy-frothy. Still, it's possible to come closer if all the ingredients are very cold when mixing begins. Freeze the milk until it's partially frozen and the banana until it's completely frozen. Also, thoroughly chill the chocolate syrup. The ice cream itself should be frozen but not hard; otherwise, the blender motor may labor excessively and overheat.

²/₃ cup whole milk or half-and-half, partially frozen

¹/₄ cup cold Crown Candy Kitchen's Chocolate Syrup (page 312)

1 generous tablespoon plain malted milk powder (not chocolate-flavored)

¹/₂ ripe medium banana, peeled, chopped, and frozen until firm

3 scoops top-quality vanilla ice cream, slightly softened

Whipped cream and freshly grated nutmeg (optional)

In a blender, combine the milk, chocolate syrup, malted milk powder, and chopped banana. Blend until the mixture is very smooth and frothy. With the blender running, gradually add the ice cream. Blend until completely smooth, about 1 minute. Divide the shake between two tall, frosty ice cream soda glasses. Top with whipped cream dusted with nutmeg, if desired. Serve immediately with straws and long-handled spoons.

"Then there was the
fountain with its marble top
front of a massive mirror, shiny
spouts and gleaming metal work
area where a prince in white
jacket presided . . . He was . . . a
fellow of infinite skill, able to
produce a milkshake with a few
deft moves with large containers
and a mixing machine. His sorcery
done, he poured with a flourish,
usually at arm's length from great
height."

–Kay Houston,
"Of Soda Fountains
and Ice Cream Parlors,"
Detroit News (2002)

ReaL HOT FuDge sauce

It was a great treat when my family made the trek from the farming country west of Baltimore to the Tommy Tucker dime store and soda fountain on the edge of the city. I'd climb up on one of the tall stools, request a hot fudge sundae, and then spin around on my perch as I watched the clerk prepare my order. Like bartenders, the soda jerks enjoyed making a show of their trade—dramatically dipping into the metal warming pot and ladling the hot fudge over the ice cream, squirting on lavish rosettes and swirls of whipped cream, and, finally, plopping a maraschino cherry on top.

In a few quaint corners of America, old-time soda fountains are still on the scene, but for the most part, a good hot fudge sauce is hard to find. To remedy this, I set to work creating a recipe that would measure up to the best hot fudge sauces I remembered from childhood. After a lot of experimenting I came up with this one. It's shiny, becomes chewy-gooey as it cools over the ice cream, is faintly bittersweet, and has a distinctive, mellow flavor that comes from unsweetened chocolate blending with cooked-down, slightly caramelized sugar and cream. This is exactly the way real, old-fashioned fudge is prepared, except that it's cooked to a firmer stage and then stirred until set.

You can use a candy thermometer to check the doneness of the sauce, but the recipe is designed to be made without one. Sauce that's undercooked will just require less thinning with water; sauce that's overcooked will need more thinning to obtain the desired fluid consistency. It is important to use a heavy flat-bottomed saucepan. A flimsy pan may not conduct heat evenly and increases the chance that the boiling sugar-cream mixture will scorch on the bottom.

1 cup heavy (whipping) cream	5½–6 ounces unsweetened chocolate, broken up or coarsely chopped
1⅓ cups sugar	Generous ½ cup hot water, plus more if necessary
⅓ cup light corn syrup	2 teaspoons vanilla extract
8 tablespoons (1 stick) unsalted butter, cut into chunks	
Generous ¼ teaspoon salt	

In a heavy, flat-bottomed 3- to 4-quart saucepan, thoroughly stir together the cream, sugar, corn syrup, butter, and salt. Bring to a boil over medium-high heat, stirring; it will boil up some, then gradually subside. Continue to boil briskly, stirring occasionally, for 2½ to 3 minutes, or until the mixture begins to thicken slightly. Immediately lower the heat so the mixture boils steadily but not hard. Continue cooking, stirring constantly and watching carefully to prevent scorching, until the mixture turns a light caramel color (a little lighter than caramel candies) and thickens to a gravylike consistency, 8 to 9 minutes. (If you wish to check with a candy thermometer, it should register 236 to 238 degrees F.) Remove from the heat.

Add the chocolate all at once, stirring until completely melted and smooth. Slowly stir in the hot water until the sauce is well blended and fluid. Add the vanilla, stirring well. At this point, the sauce should be very fluid but not quite runny. If necessary, stir in 1 to 2 tablespoons more hot water to thin it further.

Let the sauce cool to warm. If it has stiffened during standing, gradually thin it with more hot water and serve.

The sauce will keep, tightly covered, in the refrigerator for up to 3 weeks. It will stiffen too much to pour, so store it in a wide-mouthed container. To serve, transfer the sauce to a microwave-safe container and microwave on medium power, rotating the container, stirring, and checking the temperature at 30-second intervals, until very warm but not hot. (Alternatively, rewarm it in a double boiler over simmering water.) If necessary, thin with warm water after rewarming.

TIPS

For an intensely chocolatey sauce, use 6 ounces unsweetened chocolate. For a slightly milder, sweeter sauce, reduce the chocolate to 5½ ounces.

Chilled or room-temperature sauce is too stiff to pour, so it must be warmed until fluid. Don't heat it to hot, however; the heat will make the ice cream melt too fast.

crown candy kitchen's chocolate syrup

I am grateful to Andy Karandzieff, a third-generation owner of Crown Candy Kitchen, St. Louis's oldest soda fountain, for sharing this recipe with me. Crown Candy Kitchen uses this syrup in its popular chocolate-banana malted (see page 308) and in sodas. I find it convenient for drizzling over ice cream and making hot chocolate, too.

1¼ cups sugar

¾ cup unsweetened, nonalkalized American-style cocoa powder, sifted after measuring

3 tablespoons unsweetened Dutch-process cocoa powder, sifted after measuring

Scant 1¼ cups hot water

½ cup light corn syrup

¾ teaspoon vanilla extract

In a heavy medium saucepan, thoroughly stir together the sugar and cocoas until well mixed. Stir in the hot water until well blended and smooth. Stir in the corn syrup. Heat the mixture over medium heat, stirring constantly and watching carefully, until the sugar dissolves and the mixture is steaming hot; do not boil. Immediately remove from the heat. Stir in the vanilla. Let cool to room temperature. Transfer to an airtight storage jar or container.

The syrup will keep in the refrigerator for up to 3 weeks. Stir before using.

HOT CHOCOLATE WITH MARSHMALLOWS

In a microwave-safe mug, stir together 1 cup milk and 3 to 4 tablespoons Crown Candy Kitchen's Chocolate Syrup or a good store-bought chocolate syrup. Microwave on high power for 1 minute. Stop and stir. Microwave on medium power, stopping and stirring every 30 seconds, just until hot. Float 2 marshmallows on the hot chocolate. If desired, microwave for 10 seconds to soften the marshmallows slightly; the heat of the milk will do the rest.

marshmallow sundae topping

Homemade always tastes better, and that's certainly true of this topping. It is one of the sauces traditionally offered by ice cream parlors and many snow cone (also called snow-ball) stands (see page 371). In Baltimore and environs, marshmallow is the standard topping for the chocolate snowball, perhaps the city's most frequently ordered flavor. I can attest that the combination of mild, gooey-smooth sauce and chocolatey, slightly crunchy ice is pure heaven on a sultry day. Marshmallow topping is also excellent spooned over brownies or chocolate cake.

- 2 teaspoons unflavored gelatin (about 1 scant packet)
- ⅓ cup cold water, plus more as needed
- 1 cup sugar
- ⅔ cup light corn syrup
- ⅛ teaspoon salt
- 2 tablespoons warm water
- 1 teaspoon vanilla extract
- 2 drops almond extract (optional)

In a small bowl, stir the gelatin into the cold water. Let stand, stirring once or twice, until the gelatin softens, about 5 minutes.

Using a wooden spoon, stir together the sugar, corn syrup, salt, and warm water in a heavy 2-quart saucepan over medium-high heat until well blended. When the sugar is fully incorporated, raise the tempera-ture and bring the mixture to a full boil, stirring. Continue boiling and stirring for 20 seconds. Stir in the gelatin mixture, vanilla, and almond extract (if using) and cook, stirring, for 30 seconds longer.

Pour the mixture into a larger bowl. Using a mixer (with a whisk-shaped beater, if available), beat on low speed until the mixture begins to thicken; this presents hot splatters. Gradually raise the speed to high and beat until the mixture is gooey, thick, white, and very fluffy, 4 to 7 minutes. Beat in 3 to 4 tablespoons cold water to thin the topping to a fluid consistency. (The topping will stiffen somewhat during storage.) Let cool to room temperature before serving.

The topping will keep, tightly covered, in the refrigerator for up to 2 weeks. Let come almost to room temperature before using.

proud to be a jerk

Originally, the term "soda jerker" referred to the action of the fountain clerk pulling back on the soda spigot levers. Octogenarian Bryce Thomson, who began working as a jerk in Bellevue, Michigan, in 1930, says he likes being referred to as "one of the world's oldest soda jerks." He has always taken pride in the title because of the skill and show-manship the job required: "I was kind of a show-off and an amateur magician, so it suited me fine."

Butterscotch sauce

One of my most eagerly anticipated childhood treats was a visit to Giffords, a popular candy store and ice cream parlor that for many years stood right across from the train depot in the Washington, D.C., suburb of Silver Spring, Maryland. (That branch of the shop is gone, but there is still one in the suburb of Bethesda.) Since most of the outings coincided with family trips in from the country to pick up or drop off someone at the railroad station, I was always wildy excited when the train was late: we would have to kill time at Giffords.

I usually chose the butterscotch sundae. The sauce was different from most of today's commercial renditions, which have a stronger but less natural taste. Giffords' butterscotch sauce isn't homemade anymore, but I've come up with one that reminds me of the original. It's mellow, buttery, and slightly chewy. Spoon it over ice cream, gild the lily with a dollop of whipped cream (if you wish), and dig in!

6 tablespoons (3/4 stick) unsalted butter, cut into chunks
1 1/4 cups packed light brown sugar
1/2 cup light corn syrup
1 cup heavy (whipping) cream
3 tablespoons dark rum or bourbon, or 2 1/2 tablespoons water plus 1/2 teaspoon rum extract

1 1/2 teaspoons vanilla extract
1 teaspoon fresh lemon juice
Pinch of salt

In a heavy 3- to 4-quart saucepan, melt the butter over medium-high heat. Cook for 1 minute, stirring. Stir in the brown sugar and corn syrup and cook, stirring, for 2 minutes longer. Immediately remove from the heat. Using a long-handled wooden spoon and standing back to avoid splatters and steam, gradually stir in the cream, then the rum, until fully incorporated. Cook over medium-high heat, stirring, until any brown sugar lumps completely dissolve and the mixture comes to a boil.

Using a pastry brush dipped in warm water or a damp paper towel, wipe any sugar from the pan sides. Rinse off the stirring spoon to remove any sugar crystals. Boil the mixture briskly, stirring, for 3 minutes longer, or until the sauce thickens a bit and its color deepens slightly. Immediately remove from the heat. Let cool slightly. Stir in the vanilla, lemon juice, and salt. Pour through a fine sieve into a heatproof storage container.

Let cool to warm and serve.

The sauce will keep, tightly covered, in the refrigerator for up to 2 weeks. Let come to room temperature before serving. (Or remove the lid and gently heat to warm in a microwave oven on medium power, stirring every 30 seconds.) If the sauce is too stiff to flow readily, thin it slightly with a few teaspoons of hot water.

sundae school

The sauces and syrups that top our sundaes have their origins in the early temperance-approved soft-drink industry. As is suggested by the title of a 1863 handbook, *The American Dispenser's Book . . . Containing Choice Formulas for Making Soda Water Syrups and Fancy Drinks; or, How to Make a Soda Fountain Pay,* soda fountain operators were already busy devising increasingly rich concoctions to attract customers by the mid-nineteenth century.

Soon they began adding shaved ice and cream to their syrup and soda water beverages, and several decades later, they replaced the shaved ice and cream with ice cream. The next step was to jettison the soda water completely in favor of syrup and ice cream. Perhaps the resulting "sundae" was first served on Sunday. There's no proof, but nobody has come up with a better explanation.

Maple-Butter Pecan sauce

Maple and pecans are one of America's most delicious culinary pairings, and this sauce brings out the best in both. Boiling down the maple syrup with cream intensifies and smooths the flavor and adds body. Briefly sautéing the pecans in butter accentuates their taste and makes them crispy-crunchy. All that's needed is a scoop or two of Vanilla Frozen Custard (page 284) or a good vanilla ice cream, and you've got a spectacular sundae.

1½ tablespoons unsalted butter

½ cup coarsely chopped pecans

1 cup maple syrup, preferably medium or dark amber

¾ cup heavy (whipping) cream

¼ cup sugar

⅓ cup light corn syrup

Pinch of salt

½ teaspoon vanilla extract

Warm water, if needed

In a heavy 2-quart saucepan, melt the butter over medium-high heat. Add the pecans and cook, stirring, until fragrant and lightly browned, 1 to 2 minutes; do not burn. Immediately turn out the pecans and butter into a small bowl.

In the saucepan, using a long-handled wooden spoon, thoroughly stir together the maple syrup, cream, sugar, corn syrup, and salt. Bring to a simmer over medium-high heat, stirring until the sugar dissolves. Using a pastry brush dipped in warm water or a damp paper towel, wipe any sugar crystals from the pan sides. Wash any sugar from the stirring spoon. Adjust the heat so the mixture boils. Continue boiling briskly, stirring occasionally, for 5 minutes, or until thickened and slightly darkened. Remove from the heat. Stir in the vanilla and butter-pecan mixture. Let cool to warm. If the sauce seems too thick, thin it to the desired consistency by stirring in a few teaspoons of warm water. Serve immediately.

The sauce will keep, tightly covered in a heatproof, microwave-safe container, in the refrigerator for up to 2 weeks. At serving time, remove the lid and gently heat to warm in a microwave oven on medium power, stirring and checking the temperature every 30 seconds. If the sauce seems too thick, thin it slightly with a few teaspoons of hot water.

quick strawberry sauce

makes about 2 cups sauce
(more if fresh
strawberries are added)

At its best, strawberry sauce is a light, flavorful mix of freshly sliced or crushed berries and sugar. All too often, though, commercial sauces are reminiscent of thinned strawberry jam.

The following quick-to-make version takes advantage of frozen strawberries in sugar, making it possible to enjoy a fresh taste even when strawberries aren't in season. When they are, a few sliced and stirred in just before serving brightens both the flavor and the texture of the sauce. If you do plan to add the fresh berries, you may want to incorporate several more tablespoons of sugar into the sauce before refrigerating it.

2   10-ounce packages frozen sliced strawberries in sugar, thawed, or 2 cups frozen (thawed) strawberries in syrup

2   teaspoons arrowroot powder or cornstarch

1–2   tablespoons sugar, to taste (optional)

¼–½   teaspoon fresh lemon juice, to taste (optional)

½–¾   cup thinly sliced fresh strawberries (optional)
     Water, if needed

Drain the syrup from the strawberries into a heavy, nonreactive 2-quart saucepan. Stir the arrowroot powder into the syrup until completely smooth and lump-free. Stirring constantly, bring to a boil over medium-high heat. Gently boil, stirring, until the mixture thickens and clears, 1½ to 2 minutes. Immediately remove from the heat. Stir in the thawed strawberries just until evenly incorporated. Taste and adjust the sweetness by stirring in sugar or lemon juice, if desired.

Transfer the sauce to a storage container. Refrigerate, covered, until cold, at least 1 hour and up to 3 days.

At serving time, stir in the fresh strawberries, if using. Stir in a little water if a slightly thinner sauce is desired.

fresh pineapple sauce

makes about
2½ cups sauce

Serve this as one of the toppings on a banana split (see page 300) or over Vanilla Frozen Custard (page 284) or vanilla ice cream. (It makes a great topping for vanilla or lemon cheesecake, too.)

Because Del Monte's trademarked Gold Pineapples are the sweetest and yellowest variety, I like to use them whenever they are available. However, any ripe, flavorful pineapple will do nicely.

¼ cup sugar, or more to taste

2 teaspoons arrowroot powder or cornstarch

⅓ cup water

½ cup frozen (unreconstituted) pineapple juice concentrate

1 fresh pineapple, peeled, cored, and finely chopped (about 2¼ cups)

½ teaspoon vanilla extract

In a nonreactive medium saucepan, stir together the ¼ cup sugar and arrowroot powder until thoroughly blended. Stir in the water until the mixture is smooth and lump-free. Bring to a simmer over medium heat, stirring. Adjust the heat so the mixture boils gently. Cook, stirring, for 2 to 3 minutes, or until slightly thickened and clear. Stir in the pineapple juice concentrate, chopped pineapple, and any pineapple juice. Cook, stirring occasionally, until the mixture returns to a boil, about 3 minutes.

Remove from the heat. Stir in the vanilla. Taste and stir in a tablespoon or two more sugar, if desired. Transfer to a nonreactive storage container and refrigerate for at least 1 hour, or until chilled, before serving.

The sauce will keep, tightly covered, in the refrigerator for up to 5 days. Stir briefly before using.

Tip

Arrowroot powder and cornstarch have about the same thickening power, but the arrowroot yields a clearer sauce. Arrowroot is usually stocked with the spices or baking supplies.

Blackberry sauce

This sauce is easy to prepare but delivers spectacular blackberry flavor. It makes a great blackberry sundae and is also delicious used in place of strawberry sauce in a banana split.

Both fresh and unsweetened frozen blackberries yield excellent results, so the sauce can be made any time of the year. (Economical 1-pound packages of unsweetened, loose-packed frozen blackberries are often stocked in supermarkets. One package yields the 3 cups required for this recipe.) The brief cooking produces a sauce with fuller flavor, more body, and more brilliant color than an uncooked sauce.

6 tablespoons sugar

1 tablespoon arrowroot powder or cornstarch

3 cups blackberries

3 tablespoons blackberry brandy, apricot brandy, peach brandy, or orange juice

Generous pinch of finely grated lemon zest (yellow part of skin)

1 tablespoon fresh lemon or lime juice

In a heavy, nonreactive medium saucepan, stir together the sugar and arrowroot powder until well blended. Stir in the berries, brandy, lemon zest, and lemon juice. Bring to a gentle boil over medium-high heat, stirring. Cook, stirring, until the mixture thickens and clears, about 2 minutes. Remove from the heat. Let cool slightly.

Press the mixture through a fine sieve, forcing through as much juice and pulp as possible into an airtight storage container; discard the seeds. Refrigerate the sauce for at least 1½ hours. Stir briefly before using.

The sauce will keep, tightly covered, in the refrigerator for up to 5 days.

Candies and Confections

7

candy-making Tips

Read This

Getting Started: Ready, Set, Read!

- Candy making isn't difficult, but it requires precision. Follow the directions of each recipe carefully, don't make substitutions, don't stir any more than directed (which can cause graininess), and cook the candy to the specified temperature. In most cases, you can check the temperature either by using a candy thermometer or by doing an ice water test (see page 323), although some recipes require a thermometer.

- Many of the recipes call for large heavy pots that distribute the heat evenly, reduce the risk of scorching, and provide enough room so the mixture won't boil over. Don't use a smaller pot than the recipe calls for. Also, have on hand kitchen mitts or heavy potholders for lifting the pot and pouring out the candy; both the container and the candy will be very hot.

- "The success of fudge depends upon its being removed from the fire at the right moment," said Frank A. Dupuy in his 1900 *New Century Home Book,* and the same is true for all candy. Especially if you're a novice, it's helpful to have a candy thermometer (see below). Never try to check the consistency of candy by dipping your finger in or by taking a taste; the mixture is too hot.

Is It Done Yet?

USING A CANDY THERMOMETER

- Be sure you're actually using a *candy* thermometer—one that can register as high as 350 to 400 degrees F. (Some cooking thermometers, such as those designed for meats, can only check to 190 degrees F and are not suitable.) Although digital candy thermometers are a little more expensive than the traditional models, they are far easier to read. They are not nearly as durable, however.

- Occasionally check the accuracy of your candy thermometer by inserting it into boiling water. If it doesn't register 212 degrees, note how much higher or lower it reads, then adjust accordingly.

- If using a glass thermometer, prewarm it by standing it in a pitcher or tall glass of warm water. After testing the candy, return the thermometer to the water to prevent sticky drips and to allow it to cool down gradually. With a digital thermometer, you can skip the prewarming step. After testing, place only the metal probe in water. The digital component is not usually waterproof, and submerging it in water or even splashing it can cause damage.
- If possible, clip the thermometer to the pan side, adjusting it so the tip is submerged in the candy but not touching the bottom of the pan.
- Watch carefully as the candy cooks. The temperature can rise slowly, then shoot up quickly.
- If the air is very dry, cook to the lower end of the temperature range specified in the recipe. If the air is humid, cook to the higher end of the range given, or even a degree beyond that. It's best not to make candy in very humid or rainy weather, since it may not set up properly or may be too sticky.

USING THE ICE WATER TEST

- Set out a measuring cup of cold water. Add 3 or 4 ice cubes to keep the water ice-cold during testing.
- Set out several clean metal teaspoons and a saucer to hold them between checks.
- Scoop up a generous ½ teaspoon of the mixture using a heatproof spoon and drop the candy into the ice water. Wait for 10 seconds, then squeeze the mixture into a ball with your fingertips. Remove the ball from the water and squeeze again. Each recipe indicates the consistency sought; if the mixture is too soft, keep cooking and frequently testing with new bits dropped into the water until the right consistency is obtained.

CLassic chocoLate fudge

makes about 2 pounds
pLain fudge
or 2¼ pounds nut fudge

On Sunday afternoons when the weather was too cold and blustery to go outside, my brother and sister and I would get out the fudge pot and wooden spoons and flip through fudge recipes in my mother's dog-eared cookbooks. My mother did the cooking herself when we were very young, but at age eleven I, being the oldest, was allowed to take over.

The beating, which causes the fudge to form fine crystals and set up, was always a family activity. None of us minded taking turns during the fifteen or so minutes re-quired—perhaps because we got to sneak a taste.

This fudge is roughly based on early versions that began turning up in American cookbooks in the late nineteenth century. However, those recipes rarely included vanilla and never called for corn syrup, a modern addition that discourages graininess. Beating fudge once required considerable elbow grease, but this task can now be ac-complished using a heavy-duty stand mixer fitted with a paddle (if available). My ver-sion is smooth, has a slight chew, and has full chocolate flavor. The photograph is on page 320.

5½ ounces unsweetened chocolate, broken up or coarsely chopped	⅛ teaspoon salt
1¾ cups heavy (whipping) cream	2½ teaspoons vanilla extract
2 cups sugar	Warm water, if needed
⅓ cup light corn syrup	1 cup chopped walnuts or pecans (optional)
½ tablespoon unsalted butter, slightly softened	

Line an 8-inch square pan with aluminum foil, allowing the foil to over-hang two sides. Grease the foil or coat with nonstick spray.

Put the chocolate in a large heatproof bowl or a large mixer bowl. In a heavy 4- to 5-quart saucepan, combine the cream, sugar, corn syrup, but-ter, and salt. Bring to a boil over medium-high heat, stirring with a wooden spoon. Immediately cover the pan with a tight-fitting lid and boil for 3 minutes to allow steam to wash any sugar crystals from the pan sides. Meanwhile, carefully wash off all the sugar from the spoon.

Remove the lid and lower the heat so the mixture boils briskly but not hard. If any sugar remains on the pan sides, carefully wipe it away with a pastry brush dipped in warm water or a damp paper towel. If you have a candy thermometer, clip it to the pan side, with the tip immersed but not touching the bottom. Continue cooking, occasionally gently stirring and scraping the pan bottom, for 3 to 7 minutes longer, or until the mixture is 235 to 237 degrees F. Or use the ice water test and cook until a teaspoon of the mixture dropped into ice water forms a soft, flexible ball that holds together when squeezed in the water and loses its shape when removed from the water and squeezed. Using oven mitts or potholders, immediately remove the pan from the heat and pour the mixture over the chocolate. Do not stir.

Let cool for about 1 hour, or until the mixture has cooled to just barely hot. If desired, speed up the cooling by setting the bowl in a large bowl of cold water. Stir with a clean wooden spoon or beat on low speed with a heavy-duty stand mixer until the chocolate is fully melted and incorporated. Add the vanilla. Continue stirring or beating vigorously until the mixture lightens in color, begins to thicken, and gradually loses most of its shine, 5 to 10 minutes. (If at any point the mixture begins to separate and looks oily, add a few teaspoons of warm water and beat until it is smooth again.) Quickly stir in the nuts, if using.

Immediately scrape the mixture out into the pan. Working quickly and using a lightly greased table knife, spread and smooth it into an even layer. Let cool on a wire rack until thoroughly set. Lift the foil and fudge out of the pan. Refrigerate until chilled, at least 30 minutes. Carefully peel off the foil and place the fudge on a cutting board. If desired, trim away uneven edges from the slab using a large sharp knife. The slab will keep, stored airtight, in the freezer for up to a month. Thaw in the refrigerator before cutting. Cut the fudge crosswise and lengthwise into 1-by-2-inch pieces (or as desired). Pack airtight.

The fudge will keep in a cool place or the refrigerator for up to a week. Let come to room temperature before serving.

THE FUDGE FILES

The first known mention of fudge is in files in the Vassar College archives, according to Lee Edwards Benning, the author of *Oh Fudge*. Vassar graduate Emelyn Hartridge wrote that in 1886 she had obtained a recipe while visiting a classmate's family in Baltimore. She added that she made thirty pounds of fudge for the 1888 Vassar senior auction. Fudge immediately became popular on the campus and also caught on at other schools in the region. In 1894, a Wellesley student mentioned making a dorm dweller's version over a chimney lamp.

Traditional penuche

MAKES 1¾ POUNDS
PLAIN FUDGE
OR 2 POUNDS NUT FUDGE

Like chocolate fudge, penuche, or brown sugar fudge, is an American creation, and recipes for it began turning up in cookbooks in the late nineteenth and early twentieth centuries. This one has a slightly soft, chewy consistency and a distinctly mellow brown sugar–caramel taste and aroma. Although the nuts are optional, they complement the caramel flavor and balance the sweetness of the candy nicely. The fudge can be beaten by hand or with a heavy-duty stand mixer.

Unless you are experienced at checking for doneness by dropping a bit of candy into ice water, it's best to rely on a candy thermometer for this recipe.

1 1-pound package light brown sugar	2 teaspoons vanilla extract
1 cup granulated sugar	Warm water, if needed
⅓ cup light corn syrup	1 cup chopped pecans or walnuts (optional)
1⅓ cups heavy (whipping) cream	
⅛ teaspoon salt	

Line an 8-inch square pan with aluminum foil, allowing the foil to over-hang two sides. Grease the foil or coat with nonstick spray.

In a heavy 4-quart (or slightly larger) saucepan, combine the sugars, corn syrup, cream, and salt. Bring to a boil over medium-high heat, stir-ring with a wooden spoon. Immediately cover the pan with a tight-fitting lid and boil for 2½ minutes to allow steam to wash any sugar crystals from the pan sides. Meanwhile, wash off all the sugar from the spoon.

Remove the lid and lower the heat so the mixture boils briskly but not hard. If any sugar remains on the pan sides, carefully wipe it away with a pastry brush dipped in warm water or a damp paper towel. Continue cooking, frequently stirring and scraping the pan bottom, for 2 to 4 min-utes longer, or until the mixture is 238 to 239 degrees F. Or use the ice water test and cook until a teaspoon of the mixture dropped into ice water forms a firm, flexible ball that holds its shape when squeezed in the water and softens slightly when removed from the water and squeezed. Using oven mitts or potholders, immediately remove the pan from the heat.

Carefully pour the mixture into a large heatproof bowl or a large mixer bowl without scraping the pan. Set the bowl in a larger bowl of ice-cold

326 ★ ★ ★ ★ ★ ★ ★ ★ ★ ★ ★ ★ ★ ★
THE ALL-AMERICAN DESSERT BOOK

water to speed the cooling. (After the water warms up, replace it with more cold water, if desired.) Let cool for about 1 hour, or until the mixture reaches 110 to 115 degrees F in the deepest part. (If checking by hand, the bottom of the bowl should be just slightly warm.)

Loosen the mixture from the sides of the bowl by dipping the bowl into a larger bowl of hot water for about 30 seconds, then scrape down the sides of the bowl. Begin beating with a metal spoon or on medium-low speed with a heavy-duty stand mixer, scraping down the sides of the bowl as needed. Add the vanilla. (The mixture may be very fluid.) Continue beating until the mixture gradually thickens, lightens in color, and begins to lose its shine; it may take 10 to 15 minutes or more, but watch carefully, as it can also happen quickly. If the mixture looks crumbly and dry, stir in a teaspoon or two of warm water. Quickly stir in the nuts, if using.

Immediately scrape the mixture out into the pan. Working quickly and using a lightly greased table knife, spread and smooth it into an even layer. Let cool on a wire rack until thoroughly set. Refrigerate until chilled, at least 30 minutes. Carefully peel off the foil and place the penuche on a cutting board. If desired, trim away uneven edges from the slab using a large sharp knife. The slab will keep, stored airtight, in the freezer for up to a month. Thaw in the refrigerator before cutting. Let come to room temperature before serving. Cut the penuche crosswise and lengthwise into 1-by-2-inch pieces (or as desired). Pack airtight.

The fudge will keep in a cool place or the refrigerator for up to a week.

Nobody knows exactly who first named brown sugar fudge "panocha." Mexicans called a flavorful coarse brown, or raw, sugar that came into use in the mid-nineteenth century *panocha*, and a recipe for a fudge by this name appeared in *Mrs. Rorer's New Cook Book* in 1898. The original spelling was quickly corrupted, however, turning into ponouchi, pinoche, panoche, penuchi, penuche, penuci, and several other variants. In 1909, a brown sugar fudge called "ponouchi" appeared in a pamphlet put out by Walter Baker & Company, in Dorchester, Massachusetts. Across the country, three similar recipes called "pinoches" were published in *Tried and True Recipes of Prineville (Oregon) Ladies* in 1909. Another "pinoche" appeared in *The Portland (Oregon) Woman's Exchange Cook Book* in 1913. All of the variations were pronounced the same — "puh-NOO-chee."

chocolate-ROCKY ROAD FUDGE

Makes about 2 pounds fudge or 2¼ pounds nut fudge

This is the recipe I turn to when I want a great "no beating required" fudge. It has a shiny surface and is studded with puffy, slightly chewy marshmallows. Avoid the temptation to stir vigorously during cooking: the more stirring, the grainier the fudge.

The recipe can be made without a candy thermometer, but it's best to use one. If you have no thermometer, see the tips on page 323.

3½ ounces unsweetened chocolate, broken up or coarsely chopped	2 cups sugar
1 10½-ounce bag miniature marshmallows (divided)	¼ cup light corn syrup
8 tablespoons (1 stick) unsalted butter (divided)	2 teaspoons vanilla extract
⅔ cup heavy (whipping) cream	1 cup chopped walnuts or pecans (optional)

Line an 8- or 9-inch square baking pan with aluminum foil, allowing the foil to overhang two sides. Generously grease the foil or generously coat with nonstick spray.

In a large microwave-safe bowl, combine the chocolate, 3½ cups of the marshmallows, and 4 tablespoons of the butter. Microwave on medium power for 30 seconds. Stop and stir. Continue microwaving, stopping and stirring at 30-second intervals, until the mixture is just melted. (Alternatively, melt the chocolate, 3½ cups of the marshmallows, and 4 tablespoons of the butter in a double boiler over gently simmering water, stirring occasionally.)

In a heavy 3- to 4-quart saucepan, stir together the remaining 4 tablespoons butter, the cream, sugar, and corn syrup. Heat over medium heat, stirring with a wooden spoon, until the butter melts and the mixture just comes to a boil. Cover the pan with a tight-fitting lid and boil for 2½ minutes to allow steam to wash any sugar crystals from the pan sides. Meanwhile, thoroughly wash and dry the spoon.

Remove the lid and adjust the heat so the mixture boils briskly but not hard. If any sugar remains on the pan sides, wipe it away with a pastry brush dipped in warm water or a damp paper towel. If you have a candy thermometer, clip it to the pan side, with the tip immersed but not touching the bottom. Boil the mixture for 3 minutes, frequently gently stirring and scraping the pan bottom just enough to prevent sticking. Begin frequently checking the thermometer and cook until the mixture is 246 to 247 degrees F. Or use the ice water test and cook until a teaspoon of the mixture dropped into ice water forms a firm, flexible ball that holds its shape when squeezed in the water and softens slightly but holds its shape when removed from the water and squeezed.

Using oven mitts or potholders, immediately remove the pan from the heat and transfer to a wire rack. Quickly but gently stir in the chocolate mixture and vanilla until just blended. Gently fold in the nuts, if using, then stir in the remaining marshmallows for a few seconds, or until they just begin to melt.

Immediately scrape the mixture out into the pan (before the marshmallows melt completely). Quickly shake the pan and rap it on the counter several times to even the surface; don't try to spread the mixture with a knife, as it will already be setting up. Let cool on the wire rack until thoroughly set, about 2½ hours. (To speed cooling, let stand for 20 minutes, then refrigerate until firm, at least 1½ hours.)

Carefully peel off the foil and place the fudge on a cutting board. If desired, trim away uneven edges from the slab using a large sharp knife. The slab will keep, stored airtight, in the freezer for up to a month. Thaw in the refrigerator before cutting. Wiping off the knife between cuts, cut the fudge into 1-by-2-inch pieces (or as desired). Pack airtight, with wax paper between the layers.

The fudge will keep in a cool place for up to a week or in the refrigerator for up to 2 weeks. Let warm up slightly before serving.

Honey taffy and chocolate-honey taffy

Pulling taffy provides good old-fashioned fun for children, but the process of folding and stretching the warm candy into long ropes also serves a practical purpose, cooling it, lightening its texture, and making it sensuously glossy and opaque. Great for a taffy-pulling party, this recipe makes plenty for six to eight people to pull. (The pulling can be done by two people working together or by one person.) If you like, the finished ropes of the two flavors, which are prepared from the same batch, can be plaited together to produce two-toned taffy. For convenience, boil the candy in advance, then at party time rewarm it until it is soft and elastic enough to pull. Most children over the age of six or seven can help with pulling and wrapping the taffy, but the boiling of the candy should be done by an adult.

Be assured that the pulling technique doesn't have to be perfect. With very lightly buttered hands, just stretch out taffy portions and fold them back onto themselves.

5 cups sugar	2 teaspoons vanilla extract
1¼ cups light corn syrup	2½ ounces unsweetened chocolate, broken up or coarsely chopped
1¼ cups hot water	⅛ teaspoon instant coffee powder or granules, dissolved in 1 teaspoon hot water
1 cup honey	
½ teaspoon fresh lemon juice	
¼ teaspoon salt	
6 tablespoons (¾ stick) unsalted butter, cut into bits, plus 4–6 tablespoons (½–¾ stick), softened, for pulling taffy	

Set two 9-by-13-inch baking dishes or two large heatproof platters on wire racks. Lightly but evenly butter or coat with nonstick spray.

In a heavy 6-quart or larger pot, thoroughly stir together the sugar, corn syrup, hot water, honey, lemon juice, and salt using a wooden spoon. Bring to a boil over medium-high heat, stirring. Initially, the mixture will foam excessively, but gradually it will subside; it's normal for the foam to have brown flecks. If you have a candy thermometer, clip it to the pot side, with the tip immersed but not touching the bottom. Adjust the heat so the candy boils but doesn't rise high up the pot sides, stirring as needed to reduce foaming. As the foaming subsides, increase the heat and boil briskly. Cook for 12 to 14 minutes longer, or until the mixture reaches to 264 to 266 degrees F. Or use the ice water test and cook until

tip

Particularly during the early stages of cooking, taffy made with honey foams and boils up a great deal, so be sure to use a 6-quart or larger pot. You'll also need to watch the pot carefully and stir frequently to control the foaming.

a teaspoon of the mixture dropped into ice water forms a very firm, almost brittle ball that holds its shape when squeezed in the water and stays very firm when removed from the water and squeezed. The temperature will rise rapidly near the end of cooking. Using oven mitts or potholders, immediately remove the pot from the heat.

Using a clean wooden spoon, immediately stir in the bits of butter and the vanilla just until the butter melts. Carefully turn out a generous half of the taffy (this needn't be exact) into a baking dish. Add the chocolate to the remaining taffy; do not stir. Let stand for 15 minutes, or until the chocolate melts, then stir until well blended and smooth. Stir in the coffee mixture. Carefully turn out the chocolate taffy into the second dish; don't scrape out the pot.

Let the taffy cool for at least 1 hour, or until cool enough to handle comfortably. Pull immediately, or cover with aluminum foil and set aside at room temperature for up to 4 days. (If working with completely cooled taffy, place the baking dishes in a preheated 175 degree F oven and let warm up until the taffy is just warm and softened, 2 to 3 minutes, before pulling. Check the temperature by pressing down in the center. If necessary, using a greased metal or wooden scraper or spoon, scrape the taffy from the edges to the center to redistribute the heat and continue warming.)

TO PULL THE TAFFY: Lay out one 30-inch-long sheet of wax paper for each person and lightly coat with nonstick spray. Set out the softened butter for greasing the pullers' hands. Using lightly buttered kitchen shears or a sharp knife, divide each taffy flavor into 3 or 4 portions, placing each portion on a sheet of wax paper. Working singly or in pairs, with very lightly buttered hands, pull a portion by continuously stretching it out to about 6 inches, folding and kneading it back into a mass, and then pulling it out again. Don't pull it out so far that the taffy becomes stringy. As needed, rub a dab or two more butter on your hands; the taffy shouldn't get greasy. Continue pulling until the taffy is opaque and slightly shiny and stiffens slightly, 3 to 5 minutes.

ALL TOGETHER NOW, PULL!

The American custom of pulling candy as entertainment dates back to the Victorian era and remained popular through the first few decades of the twentieth century. It was a favorite activity for family get-togethers, children's gatherings, and even young adult "socials." In *Fulton County Folks, Volume 1,* a compilation of nineteenth-century letters and reminiscences assembled for the Fulton County Historical Society of Indiana, Marie Gast Talbot writes that "there were . . . parties usually of young people, who amused themselves by a boy and girl teaming to pull ropes of the elastic candy . . . Sometimes uninvited jealous boys stole the candy as it cooled on the windowsill preparatory to pulling."

Mabel Jones, who lives near Geneva, Alabama, remembers that in the 1920s, her family threw cane-syrup taffy pulls on Halloween instead of going trick-or-treating: "We knew when the crowd was coming, and we had the syrup already cooked down to the right consistency for pulling . . . We needed a partner so the two of us could pull the candy back and forth . . . Lots of good clean, wholesome fun."

Divide each pulled portion into thirds or quarters, then pull each third or quarter into a ⅓-inch-diameter even rope. Cut very long ropes into more manageable lengths. Lay the ropes on the wax paper. If desired, chocolate and honey ropes can be plaited together, then pulled out to ⅓-inch-thick ropes again to make two-toned chocolate-honey twist taffy. Generously rub the finished ropes all over with butter; this will make them easier to cut and keep the candies from sticking to their wrappers during storage.

Using lightly buttered shears or a sharp knife, cut each finished rope into 2-inch lengths (or as desired). Wrap each piece in a 3½-by-5-inch rectangle of wax candy paper or regular wax paper, twisting the ends to keep the paper from unrolling.

The taffy will keep, stored airtight, in the refrigerator for up to a month or in the freezer for up to 3 months. Let come to room temperature before serving.

Taffy Time

"Mostly, we made taffy on Sunday afternoons. We would all come together, after it was cooked and cooled enough to handle, to pull it. You had to pull the taffy until it was cool and shiny. We worked in twos pulling the sweet, stringy stuff across the entire room, putting it back together again and pulling until it was just right. Then we would snip it into bite size pieces, wrap each luscious piece in wax paper and keep them, but only for a little while. This did not last long at all in our house."

—Janey Deal, "Memories of Mama," unpublished essay, Hickory (North Carolina) Public Library (circa 2000)

peppermint-twist saltwater taffy

This taffy is chewy-smooth and pleasingly pepperminty. The recipe calls for stirring together water and salt before adding them to the pot, so you can legitimately say, "Yes, indeed, this is salt water taffy," even if you live nowhere near the ocean. This recipe makes enough for four people to pull.

2³/₄ cups sugar

1¹/₂ cups light corn syrup

³/₄ cup water, combined with ¹/₈ teaspoon salt

¹/₄ teaspoon fresh lemon juice

3 tablespoons unsalted butter, cut into bits, plus 2–3 tablespoons, softened, for pulling taffy

Red liquid food color

4–6 drops oil of peppermint, to taste

Set a 9-by-13-inch baking dish or large heatproof platter on a wire rack. Lightly but evenly butter or coat with nonstick spray.

In a heavy 3- to 4-quart saucepan, thoroughly stir together the sugar, corn syrup, salt water, and lemon juice using a wooden spoon. Bring the mixture to a boil over medium-high heat, stirring. Cover and boil briskly for 2 minutes. Uncover, and if you have a candy thermometer, clip it to the pan side, with the tip immersed but not touching the bottom. Cook, without stirring, for 5 to 7 minutes longer, or until the mixture reaches 260 to 262 degrees F. Or use the ice water test and cook until a teaspoon of the mixture dropped into ice water forms a very firm, almost brittle ball that holds its shape when squeezed in the water and stays very firm when removed from the water and squeezed. The temperature will rise rapidly near the end of cooking. Using oven mitts or potholders, immediately remove the pan from the heat.

Using a clean wooden spoon, immediately stir in the 3 tablespoons butter and oil of peppermint until the butter melts. Carefully turn out the taffy into the baking dish; don't scrape out the pan.

Let the taffy cool for 45 to 55 minutes, or until cool enough to handle comfortably. Pull immediately, or cover with aluminum foil and set aside at room temperature for up to 3 days. (If working with completely cooled taffy, place the baking dish in a preheated 175 degree F oven and let

tip

If you have oil of spearmint or cherry, or another appealing candy flavoring oil, it will work as well as the peppermint oil. These flavoring oils are stocked with cake-decorating or candy-making supplies in specialty shops and discount department stores. (Don't use extracts; they are too mild.) Tint each flavor with the appropriate food color.

warm up until the taffy is just warm and softened, 3 to 5 minutes, before pulling. Check the temperature by pressing down in the center. If necessary, using a greased metal or wooden scraper or spoon, scrape the taffy from the edges to the center to redistribute the heat and continue warming.)

TO PULL THE TAFFY: Lay out one 30-inch-long sheet of wax paper for each person and lightly coat with nonstick spray. Set out the softened butter for buttering the pullers' hands. Using lightly buttered kitchen shears or a sharp knife, divide the taffy into 3 or 4 portions, placing each portion on a sheet of wax paper. Working singly or in pairs, with very lightly buttered hands, pull a portion by continuously stretching it out to about 6 inches, folding and kneading it back into a mass, and then pulling it out again. Don't pull it out so far that the taffy becomes stringy. As needed, rub a dab or two more butter on your hands; the taffy shouldn't get greasy. Continue pulling until the taffy is opaque and slightly shiny and stiffens slightly, 3 to 5 minutes.

Divide each pulled portion in half, then pull each half into a ⅓-inch-diameter even rope. Rub the ropes very lightly with butter to reduce stickiness, then lay 2 ropes on each sheet of wax paper. Working with one rope in each pair, add drops of red food color along the length and on all sides, then pull it out and fold it back onto itself several times until the red color is just incorporated but still streaky. Pull out each colored portion until it's the same length as the uncolored portion it's paired with. Wash the food color from your hands, then dry and rebutter them. Immediately twist and stretch a white and a red rope together so they intertwine and form an even ⅓-inch-diameter red-and-white rope. Generously rub the finished ropes all over with butter; this will make them easier to cut and keep the candies from sticking to their wrappers during storage.

Using lightly buttered shears or a sharp knife, cut each finished rope into 1½-inch lengths (or as desired). Wrap each piece in a 3½-by-4½-inch rectangle of wax candy paper or regular wax paper, twisting the ends to keep the paper from unrolling.

The taffy will keep, stored airtight, in the refrigerator for up to a month or in the freezer for up to 3 months. Let come to room temperature before serving.

New Mexico caramels

Makes 2 pounds plain caramels or 2¾ pounds nut caramels

Roswell, New Mexico, is much more famous for its UFO sightings than its superb caramels, but it shouldn't be. For years, the women in the Altar Guild of Roswell's St. Andrews Episcopal Church were well known for their annual Christmas caramels fundraiser. (Eventually, the event got to be too much, and after more than fifty years, it finally ceased in the 1990s.) According to guild member Mary Ely, the caramels were originally created by a confectioner named Felix who worked for a popular sweet shop in the town in the 1920s. The candies are known locally as "fours," probably because the recipe calls for equal amounts of four of the ingredients.

The following caramels are adapted from a recipe shared with me by Linda Behrends, a St. Louis recipe developer who grew up in Roswell. She has kept her formula secret until now.

The caramels have a delectable flavor and aroma and an appealing creamy-chewy-soft texture. When cooked to the right temperature (a candy thermometer is required to ensure this), they don't stick to your teeth.

Although it is traditional in Roswell to dip these caramels in chocolate and to always include pecans (the nuts are native to New Mexico), they are also good plain. If you wish to dip them, see page 339.

1 cup granulated sugar	2 cups heavy (whipping) cream
1 cup packed light brown sugar	1 tablespoon vanilla extract, combined with 1 tablespoon hot water
1 cup dark corn syrup	2½ cups chopped pecans (optional)
16 tablespoons (2 sticks) unsalted butter, cut into chunks	
⅛ teaspoon salt	

Line a 9-by-13-inch baking dish with aluminum foil, allowing the foil to overhang two sides. Grease the foil or evenly coat with nonstick spray. Set the baking dish on a wire rack.

In a heavy, nonreactive 6-quart pot, thoroughly stir together the sugars, corn syrup, butter, and salt. Stir in the cream until the sugars dissolve. Bring to a boil over medium-high heat, stirring constantly with a wooden spoon. If any sugar remains on the pot sides, wipe it away with a pastry brush dipped in warm water or a damp paper towel.

Adjust the heat so the mixture boils briskly. Clip a candy thermometer to the pot side, with the tip immersed but not touching the bottom. Continue boiling briskly, occasionally gently stirring and scraping the pot bottom, until the mixture thickens and darkens somewhat, 8 to 9 minutes. Reduce the heat slightly and continue boiling, gently stirring and scraping the pot bottom to prevent scorching, until the caramel reaches 246 to 247 degrees F. Watch carefully, as the temperature may rise rapidly near the end of cooking. Immediately remove from the heat. Working carefully to avoid splattering, gently stir in the vanilla mixture and the pecans, if using, just until evenly distributed. Carefully pour the caramel into the baking dish; do not scrape out the pot.

Let cool until thoroughly set, at least 1½ hours. To aid in cutting the caramels, refrigerate for 15 to 20 minutes, or until firmed up slightly. (Do not refrigerate longer, or the caramel will become too hard.) Carefully peel off the foil. Wipe any excess oil from the slab using a paper towel. Place the slab on a cutting board. Using a lightly greased, large sharp knife, trim away uneven edges, if desired. Score and cut the slab into eighths lengthwise and twelfths crosswise (or as desired). Wrap each caramel in a 4-inch square of wax paper, twisting the ends to keep the paper from unrolling.

The caramels will keep in the refrigerator for up to 3 weeks. Let come almost to room temperature before serving.

MiLton HersHey, caraMeL Man

Today nearly everybody in America associates Milton Hershey with the chocolate industry, but caramels were his first claim to fame. After selling his struggling Philadelphia confectionary shop in 1882 when he was still in his early twenties, Hershey went to work for a Denver caramel manufacturer. With money from an aunt, he eventually set up the Lancaster Caramel Company in Pennsylania. The business languished initially, but eventually his commitment paid off. The Lancaster Caramel Company became a profitable manufacturer of top-quality caramels.

In 1893, Hershey attended the World's Columbian Exposition in Chicago and saw a German manufacturer's exhibit of chocolate-making equipment. He was so impressed that he immediately purchased the machinery and decided to embark on a new business.

"Caramels are only a fad," he is quoted as saying. "Chocolate is a permanent thing. I'm going to make chocolate." In 1900, he sold his caramel company. Caramels didn't fade away as Hershey expected, but his prediction of a great future for chocolate in America came true.

chocolate-dipped caramels

Makes about 3¾ pounds chocolate-dipped caramels

Hand-dipping caramels in chocolate is a confectionary skill that requires attention to detail, but the reward is an extraordinary treat. The actual dipping is not really tricky; the challenge is melting and cooling the chocolate properly so that it will set up smooth and firm.

When dipping candies in chocolate, be sure to work on a cool day or in an air-conditioned kitchen, or the chocolate may not set up properly.

New Mexico Caramels (page 336), cut neatly into 1-inch squares (or as desired)

2 pounds plus 5–8 ounces bittersweet (not unsweetened) or semisweet chocolate (divided)

2 tablespoons corn oil or other flavorless vegetable oil

Line two 10-by-15-inch or similar rimmed baking sheets with aluminum foil. Lay the caramels, slightly separated, on the baking sheets. Refrigerate until slightly cool and firm, about 30 minutes. Line several small trays or baking sheets with aluminum foil.

Break up or chop 2 pounds of the chocolate into 1-inch chunks; leave the remaining amount in blocks or large chunks.

In a large microwave-safe bowl, microwave the chopped chocolate and oil on high power for 1½ minutes. Stop and stir. Continue microwaving on medium power, stopping and stirring every 30 seconds, until most of the chocolate is melted. (Alternatively, heat the chopped chocolate and oil in a heavy medium saucepan over lowest heat. Stir and watch carefully until most of the pieces are melted. Immediately remove from the heat. Transfer the chocolate to a large bowl.) Continue stirring until the chocolate completely melts, several minutes longer.

Stir in 5 ounces of the chocolate blocks until melted and the mixture is almost cool to the touch; this may take some time. Touch the spoon to right above your upper lip; the melted mixture should feel almost cool. (Or insert a thermometer into the deepest part of the bowl. Wait 30 seconds. The temperature should be 89 degrees F or cooler.) If the added

candies and confections

339

pieces have completely melted and the mixture is still too warm, stir in the remaining 3 ounces chocolate blocks and continue to stir. When the chocolate has cooled enough, push any unmelted chunks to the side.

Set the bowl in a flat pan with 1 inch of hot water; be careful not to splash water into the chocolate. Stir the chocolate every 2 minutes to keep it blended and to redistribute the warmth. Change the water if it cools during the dipping process. (Alternatively, place the bowl on a heating pad set to low heat.)

Work with about a dozen chilled caramels at a time, removing each batch from the refrigerator about 5 minutes before dipping them. Using a large dinner fork, place a caramel on the tines and lower it into the chocolate. Tap the fork against the edge of the bowl several times, then scrape it against the edge to remove as much excess chocolate from the caramel as possible. Occasionally wipe off the fork with paper towels as chocolate builds up on it and stir the chocolate to keep it well blended.

Set the dipped caramels slightly separated on the baking sheets. (If necessary, push each caramel off the fork with the tines of another fork.) If desired, immediately draw the fork lightly back and forth in the chocolate to mark the surface of the caramel with a decorative zigzag. If a pool of chocolate forms a "foot" around the base of each caramel, tap off more excess chocolate as you dip subsequent caramels. When a baking sheet is full, transfer it to the refrigerator for 30 minutes to firm up the chocolate completely.

When the caramels are chilled, gently lift them off the foil using a table knife. Don't use your fingers, as this will leave fingerprints. If desired, use a paring knife to trim off uneven edges on the bottoms of the caramels. Place in individual fluted paper bonbon cups, if desired.

The caramels will keep, stored airtight (in a flat container with wax paper underneath and between the layers) and refrigerated, for up to 3 weeks. Let warm up to room temperature before serving.

caramel-pecan turtlettes

The combination of chocolate, caramel, and nuts, one of America's contributions to the sweets hall of fame, started appearing in commercial candy bars in the early twentieth century. Turtles, the candies that inspired this recipe, were created in the 1920s by a Chicago company called DeMets.

The caramel in these homemade turtlettes has a wonderfully rich flavor and aroma, and when cooked to the right stage, it has a firm, smooth, slightly chewy texture as well. To simplify what would otherwise be a fairly ambitious undertaking, this recipe calls for preparing a pan of candy that is cut into bite-size pieces rather than making the usual turtle-shaped patties. The chocolate is on the bottom and the pecans on top to avoid the challenge of enrobing the candies.

Using milk chocolate morsels will give you candies that are closest to commercial turtles, but I think the slightly bolder semisweet chocolate tastes even better.

$2^1/_2$ cups pecan halves

$1^2/_3$ cups heavy (whipping) cream

1 cup light corn syrup

1 cup granulated sugar

$^2/_3$ cup packed light brown sugar

8 tablespoons (1 stick) unsalted butter, cut into chunks

$^1/_8$ teaspoon salt

$1^1/_2$ teaspoons vanilla extract, combined with 3 tablespoons hot water

$2^2/_3$ cups (16 ounces) milk chocolate or semisweet chocolate morsels

Position a rack in the middle of the oven and preheat to 350 degrees F. Line a 9-by-13-inch baking dish with 18-inch-wide aluminum foil, allowing the foil to overhang all sides by at least 2 inches. Evenly coat the foil with nonstick spray. Set the baking dish on a wire rack.

Spread the pecans on a large rimmed baking sheet. Toast, stirring every 3 or 4 minutes, until lightly browned, 7 to 11 minutes. Set aside; turn off the oven.

In a heavy, nonreactive 6-quart pot, thoroughly stir together the cream, corn syrup, sugars, butter, and salt. Bring to a boil over medium-high heat, stirring with a wooden spoon until the sugars dissolve and the butter melts. With a pastry brush dipped in warm water or a damp paper towel, wash any sugar crystals from the pot sides. Carefully wash off all the sugar from the spoon.

Adjust the heat so the mixture boils briskly. Clip a candy thermometer to the pot side, with the tip immersed but not touching the bottom. Continue boiling briskly, gently stirring and scraping the pot bottom, until the mixture turns a medium-light caramel color and thickens somewhat, 8 to 9 minutes. Reduce the heat slightly and continue cooking—gently stirring, scraping the pot bottom, and watching carefully for signs of scorching—until the candy turns a rich caramel color and reaches 250 to 252 degrees F, 2 to 4 minutes longer. Watch carefully, as the temperature may rise rapidly near the end of cooking. Immediately remove from the heat. Standing back to avoid splattering and steam, and using a long-handled wooden spoon, gently stir in the vanilla-water mixture until well blended. Immediately pour the caramel into the baking dish; do not scrape out the pot.

Evenly sprinkle the pecans over the caramel. Using a fork, lightly rearrange and press the pecans down firmly so they are evenly distributed and embedded in the top. Let cool until warm and slightly stiffened, 20 to 30 minutes. Refrigerate until thoroughly chilled, about 1 hour.

Lift the caramel layer from the baking dish using the foil as handles. Line the same dish with another sheet of foil, again overhanging all sides by at least 2 inches. Evenly sprinkle the chocolate morsels on the foil. Transfer the dish to the oven, then turn the oven to the lowest setting. Heat for 3 minutes, then turn off the oven and let the dish stand in the oven until the morsels are just barely melted, about 8 minutes longer. Meanwhile, carefully peel the foil off the caramel layer. Lightly blot any excess oil from the caramel using a paper towel. Remove the baking dish from the oven. Immediately press the caramel layer, pecan side up, firmly onto the chocolate. Press down evenly over the entire layer so the caramel and chocolate stick together all over.

Immediately refrigerate for at least 1 hour and up to 12 hours, or until the chocolate sets completely. Carefully peel the foil off the chocolate. Let stand on a cutting board until the slab warms almost to room temperature. Using a lightly greased, large sharp knife, trim away uneven edges. Cut the slab into sixths lengthwise and eighths crosswise (or as desired).

The candies will keep, stored airtight (in a flat container with wax paper between the layers), in a cool place for up to a week or in the refrigerator for up to a month. Let come to room temperature before serving.

AT RIGHT

MERB'S CARAMEL
APPLES

PAGE 344

Merb's caramel apples

I've been a fan of caramel apples all my life, and these are the best I've ever eaten. They are very similar to the ones I sampled at Merb's, a well-known candy shop in St. Louis. Those apples, which are always crisp, tart, and huge, are dipped in a creamy, slightly chewy, not-too-sweet caramel, then rolled in a generous coating of chopped pecans. Merb's calls them "bionic," because they are almost grapefruit-size and weigh about a pound apiece. Although the apples are a seasonal item available only from the end of August through Thanksgiving, the company sells about seventy thousand a year.

This recipe is slightly adapted from one generously provided by Linda Behrends, a St. Louis food stylist and product development specialist, who credits her sister with creating it. Although the Merb's apples are always extra-large, I've called for medium ones here because they are easier to dip and make a more manageable serving. Merb's also uses only Granny Smith apples, but any firm, tangy variety works well.

This recipe requires a candy thermometer and a very large cooking pot.

3½–4 cups chopped pecans (optional)
1¼ cups granulated sugar
1¼ cups packed light brown sugar
1¼ cups dark corn syrup
8 tablespoons (1 stick) unsalted butter

2 cups heavy (whipping) cream (divided)
¼ teaspoon salt
2½ teaspoons vanilla extract
9–12 tart, crisp, well-chilled medium apples (6–7 ounces each), stems removed if desired

Line several rimmed baking sheets with aluminum foil and coat with nonstick spray (or use nonstick foil). If using the pecans, spread them on a large plate.

In a heavy 5- to 6-quart pot, thoroughly stir together the sugars, corn syrup, butter, 1 cup of the cream, and the salt. Bring to a boil over medium-high heat, stirring constantly with a wooden spoon. Adjust the heat so the mixture boils briskly. Using a long-handled wooden spoon, stir in the remaining 1 cup cream, adding it in a slow, thin stream so that the mixture keeps boiling. Wipe any sugar from the pot sides using a pastry brush dipped in warm water or a damp paper towel. Carefully wash off all the sugar from the spoon. Clip a candy thermometer to the pot side, with the tip immersed but not touching the bottom. Boil briskly, occasionally gently stirring and scraping the pot bottom, until the mixture is 247 to 248 degrees F, 8 to 10 minutes. Immediately remove from the heat. Gently stir in the vanilla just until evenly blended. Using oven mitts or potholders, pour the caramel into a heatproof medium bowl; do not scrape out the pot. Let cool for 4 to 5 minutes.

Meanwhile, insert a Popsicle stick or caramel-apple stick in the center top of each apple. Holding an apple by the stick, dip and roll it in the caramel until coated, letting any excess drip back into the bowl. (If the caramel runs off quickly and the coating seems thin, it is too hot. Let cool further before dipping more apples.) Hold the apple upside down and slowly twirl it so the remaining caramel flows evenly over the surface. If using the pecans, immediately dip the bottom half of the apple in them until coated as desired. If necessary, pat the nuts into place. Put the apple stick side up on a baking sheet. Continue with the remaining apples, spacing them a bit apart on the sheets. (As the caramel cools during dipping, it may stiffen and coat the apples too thickly or begin to slide off instead of adhering. Reheat in the microwave on high power, stirring and checking at 10-second intervals, for 20 to 30 seconds, or until fluid again.)

Let the apples cool until the caramel is firm. If the weather is warm, refrigerate for a few minutes to firm up. Wrap each apple in plastic or place in a plastic bag. Pull the plastic up around the stick and tie it in place with a ribbon or twist tie.

The apples will keep in the refrigerator for up to 2 days.

APPLES ON A STICK

"Take small apples and stick in each one at the top, a small wooden skewer, such as butchers use to pin roasts. Now cook a batch of Molasses Taffy to 280 degrees F. Then dip the apple in the hot batch so as to cover it completely. Let the surplus syrup drip off, then stand them on a slab until cold. "

—W. O. Rigby,
Rigby's Reliable Candy Teacher (1919)

Homemade Honey marshmaLLows

Considering how easy it is to make marshmallows and how appealing they are, it's surprising that they are so infrequently made at home. They are moister, tenderer, and more flavorful than the store-bought kind, especially when a little honey is incorporated to round out the taste. Use them to make Indoor S'mores (page 378) or Heavenly Hash Faux Fudge (page 376), toast them in the fireplace, or float them on mugs of steaming hot chocolate (see page 312).

It's easy to produce a variety of marshmallow flavors and colors simply by adding some citrus, mint, or other flavoring oils (not extracts) and an appropriate food color to the basic recipe. You can also turn out eye-catching "gourmet-shaped" marshmallows using whatever cookie cutters you desire (see the variation). Homemade marshmallows are wonderful dipped in chocolate (see page 349).

2½ tablespoons unflavored gelatin (3–4 packets)	3–4 drops almond extract, to taste (optional)
Generous ½ cup plus 3 tablespoons water (divided)	3–5 drops candy flavoring oil, such as oil of lemon, lime, peppermint, or crème de menthe, to taste (optional)
2 cups granulated sugar	2–4 drops liquid food color, as desired (optional)
1 cup light corn syrup	About ¾ cup powdered sugar for dusting marshmallows
¼ cup honey	
⅛ teaspoon salt	
2½ teaspoons vanilla extract	

Line a 9-by-13-inch baking dish with wax paper, allowing the paper to overhang the ends by about 1 inch. Evenly coat the paper with nonstick spray.

In a small bowl, sprinkle the gelatin over the ½ cup cold water. Let stand, stirring once or twice, until the gelatin softens, about 6 minutes.

In a heavy 3- to 4-quart saucepan over medium-high heat, stir together the sugar, corn syrup, honey, the remaining 3 tablespoons warm water, and salt until well blended. When the sugar dissolves, raise the heat and bring the mixture to a full boil, stirring. Boil for 20 seconds. Stir in the gelatin mixture, vanilla, and almond extract (if using) and cook, stirring, for 30 seconds longer. Remove from the heat and continue stirring until the gelatin completely dissolves.

tip

Be sure to let the marshmallow mixture stand for at least 6 hours and preferably 24 hours before cutting. Otherwise, it may be sticky and hard to work with.

Pour the mixture into a large bowl. Add the flavoring oil and/or food color, if desired. Using a mixer (with a whisk-shaped attachment, if available) and gradually raising the mixer speed from low to high speed, beat until the mixture is stiffened, lightened, and very fluffy, 5 to 7 minutes.

Using a rubber spatula coated with nonstick spray, scrape out the marshmallow mixture into the baking dish, spreading it evenly to the edges. Very evenly coat a sheet of wax paper with nonstick spray, then pat it down on the marshmallow surface. Let the mixture cool and firm up, at least 6 hours and preferably 24 hours. (The mixture will become firmer and easier to handle if left for the full 24 hours.)

TO CUT THE MARSHMALLOWS: Sift about one third of the powdered sugar onto a cutting board. Lift the marshmallow slab out of the baking dish. Peel off the top sheet of paper. Invert the slab on the sugar and peel off the other sheet. Sift about a third of the remaining powdered sugar over the top. Using lightly greased kitchen shears or a lightly greased, large sharp knife, cut the slab crosswise into twelfths and lengthwise into eighths to form generous 1-inch marshmallows (or as desired). Generally dust all the cut surfaces with powdered sugar to reduce their stickiness. As necessary, clean off and regrease the knife.

The marshmallows will keep, stored loosely packed in an airtight container (with wax paper between the layers) in the refrigerator, for up to 2 weeks. Let come to room temperature before serving.

VARIATION: Gourmet-Shaped Marshmallows

Prepare the marshmallows as directed, except use a 10-by-15-inch rimmed baking sheet instead of the baking dish.

To cut, lightly oil sharp metal cookie cutters. Cut out the gourmet shapes by pressing the cutters down through the marshmallow layer. Clean off and re-oil the cutters as needed. Dust the cut marshmallows all over with a little more powdered sugar so they don't stick together during storage.

confessions of a marshmallow epicure

"When we roasted marshmallows on a fire, I always made sure to get them perfectly brown on the surface and melted through and through. Robert stuck his right into the flame and carbonized it in an engulfing fireball. He would be on his third while I was still fussing over my first."

–John Kessler, "Fluff over Substance," *Atlanta Journal-Constitution* (March 14, 2002)

TAKE ONE MARSHMALLOW AND CALL ME IN THE MORNING

Introduced from Europe, marshmallows have been on the American scene for several centuries, though not in their present form. Originally prepared from the marsh mallow plant, a swamp-loving relative of the hollyhock, they were once used as a medicinal candy for sore throats. Thomas Jefferson included "marshmellow" among his list of "Objects for the Garden" in 1794, and according to seed packets available at Monticello today, the plant still adds "modest ornament" to the yard. In his 1869 work, *The Physiomedical Dispensatory,* the American physician William Cook described the sap from the plant as "agreeable to the taste and soothing to all mucous membranes." He recommended it as "useful in irritable coughs" as well as numerous digestive ailments best left unmentioned here.

By the 1850s, commercial confectioners in America were beginning to replace mallow sap with gelatin, a step that improved the texture of the candies but stripped them of any medicinal value. The marshmallow as a light and puffy delivery system for sugar was born.

chocolate-covered Homemade Marshmallows

It's amazingly easy to make your own chocolate-covered marshmallows at home. They make an impressive, eagerly received gift—if you can bear to part with them.

Homemade Honey Marshmallows (page 346)

2 pounds semisweet or milk chocolate, or a combination, broken up or coarsely chopped

½ cup corn oil or other flavorless vegetable oil

Freeze the marshmallows in an airtight container for at least 1 hour and up to 24 hours. Line several large rimmed baking sheets with aluminum foil and coat with nonstick spray (or use nonstick foil).

In a large microwave-safe bowl, combine the chocolate and oil. Microwave on high power for 2 minutes. Stop and stir well. Continue microwaving on medium power, stopping and stirring at 1-minute intervals, until most of the chocolate melts. Stir until the remaining chocolate melts and the mixture is smooth. (Alternatively, heat the chocolate and oil in the top of a double boiler over gently simmering water, stirring occasionally, until mostly melted. Transfer to a large bowl.)

Remove about a dozen frozen marshmallows at a time from the freezer. Using a large dinner fork, place a marshmallow on the tines and lower it into the chocolate. Tap the fork against the edge of the bowl several times, then scrape it against the edge to remove as much excess chocolate from the marshmallow as possible. Occasionally wipe off any chocolate that builds up on the fork with paper towels.

Set the dipped marshmallows slightly separated on the baking sheets. (If necessary, push each marshmallow off the fork with the tines of another fork.) If a pool of chocolate forms a "foot" around the base of each marshmallow, tap off more excess chocolate as you dip subsequent marshmallows. When a baking sheet is full, transfer it to the refrigerator for 30 minutes to firm up the chocolate completely. When the marshmallows are chilled, gently lift them off the foil.

The marshmallows will keep, stored airtight (in a flat container with wax paper between the layers) in the refrigerator for up to a month.

Tip

A combination of semisweet and milk chocolate complements the mild-tasting marshmallows best. Big fans of milk chocolate may want to use it alone. Don't be tempted to add vanilla extract or any other liquid to the chocolate-oil mixture. Chocolate contains a natural starch and may "seize up" and become completely unworkable when moisture is introduced.

peanut brittle

makes about
2½ pounds brittle

Alan Richardson, the photographer for this book, knows a winner when he tastes one. He passed along this fine peanut brittle recipe from his uncle and aunt, Bob and Bonnie McKay of Carthage, Mississippi. I've adapted it slightly, doubling the original to produce a bigger batch and adding some dark corn syrup and butter to heighten the rich, caramelized-sugar taste even more. The candy has a crunchy-brittle consistency and doesn't stick to your teeth.

It's important to note that the recipe calls for raw, skinless, unsalted peanuts, not roasted ones; the latter would overcook and burn. As the peanuts cook in the hot sugar mixture, they infuse it with their nutty flavor. Raw peanuts are usually labeled as such, but if not, they can be distinguished from roasted ones by their light beige color and earthy, noticeably uncooked taste.

As with many candy recipes, it is helpful, though not absolutely essential, to use a candy thermometer to determine doneness. Don't make the brittle on rainy or very humid days, as it may come out sticky.

3 cups sugar
1 cup light corn syrup
½ cup dark corn syrup
¾ cup water
4 cups raw, skinless, unsalted peanuts (about 1⅓ pounds)

2½ tablespoons unsalted butter, cut into bits
1½ teaspoons vanilla extract
½ teaspoon salt
2 teaspoons baking soda

Lightly coat two 12-by-18-inch rimmed baking sheets or similar large rimmed baking pans with nonstick spray. Line the pans with aluminum foil and coat with nonstick spray (or use nonstick foil). Set the sheets in the oven and turn the oven to the lowest setting.

In a heavy 4-quart saucepan, stir together the sugar, corn syrups, and water until well blended. Bring to a boil over medium-high heat, stirring frequently with a wooden spoon. Using a pastry brush dipped in warm water or a damp paper towel, wash any sugar crystals from the pan sides. Carefully wash off all the sugar from the spoon.

Adjust the heat so the mixture boils briskly. If you have a candy thermometer, clip it to the pan side, with the tip immersed but not touching the bottom. Continue boiling briskly, without stirring, until the mixture is 240 to 241 degrees F, 5 to 6 minutes longer. Or use the ice water test

tip
Raw peanuts are fairly easy to find in much of the South, but not in other parts of the country. Health food stores and gourmet shops are the best places to look.

and cook until a teaspoon of the mixture dropped into ice water forms a slightly firm, flexible ball that holds its shape when squeezed in the water but loses its shape and flattens when removed from the water and squeezed. With a clean spoon, immediately stir the peanuts into the mixture. Continue boiling briskly, gently stirring and scraping the bottom to prevent scorching, until the mixture is 312 to 316 degrees F, or until the peanuts look cooked through and are a toasty, medium amber color, 11 to 14 minutes longer. Immediately remove the pan from the heat. Stir in the butter, vanilla, and salt until evenly incorporated. Thoroughly stir in the baking soda; the mixture will foam and lighten in color.

Quickly turn out the mixture onto the baking sheets; don't scrape out the pan. Using the back of a large greased spoon or long-bladed metal spatula, press out the mixture into as thin a layer as possible. Work quickly, as the mixture will stiffen, then harden rapidly.

Let cool to room temperature. Gently lift up the foil and invert the brittle on the baking sheets. Gently peel off the foil. If the brittle seems at all oily, wipe it off with a paper towel. Break the brittle into large bite-size pieces (or as desired).

The brittle will keep, stored airtight, at room temperature for up to 2 weeks or refrigerated for up to 6 weeks. Let come to room temperature before serving.

VARIATION: Chocolate-Coated Peanut Brittle
Makes about 3⅓ pounds chocolate-coated brittle

Follow the recipe above until the brittle is cooled. Gently lift up the foil and set the slabs down on the counter. Line the baking sheets with more foil and coat with nonstick spray (or use nonstick foil). Invert the brittle on the sheets and gently peel the foil off the brittle. Sprinkle each slab evenly with 1 cup (6 ounces) semisweet chocolate morsels. Place the slabs in a cold oven, then turn the oven to the lowest setting. Let warm up for 2 to 3 minutes, or until the morsels are almost melted. Do not overheat, or the chocolate may not harden and set up properly. Using a narrow-bladed spatula or a table knife, spread the chocolate in an even layer. Lay a clean sheet of foil directly on the chocolate, smoothing and lightly pressing down all over so the two make contact evenly over the entire surface. Refrigerate for 25 to 30 minutes, or until the chocolate has set up. Gently peel the foil off the chocolate. Break the brittle into large bite-size pieces (or as desired). Store as for regular brittle.

peppermint-
chocolate bark

Taking my cue from the candy manufacturers, I've started making peppermint-chocolate bark to give out at Christmas. It's always a hit. Besides being far less expensive than the purchased product, it tastes much fresher.

Although making peppermint-chocolate bark isn't difficult, there is one trick: follow the directions for melting and cooling the chocolate carefully to ensure that it will set up quickly and have a smooth, crisp texture and sheen. The procedure is called "tempering." If you don't handle the chocolate properly, it can come out crumbly, blotchy, or streaked.

Since chocolate doesn't mix readily with tiny amounts of liquid, don't be tempted to add peppermint extract or any other liquid to the melted chocolate. If you want an extra hit of peppermint flavor, add some oil of peppermint. It's often stocked with candy-making and cake-decorating supplies in discount department stores and gourmet shops. Broken-up peppermint candy canes or peppermint sticks or peppermint pinwheel hard candies all work well in this recipe.

1 pound 6 ounces bittersweet (not unsweetened) or semisweet chocolate (divided)

1 tablespoon corn oil or other flavorless vegetable oil

2 drops oil of peppermint (optional)

½ cup crushed peppermint candy (about 4½ ounces)

Line a 10-by-15-inch rimmed baking sheet with aluminum foil, allowing the foil to overhang the ends by 2 inches. Try not to wrinkle the foil.

Break up or chop 1 pound of the chocolate into 1-inch chunks; leave the remaining 6 ounces in blocks or large chunks. In a microwave-safe medium bowl, microwave the chopped chocolate and oil on high power for 1 minute. Stop and stir. Continue microwaving on medium power, stopping and stirring every 30 seconds, until most of the chocolate is melted. (Alternatively, heat the chopped chocolate and oil in a heavy medium saucepan over lowest heat, stirring, until most of the chocolate is melted. Immediately remove from the heat. Transfer the chocolate to a medium bowl.) Continue stirring until the chocolate completely melts, about 5 minutes longer.

tip

To crush the candy, place the unwrapped pinwheel candies or broken-up sticks or canes in a triple layer of heavy plastic bags, closing the bags tightly. Using a kitchen mallet or the back of a heavy spoon, whack the candy into ⅛-inch or smaller pieces.

Stir in the oil of peppermint, if using, and 4 ounces of the remaining blocks or large chunks of chocolate until melted and the mixture is almost cool to the touch. To judge the warmth, insert a thermometer into the deepest part of the bowl. Wait 30 seconds. The temperature should be 89 degrees F or cooler. (Alternatively, touch the chocolate stirring spoon to just above your upper lip; the melted mixture should feel almost cool.) If the added pieces have completely melted and the mixture is still too warm, stir in the remaining 2 ounces chocolate and continue stirring. When the melted chocolate has cooled enough, lift out any unmelted chunks with a fork and discard.

Put the crushed candy in a medium-fine sieve or strainer. Hold it over the chocolate and shake the sieve back and forth until all the finely crushed candy falls into the chocolate. Stir well. Remove any peppermint bits larger than ⅛ inch from the sieve and discard (or eat) them. Reserve the remaining bits in the sieve.

Immediately turn out the chocolate mixture onto the baking sheet. Working quickly and using an offset spatula or a table knife, spread the chocolate in an even layer to the edges. Rap the sheet on the counter to even the surface. Immediately sprinkle the peppermint left in the sieve evenly over the chocolate. Work quickly, since the chocolate may set up rapidly. Shake the sheet back and forth and rap it on the counter several times to embed the candy bits in the chocolate. Immediately refrigerate for 15 to 20 minutes, or until the chocolate is completely set. Break the bark into 2- to 3-inch irregular pieces.

The bark will keep, stored airtight, in a cool place for up to a month.

VARIATION: Double Recipe
Makes about 2¾ pounds bark

Follow the basic directions, except prepare two 10-by-15-inch rimmed baking sheets. Break up or chop 2 pounds chocolate into 1-inch chunks; have 8 ounces unchopped chocolate blocks or large chunks on hand. In a large microwave-safe bowl, microwave the chopped chocolate and 2 tablespoons corn oil or other flavorless vegetable oil on high power for 2 minutes. Stop and stir. Continue microwaving on medium power, stopping and stirring every 30 seconds, until most of the chocolate is melted. Continue stirring until the chocolate completely melts. Stir in 4 drops oil of peppermint, if using, and 5 ounces of the unchopped chocolate. Proceed as in the original recipe, except if the mixture is still too warm, stir in 3 ounces more unchopped chocolate. Divide the mixture evenly between the two baking sheets.

A crooked History

As candy canes have become ever more popular at Christmas, colorful lore has sprung up suggesting that they are Christian in origin. One widely circulated tale is that a seventeenth-century choirmaster in Cologne, Germany, handed out plain white sugar sticks to keep the children quiet during the long Nativity service. In honor of the occasion, he supposedly had the candies bent to resemble shepherds' crooks, or perhaps upside-down Js (for Jesus).

Another story says that the German-Swedish immigrant August Imgard brought the tradition of decorating a Christmas tree with candy canes, paper ornaments, candles, and a tin star with him from Germany to Wooster, Ohio, in 1847. It's said that candy canes in that era were plain white, not striped as they are today.

Imgard's grave and former home (now the rectory of St. Mary's Catholic church) are indeed in Wooster, and he reportedly often recounted his story of introducing the custom of the Christmas tree and decorating it with candles and paper, but it's doubtful that candy canes were among the ornaments. They don't appear in holiday photographs, illustrations, or writings until much later, around 1910, nor is there any evidence that they existed in Germany. During the four years that I lived in Germany, I never saw any sign of them, and the few Germans who had heard of them told me they are an American sweet.

Lack of evidence notwithstanding, the candy cane legend has flourished. Today in parts of Ohio, it's possible to buy plain "old-fashioned" white candy canes at Christmastime. Some folks hang these supposedly authentic treats on their holiday trees to commemorate the first time August Imgard used candy canes as Christmas tree decorations—an event that likely never occurred.

8

Family Fun: Easy Gifts and Treats

kitchen Maple kettle corn

Salty, smoky-sweet, and thinly glazed with a slightly caramelized maple coating, this incredibly munchable popcorn treat is a takeoff on the kettle corn often sold at country fairs and festivals. It's vaguely like caramel corn, but lighter, fresher, less sugary, and much more natural-tasting. The popcorn is made the old-fashioned way—by heating oil and popping the kernels in a large pot. Then a maple syrup, salt, and sugar mixture is prepared, and the popcorn is quickly stirred back into the syrup. It's tempting enough that nobody can stop eating until the bowl is empty.

3 tablespoons maple syrup, preferably medium or dark amber

3 tablespoons corn oil or other flavorless vegetable oil (divided)

1 tablespoon sugar

¾ cup unpopped popcorn

Generous ¼ teaspoon salt, or more to taste

In a small bowl, stir together the maple syrup, 1 tablespoon of the oil, and the sugar. Set aside.

In a 6-quart or larger pot, heat the remaining 2 tablespoons oil and 3 or 4 kernels of the corn over medium-high heat until the kernels pop. Discard them, then stir the remaining corn and the salt into the oil. Cover the pot and cook, frequently shaking the pot, until the corn begins to pop. If the pot begins to smoke, lower the heat slightly. Continue cooking, shaking the pot constantly, until the popping mostly subsides, about 2 minutes longer. (Don't keep cooking until all the kernels pop, as the bottom layer may scorch.) Immediately turn out the popcorn into a large serving bowl, discarding any unpopped kernels, if desired.

Rinse out the pot and wipe it dry with paper towels. Add the maple syrup mixture to the pot. Cook, uncovered, over medium-high heat, stirring constantly with a wooden spoon, until the mixture boils and slightly thickens, 3 to 4 minutes. Immediately remove from the heat. Quickly and vigorously stir the popcorn into the maple syrup mixture until evenly coated. Turn out the corn into the serving bowl. If desired, add a little more salt to taste; stir well to incorporate.

Homemade kettle corn is best when very fresh, as it loses its crispness after a few hours.

tip

If desired, you can prepare a 3- to 3.5-ounce bag of regular microwave popcorn (follow the package instructions) instead of popping the corn on the stove. Home-style, natural light, and old-fashioned flavors all work well. Avoid using popcorn with extra butter or special flavorings. Since the commercial packages include salt, omit the salt from the recipe. (You will need 6 to 7 cups popped corn, the yield of most microwave bags.)

BUCKET OF INVENTION

I was introduced to the remarkably addictive treat called maple kettle corn by Burr Morse, a sixth-generation sugar maker in Montpelier, Vermont, who operates a maple retail store that's a popular destination for both natives and tourists. (More than three hundred bus tours visit Morse Farm Maple Sugarworks each year.)

Morse came up with the idea after discovering plain kettle corn at a farmers' market in Florida several years ago.

"I'd ordered over seventeen thousand custom-made cardboard tubs to hold maple gift assortments," Morse recalls, "and my customers weren't taking to the gift buckets like I anticipated. As soon as I tasted the regular kettle corn, I had a brainstorm—I'd make a maple version and sell it in the Morse Farm Maple Sugarworks buckets."

Morse makes his corn outside in the same kind of huge, gas-fired commercial kettle that regular kettle-corn purveyors use. He adds all the ingredients—popcorn kernels, oil, maple syrup, salt, and sugar—to the heated pot, then stirs furiously with a canoe paddle until the corn pops and scents the air. The popcorn has been a big hit, and the troublesome stack of tubs is now rapidly disappearing.

You can buy his kettle corn directly from Morse Farm by calling (800) 242-2740 or going to www.morsefarm.com.

spiced Frosted nuts

These temptingly sweet and crispy frosted nuts seem quite modern but are much like those that were typical on dessert tables several centuries ago. They are easy to prepare, even for fairly young children, and they make a great gift and fit nicely on a dessert table or cocktail tray.

- 1 large egg white
- ⅛ teaspoon salt
- 1 pound (about 4¼ cups) walnut or pecan halves
- ¼ cup granulated sugar
- ¼ cup packed light brown sugar
- ½ teaspoon ground cinnamon

Position a rack in the middle of the oven and preheat to 300 degrees F. Lightly grease a 10-by-15-inch rimmed baking sheet or coat with non-stick spray.

In a large bowl using a fork, beat together the egg white and salt until frothy. Stir in the nuts until thoroughly coated. In a large bowl, stir together the sugars and cinnamon until well blended. Add the nut mixture to the sugar mixture, stirring until the nuts are thoroughly coated.

Turn out the nuts onto the baking sheet, spreading out to form an even layer. Bake, stirring every 10 minutes, until crisp and dry, 30 to 40 minutes. Stir. Transfer the sheet to a wire rack. Let cool completely. Pack in tins, jars, or other airtight containers.

The nuts will keep at room temperature for up to a week, or refrigerated for up to a month.

ROCK crystal candy LoLLies

Besides being fun, making rock candy offers children the opportunity to create glittering sugar crystal lollipops (or sweet swizzle sticks) that can be used as special gifts for family or friends. At the same time, the project can serve as a fascinating lesson in the chemical phenomenon of supersaturation and how certain molecules naturally crystallize in striking jewel-like formations and patterns. For safety, an adult needs to do the boiling, but the rest of the steps can be managed by older elementary school and middle school children.

Pure cane sugar rock candy became a popular product in the late Victorian era. Rough chunks of it that had been "grown" on fine strings were sold in penny candy cases, and pharmacies relied on it in both crystal and syrup form to concoct cough remedies. Soda fountains used it in their flavoring syrups, and saloons combined it with rye whiskey to concoct a potent popular potion called "rock-and-rye," which barkeeps touted as a cold and stomach remedy.

With the arrival of Prohibition and the competition from lower-cost corn sweeteners in the early twentieth century, rock candy fell on hard times. Now its retro charm is resulting in a resurgence of popularity, and rock crystal lollies and swizzle sticks are available in many fancy shops.

12–16	6- to 8-inch-long sturdy paper lollipop sticks or Popsicle sticks
	Candy flavoring oils, such as oil of cinnamon, peppermint, clove, lemon, orange, cherry, or grape (optional)
	Assorted liquid food colors (optional)
1½	cups hot water, plus more as needed
3⅔	cups sugar, plus 2 tablespoons for coating sticks
	A cup of water for dipping sticks

Set out some 6- to 8-ounce preserving jars, very sturdy small jelly or condiment jars, or small heatproof containers such as custard cups. If preparing plain lollies, set out four jars; if preparing a variety of colors and flavors, set out enough jars (up to six) to prepare the selection of colors and flavors desired. Add a drop or two of the desired flavoring to each jar. Stir in the associated food color and ½ teaspoon hot water.

In a large heavy saucepan using a wooden spoon, stir together the sugar and the 1½ cups hot water until well mixed. Bring to a full boil, stirring, over medium-high heat. Boil for 1 minute, or until the sugar is completely dissolved and the syrup is clear. Remove from the heat. Let cool

Tip

Candy flavoring oils are found with cake-decorating or candy-making supplies in specialty shops and discount department stores.

for about 5 minutes. Carefully pour the syrup into the jars until it is a generous 2½ inches deep in each jar. It's important not to stir the syrup or agitate the jars, or the mixture can turn sugary too soon. Let cool, without any stirring, to room temperature.

Meanwhile, lay out a sheet of wax paper or aluminum foil. Put 2 table-spoons sugar in a small saucer. Dip 2½ inches of each stick in a cup of water. Shake off the excess, then roll the stick in sugar until the damp-ened area is coated. These sugar crystals will encourage larger ones to form around them. Tap off the excess sugar and set the sticks aside on the paper.

When the preserving jars are completely cool to the touch, gently stir each to evenly incorporate the color and flavoring (if using). Gently place several sugared sticks in each jar, spacing them apart. Tent all the jars loosely with aluminum foil. Let stand for 4 to 8 days, checking and lift-ing up the sticks at least once and preferably twice a day to make sure they aren't sticking to the bottom or to one another, until the submerged parts are encrusted with a ¼- to ⅓-inch-thick layer of crystals (or more if thicker lollipops are desired). Remove the sticks from the syrup, shak-ing off the excess, and lay the candies slightly separated on a sheet of wax paper or aluminum foil.

Let stand for at least 1 hour, or until dry, before packing airtight. The candies may be packed individually or in groups in plastic bags, clear plastic boxes, or plastic wrap.

The candies will keep, stored airtight, at room temperature for 3 months.

TIP

Sometimes the sugar solution becomes cloudy, thick, and sugary before the crystals have built up sufficiently on the sticks. If this happens, remove the lollies and set aside on wax paper. If the mixture is hard and crystallized, heat in a microwave on medium power for 1 minute to soften it. Scrape the sugar solution into a saucepan, add 1 teaspoon water, and bring to a boil, stirring. Boil until the mixture is clear and all the sugar has dissolved. Let stand for 5 minutes. Gently pour the mixture into a clean heatproof jar. Let cool completely, then return the lollies to the mixture and continue as originally directed. This method can also be used *one time* to recycle the solution to make a second batch of lollies.

The science Behind the Magic

How does plain granulated sugar disappear into water, then magically come back out of the water and form hard, shiny crystals? It's a chemical process called crystallization. It works like this: When sugar and water are mixed together, sugar crystals dissolve and form a sugar solution. Heating the water, especially to boiling, makes dissolving the sugar crystals easier, so many more of them dissolve into the solution than normal. The super-sugary solution is then said to be supersaturated. Supersaturation is not a normal state, so the sugar molecules have a strong tendency to turn back into a solid again. Particularly when the solution is hot, stirring or jostling of any kind can cause the sugar to begin instantly crystallizing into grains.

Once the sugar solution cools down, it can't hold the extra sugar that was incorporated, so gradually the sugar starts to fall out, or precipitate. Granulated sugar, or sucrose, is composed of glucose and fructose molecules that naturally bond together in pairs. The slow, gradual precipitation provides time for the pairs to link and build up in orderly geometric patterns that become visible as shimmery rock crystal formations.

chocolate-dipped banana pops

Chocolate-covered banana pops are easily made by middle-schoolers and teenagers and by younger children with the help of an adult. A good part of the appeal is that each child can custom-coat his or her own pop, so offer several choices: chopped nuts, toasted coconut, and colorful tiny candies all work well. (Avoid large candy sprinkles, which freeze too hard.)

It's best to use wooden Popsicle sticks (available in craft shops) for this recipe. You can substitute sturdy cardboard lollipop sticks, which are sometimes sold with cake-decorating supplies, if you wish. Never use thin skewers or pointed sticks, as these can splinter.

3 or 4 unbruised ripe or slightly overripe small or medium bananas

6 or 8 wooden Popsicle sticks

8 ounces bittersweet (not unsweetened) or semisweet chocolate, broken up or coarsely chopped

3 tablespoons corn oil or other flavorless vegetable oil

Assorted garnishes, such as finely chopped roasted peanuts (salted or unsalted), walnuts, pecans, or macadamia nuts; toasted coconut; or fine sprinkles (optional)

Peel the bananas, discarding the stringy fibers. Cut each banana in half crosswise. Push a Popsicle stick about 1½ inches into the cut end of each half. Place each in a small plastic bag or wrap in plastic. Freeze for at least 3 hours and up to several days.

In a microwave-safe medium bowl, combine the chocolate and oil. Microwave on high power for 1 minute. Stop and stir. Continue microwaving on medium power, stopping and stirring at 30-second intervals, until the chocolate is just melted. (Alternatively, in a heavy medium saucepan, warm the chocolate and oil over lowest heat, stirring, until just melted. Immediately remove from the heat.)

TO MAKE GARNISHED POPS: Pour the chocolate mixture into a jar or sturdy drinking glass tall enough to hold it and wide enough that the bananas can be easily dipped. Line a baking sheet with wax paper. Place each garnish in the middle of a sheet of wax paper.

Working with one banana half at a time and holding it by the stick, dip it in the chocolate, tipping the jar to one side and quickly rotating the banana until it is covered. Hold the banana upright so any excess chocolate drips toward the stick. Immediately roll the dipped banana in one or more of the garnishes, turning until lightly coated. Work quickly, as the chocolate will set up rapidly. Lay the finished pops on the baking sheet. Freeze until completely frozen, at least 20 minutes.

TO MAKE UNGARNISHED POPS: Pour the chocolate mixture into a jar or sturdy drinking glass as for the garnished pops. Refrigerate the chocolate, stirring occasionally, for 5 to 10 minutes, or until slightly cooled but not stiff. Line a baking sheet with wax paper and chill it briefly in the refrigerator or freezer.

Grasping a banana half by the stick, dip it in the chocolate, tipping the jar to one side and quickly rotating the banana until it is covered. Hold the banana upright for about 1 minute, or until the chocolate partially sets. Immediately transfer it to the chilled baking sheet. Continue until all the bananas are covered. Freeze for at least 20 minutes, or until completely frozen.

The pops will keep, stored airtight, in the freezer for up to a week.

The Good Stick Lollipop

The word "lolly-pop" dates back to eighteenth- and nineteenth-century England, where it referred to a sweetmeat or lozenge, not a candy on a stick. (According to the *Old English Dictionary,* the word "lolly" once meant tongue in a northern English dialect.)

Lollipops of the lickable, stickable sort came on the scene much later, probably in the early twentieth century. No one knows for sure, but the novel idea of adding a stick likely originated in America. A confectionery machinery company in Racine, Wisconsin, is said to have invented equipment that inserted sticks into candies in 1908, at the request of a candy manufacturer. U.S. patent records indicate that the "first use" for the Dum Dums Pops brand name was in 1924.

sugar cookie pops

This tasty all-purpose sugar cookie recipe can be used to prepare rolled cookie pops in various cut-out shapes or large, hand-shaped round lollipops formed from flattened balls of dough. The latter method is more fun for youngsters, since they don't usually need a lot of adult help. The round cookie pops can be iced and decorated to resemble smiley faces, jack-o'-lanterns, balloons, trimmed Christmas balls, flowers, or spiral-patterned all-day suckers. This dough is fairly sturdy and not too sweet, making it a good choice for icing.

You'll notice that the directions for attaching the Popsicle sticks to the cookies are very specific and call for sandwiching the sticks between two layers of dough. This is because the most obvious method—simply laying the dough over the sticks and pressing down—doesn't work very well.

To inspire the creativity of young decorators, you may want to provide an array of colors for the icing by dividing it among several smaller bowls and adding a different food color to each.

3¼ cups all-purpose flour, plus more if needed

¾ teaspoon baking powder

¾ teaspoon salt

16 tablespoons (2 sticks) unsalted butter, slightly softened

2 tablespoons corn oil or other flavorless vegetable oil

1 cup granulated sugar, plus about 3 tablespoons (if making hand-shaped cookies) for topping cookies

1 large egg

3 tablespoons half-and-half or whole milk

2½ teaspoons vanilla extract

24 wooden Popsicle sticks

Assorted sprinkles or edible glitter (optional)

ICING (OPTIONAL)

1 1-pound package powdered sugar, sifted if lumpy, plus more if needed

¼ cup warm water, plus more if needed

1 tablespoon corn oil or other flavorless vegetable oil

2 teaspoons light corn syrup

⅛ teaspoon vanilla extract

Assorted liquid or paste food colors (optional)

tip
Paste food colors are found in gourmet shops and discount department stores.

In a large bowl, stir together the flour, baking powder, and salt. In a large bowl using a mixer on medium speed, beat together the butter, oil, and granulated sugar until very light and fluffy, 2 to 3 minutes. Beat in the egg, half-and-half, and vanilla until well blended and smooth. Gradually beat or stir the flour mixture into the butter mixture to form a smooth, slightly firm dough. Let the dough stand for 10 minutes to firm up a little more. If the dough seems soft, work in up to 3 tablespoons more flour to make it slightly firmer but not at all dry. Divide the dough in half, then proceed as directed for either hand-shaped round cookie pops or rolled, cut-out cookie pops. The dough will keep, tightly covered, in the refrigerator for up to 3 days.

TO MAKE HAND-SHAPED ROUND COOKIE POPS: Cover the dough and refrigerate until well chilled and fairly firm, 30 to 45 minutes, or freeze for 20 to 25 minutes.

Position a rack in the upper third of the oven and preheat to 375 degrees F. Generously grease several large baking sheets or generously coat with nonstick spray. Put 3 tablespoons granulated sugar in a saucer. Lightly oil the bottom of a large, flat-bottomed drinking glass. Working on a sheet of baking parchment or wax paper with half the dough (keep the other half refrigerated), divide it into 12 equal portions. Working with one portion at a time with lightly greased hands, pull off and roll one fourth of the portion into a small ball, then roll the remaining three fourths into a larger ball. Set the smaller ball on a baking sheet, then center the end of a Popsicle stick over the ball; do not press down. Stack the larger ball, centered, over the stick and the smaller ball. Dip the bottom of the glass into the granulated sugar and shake off the excess, then firmly press down the larger ball until it is about 2¾ inches in diameter. Repeat the shaping process with the remaining dough portions. If desired, decorate the cookie tops with sprinkles. (Or leave undecorated and add icing and other decorations after baking.) Remove the remaining dough from the refrigerator and repeat the shaping process.

Bake one sheet at a time for 10 to 15 minutes, or until the cookies are lightly colored on top and slightly darker at the edges. Reverse the sheet from front to back halfway through baking, if necessary, to ensure even browning. Transfer the sheet to a wire rack. Let the cookies stand for 1 to 2 minutes to firm up. Using a wide spatula, transfer to the rack. Let cool completely. Don't try to pick up the cookies using their sticks until they are completely cooled.

TO MAKE ROLLED, CUT-OUT COOKIE POPS: Divide the dough in half. Roll out each portion between sheets of baking parchment or wax paper until ⅛ inch thick. Occasionally check the underside of the dough during rolling and smooth out any wrinkles. Stack the rolled portions (paper still attached) on a baking sheet. Refrigerate for

Tips

As added insurance that the cookies stay on their sticks, brush the bottom layer of dough with a little lightly beaten egg white and top with the stick as directed. Then brush with a little more beaten egg white, top with the remaining dough, and proceed as directed.

You can use this recipe to form regular plain or iced sugar cookies (without sticks) by rolling the dough out a scant ¼ inch thick between sheets of baking parchment or wax paper. Refrigerate the dough, then cut out the cookies and bake.

about 45 minutes, or until cold and firm, or freeze for about 20 minutes. (The dough may be frozen for up to 2 days.)

Position a rack in the upper third of the oven and preheat to 375 degrees F. Generously grease several large baking sheets or generously coat with nonstick spray. Working with one dough portion at a time and leaving the other refrigerated, gently peel off the top sheet of paper, then pat loosely back into place so it will be easy to remove later. Invert the dough and peel off the second sheet.

Using 2½- to 3-inch cookie cutters, cut out 2 of each cookie desired. (Each pair will be sandwiched together with the stick in the middle.) If at any point the dough softens too much to handle easily, transfer the paper and dough to a baking sheet and refrigerate or freeze until firm.

Using a spatula, carefully transfer half the cookies (to serve as the bottoms) to the baking sheets, spacing them about 1¼ inches apart. Center the Popsicle sticks over on the bottoms, pressing to embed them slightly. Place the cookie tops directly over the sticks and bottoms and pat down lightly but evenly all over. If desired, garnish the cookies with sprinkles. (Or leave the pops plain and add icing and other decorations after baking.) Re-roll any dough scraps. Continue cutting out and forming cookies until all the dough is used.

TO BAKE THE COOKIES: Bake one sheet at a time as directed for hand-shaped cookies.

The cookie pops will keep, stored airtight, at room temperature for up to 2 weeks or frozen for up to a month. Let thaw at room temperature before icing and decorating.

TO MAKE THE ICING (IF USING): In a large bowl with a mixer on low speed or by hand, beat together the powdered sugar, water, oil, corn syrup, and vanilla. Raise the speed to medium and beat until well blended and smooth. Adjust the icing consistency as needed by adding a bit more water to thin it or a bit more powdered sugar to stiffen it. A fairly fluid consistency is needed to spread the icing easily and form a perfectly smooth, glossy surface. A stiff consistency is needed to pipe and form lines that hold their shape. If desired, divide the icing into several bowls and tint each a different color by stirring in a drop or two of food color. The icing gradually dries out as it stands; add a drop or two of water to thin it as necessary, and cover with plastic wrap when not in use. The icing will keep, covered tightly, in the refrigerator for 3 or 4 days. Let come to room temperature and stir before using. You'll have enough icing to completely cover the cookie pops, then to add generous amounts of decorative piping to them.

TO ICE THE COOKIES: Using a small wide-bladed spatula, spreader, or table knife, ice the cookies. To prevent the piping from running on the iced cookies, be sure the icing layer is completely set, at least 6 hours and preferably longer, before adding piping. To apply piped icing outlines or trims to cookies, spoon the icing into paper decorating cones or pastry bags fitted with fine writing tips.

The iced cookie pops will keep, stored airtight, at room temperature for up to 2 weeks.

snow cones

Whether shaved or crushed ice is better is hotly debated among serious fans of snow-balls. The two do yield noticeably different textures, but preference mostly depends on what you're used to. Whichever you choose, the ice must be relatively fine, or it won't blend well with the syrup. If you plan to make snowballs often, consider purchasing an electric ice-shaving machine, specifically designed for this purpose. (These appliances usually work with regular ice cubes and often come with a starter supply of paper cones and syrups.) If you have a refrigerator with a crushed-ice dispenser, you can probably start with that and get it fine enough by grinding it in a sturdy food processor. Bags of crushed ice also can usually be ground finely enough in a food processor.

Snowballs don't have a reputation for being nutritious, but I make mine with undi-luted frozen fruit juice concentrates with no artificial dyes and flavorings, so they are reasonably healthful. I like to use real berry, cherry, and fruit blends, since they have kid-pleasing colors and flavors. For chocolate snowballs, I start with a batch of choco-late syrup.

1¼–1½ cups finely crushed, shaved, or ground ice

1 8-ounce paper cone or paper (not Styrofoam) cup

3–4 tablespoons undiluted frozen (thawed) fruit juice concentrate or Crown Candy Kitchen's Chocolate Syrup (page 312)

3–4 tablespoons Marshmallow Sundae Topping (page 313; optional)

If using crushed ice, grind it in a food processor until finely ground and snowlike, stopping and stirring to redistribute it as necessary. Put the ice in the cone. Pour the juice concentrate or syrup over the ice, or use several syrups, separated or overlapped, as desired. Garnish with marsh-mallow sauce, if desired. Serve immediately, preferably with both a spoon and a straw.

Leftover fruit juice concentrate, chocolate syrup, or marshmallow sauce will keep, stored in airtight jars, in the refrigerator for up to 2 weeks.

Baltimore and New Orleans, two of America's most enthusiastic snowball cities (the icy treats are never called snow cones there), have numerous stands and syrup suppliers, some with names as colorful as the wares they sell. In the Baltimore area, there's Chilly Willy's, Icy Delights, Koldkiss, Jay's Shave Ice, and Sweet Shivers. New Orleans is home to SnoWizard, Sno-Blitz, Pandora's Ice Box, and the Nectar Soda Company (which makes just one flavor, a shocking pink vanilla-almond blend called New Orleans Nectar Soda Syrup).

Tom Fitzmorris, a longtime restaurant reviewer, newsletter publisher, and radio talk show host in New Orleans, grew up loving the cherry snowballs sold at a stand near his house. He says that for every ice cream cone consumed in the city, at least ten snowballs are eaten. (What's known as an ice cream headache in the rest of the country is a snowball headache there.)

Fitzmorris objects to some of the innovations in the snowball business since his childhood. The foam cup that replaced the thin paper cone about twenty years ago, he says, "upsets the balance of ice and snowball juice because it prevents the ice from melting quickly enough." However, as he wrote in the *New Orleans Menu Daily,* the worst is the "spoon-straw," which "looks like a tiny spoon but in no way functions like one. It's a conspiracy that probably has the Communists, the Illuminati, the Jesuits, or all three behind it."

MapLe sugar on snow

Making a simple maple candy variously called sugar on snow, maple on snow, or jack wax is a favorite family activity in America's maple sugar country. The Harold J. Howrigan family of Fairfield, in northern Vermont, introduced me to the tradition in their comfortable farmhouse kitchen on a frigid March day. "Basically, you just boil maple syrup, then drizzle it over snow," Harold, the quiet-spoken patriarch of the clan, said as he tended the pot of syrup bubbling on the stove.

A few minutes later, with a cloud of sweet steam filling the room, Harold checked the syrup with a candy thermometer, pronounced it ready, and drizzled it over a pan of waiting snow. The syrup stiffened immediately, and we forked it into our mouths. It was chewy but smooth, with a pure, concentrated maple taste. Following the long-established custom of sugar-on-snow parties, Harold's wife, Anne, passed around sour pickles, explaining that they counteract the candy's sweetness. (Some people serve crackers or plain doughnuts.)

Since the temperature of the syrup doesn't have to be exact, a candy thermometer isn't essential. You can simply check the syrup by drizzling a little on a small amount of snow: when it hardens to the right consistency—soft chewy, firm chewy, or very firm, depending on your taste—it's done.

6–8 cups fresh, clean snow or shaved or finely ground ice

3/4 cup maple syrup, preferably light or medium amber

Sour pickles, crackers, and/or plain unglazed doughnuts for serving (optional)

Spread the snow in a 9-by-13-inch baking dish; it should be at least 1 inch deep. Pat the snow down to form an even layer. If you don't have a candy thermometer, set a small mound of snow aside in a shallow heatproof bowl. Place both in the freezer while you boil the maple syrup.

In a heavy, nonreactive 1-quart saucepan, bring the maple syrup to a boil over medium-high heat. If you have a candy thermometer, clip it to the pan side, with the tip immersed but not touching the bottom. Adjust the heat slightly and boil briskly for 3 to 4 minutes. When the syrup reaches 239 to 240 degrees F (or stiffens to a chewy taffy consistency when a small amount is drizzled over the small bowl of snow), it is almost done. For a slightly firmer consistency, cook to 242 to 243 degrees, about 1 minute longer. Slowly drizzle the syrup back and forth on the large dish

tip

If you don't have snow, I suggest making a substitute: use a food processor to grind ice from the crushed-ice dispenser of your refrigerator or buy ground chipped ice from the supermarket. It's coarser than the aficionados prefer, but it does the job. If you have an ice-shaving machine for making snow cones, that will yield an even better substitute.

of snow, forming small clumps or ropes. Let cool for a minute or two, until the maple stiffens and becomes taffylike. Lift the clumps off with forks or your fingertips and enjoy. Serve with sour pickles, crackers, and/or doughnuts, if desired.

Nature's Brief Treat

Many American sugar makers today have abandoned the traditional method of harvesting maple syrup, but the Howrigan family is proud to do it the old-fashioned way. Several years ago, in the middle of sugaring season, Anne and Harold Howrigan and their son Mike and ten-year-old grandson Ryley gathered in the senior Howrigans' home to acquaint me with the basics of their operation.

They explained that the actual harvesting, or gathering, of the sap from which maple syrup is made can occur only when the sap is running. This happens in periods of warm days and cold nights, when winter is on the wane but spring hasn't yet arrived. (The flow of sap up and down the trees is a phenomenon scientists still don't fully understand.) When the conditions are right, sugar makers work at a frenetic pace.

Collecting sap is extremely labor-intensive, Mike said, ticking off just some of the tasks. First, experienced family members drive spoutlike taps into thousands of maple trees—carefully, so the trees are not damaged. Then they hang more than 10,000 buckets, check them every day or so, and empty the sap into 150-gallon gathering tubs. The Howrigans use teams of horses to carry the tubs of sap to the evaporator. (Most large-scale sugar makers have replaced their sap-gathering buckets with a network of plastic tubing that runs directly from the taps to the collecting tanks, and even those who use buckets rarely rely on real horsepower anymore.) "The horses can get up into areas where tractors can't go," explained Harold, "and there aren't any ruts left to show they were ever there."

Later the Howrigans showed me their sugarhouse, where the "sugaring off" takes place. The faintly sweet, watery liquid is boiled down in an evaporator until only full-bodied syrup—about 2 percent of the original volume—remains. Ryley said his favorite job is to look after the firebox, adding the wood that fuels the evaporator. (The family splits and stacks 150 cords of firewood each year for sugarhouse fuel.)

The sugaring season ends when the maple trees bud, because this causes the sap to develop a strong, unpleasant taste. (Depending on the weather, budding occurs four to six weeks after the first sap run.) Then the Howrigans put the horses out to pasture for another year.

buckeyes

Buckeyes are easy-to-make, no-cook peanut butter and chocolate candies cleverly fashioned to look like the glossy brown nuts of our indigenous buckeye trees. The candies are prepared by shaping a rich peanut butter filling into little balls, then dipping all but a small portion of the chilled balls into melted chocolate. The finished candies are dark and smooth, except for the undipped "eye" portion, where the tan-colored peanut butter shows through; their resemblance to the real nuts is unmistakable. Buckeyes taste like good homemade peanut butter cup candies.

This recipe is adapted from one created by Connie Hay, a food writer friend who also happens to be from Ohio, where it appears the buckeye candies originated. (The buckeye is the Ohio state tree, as well as the state nickname and the Ohio State University team name.) Connie says the candies are probably a late-twentieth-century creation, since no one she's asked can remember eating them before the 1970s or 1980s. Originally, she says, they were a home-kitchen sweet and most often prepared in autumn, although now some commercial candy companies sell them year-round. Some Kentucky and other regional cookbooks call these confections "buck's eyes" or "doe's eyes," but they look like buckeyes just the same.

1½ cups creamy peanut butter

6 tablespoons (¾ stick) unsalted butter, slightly softened

1 teaspoon vanilla extract

3 cups powdered sugar, plus more if needed

Water, if needed

2 cups (12 ounces) semisweet chocolate morsels

¼ cup solid white shortening

TO MAKE THE CANDY CENTERS: In a large bowl using a mixer, beat the peanut butter and butter on medium speed until well blended, about 2 minutes. Beating on low speed, add the vanilla and powdered sugar. Beat on medium speed until the mixture holds together. If the mixture is too dry and crumbly, beat in a teaspoon or two of water until the mixture holds together smoothly. If the mixture seems slightly wet, beat in a few tablespoons more powdered sugar to stiffen it. Tightly cover the mixture and refrigerate until cool and slightly firm, at least 1 hour and up to 24 hours, or freeze for 30 to 40 minutes.

Line several rimmed baking sheets with wax paper. Working with about a quarter of the peanut butter mixture and keeping the rest in the refrigerator, scoop up portions using a teaspoon or very small scoop and roll into 1-inch balls. Place on the baking sheets, spacing them about 1 inch apart. Repeat with the remaining mixture until all the balls are formed. Cover and freeze until well chilled and firm, at least 1½ hours and up to 24 hours.

TO PREPARE THE CHOCOLATE: In a microwave-safe medium bowl, microwave the chocolate morsels and shortening on high power for 1 minute. Stir well. Continue microwaving on medium power, stirring and checking the consistency at 30-second intervals, until the chocolate is about two-thirds melted. Stir until the residual heat finishes the job and the chocolate mixture is smooth and has cooled to warm. (Alternatively, in a heavy medium saucepan over lowest heat, warm the chocolate and shortening, stirring until barely melted.) Transfer to a small bowl.

Line several large rimmed baking sheets with wax paper. Remove about 12 candy centers from the freezer at a time for dipping. Using a toothpick, dip a ball partially into the chocolate, leaving about one quarter of the ball (around the pick) uncovered so that the peanut butter mixture shows. Shake off as much excess chocolate as possible. As you work, place the candies on the wax paper, spacing them about 1 inch apart with the "eyes" up. Patch the tiny hole left by the toothpick by smoothing the peanut butter filling with a fingertip. If the chocolate cools and stiffens too much for dipping, reheat it in the microwave on medium power (or in the saucepan over lowest heat), stirring every few seconds, until just warm enough to use. As each sheet of buckeyes is prepared, transfer it to the refrigerator. Refrigerate until cold and firm, about 30 minutes. Pack in airtight containers with wax paper between the layers.

The buckeyes will keep in the refrigerator for up to 3 weeks or in the freezer for up to 2 months. Serve lightly chilled; they should not come to room temperature. If frozen, let thaw in the refrigerator.

Heavenly Hash Faux Fudge

makes 50 to 60 pieces, or 2¼ pounds candy

If you're looking for a homemade holiday treat or last-minute chocolate gift that even kids can make successfully, this quick, no-boil candy is a perfect choice. The name "heavenly hash" usually indicates that a recipe combines fruit, marshmallows, and nuts. In the early twentieth century, the moniker often referred to a creamy marshmallow–maraschino cherry cup or compote, but within the past twenty to thirty years, American candy makers have applied it to various chocolate-marshmallow-fruit concoctions.

This candy tastes and looks a lot like chocolate fudge, but no cooking or beating is involved. Instead, briefly heated sweetened condensed milk stands in for the boiled-down caramelized milk-sugar mixture of real fudge recipes. The faux version has a rich, fudgy consistency and is abundantly studded with chewy dried cranberries or cherries, puffy miniature marshmallows, and crunchy nuts.

- 1 14-ounce can sweetened condensed milk
- 2 tablespoons unsalted butter, cut into chunks
- 2 cups (12 ounces) semisweet chocolate morsels
- 2 ounces unsweetened chocolate, broken up or coarsely chopped
- 1 teaspoon vanilla extract
- 3 cups miniature marshmallows
- 1 cup dried sweetened cranberries or cherries
- 1 cup chopped walnuts or pecans

Line an 8- or 9-inch square pan with aluminum foil and coat with non-stick spray (or use nonstick foil), allowing it to overhang two sides.

In a large microwave-safe bowl, microwave the condensed milk and butter on high power for 1½ minutes. Stir in the chocolate morsels and unsweetened chocolate. Microwave on medium power for about 1 minute longer, stopping and stirring at 30-second intervals just until the chocolate is melted. (Alternatively, in a heavy 4-quart saucepan, heat the condensed milk and butter over medium-low heat just until hot, stirring constantly and taking care not to scorch; do not boil. Add the chocolate morsels and unsweetened chocolate. Lower the heat to the lowest setting and heat, stirring, just until the chocolate is melted. Remove from the heat.) Stir until completely smooth.

Stir the vanilla, then the marshmallows, cranberries, and nuts, into the chocolate until evenly incorporated. Immediately turn out the mixture into the pan. Smooth the surface with a lightly greased table knife. With lightly greased hands, press the mixture into the pan until evenly thick and compact. Let cool slightly. Cover and refrigerate for at least 1½ hours and up to 24 hours.

Lift the slab from the pan and peel off the foil. If desired, trim off uneven edges using a sharp knife. Cut the slab crosswise and lengthwise into squares. Pack airtight with wax paper between the layers.

The candy will keep in the refrigerator for up to a week. Let warm up slightly before serving.

words of
kitchen wisdom

"The fudge pot is responsible for the beginnings of many a good cook. So be tolerant when, some rainy day, your children take an interest in the sweeter side of kitchen life."

–Irma S. Rombauer,
Joy of Cooking (1931)

indoor s'mores

Initially, I wondered if marshmallows toasted in an oven would be as good in s'mores as the ones I cooked on sticks over crackling campfires years ago. The answer is yes. In fact, it's possible to obtain the desired amount of marshmallow browning (or in my case, charring) just by watching carefully and controlling their time in the oven. (In the indoor version, the marshmallows go on top of the graham crackers, not between them, to facilitate browning.)

Although traditional s'mores have a no-fuss, no-frills reputation, upscale restaurants around the country have recently been turning out fancy variations on this classic. Anago in Boston used to offer a s'mores takeoff that included a buttery crust, rich chocolate ganache filling, and mascarpone–whipped cream topping. The French Laundry restaurant in Yountville, California, serves a more true-to-type version featuring house-made graham crackers and marshmallows, along with top-quality chocolate.

15 whole graham crackers
12 ounces bittersweet (not unsweetened), semisweet, or milk chocolate bars, or one 12-ounce package milk chocolate or semisweet chocolate morsels

About 45 Homemade Honey Marshmallows (page 346) or store-bought marshmallows (most of a 1-pound bag)

Position a rack in the middle of the oven and preheat to 350 degrees F. Lightly grease a 9-inch square or 7-by-11-inch baking dish or coat with nonstick spray. Arrange half the graham crackers so they neatly cover the pan bottom, cutting or breaking them into the right size and overlapping them slightly as needed.

Lay the chocolate bars (or sprinkle the morsels) over the graham crackers, cutting or breaking the bars to cover the crackers completely. Bake until the chocolate is just melted, 3 to 6 minutes. If using chocolate morsels, smooth the chocolate into an even layer with a greased table knife. Transfer to a wire rack and reset the oven to 475 degrees F. Reposition the rack in the upper third of the oven.

Tips

My taste testers and I prefer semisweet or bittersweet chocolate to the milk chocolate traditionally used in this recipe.

Not surprisingly, we also preferred homemade marshmallows, since they produce moister and more flavorful s'mores than those made with store-bought ones.

Press another layer of graham crackers onto the chocolate layer. Arrange the marshmallows on the crackers, spacing them fairly close together. Bake, checking frequently, until the marshmallows are well browned and crispy on top, 4 to 8 minutes. Transfer the dish to a wire rack. For easier cutting and serving, let cool to barely warm. Cut crosswise and lengthwise into 6 to 8 servings, as desired. You can quickly reheat individual servings in the microwave on medium power for about 30 seconds. Or reheat in the upper third of a preheated 350 degree F oven until the marshmallows are just heated through, 3 to 4 minutes.

The s'mores will keep, stored airtight, at room temperature for 3 or 4 days.

The taste of more

Exactly who came up with s'mores is unknown, although this sweet has most often been associated with camping trips and scouting events. One early recipe, published in 1927 in *Tramping and Trailing with the Girl Scouts,* perfectly captures the pleasure:

> Toast two marshmallows over the coals to a crispy gooey state and then put them inside a graham cracker and chocolate bar sandwich. The heat of the marshmallow between the halves of chocolate bar will melt the chocolate bar a bit. Though it tastes like "some more" one is really enough.

brownie Bars in a jar

Attractively layered jars of bar cookie and brownie mixes are popular gift items in gourmet shops, but they're much better when made at home. Not only are they economical and fun to prepare, but you can be confident that the ingredients are fresh and the bars will taste great.

Looking vaguely like multilayered sand art creations, the finished jars make thoughtful gifts for favorite family members, friends, or teachers. Children can help measure ingredients and fill the jars. Remember to include a tag or card with the mixing and baking instructions. (You may want to use colorful construction paper and a computer for a festive presentation.)

For each batch of mix, you will need a 1-quart jar. (If you aren't sure of your jar's size, fill it with water; it should fill a 4-cup measure.) You can paint the outsides of the lids with bright enamel or acrylic paint. (Enamel is more durable, but acrylic is easier to clean.) Once the base coat is dry, dab on cream-colored splotches for an attractive spongeware look.

Brownie Mix
makes 1 quart mix (enough for 1 pan of bars)

- 1 cup (6 ounces) semisweet chocolate morsels
- ½ cup chopped walnuts or pecans, or ½ cup white chocolate morsels
- 1 cup all-purpose flour
  Scant ½ cup unsweetened Dutch-process cocoa powder
- 1⅓ cups sugar (divided)
- ½ teaspoon salt

Put the semisweet morsels and nuts in a 1-quart jar and stir until mixed. Rap the jar on the counter several times to compact the mixture. Wipe down the jar sides with a dry cloth or paper towel. Add the flour to the jar, smoothing it with a spoon, then rap the jar to create an even layer. Wipe down the jar sides. Sift the cocoa into a medium bowl. Thoroughly stir ⅔ cup of the sugar and the salt into the cocoa until well blended. Add the cocoa mixture to the jar, then rap the jar to even the surface. Wipe down the jar sides again. Top the jar with the remaining ⅔ cup sugar, smoothing it with a spoon. Rap the jar to even the surface further. Close the jar tightly. Attach a tag or card with the Brownie Recipe instructions to the jar.

The mix will keep for up to 2 months.

Brownie Recipe
Makes 12 bars

> 3/4 cup (1½ sticks) unsalted butter, very soft but not melted
> 3 large eggs
> 1 1-quart jar Brownie Mix

Position a rack in the middle of the oven and preheat to 350 degrees F. Grease an 8-inch square baking dish. In a large bowl, beat the butter and eggs until blended. Add the first two jar layers from the jar and mix well. Add the rest of the ingredients and stir until evenly incorporated. Spread evenly in the baking dish. Bake for 25 to 35 minutes, or until a toothpick inserted in the center comes out clean. Let cool completely before cutting.

The bars will keep, covered, at room temperature for 2 or 3 days.

Toffee-Berry Bars in a Jar

These bars have a mellow flavor from the toffee bits, pecans, and coconut, and a nice color and pleasant chew from the berries. The layers look very festive in a jar.

Note that this recipe calls for Brownulated sugar, not brown sugar. (This is normally stocked with regular brown sugar.) Brownulated sugar has a brown sugar taste but a dry, granular consistency, so it stays softer when packed in a jar. Don't try to substitute regular brown sugar; it will soon harden and become too difficult to mix.

Toffee-Berry Mix
makes 1 quart mix (enough for 1 pan of bars)

- 1   cup all-purpose flour
- ½   teaspoon baking powder
- ¾   cup Brownulated sugar
- ¾   cup dried sweetened cranberries or cherries
- ½   cup chocolate-toffee bits or chopped toffee candy bars
- ½   cup chopped pecans or ½ cup semisweet chocolate morsels
- ¾   cup flaked sweetened coconut

On a sheet of wax paper or aluminum foil, thoroughly stir together the flour and baking powder. Using the paper as a funnel, pour the mixture into a 1-quart jar. Rap the jar on the counter several times to compact the mixture. Wipe down the jar sides with a dry cloth or paper towel, if necessary. Add the Brownulated sugar to the jar, smoothing it with a spoon. Rap the jar to even the surface. Repeat with the dried cranberries, then the toffee bits, and then the pecans. Top with the coconut, smoothing out the surface with a spoon. Rap the jar to even the surface further. Close the jar. Attach a tag or card with the Toffee-Berry Bar Recipe instructions to the jar.

The mix will keep for up to 2 months.

Toffee-Berry Bar Recipe
Makes 12 bars

    8 tablespoons (1 stick) unsalted butter, very soft but not melted
    2 large eggs
    1 1-quart jar Toffee-Berry Mix

Position a rack in the middle of the oven and preheat to 350 degrees F. Grease an 8-inch square baking dish. In a large bowl, beat the butter until soft and lightened. Add the eggs and beat well. Add all the jar ingredients and stir until well blended. Spread evenly in the baking dish. Bake for 25 to 30 minutes, or until a toothpick inserted in the center comes out clean. Let cool completely before cutting.

The bars will keep, covered, at room temperature for 3 or 4 days.

AT RIGHT

GRAHAM CRACKER
HOLIDAY COTTAGES

PAGE 386

graham cracker HOLiday cottages

Children of all ages enjoy making festive, edible miniature houses from graham crackers. Elementary school kids can make a house with adult assistance, and middle-schoolers and teens can do it on their own. Although Christmasy edible houses adorned with white royal icing snow and icicles and red-and-white candies are most common, you can create a nontraditional "winter wonderland" look by using sparkling sugar, silver edible glitter, and ice-blue frosting. (See page 390 for other decorating ideas.) The following icing recipe makes enough to glue together and decorate three little houses.

ROYAL ICING

- 2/3 cup egg whites (5–6 large), completely free of yolk and at room temperature
- 2 1/2 teaspoons fresh lemon juice (divided)
- Generous pinch of salt
- 5 cups powdered sugar, plus more if needed
- 1/2 teaspoon vanilla extract
- Water, if needed
- Assorted liquid or paste food colors (optional)

GRAHAM CRACKER COTTAGES

- 10–12 whole graham crackers for each cottage (to allow for breakage)
- Assorted candies, dried fruit, and nuts
- Assorted sprinkles, nonpareils, colored decorating sugar, crystal sugar, and edible glitter

TO MAKE THE ROYAL ICING: In a large bowl using a mixer on low speed (with a whisk-shaped beater), beat the egg whites, 1/2 teaspoon of the lemon juice, and the salt until frothy and opaque. Raise the speed to medium and beat until the mixture begins to form soft peaks, several minutes longer. Lower the speed and gradually beat in the powdered sugar 1/2 cup at a time until fully incorporated and free of lumps.

Raise the speed to high, add the remaining 2 teaspoons lemon juice and the vanilla, and beat until the mixture increases in volume and stands in stiff peaks, about 3 minutes. If the mixture is too stiff to pipe or spread, beat in water a teaspoon at a time. If it is too runny, beat in a little more powdered sugar. The icing will keep, tightly covered, in the refrigerator for up to 4 days. Let come almost to room temperature and beat for a minute or two to refluff before using.

Keep a damp kitchen towel draped over the bowl to prevent the icing from drying out as you work. If it stiffens upon standing, thin it with a

TiPS

For icing that is safe for those with compromised or weak immune systems, use dehydrated egg whites especially designed for making royal frosting. (Follow the directions on the package.) Dehydrated whites are sometimes stocked with the cake decorating supplies in discount department stores and craft stores.

It's easier to add decorative piping to the graham cracker doors, shutters, and other decorative accents before you attach them to the cottage.

few drops of water. If several colors of icing are desired, divide it among as many bowls as needed, then stir in food color until the desired color is obtained. (For very intense shades, paste colors work best.) Food colors can be mixed together for virtually any custom color.

TO MAKE A GRAHAM CRACKER COTTAGE: Lay 3 whole graham crackers, long sides touching, on a sheet of nonstick aluminum foil. These will serve as the cottage platform (see Figure 1, page 389). Completely cover the crackers with a generous ⅛-inch-thick layer of icing, being sure they stay fitted together. Center another whole cracker lengthwise on the platform, pressing it lightly into the icing. This will be the cottage floor (see Figure 2). Add a ⅛-inch-thick line of icing around the outside edge of the floor. Set out 2 whole crackers and 2 cracker halves for the cottage walls. If desired, cut away a rectangle for a 1-by-2-inch door from one cracker half, using a sharp paring knife (see Figure 3). The cracker will be less likely to break apart if microwaved at 50 percent power until warm to the touch. (Or simply cut out a door-sized rectangle to glue in place where the front door should be. Decorate it before attaching it to the house.) Set the cottage walls in place around the edge of (not on) the floor, propping them up with small jars or salt and pepper shakers if necessary. Using a table knife or a piping cone or pastry bag fitted with a plain ¼-inch-diameter tip, add generous lines of icing to all the inside seams to cement the walls and floor together. Let stand for at least 15 minutes so the icing begins to set up. Use a wide, thin spatula to lift up the house (and platform) very carefully and transfer to a clean sheet of nonstick foil.

Using the table knife or piping bag, add a very thick line of icing to the top edges of the house walls all the way around (see Figure 4). Place 2 roof crackers over the house, adjusting them so that they butt together neatly at the center peak. Add a thick line of icing all along the center peak, pressing the roof pieces together. Brace the roof on each side with small jars slipped under the edge. Cut 2 triangular ends off a cracker, adjusting the size so the triangles will fit into the open area below the front and back roof peaks (see Figure 5). Again, the cracker will cut better if warmed in the microwave first. Add a line of icing all around the triangles, then slide them into place in the upper front and back. Before removing the braces and beginning the decorating, let the cottage stand for at least 30 minutes and preferably 1 hour so the icing can set up.

TO DECORATE THE COTTAGE: Use plain white royal icing everywhere snow and ice are wanted. As you spread it on, sprinkle with edible glitter or crystal sugar if a sparkling look is desired. Divide some of the icing among bowls and tint portions with food color as desired to add colored trim or piping accents; to paint walls, doors, or the roof; or to create a green "yard" or fantasy-colored ground around the cottage.

Thin the icing slightly with water to paint walls and other surfaces. Use clean artist's brushes to paint these surfaces.

Cut out and decorate graham cracker pieces to serve as windows, shutters, and decorative trim.

Sprinkle on sparkling sugar, colored sprinkles, nonpareils, and the like immediately after you apply the icing. After the icing begins to dry and set up (which happens almost immediately), the bits won't stick.

Keep decorative accents fairly small. If desired, use tweezers to put them in place. Sprinkles, tiny candies such as Dots and Red Hots, diced or slivered dried fruit (dried apricots and candied cherries are particularly colorful), and small nuts such as pistachios and chopped or slivered almonds and walnuts look more in scale with these cottages than large items. Also, large pieces are often heavy and don't stick as well. If you do use heavier items, add generous dabs of icing to glue them in place.

Long, vertical candies such as peppermint sticks, licorice sticks, or striped candy sticks all work well to cover (and decorate) corner and roof peak seams.

Although seams look tidiest when piped using a pastry bag fitted with a small plain tip, most children (and some adults) will be more comfortable simply spooning icing into place or smoothing it on with a knife. Encourage decorators not to worry about imperfections and just to have fun.

The cottage will keep in a cool, dry place for up to a year.

1

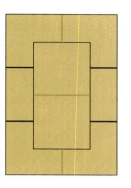

2

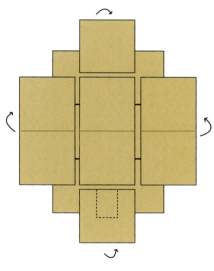

3

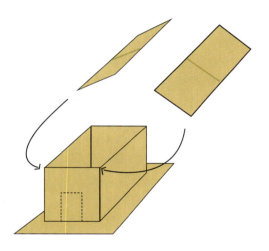

4

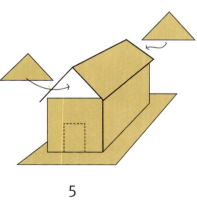

5

OTHER IDEAS FOR HOLIDAY COTTAGES

- For a charming Valentine's Day decoration or gift, pair edible gold or silver glittery details with romantic lavender, pink, or red, and add some heart-shaped candies as exterior accents. (This makes a particularly wonderful present if you tuck chocolates and other candies inside the structure.)

- For an Easter theme, make a bunny hutch, replacing the white icing snow with pastel-tinted icing to cover seams and decorate rooflines. For accents, use candies such as miniature eggs, jellybeans, Jordan almonds, and tiny chocolate bunnies. Achieve a grassy "yard" by using green liquid food color to tint shredded coconut.

- For Halloween, make a Hansel and Gretel–style witch's cottage topped with a thatched roof (Life cereal or bits of shredded wheat) and decorated with orange icing and tiny pumpkin-shaped candies, licorice sticks, peanuts, and candy corn.

- For a housewarming gift, make a cottage and decorate it fancifully, or copy the color scheme of the actual house.

- To celebrate the Jewish harvest festival of Sukkoth, you can make miniature huts by modifying the basic cottage plan a bit. Because the structure's top must offer a view of the stars at night, skip the peaked roof and make a flat covering of pretzel stick "logs" spaced slightly apart. Decorate the hut amply with bits of dried fruit and nuts, and tint the royal frosting harvest yellow, green, or brown (use cocoa powder to create this color).

Bibliography

Allen, Ida Bailey. *Best Loved Recipes of the American People.* Garden City, N.Y.: Doubleday, 1973.

Anderson, Jean. *The American Century Cookbook.* New York: Clarkson Potter, 1997.

Anderson, Jean, and Elaine Hanna. *The Doubleday Cookbook.* Garden City, N.Y.: Doubleday, 1975.

Barnum, Mrs. A. L., and Mrs. S. I. Delavan, eds. *1902 Cook Book.* Estherville, Iowa, 1902.

Beecher, Catharine E. *Miss Beecher's Domestic Receipt Book.* Third ed. New York: Harper & Brothers, 1858. (Facsimile edition, Mineola, N.Y.: Dover, 2001.)

Beeton, Mrs. *Mrs. Beeton's Everyday Cookery and Housekeeping Book.* London: Ward, Lock, 1865. (Facsimile edition, London: Bracken Books, 1984.)

Bell, Wm. M. *The Pilot: Candy-Ice Cream and Soda Fountain Formulae.* 5th ed. Chicago: Wm. M. Bell, 1922.

Benes, Peter, ed. *Foodways in the Northeast.* Vol. 7, Annual Proceedings of the Dublin Seminar for New England Folklife. Boston: Boston University, 1984.

Benson Woman's Club. *Benson Woman's Club Cook Book.* Omaha, Neb.: Douglas Printing Company, 1915.

Bolsterli, Margaret Jones, ed. *Vinegar Pie and Chicken Bread: A Woman's Diary of Life in the Rural South, 1890–1891.* Fayetteville: University of Arkansas Press, 1982.

Bradford, William. *Of Plymouth Plantation 1620–1647.* New York: Modern Library College Editions, 1981. (First published under the title History of Plymouth Plantation, 1856.)

Brenner, Joel Glenn. *The Emperors of Chocolate: Inside the Secret World of Hershey and Mars.* New York: Broadway Books, 2000.

Brenner, Leslie. *American Appetite: The Coming of Age of a Cuisine.* New York: Avon Books, 1999.

Bryan, Lettice. *The Kentucky Housewife.* Cincinnati: Shepard & Stearns, 1839. (Facsimile edition, Paducah, Kentucky: Image Graphics, n.d.)

Carson, Gerald. *Cornflake Crusade.* New York: Rinehart & Company, 1957.

Child, Mrs. Lydia Maria *The American Frugal Housewife.* 12th ed. Boston: Carter, Hendee, 1833. (Reprint edition, Sandwich, Mass.: Chapman Billies, n.d.)

Clarke, Mrs. *Mrs. Clarke's Cookery Book.* Toronto: Grip Printing and Publishing, 1889. (Also published as The People's Cook Book, Chicago: People's Company, 1989.)

Coe, Sophie D., and Michael D. Coe. *The True History of Chocolate.* New York: Thames & Hudson, 2000.

The Complete Bread, Cake and Cracker Baker in Two Parts. Chicago: J. Thompson Gill, Manager Confectioner and Baker Publishing, 1881.

The Complete Confectioner, Pastry-Cook, and Baker. Philadelphia: Practical Confectioners, 1864.

Corriher, Shirley O. *CookWise: The Hows and Whys of Successful Cooking.* New York: William Morrow, 1997.

Dabney, Joseph E. *Smokehouse Ham, Spoon Bread, & Scuppernong Wine.* Nashville: Cumberland House, 1998.

Damerow, Gail. *Ice Cream! The Whole Scoop.* Aurora, Colo.: Glenbridge Publishing, 1995.

De Graf, Belle. *Mrs. De Graf's Cook Book.* San Francisco: H. S. Crocker, 1922.

Denys, Nicolas. *Histoire naturelle des Peuples, des Animaux, des Arbres et Plantes de l'Amérique Septentrionale (Natural History of the People, Animals, Trees and Plants of North America).* Paris: Claude Barbin, 1672.

Dickson, Paul. *The Great American Ice Cream Book.* New York: Atheneum, 1978.

Dolby, Richard. *The Cook's Dictionary, and Housekeeper's Directory.* 2d ed. London: Henry Colburn and Richard Bentley, 1832.

Dull, Mrs. S. R. *Southern Cooking.* Atlanta: Ruralist Press, 1928. (Reprint edition, Atlanta: Cherokee Publishing, 1989.)

Dupree, Nathalie. *Nathalie Dupree's Southern Memories.* New York: Clarkson Potter, 1993.

Earle, Alice Morse. *Home Life in Colonial Days.* New York: Grosset & Dunlap, 1898. (Reprint edition, Stockbridge, Mass.: Berkshire Traveller Press, 1974.)

Egerton, John. *Southern Food: At Home, on the Road, in History.* New York: Alfred A. Knopf, 1987.

Farmer, Fannie Merritt. *The Boston Cooking-School Cook Book.* Rev. ed. Boston: Little, Brown, 1921, 1924.

——. *The Boston Cooking-School Cook Book,* revised by Wilma Lord Perkins. Boston: Little, Brown, 1965. (Also known as *The Fannie Farmer Cookbook.*)

——. *The 1896 Boston Cooking-School Cook Book.* (Facsimile edition, New York: Random House Value, 1997.)

Fisher, Mrs. Abby. *What Mrs. Fisher Knows About Old Southern Cooking.* San Francisco: Women's Cooperative Printing Office, 1881. (Facsimile edition, Bedford, Mass.: Applewood Books, 1995.)

Fowler, Damon Lee. *Classical Southern Cooking.* New York: Crown, 1995.

Funderburg, Anne Cooper. *Chocolate, Strawberry, and Vanilla: A History of American Ice Cream.* Bowling Green, Ohio: Bowling Green State University Popular Press, 1995.

Fussell, Betty. *I Hear America Cooking.* New York: Viking, 1986.

Gardiner, Anne Gibbons. *Mrs. Gardiner's Family Receipts from 1763.* Boston, n.d. (Reprint edition, edited by Gail Weesner, Boston: Rowan Tree Press, n.d., based on 1938 edition printed by the Gardiners.)

Glasse, Hannah. *The Art of Cookery Made Plain and Easy; Excelling Any Thing of the*

Kind Ever Yet Published. Alexandria, Va.: Cottom & Stewart, 1805. (First published, 1747. Facsimile edition, Bedford, Mass.: Applewood Books, 1997.)

Haber, Barbara. *From Hardtack to Home Fries: An Uncommon History of American Cooks and Meals.* New York: Free Press, 2002.

Hale, Sarah Josepha. *The Good Housekeeper.* Boston: Otis, Broaders, 1841. (Facsimile edition, *Early American Cookery,* Mineola, N.Y.: Dover, 1996.)

Hart, Cynthia, John Grossman, and Priscilla Dunhill. *Joy to the World: A Victorian Christmas.* New York: Workman, 1990.

Hawke, David Freeman. *Everyday Life in Early America.* New York: Harper & Row, 1988.

Heath, Dwight B., ed. *Mourt's Relation: A Journal of the Pilgrims at Plymouth.* Bedford, Mass.: Applewood Books, 1963. (First published as *A Relation or Journal of the English Plantation Settled at Plymouth,* 1622.)

Hess, John L., and Karen Hess. *The Taste of America.* New York: Grossman/Viking, 1977.

Hess, Karen, ed. *Martha Washington's Booke of Cookery.* New York: Columbia University Press, 1981.

Heywood, Margaret Weimer, ed. *The International Cook Book.* Boston: Merchandisers, 1929.

Hill, Annabelle P. *Mrs. Hill's Southern Practical Cookery and Receipt Book.* 1820. (Reprint edition, Columbia: University of South Carolina Press, 1955.)

Hooker, Richard J. *Food and Drink in America.* Indianapolis: Bobbs-Merrill, 1981.

Howard, Mrs. B. C. *Fifty Years in a Maryland Kitchen.* 4th ed. Philadelphia: J. B. Lippincott, 1888.

Howard, Maria Willett. *Lowney's Cook Book.* Boston: Walter M. Lowney, 1908.

James, Sydney V., Jr., ed. *Three Visitors to Early Plymouth.* Bedford, Mass.: Applewood Books, 1997.

Johnson, Mrs. W. A. *What to Cook, and How to Cook It.* Louisville, Ky.: Pentecostal Herald Press, 1899.

Jones, Evan. *American Food: The Gastronomic Story.* New York: E. P. Dutton, 1975.

Kander, Mrs. Simon. *The Settlement Cook Book.* 6th ed. Milwaukee: Settlement, 1912.

———. *The Settlement Cook Book.* 24th ed. Milwaukee: Settlement Cook Book, 1941. (First published 1901.)

Krondl, Michael. *Around the American Table.* Holbrook, Mass.: Adams Publishing, 1995.

Ladies of the First Presbyterian Church, Dayton, Ohio. *Presbyterian Cook Book.* Dayton: John H. Thomas, 1875.

Langdon, William Chauncy. *Everyday Things in American Life: 1607-1776.* New York: Charles Scribner's Sons, 1937.

Larkin, Jack. *The Reshaping of Everyday Life, 1790-1840.* New York: Harper & Row, 1988.

Le Draoulec, Pascale. *American Pie: Slices of Life (and Pie) from America's Back Roads.* New York: HarperCollins, 2003.

Lee, Mrs. N.K.M. (A Boston Housekeeper). *The Cook's Own Book.* Boston: Munroe & Francis, 1832. (Reprint edition, edited by Edmund B. Stewart, Merrifield, Va.: Rare Book Publishers, 1997.)

Leslie, Eliza. *Miss Leslie's Lady's New Receipt Book.* Philadelphia: A. Hart, 1850.

——. *Miss Leslie's Directions for Cookery.* 59th ed. Philadelphia: Henry Carey Baird, 1851. (Reprint edition, Mineola, N.Y.: Dover, 1999.)

——. *Miss Leslie's New Cookery Book.* Philadelphia: T. B. Peterson & Brothers, 1857.

Leslie, Eliza (A Lady of Philadelphia). *Seventy-five Receipts, for Pastry, Cakes, and Sweetmeats.* Boston: Munroe & Francis, 1828. (Facsimile edition, Bedford, Mass.: Applewood Books, 1993.)

Lincoln, Mrs. D. A. *Mrs. Lincoln's Boston Cook Book.* Boston: Roberts Brothers, 1887. (Facsimile edition, *Boston Cooking School Cook Book,* Mineola, N.Y.: Dover, 1996.)

Lundy, Ronni. *Shuck Beans, Stack Cakes and Honest Fried Chicken.* New York: Atlantic Monthly Press, 1991.

Lynn, Dr. Kristie, and Robert W. Pelton. *The Early American Cookbook.* Deerfield Beach, Fla.: Liberty Publishing, 1987.

McCully, Helen, and Eleanor Noderer, eds. *The American Heritage Cookbook.* New York: American Heritage Publishing, 1980.

Marsh, Dorothy B. *The New Good Housekeeping Cookbook.* New York: Harcourt, Brace & World, 1963.

Meyer, Arthur L. *Baking Across America.* Austin: University of Texas Press, 1998.

Modern Priscilla Cook Book: One Thousand Recipes Tested and Proved at the Priscilla Proving Plant. Boston: Priscilla Publishing, 1924.

Neal, Bill. *Biscuits, Spoonbread, and Sweet Potato Pie.* New York: Alfred A. Knopf, 1996.

Neil, Marion Harris. *A Calendar of Dinners with 615 Recipes: Including the Story of Crisco.* 7th ed. Cincinnati: Procter & Gamble, 1914.

Oliver, Sandra L. *Saltwater Foodways.* Mystic, Conn.: Mystic Seaport Museum, 1995.

Parloa, Maria. *The Appledore Cook Book.* Boston: Graves, Locke, 1878.

Porter, Mrs. M. E. *Mrs. Porter's New Southern Cookery Book.* Philadelphia: John E. Potter, 1871.

The Portland Woman's Exchange Cook Book. Portland, Ore., 1913. (Facsimile edition, Portland: Glass-Dahlstrom Printers, 1973.)

Randolph, Mary. *The Virginia Housewife.* Philadelphia: E. H. Butler, 1860. (Facsimile edition, New York: Avenel Books/Crown, n.d.)

Rhett, Blanche S., comp. and Lettie Gay, ed. *Two Hundred Years of Charleston Cooking.* Columbia: University of South Carolina Press, 1977.

Rombauer, Irma S. *Joy of Cooking.* St. Louis: A. C. Clayton Printing, 1931.

Root, Frank A., and William Elsey Connelley. *The Overland Stage to California.* Topeka, Kans., 1901.

bibliography

Root, Waverly, and Richard de Rachemon. *Eating in America: A History.* New York: William Morrow, 1976.

Rorer, Sarah Tyson. *Mrs. Rorer's New Cook Book.* Philadelphia: Arnold, 1898. (Reprint edition, New York: Ladies' Home Journal Cook Book Club, 1970.)

——. *Mrs. Rorer's Philadelphia Cook Book.* Philadelphia: Arnold, 1886.

Sax, Richard. *Classic Home Desserts.* Shelburne, Vt.: Chapters Publishing, 1994.

Second Auxiliary Missionary Society. *The Warren Cook Book.* 4th ed. Warren, Pa., 1912.

Seranne, Ann, ed. *America Cooks: The General Federation of Women's Clubs Cook Book.* New York: G. P. Putnam's Sons, 1967.

Simmons, Amelia. *American Cookery.* Hartford, Conn.: Hudson & Goodwin, 1796. (Facsimile edition, *The First American Cookbook,* New York: Dover, 1958.)

Smith, E. *The Compleat Housewife; or, Accomplish'd Gentlewoman's Companion.* London: R. Ware, 1753. (Facsimile edition, London: Literary Services and Production, 1968.)

Sokolov, Raymond. *Fading Feast.* Jaffrey, N.H.: David R. Godine, 1998.

——. *Why We Eat What We Eat.* New York: Simon & Schuster, 1991.

Tannahill, Reay. *Food in History.* New York: Stein & Day, 1973.

Trager, James. *The Food Chronology.* New York: Henry Holt, 1995.

Tried and True Cook Book. Deadwood, S.D.: Ladies Aid Society and Friends of First Methodist Episcopal Church, 1891.

Tyree, Marion Cabell, ed. *Housekeeping in Old Virginia.* Louisville, Ky.: John P. Morton, 1879. (Facsimile edition, Louisville: Favorite Recipes Press, 1965.)

Wakefield, Ruth. *Ruth Wakefield's Toll House Tried and True Recipes.* New York: M. Barrows, 1936.

Wallace, Lily Haxworth. *Rumford Complete Cook Book.* 41st ed. Rumford, R.I.: Rumford Chemical Works, 1947.

Wigginton, Eliot, ed. *The Foxfire Book.* Garden City, N.Y.: Anchor Books, 1972.

Wihlfahrt, Julius Emil. *Treatise on Baking.* New York: The Fleischmann Co., 1913.

Wilcox, Estelle Woods, ed. *Buckeye Cookery and Practical Housekeeping.* Minneapolis: Buckeye Publishing, 1880. (Reprint edition, St. Paul: Minnesota Historical Society Press, 1988.)

Williams, Jacqueline B. *The Way We Ate.* Pullman: Washington State University Press, 1996.

Winslow, Edward. *Good Newes from New England: A True Relation of Things Very Remarkable at the Plantation of Plimoth in New England.* Facsimile edition, Bedford, Mass.: Applewood Books. (First published 1624.)

Zimmer, Anne Carter. *The Robert E. Lee Family Cooking and Housekeeping Book.* Chapel Hill: University of North Carolina Press, 1997.

index

high-summer cobbler with buttermilk biscuit
crust, 154-56, *155*
Old Glory angel ice cream pie, 64-65
pie, lattice-topped deep-dish, 22-24
raspberry-plum crumb cobbler, 157
summer fresh fruit tart, 66-68
bourbon
-pecan fudge cake, *136,* 137-38
sauce, 230
souffléd whiskey bread pudding with meringue,
208-9
brandied dark cherry ice cream, 292, *293*
bread pudding
chocolate, 204-5
pecan-coconut, 203
pumpkin and cranberry, 206-7, *207*
roasted pear, 198-99
whiskey, souffléd, with meringue, 208-9
brittle, peanut, 350-52, *351*
brittle, peanut, chocolate-coated, 352
brownie bars in a jar, 380-81
brownie pecan-praline mousse pie, 46-49, *48*
brownies, fudge, 272-73, *273*
brownies, glazed cocoa-cheesecake, 274-75
brown sugar, 6, 12
brown sugar–orange sauce, 231
buckle, blueberry, 128-29
butter, 9, 15
buttermilk biscuit crust, high-summer cobbler
with, 154-56, *155*
buttermilk sherbet, pineapple-lemon, 307
butterscotch
-caramel baked custards, 218-19, *219*
custard pie, 41-43
sauce, 314-15

C

cake pans
removing cake layers from, 99

round, measuring, 9
substituting, 14
cake(s). *See also* cheesecake
apple-pecan coffeecake with caramel glaze,
120-21
apple-pecan coffeecake with cinnamon-sugar
topping, 121
applesauce spice, 110-11
apple stack, 122-25, *124*
banana, 115-16, *117*
black walnut pound, 107-9, *108*
blueberry buckle, 128-29
bourbon-pecan fudge, *136,* 137-38
chiffon, orange, Nana's, with orange glaze,
112-14, *113*
chocolate pudding, 142-43
chocolate soufflé, molten lava, 140-41
coconut white, triple layer, with lemon curd,
100-103, *102*
devil's food, triple-layer, 104-6, *106*
gingerbread, nicely spiced, *117,* 118-19
mini molten lava, 141
Mississippi mud, 132-34
orange chiffon, Nana's, with orange glaze,
112-14, *113*
peach upside-down, 126-27
pound, black walnut, 107-9, *108*
pound, plain, 109
pudding, chocolate, 142-43
pudding, red and black raspberry, 130-31
red and black raspberry pudding, 130-31
upside-down, peach, 126-27
white, triple layer coconut, with lemon curd,
100-103, *102*
yellow sour cream–butter layer, 98-99
candies and confections
buckeyes, 374-75
candy-making tips, 322-23
caramel-pecan turtlettes, 341-42
chocolate-coated peanut brittle, 352

hazelnut(s) (*cont.*)
    toasting, 294
honey marshmallows, homemade, 346-47, *348*
honey taffy and chocolate-honey taffy, 330-33, *331*

I

ice cream. *See also* ice cream desserts
    banana, Inn at Little Washington style, 288-89
    brandied dark cherry, 292, *293*
    chocolate, double-malted milk, 296-98, *297*
    maple frozen custard, 287
    mocha, with hazelnuts, 294-95
    strawberry-banana cheesecake, 290-91
    vanilla frozen custard, 284-86, *285*
ice cream desserts
    chocolate-banana malteds, 308, *309*
    chocolate cookie ice cream sandwiches, 280-81
    classic banana splits, *299*, 300
    coffee-nut ice cream pie, 65
    Old Glory angel ice cream pie, 64-65
ice water test, 323
icing. *See also* frosting
    lemon, 237
    lime, 237
    mocha, easy, 115-16
    royal, 386
    strawberry, 234-35
    for sugar cookie pops, 366-69
ingredients, 9-13

L

lemon
    cream cheese-butter frosting, 148
    curd, 70-71, 100-101
    curd, tangerine-, 246
    fluff pudding, 210-11
    glaze, 118-19
    icing, 237
    meringue pie, 56-59, *58*
    -pineapple buttermilk sherbet, 307
    shortbread sandwiches with tangerine-lemon
        curd, 246-49, *248*
    snowflake cookies, 254-55
    -vanilla cheesecake, classic, 75-76
lime
    icing, 237
    Key, juice, buying, 260
    Key, mousse pie, 53-54
    Key, sugar cookies, *258,* 259-60
liquids, measuring, 6
lollipops
    rock crystal candy lollies, 361-63, *362*
    sugar cookie pops, 366-69

M

malted milk, double-, chocolate ice cream,
    296-98, *297*
malteds, chocolate-banana, 305-9, *309*
maple
    -butter pecan sauce, 316
    -caramel nut crisps, 261-63, *262*
    custards, maple-glazed, 216-17
    frozen custard, 287
    kettle corn, kitchen, 358, *359*
    -rhubarb pie, meringue-topped, 32-34
    sugar on snow, 372-73
margarine, in recipes, 9
marshmallow(s)
    chocolate-rocky road fudge, 328-29
    cutting, 346
    gourmet-shaped, 347
    heavenly hash faux fudge, 376-77
    homemade, chocolate-covered, 349
    honey, homemade, 346-47, *348*
    hot chocolate with, 312
    indoor s'mores, 378-79
    sundae topping, 313